DIANA PRINCE
WONDER WOMAN

volume one

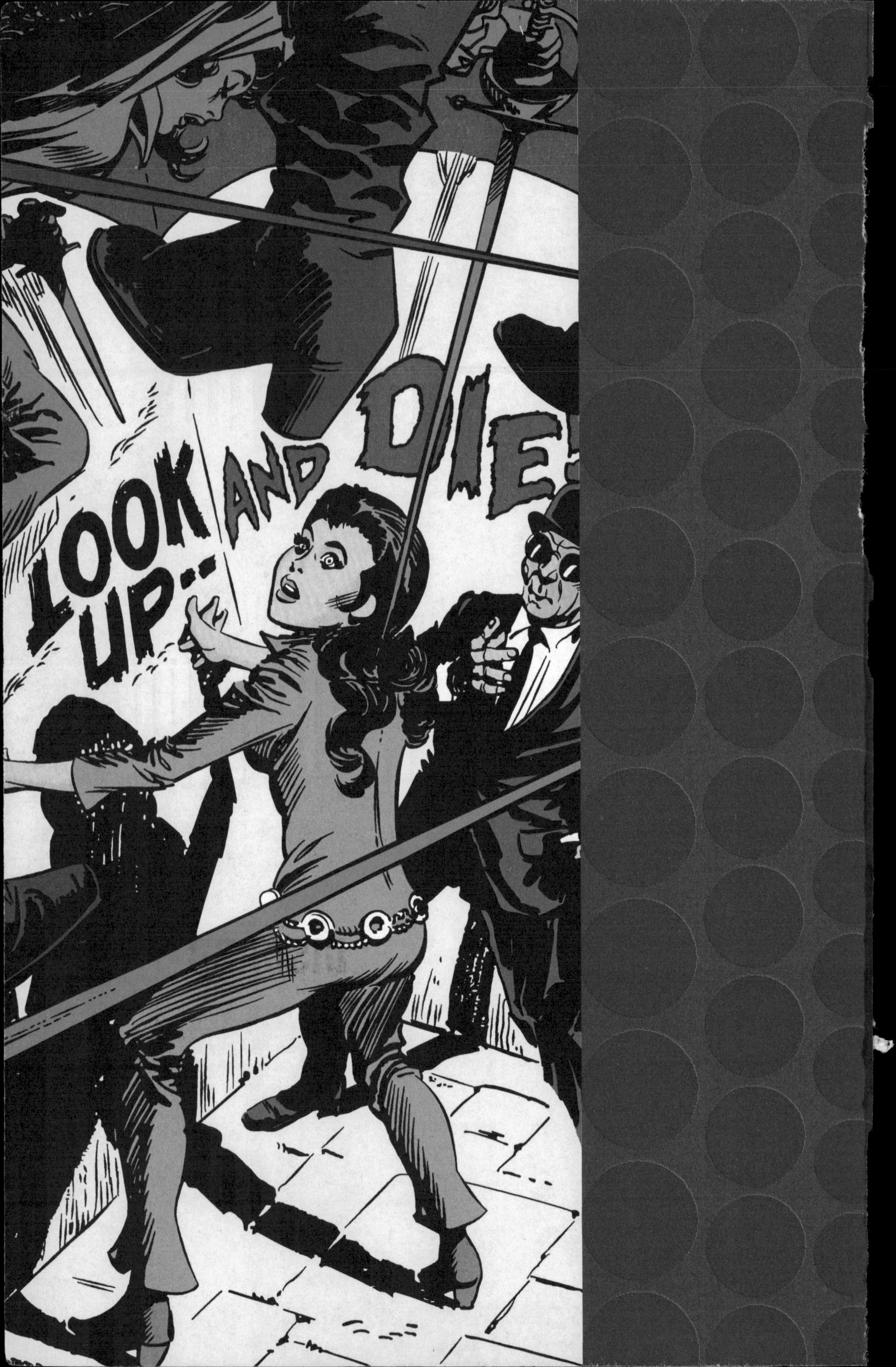
LOOK UP-- AND DIE!

DIANA PRINCE
WONDER WOMAN

Volume one

WONDER WOMAN'S RIVAL
WONDER WOMAN'S LAST BATTLE
A DEATH FOR DIANA
THE WRATH OF DR. CYBER

Written by Denny O'Neil · Pencilled by Mike Sekowsky · Inked by Dick Giordano

A TIME TO LOVE, A TIME TO DIE
RETURN TO PARADISE ISLAND
THE LAST BATTLE

Written and pencilled by Mike Sekowsky · Inked by Dick Giordano

Wonder Woman created by William Moulton Marston

DAN DIDIO Senior VP-Executive Editor
JACK MILLER MIKE SEKOWSKY Editors-original series
BOB JOY Editor-collected edition
ROBBIN BROSTERMAN Senior Art Director
PAUL LEVITZ President & Publisher
GEORG BREWER VP-Design & DC Direct Creative
RICHARD BRUNING Senior VP-Creative Director
PATRICK CALDON Executive VP-Finance & Operations
CHRIS CARAMALIS VP-Finance
JOHN CUNNINGHAM VP-Marketing
TERRI CUNNINGHAM VP-Managing Editor
ALISON GILL VP-Manufacturing
DAVID HYDE VP-Publicity
HANK KANALZ VP-General Manager, WildStorm
JIM LEE Editorial Director-WildStorm
PAULA LOWITT Senior VP-Business & Legal Affairs
MARYELLEN MCLAUGHLIN VP-Advertising & Custom Publishing
JOHN NEE Senior VP-Business Development
GREGORY NOVECK Senior VP-Creative Affairs
SUE POHJA VP-Book Trade Sales
STEVE ROTTERDAM Senior VP-Sales & Marketing
CHERYL RUBIN Senior VP-Brand Management
JEFF TROJAN VP-Business Development, DC Direct
BOB WAYNE VP-Sales

Cover art by Mike Sekowsky and Dick Giordano

DIANA PRINCE: WONDER WOMAN Volume 1

DC Comics, 1700 Broadway, New York, NY 10019
A Warner Bros. Entertainment Company
Printed in Canada. First Printing.
ISBN: 978-1-4012-1660-3

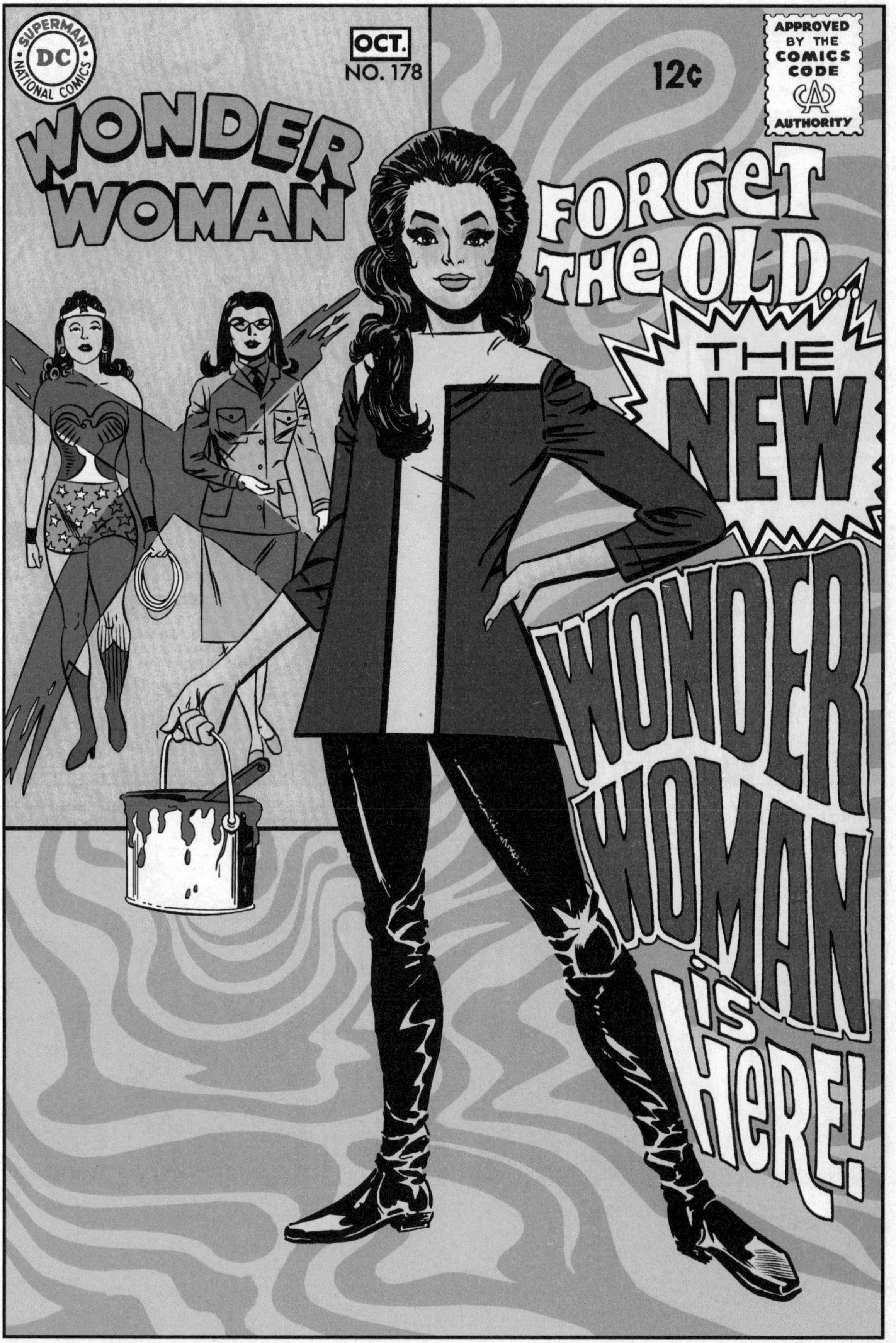
SUPERMAN DC NATIONAL COMICS
OCT.
NO. 178
12¢
APPROVED BY THE COMICS CODE AUTHORITY
WONDER WOMAN
FORGET THE OLD...
THE NEW
WONDER WOMAN IS HERE!

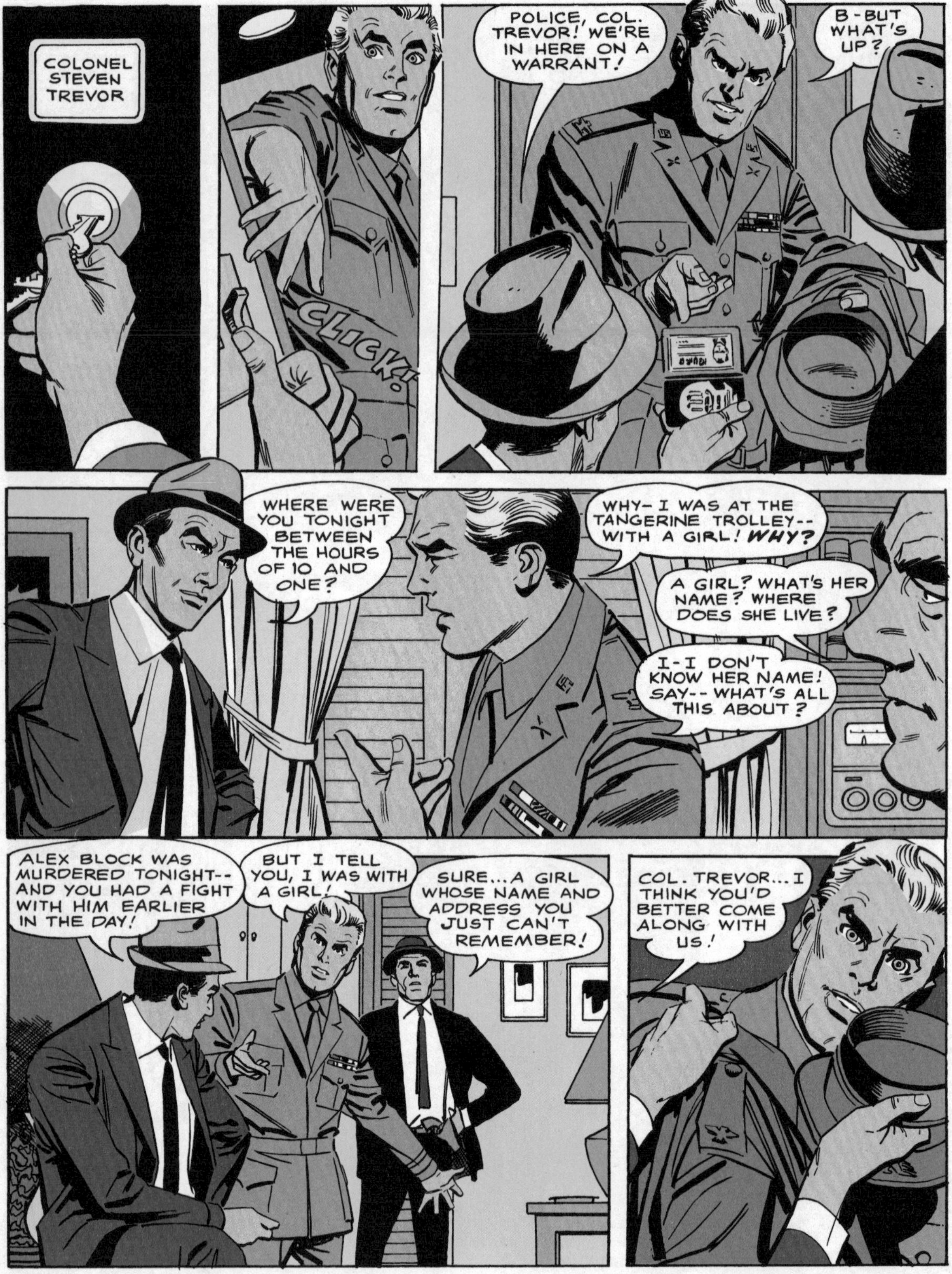
COLONEL STEVEN TREVOR
CLICK!
POLICE, COL. TREVOR! WE'RE IN HERE ON A WARRANT!
B-BUT WHAT'S UP?
WHERE WERE YOU TONIGHT BETWEEN THE HOURS OF 10 AND ONE?
WHY-- I WAS AT THE TANGERINE TROLLEY-- WITH A GIRL! WHY?
A GIRL? WHAT'S HER NAME? WHERE DOES SHE LIVE?
I-I DON'T KNOW HER NAME! SAY-- WHAT'S ALL THIS ABOUT?
ALEX BLOCK WAS MURDERED TONIGHT-- AND YOU HAD A FIGHT WITH HIM EARLIER IN THE DAY!
BUT I TELL YOU, I WAS WITH A GIRL!
SURE... A GIRL WHOSE NAME AND ADDRESS YOU JUST CAN'T REMEMBER!
COL. TREVOR... I THINK YOU'D BETTER COME ALONG WITH US!

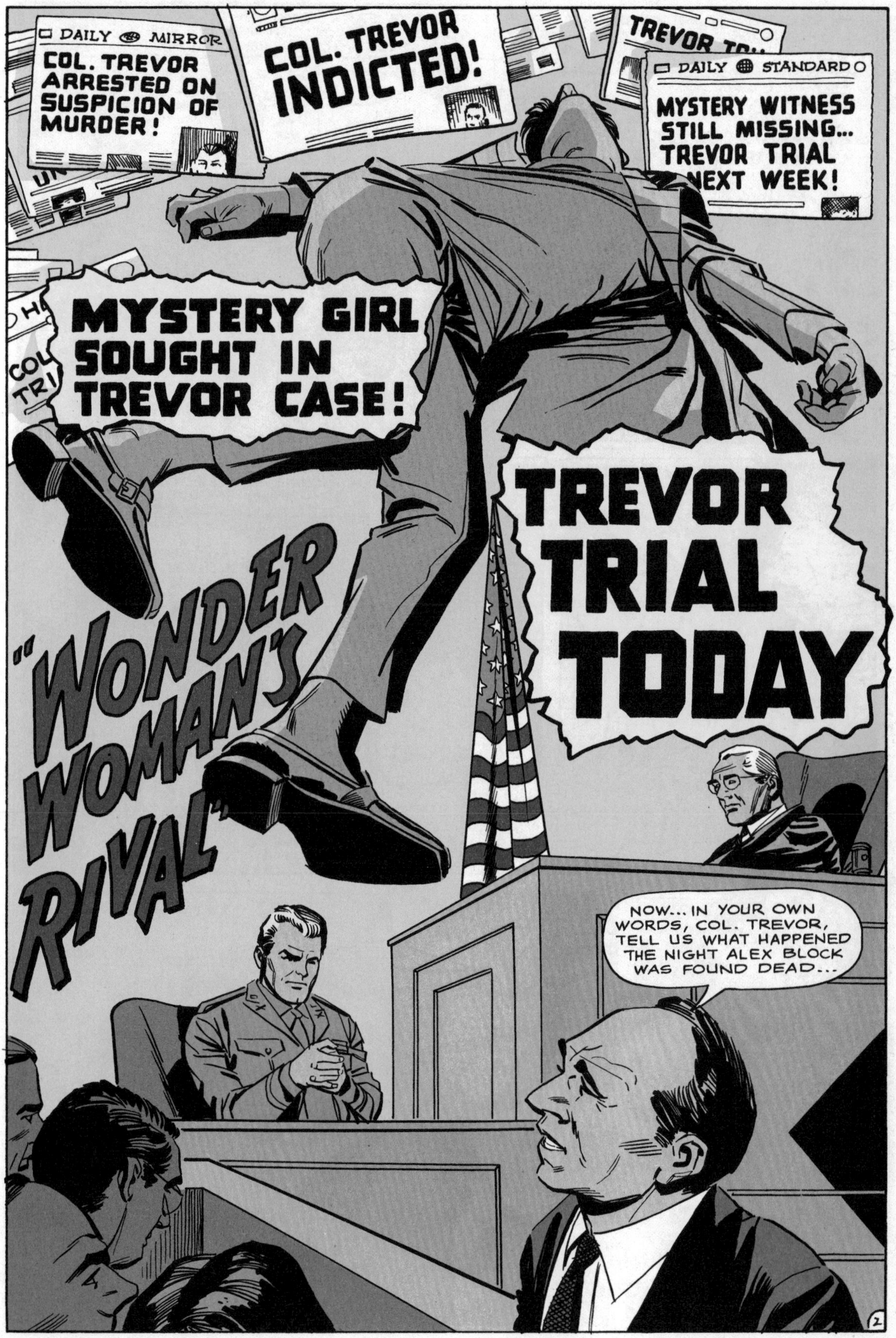
DAILY MIRROR
COL. TREVOR ARRESTED ON SUSPICION OF MURDER!
COL. TREVOR INDICTED!
DAILY STANDARD
MYSTERY WITNESS STILL MISSING... TREVOR TRIAL NEXT WEEK!
MYSTERY GIRL SOUGHT IN TREVOR CASE!
"WONDER WOMAN'S RIVAL"
TREVOR TRIAL TODAY
NOW... IN YOUR OWN WORDS, COL. TREVOR, TELL US WHAT HAPPENED THE NIGHT ALEX BLOCK WAS FOUND DEAD...
2

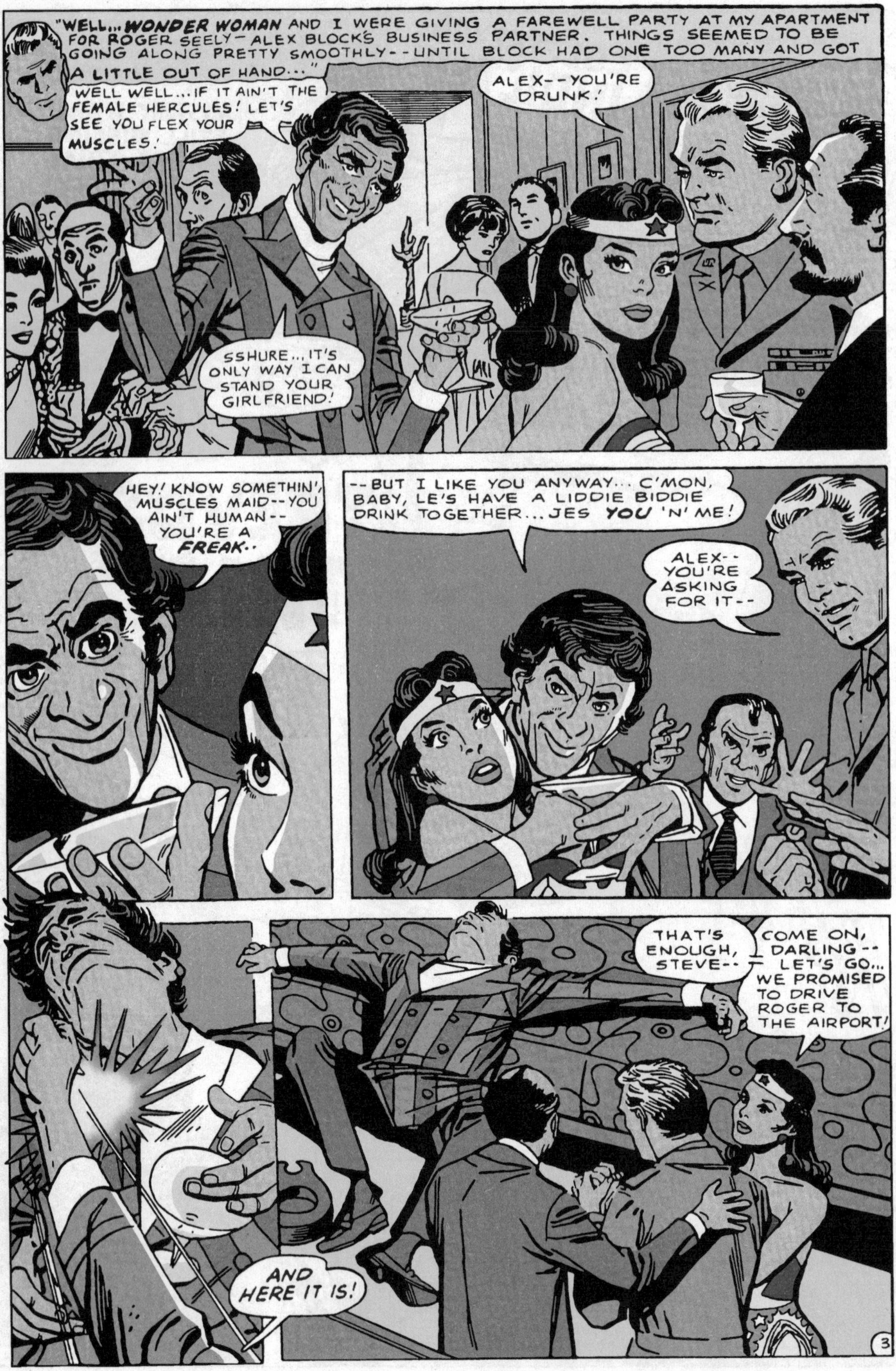
"WELL... WONDER WOMAN AND I WERE GIVING A FAREWELL PARTY AT MY APARTMENT FOR ROGER SEELY—ALEX BLOCK'S BUSINESS PARTNER. THINGS SEEMED TO BE GOING ALONG PRETTY SMOOTHLY--UNTIL BLOCK HAD ONE TOO MANY AND GOT A LITTLE OUT OF HAND..."
WELL WELL... IF IT AIN'T THE FEMALE HERCULES! LET'S SEE YOU FLEX YOUR MUSCLES!
ALEX--YOU'RE DRUNK!
SSHURE... IT'S ONLY WAY I CAN STAND YOUR GIRLFRIEND!
HEY! KNOW SOMETHIN', MUSCLES MAID--YOU AIN'T HUMAN--YOU'RE A FREAK..
--BUT I LIKE YOU ANYWAY... C'MON, BABY, LE'S HAVE A LIDDIE BIDDIE DRINK TOGETHER... JES YOU 'N' ME!
ALEX--YOU'RE ASKING FOR IT--
AND HERE IT IS!
THAT'S ENOUGH, STEVE--
COME ON, DARLING--LET'S GO... WE PROMISED TO DRIVE ROGER TO THE AIRPORT!
3

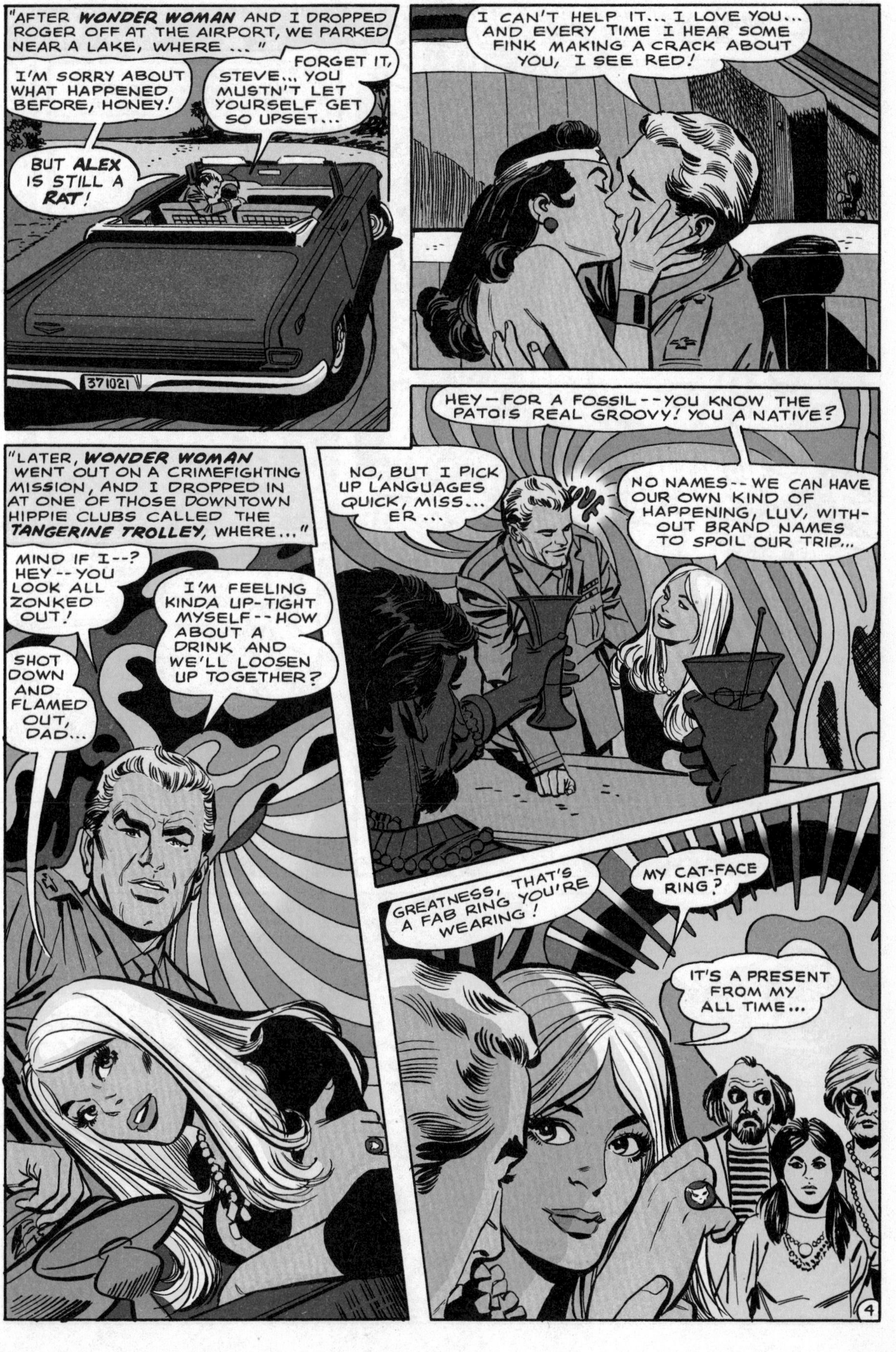
"AFTER WONDER WOMAN AND I DROPPED ROGER OFF AT THE AIRPORT, WE PARKED NEAR A LAKE, WHERE ..."
I'M SORRY ABOUT WHAT HAPPENED BEFORE, HONEY!
FORGET IT, STEVE... YOU MUSTN'T LET YOURSELF GET SO UPSET...
BUT ALEX IS STILL A RAT!
371021
I CAN'T HELP IT... I LOVE YOU... AND EVERY TIME I HEAR SOME FINK MAKING A CRACK ABOUT YOU, I SEE RED!
"LATER, WONDER WOMAN WENT OUT ON A CRIMEFIGHTING MISSION, AND I DROPPED IN AT ONE OF THOSE DOWNTOWN HIPPIE CLUBS CALLED THE TANGERINE TROLLEY, WHERE..."
MIND IF I--? HEY--YOU LOOK ALL ZONKED OUT!
I'M FEELING KINDA UP-TIGHT MYSELF--HOW ABOUT A DRINK AND WE'LL LOOSEN UP TOGETHER?
SHOT DOWN AND FLAMED OUT, DAD...
HEY--FOR A FOSSIL--YOU KNOW THE PATOIS REAL GROOVY! YOU A NATIVE?
NO, BUT I PICK UP LANGUAGES QUICK, MISS... ER...
OUF
NO NAMES--WE CAN HAVE OUR OWN KIND OF HAPPENING, LUV, WITHOUT BRAND NAMES TO SPOIL OUR TRIP...
GREATNESS, THAT'S A FAB RING YOU'RE WEARING!
MY CAT-FACE RING?
IT'S A PRESENT FROM MY ALL TIME...
4

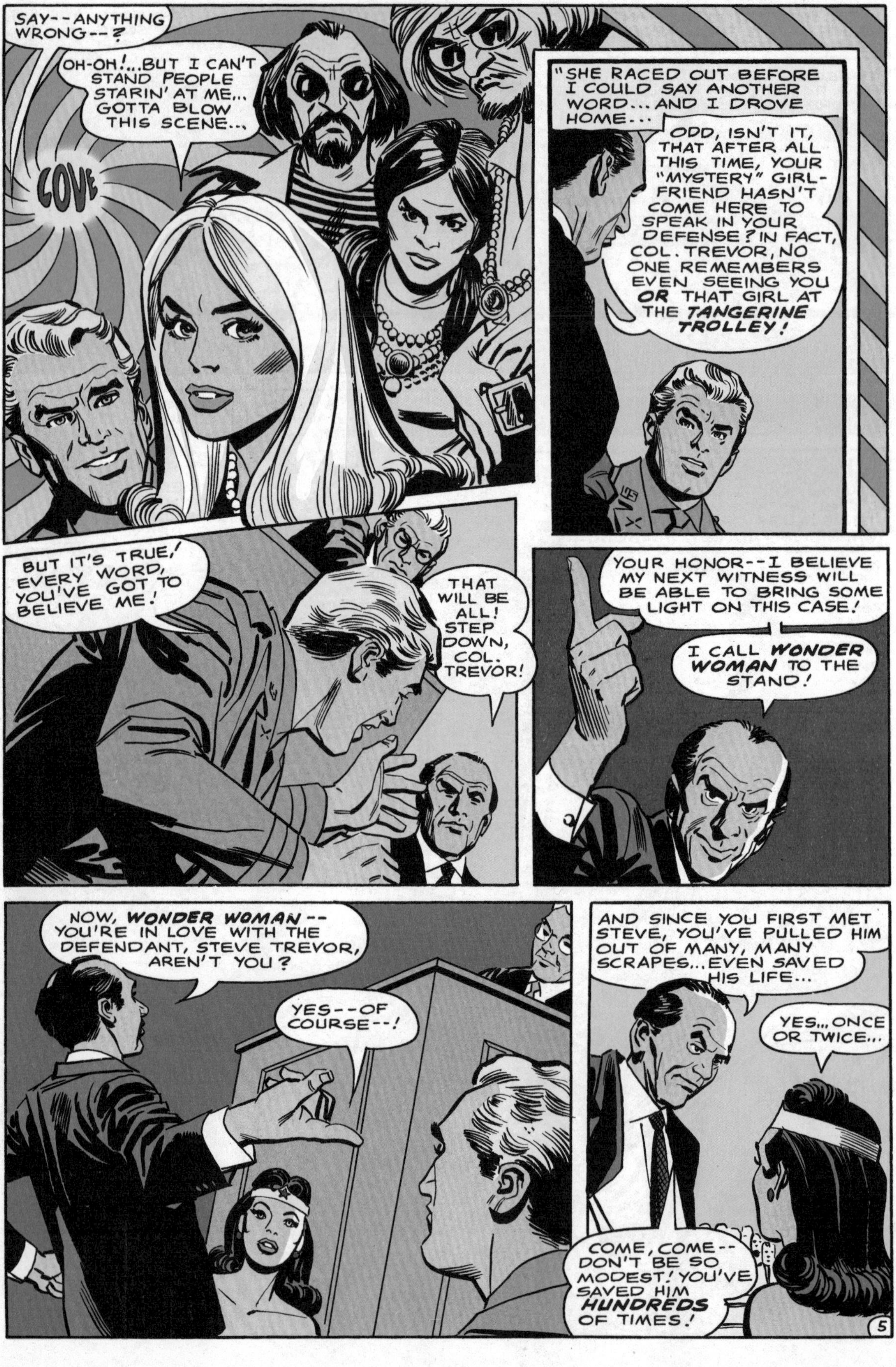
SAY--ANYTHING WRONG--?
OH-OH!...BUT I CAN'T STAND PEOPLE STARIN' AT ME... GOTTA BLOW THIS SCENE...
"SHE RACED OUT BEFORE I COULD SAY ANOTHER WORD...AND I DROVE HOME...
ODD, ISN'T IT, THAT AFTER ALL THIS TIME, YOUR "MYSTERY" GIRL-FRIEND HASN'T COME HERE TO SPEAK IN YOUR DEFENSE? IN FACT, COL. TREVOR, NO ONE REMEMBERS EVEN SEEING YOU OR THAT GIRL AT THE TANGERINE TROLLEY!
BUT IT'S TRUE! EVERY WORD, YOU'VE GOT TO BELIEVE ME!
THAT WILL BE ALL! STEP DOWN, COL. TREVOR!
YOUR HONOR--I BELIEVE MY NEXT WITNESS WILL BE ABLE TO BRING SOME LIGHT ON THIS CASE!
I CALL WONDER WOMAN TO THE STAND!
NOW, WONDER WOMAN-- YOU'RE IN LOVE WITH THE DEFENDANT, STEVE TREVOR, AREN'T YOU?
YES--OF COURSE--!
AND SINCE YOU FIRST MET STEVE, YOU'VE PULLED HIM OUT OF MANY, MANY SCRAPES...EVEN SAVED HIS LIFE...
YES...ONCE OR TWICE...
COME, COME-- DON'T BE SO MODEST! YOU'VE SAVED HIM HUNDREDS OF TIMES!
5

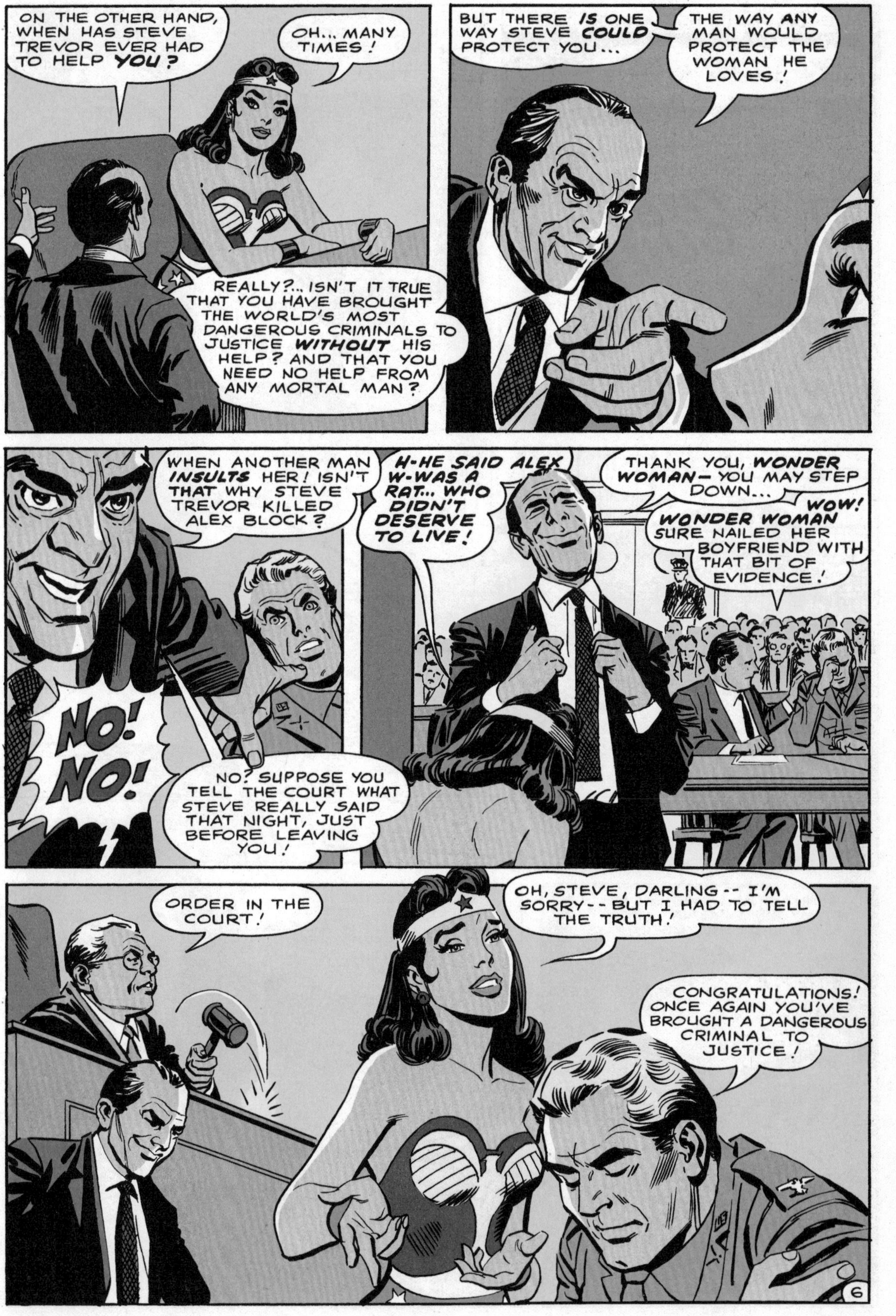
ON THE OTHER HAND, WHEN HAS STEVE TREVOR EVER HAD TO HELP YOU?
OH... MANY TIMES!
REALLY?... ISN'T IT TRUE THAT YOU HAVE BROUGHT THE WORLD'S MOST DANGEROUS CRIMINALS TO JUSTICE WITHOUT HIS HELP? AND THAT YOU NEED NO HELP FROM ANY MORTAL MAN?
BUT THERE IS ONE WAY STEVE COULD PROTECT YOU...
THE WAY ANY MAN WOULD PROTECT THE WOMAN HE LOVES!
WHEN ANOTHER MAN INSULTS HER! ISN'T THAT WHY STEVE TREVOR KILLED ALEX BLOCK?
NO! NO!
NO? SUPPOSE YOU TELL THE COURT WHAT STEVE REALLY SAID THAT NIGHT, JUST BEFORE LEAVING YOU!
H-HE SAID ALEX W-WAS A RAT... WHO DIDN'T DESERVE TO LIVE!
THANK YOU, WONDER WOMAN— YOU MAY STEP DOWN...
WOW! WONDER WOMAN SURE NAILED HER BOYFRIEND WITH THAT BIT OF EVIDENCE!
ORDER IN THE COURT!
OH, STEVE, DARLING -- I'M SORRY -- BUT I HAD TO TELL THE TRUTH!
CONGRATULATIONS! ONCE AGAIN YOU'VE BROUGHT A DANGEROUS CRIMINAL TO JUSTICE!
6

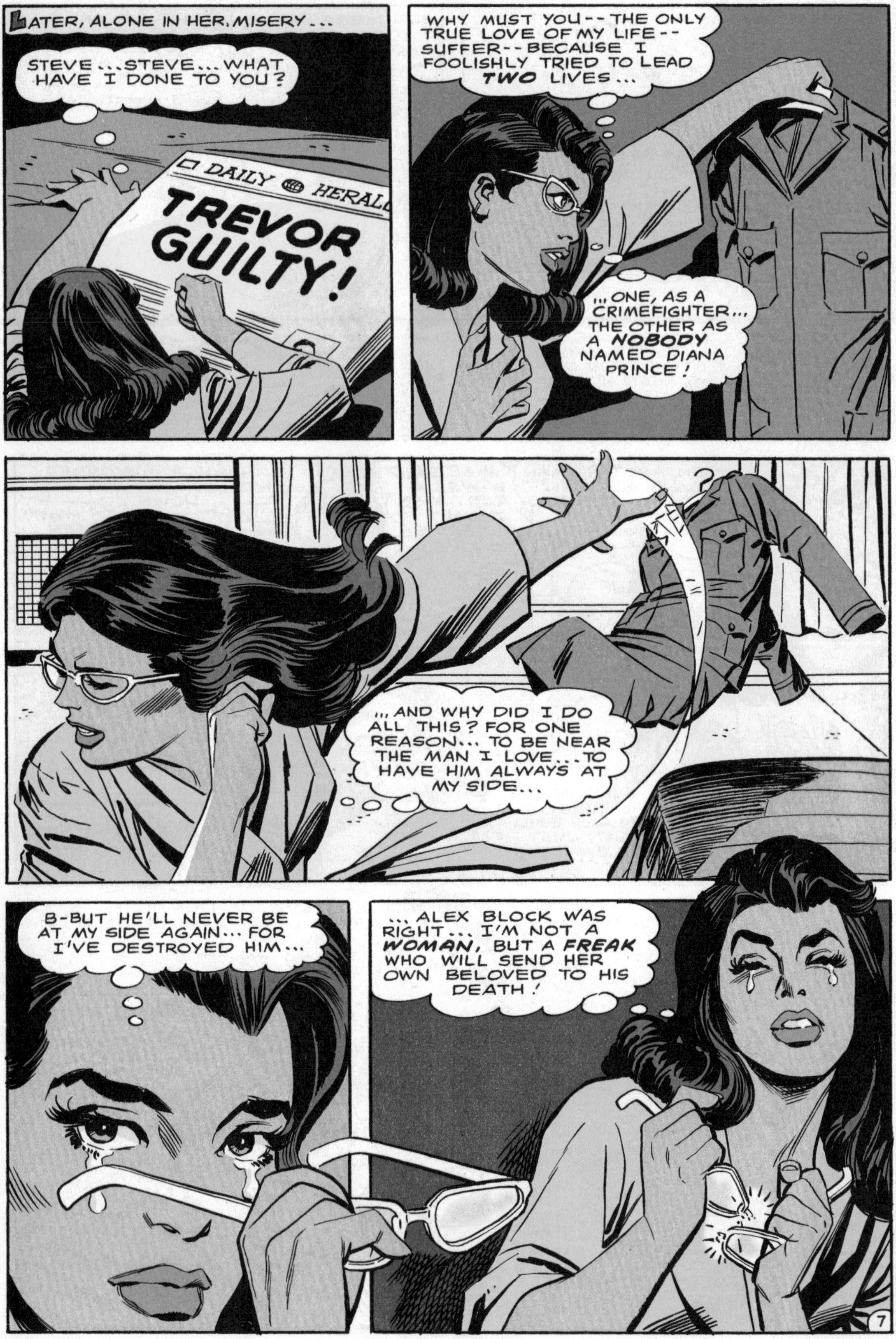
LATER, ALONE IN HER MISERY...
STEVE...STEVE...WHAT HAVE I DONE TO YOU?
DAILY HERALD
TREVOR GUILTY!
WHY MUST YOU--THE ONLY TRUE LOVE OF MY LIFE--SUFFER--BECAUSE I FOOLISHLY TRIED TO LEAD TWO LIVES...
...ONE, AS A CRIMEFIGHTER... THE OTHER AS A NOBODY NAMED DIANA PRINCE!
...AND WHY DID I DO ALL THIS? FOR ONE REASON... TO BE NEAR THE MAN I LOVE...TO HAVE HIM ALWAYS AT MY SIDE...
B-BUT HE'LL NEVER BE AT MY SIDE AGAIN... FOR I'VE DESTROYED HIM...
...ALEX BLOCK WAS RIGHT... I'M NOT A WOMAN, BUT A FREAK WHO WILL SEND HER OWN BELOVED TO HIS DEATH!
7

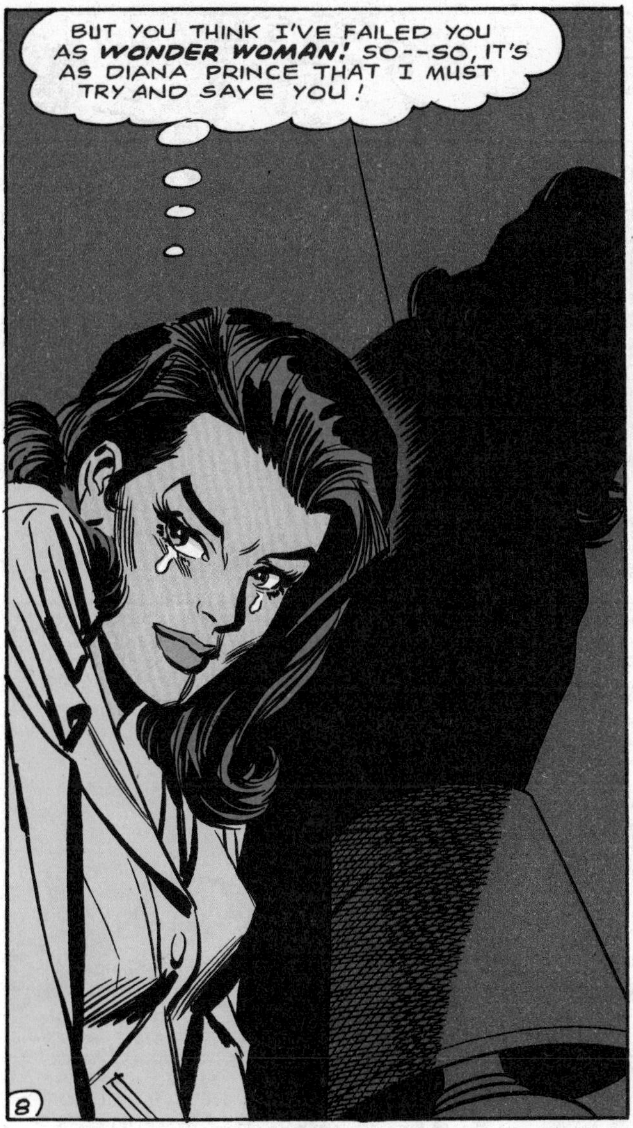
BUT YOU THINK I'VE FAILED YOU AS WONDER WOMAN! SO--SO, IT'S AS DIANA PRINCE THAT I MUST TRY AND SAVE YOU!
8

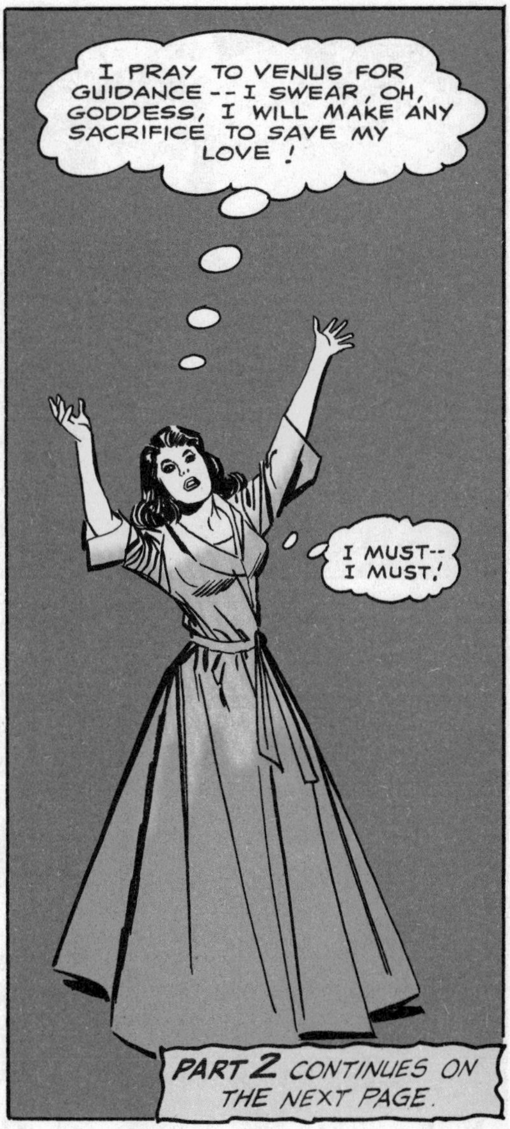
I PRAY TO VENUS FOR GUIDANCE -- I SWEAR, OH, GODDESS, I WILL MAKE ANY SACRIFICE TO SAVE MY LOVE!
I MUST-- I MUST!
PART 2 CONTINUES ON THE NEXT PAGE.

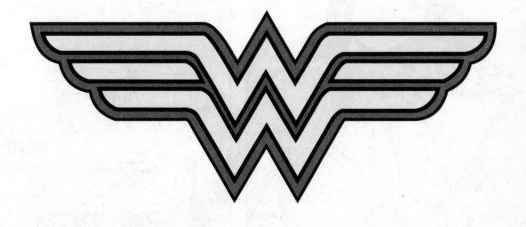

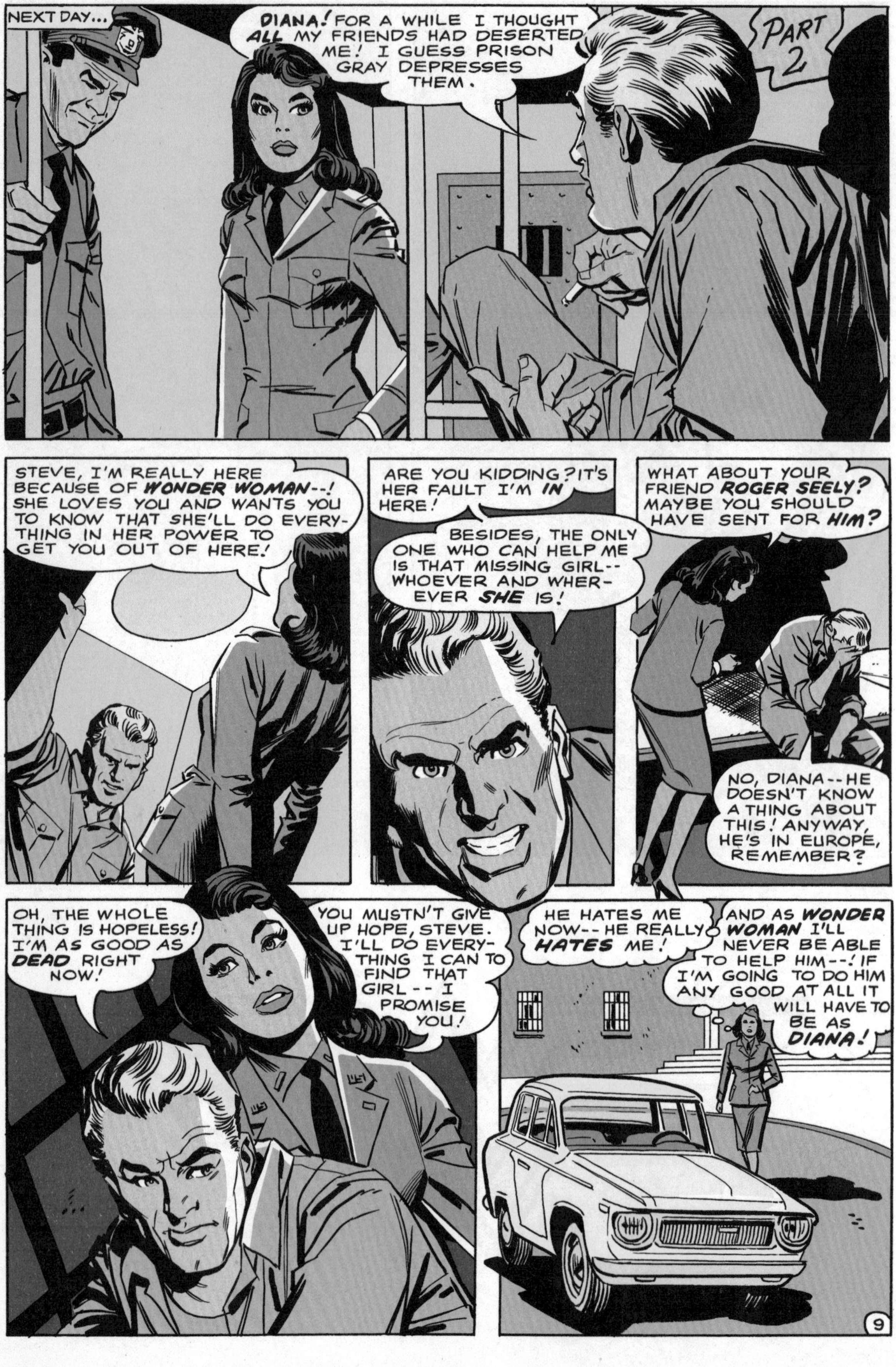
NEXT DAY...
DIANA! FOR A WHILE I THOUGHT ALL MY FRIENDS HAD DESERTED ME! I GUESS PRISON GRAY DEPRESSES THEM.
PART 2
STEVE, I'M REALLY HERE BECAUSE OF WONDER WOMAN--! SHE LOVES YOU AND WANTS YOU TO KNOW THAT SHE'LL DO EVERYTHING IN HER POWER TO GET YOU OUT OF HERE!
ARE YOU KIDDING? IT'S HER FAULT I'M IN HERE!
BESIDES, THE ONLY ONE WHO CAN HELP ME IS THAT MISSING GIRL-- WHOEVER AND WHEREVER SHE IS!
WHAT ABOUT YOUR FRIEND ROGER SEELY? MAYBE YOU SHOULD HAVE SENT FOR HIM?
NO, DIANA--HE DOESN'T KNOW A THING ABOUT THIS! ANYWAY, HE'S IN EUROPE, REMEMBER?
OH, THE WHOLE THING IS HOPELESS! I'M AS GOOD AS DEAD RIGHT NOW!
YOU MUSTN'T GIVE UP HOPE, STEVE. I'LL DO EVERYTHING I CAN TO FIND THAT GIRL -- I PROMISE YOU!
HE HATES ME NOW-- HE REALLY HATES ME!
AND AS WONDER WOMAN I'LL NEVER BE ABLE TO HELP HIM--! IF I'M GOING TO DO HIM ANY GOOD AT ALL IT WILL HAVE TO BE AS DIANA!
9

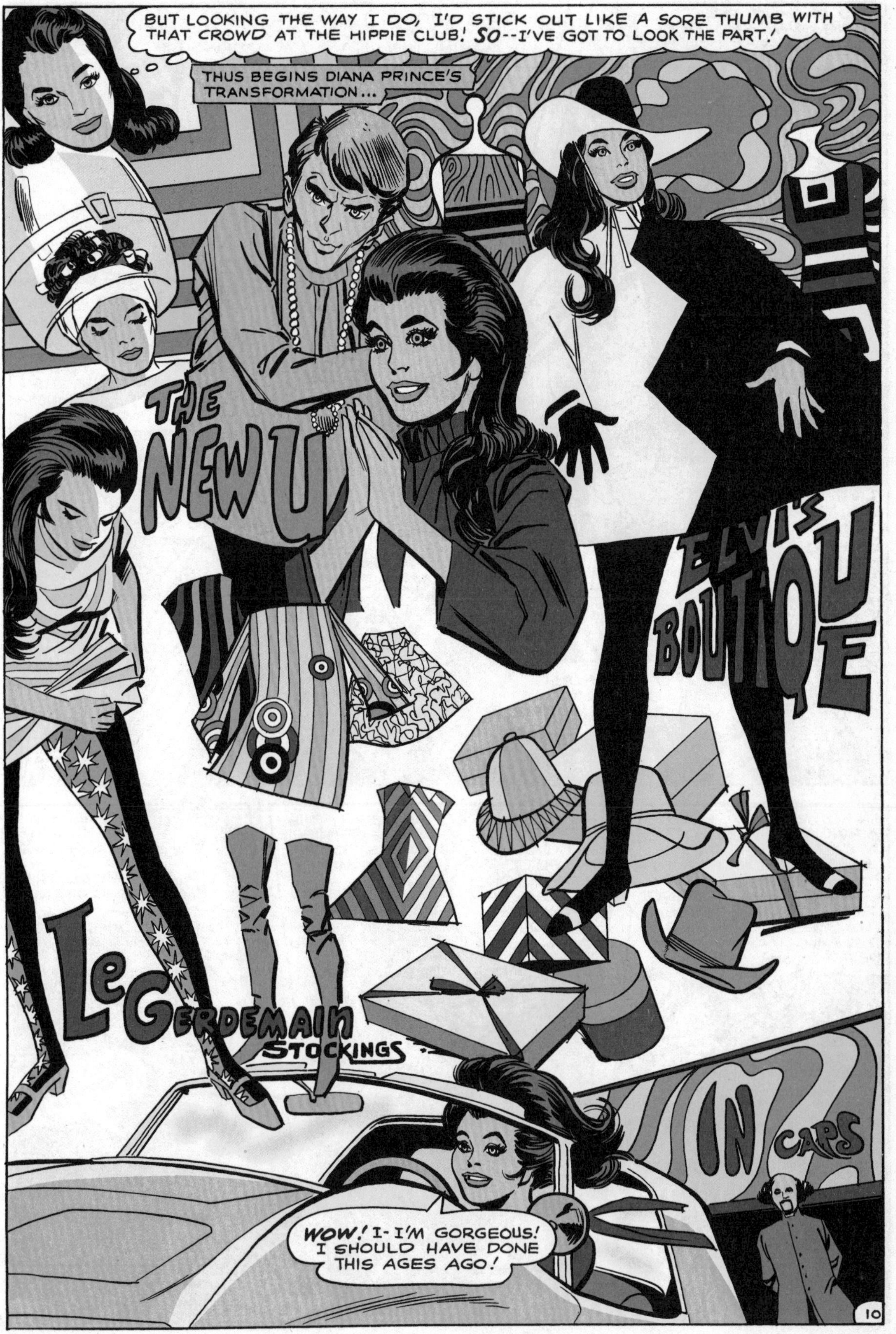
BUT LOOKING THE WAY I DO, I'D STICK OUT LIKE A SORE THUMB WITH THAT CROWD AT THE HIPPIE CLUB! SO--I'VE GOT TO LOOK THE PART!
THUS BEGINS DIANA PRINCE'S TRANSFORMATION...
THE NEW U
ELVI'S BOUTIQUE
LeGERDEMAIN STOCKINGS
IN CARS
WOW! I- I'M GORGEOUS! I SHOULD HAVE DONE THIS AGES AGO!
10

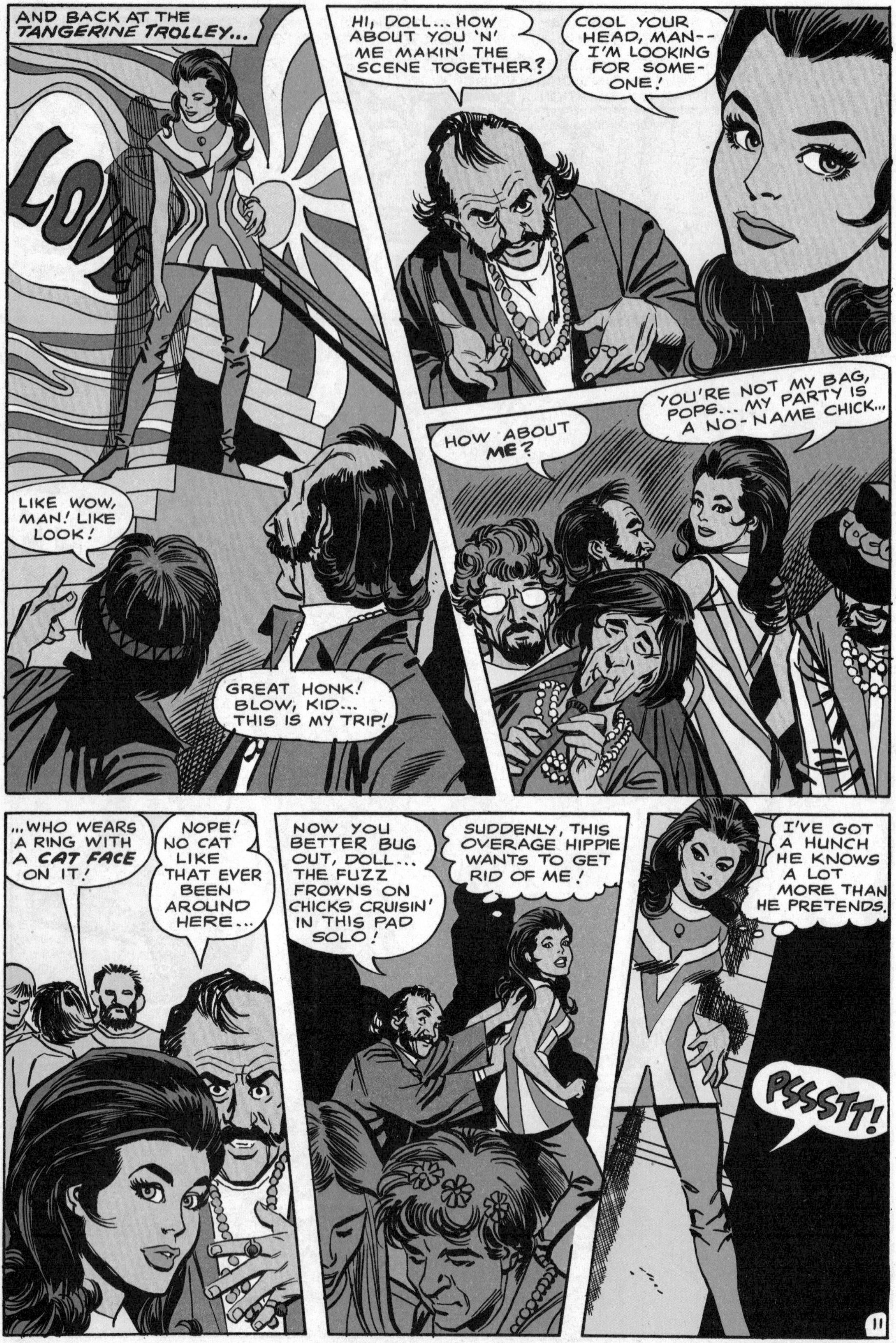

AND BACK AT THE TANGERINE TROLLEY...
LOVE
LIKE WOW, MAN! LIKE LOOK!
GREAT HONK! BLOW, KID... THIS IS MY TRIP!
HI, DOLL... HOW ABOUT YOU 'N' ME MAKIN' THE SCENE TOGETHER?
COOL YOUR HEAD, MAN-- I'M LOOKING FOR SOME-ONE!
HOW ABOUT ME?
YOU'RE NOT MY BAG, POPS... MY PARTY IS A NO-NAME CHICK...
...WHO WEARS A RING WITH A CAT FACE ON IT!
NOPE! NO CAT LIKE THAT EVER BEEN AROUND HERE...
NOW YOU BETTER BUG OUT, DOLL... THE FUZZ FROWNS ON CHICKS CRUISIN' IN THIS PAD SOLO!
SUDDENLY, THIS OVERAGE HIPPIE WANTS TO GET RID OF ME!
I'VE GOT A HUNCH HE KNOWS A LOT MORE THAN HE PRETENDS.
PSSSTT!
11

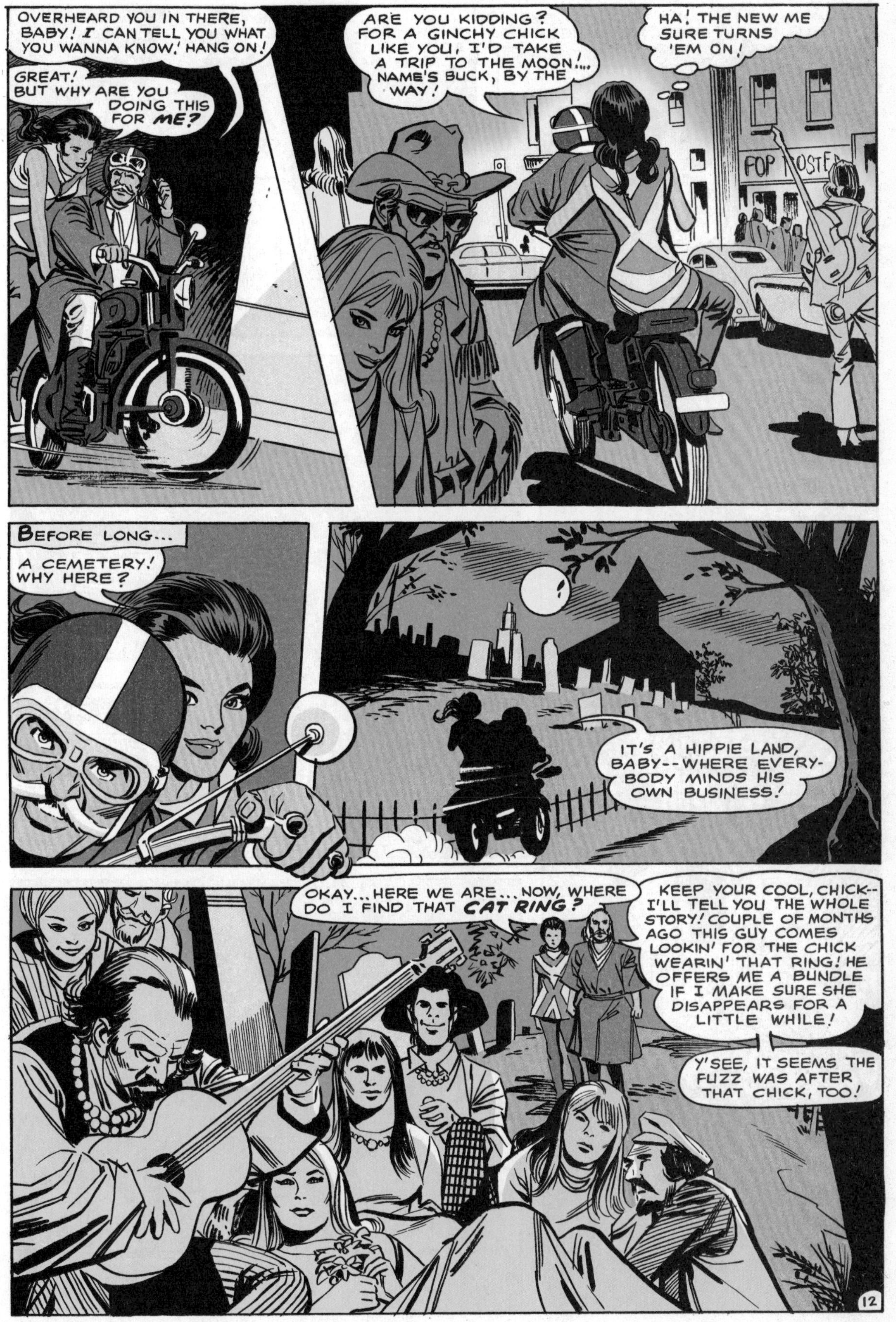
OVERHEARD YOU IN THERE, BABY! I CAN TELL YOU WHAT YOU WANNA KNOW! HANG ON!
GREAT! BUT WHY ARE YOU DOING THIS FOR ME?
ARE YOU KIDDING? FOR A GINCHY CHICK LIKE YOU, I'D TAKE A TRIP TO THE MOON!... NAME'S BUCK, BY THE WAY!
HA! THE NEW ME SURE TURNS 'EM ON!
POP POSTER
BEFORE LONG...
A CEMETERY! WHY HERE?
IT'S A HIPPIE LAND, BABY--WHERE EVERY-BODY MINDS HIS OWN BUSINESS!
OKAY... HERE WE ARE... NOW, WHERE DO I FIND THAT CAT RING?
KEEP YOUR COOL, CHICK--I'LL TELL YOU THE WHOLE STORY! COUPLE OF MONTHS AGO THIS GUY COMES LOOKIN' FOR THE CHICK WEARIN' THAT RING! HE OFFERS ME A BUNDLE IF I MAKE SURE SHE DISAPPEARS FOR A LITTLE WHILE!
Y'SEE, IT SEEMS THE FUZZ WAS AFTER THAT CHICK, TOO!
12

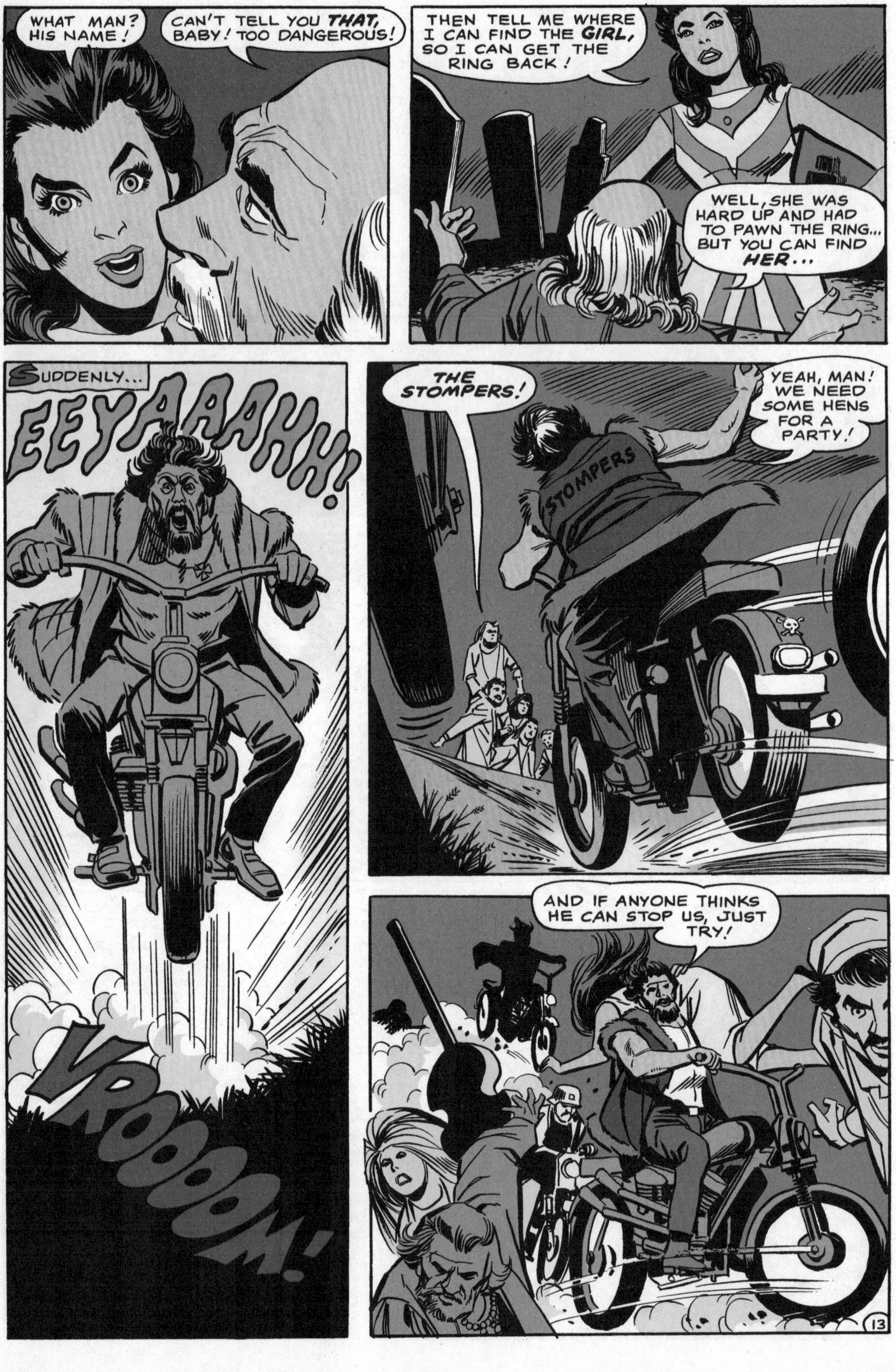
WHAT MAN? HIS NAME!
CAN'T TELL YOU THAT, BABY! TOO DANGEROUS!
THEN TELL ME WHERE I CAN FIND THE GIRL, SO I CAN GET THE RING BACK!
WELL, SHE WAS HARD UP AND HAD TO PAWN THE RING... BUT YOU CAN FIND HER...
SUDDENLY...
EEYAAAHH!
VROOOOM!
THE STOMPERS!
YEAH, MAN! WE NEED SOME HENS FOR A PARTY!
STOMPERS
AND IF ANYONE THINKS HE CAN STOP US, JUST TRY!
13

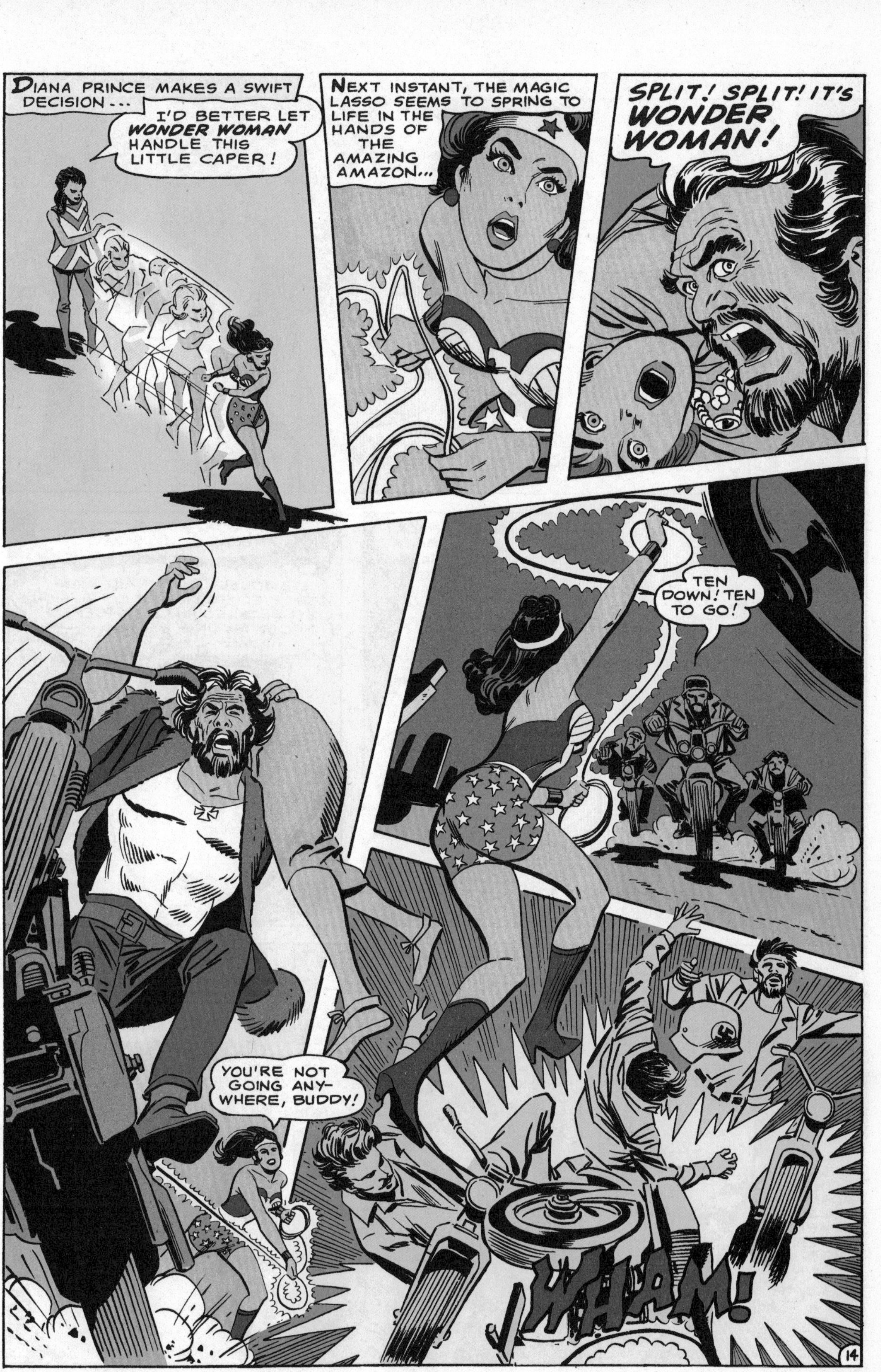
DIANA PRINCE MAKES A SWIFT DECISION ...
I'D BETTER LET WONDER WOMAN HANDLE THIS LITTLE CAPER!
NEXT INSTANT, THE MAGIC LASSO SEEMS TO SPRING TO LIFE IN THE HANDS OF THE AMAZING AMAZON...
SPLIT! SPLIT! IT'S WONDER WOMAN!
TEN DOWN! TEN TO GO!
YOU'RE NOT GOING ANY-WHERE, BUDDY!
WHAM!
14

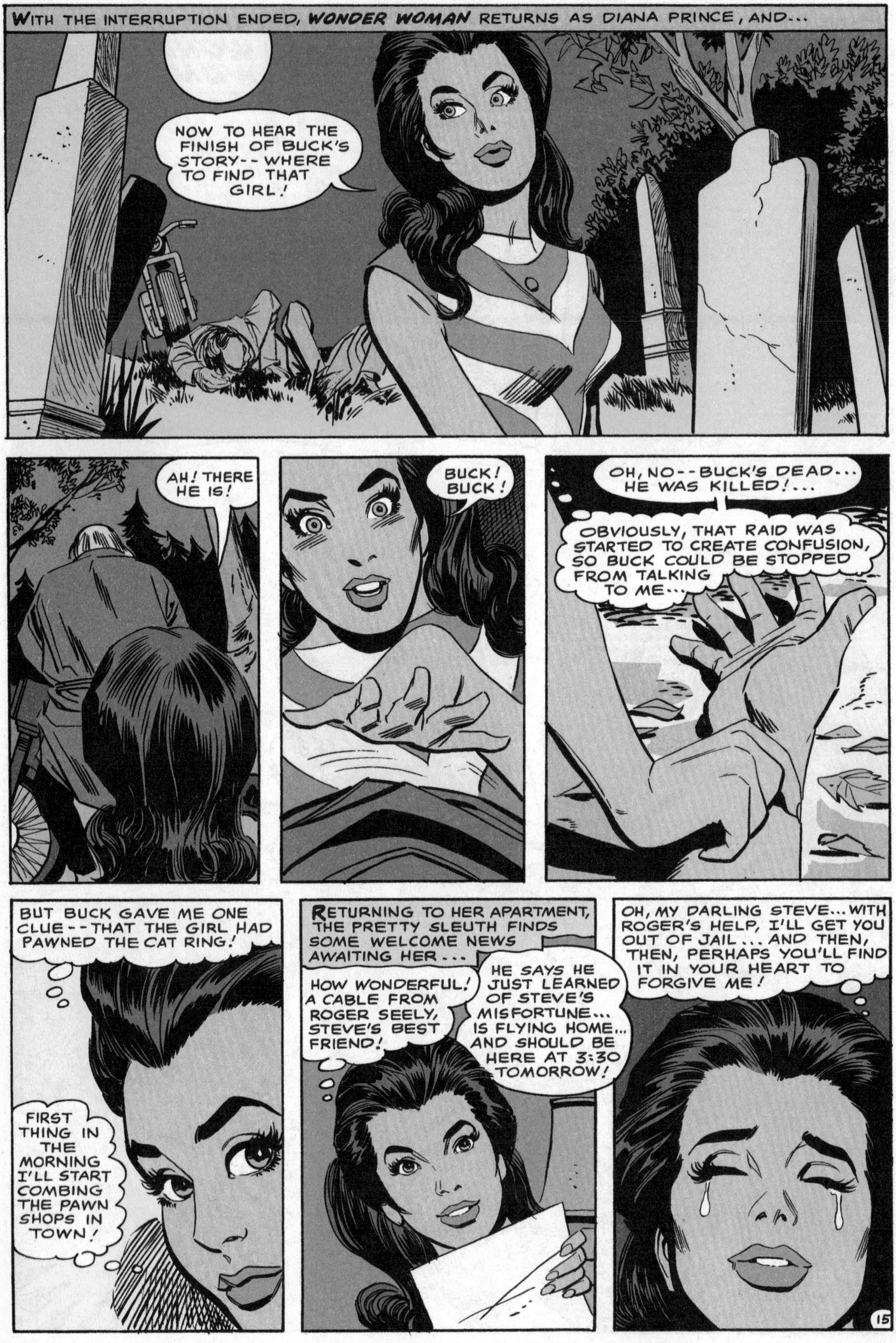

WITH THE INTERRUPTION ENDED, WONDER WOMAN RETURNS AS DIANA PRINCE, AND...
NOW TO HEAR THE FINISH OF BUCK'S STORY-- WHERE TO FIND THAT GIRL!
AH! THERE HE IS!
BUCK! BUCK!
OH, NO--BUCK'S DEAD... HE WAS KILLED!...
OBVIOUSLY, THAT RAID WAS STARTED TO CREATE CONFUSION, SO BUCK COULD BE STOPPED FROM TALKING TO ME...
BUT BUCK GAVE ME ONE CLUE--THAT THE GIRL HAD PAWNED THE CAT RING!
FIRST THING IN THE MORNING I'LL START COMBING THE PAWN SHOPS IN TOWN!
RETURNING TO HER APARTMENT, THE PRETTY SLEUTH FINDS SOME WELCOME NEWS AWAITING HER...
HOW WONDERFUL! A CABLE FROM ROGER SEELY, STEVE'S BEST FRIEND!
HE SAYS HE JUST LEARNED OF STEVE'S MISFORTUNE... IS FLYING HOME... AND SHOULD BE HERE AT 3:30 TOMORROW!
OH, MY DARLING STEVE... WITH ROGER'S HELP, I'LL GET YOU OUT OF JAIL... AND THEN, THEN, PERHAPS YOU'LL FIND IT IN YOUR HEART TO FORGIVE ME!
15

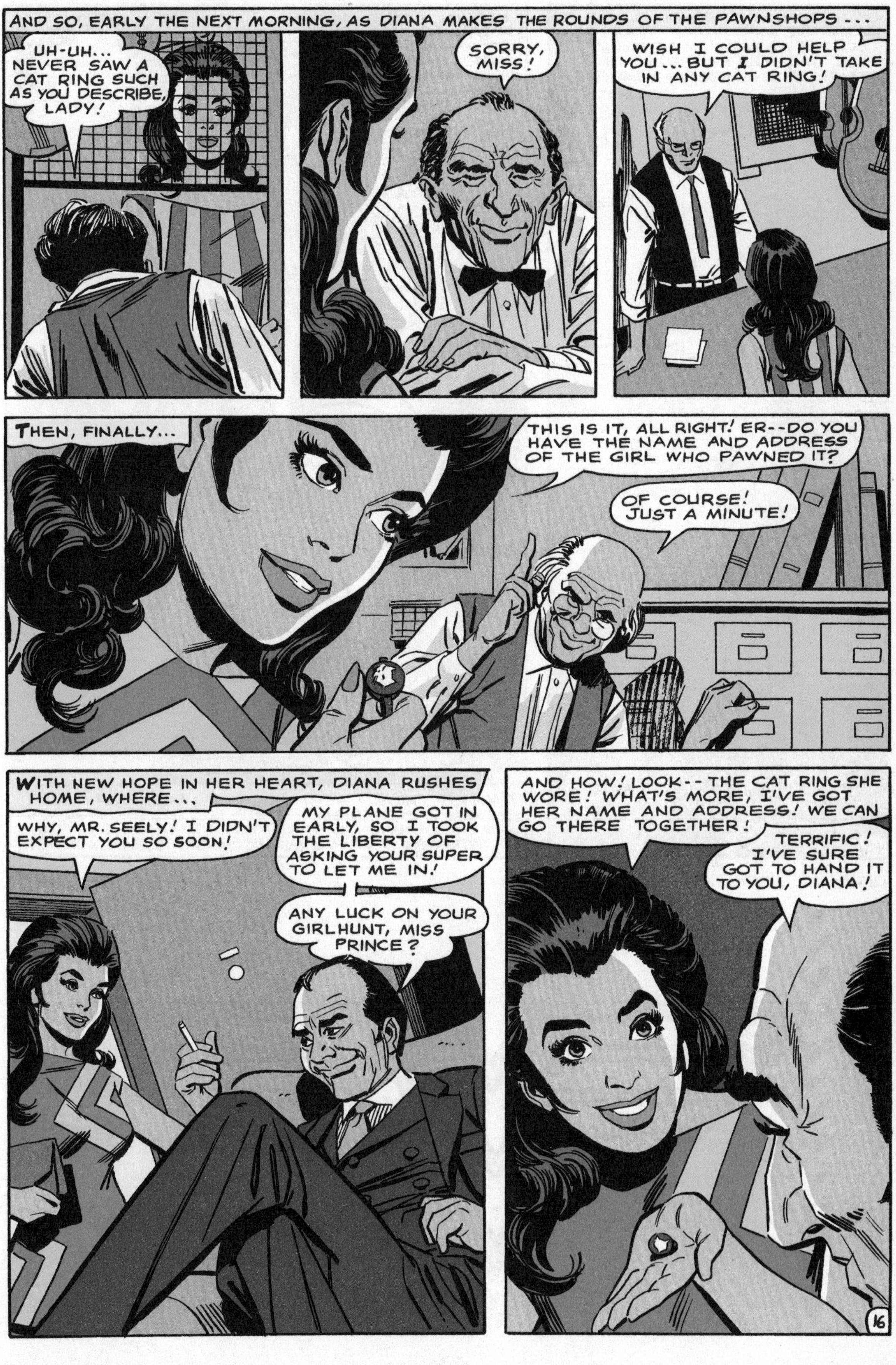
AND SO, EARLY THE NEXT MORNING, AS DIANA MAKES THE ROUNDS OF THE PAWNSHOPS ...
UH-UH... NEVER SAW A CAT RING SUCH AS YOU DESCRIBE, LADY!
SORRY, MISS!
WISH I COULD HELP YOU... BUT I DIDN'T TAKE IN ANY CAT RING!
THEN, FINALLY...
THIS IS IT, ALL RIGHT! ER--DO YOU HAVE THE NAME AND ADDRESS OF THE GIRL WHO PAWNED IT?
OF COURSE! JUST A MINUTE!
WITH NEW HOPE IN HER HEART, DIANA RUSHES HOME, WHERE...
WHY, MR. SEELY! I DIDN'T EXPECT YOU SO SOON!
MY PLANE GOT IN EARLY, SO I TOOK THE LIBERTY OF ASKING YOUR SUPER TO LET ME IN!
ANY LUCK ON YOUR GIRLHUNT, MISS PRINCE?
AND HOW! LOOK-- THE CAT RING SHE WORE! WHAT'S MORE, I'VE GOT HER NAME AND ADDRESS! WE CAN GO THERE TOGETHER!
TERRIFIC! I'VE SURE GOT TO HAND IT TO YOU, DIANA!
16

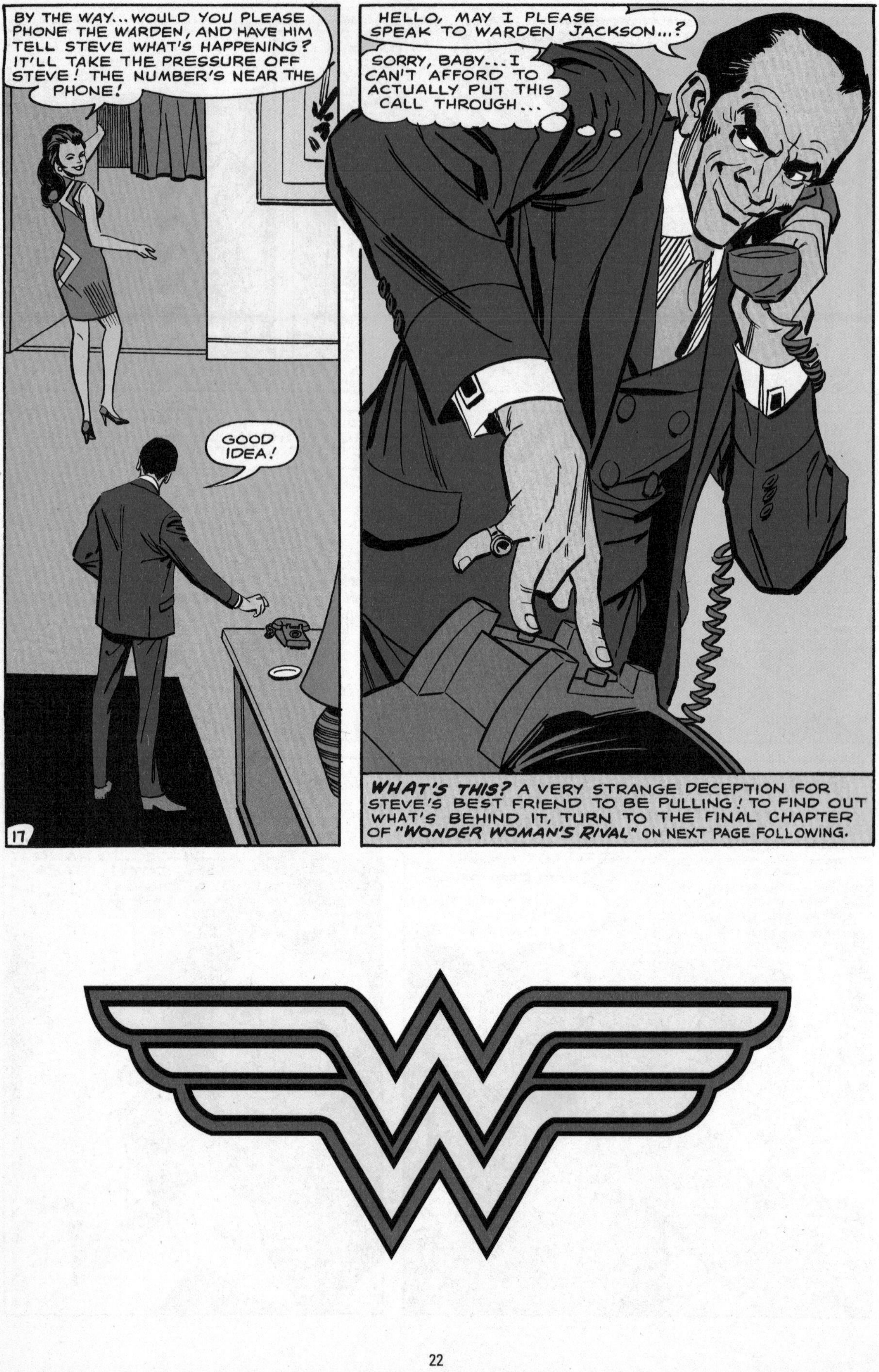
BY THE WAY... WOULD YOU PLEASE PHONE THE WARDEN, AND HAVE HIM TELL STEVE WHAT'S HAPPENING? IT'LL TAKE THE PRESSURE OFF STEVE! THE NUMBER'S NEAR THE PHONE!
GOOD IDEA!
17
HELLO, MAY I PLEASE SPEAK TO WARDEN JACKSON...?
SORRY, BABY... I CAN'T AFFORD TO ACTUALLY PUT THIS CALL THROUGH...
WHAT'S THIS? A VERY STRANGE DECEPTION FOR STEVE'S BEST FRIEND TO BE PULLING! TO FIND OUT WHAT'S BEHIND IT, TURN TO THE FINAL CHAPTER OF "WONDER WOMAN'S RIVAL" ON NEXT PAGE FOLLOWING.

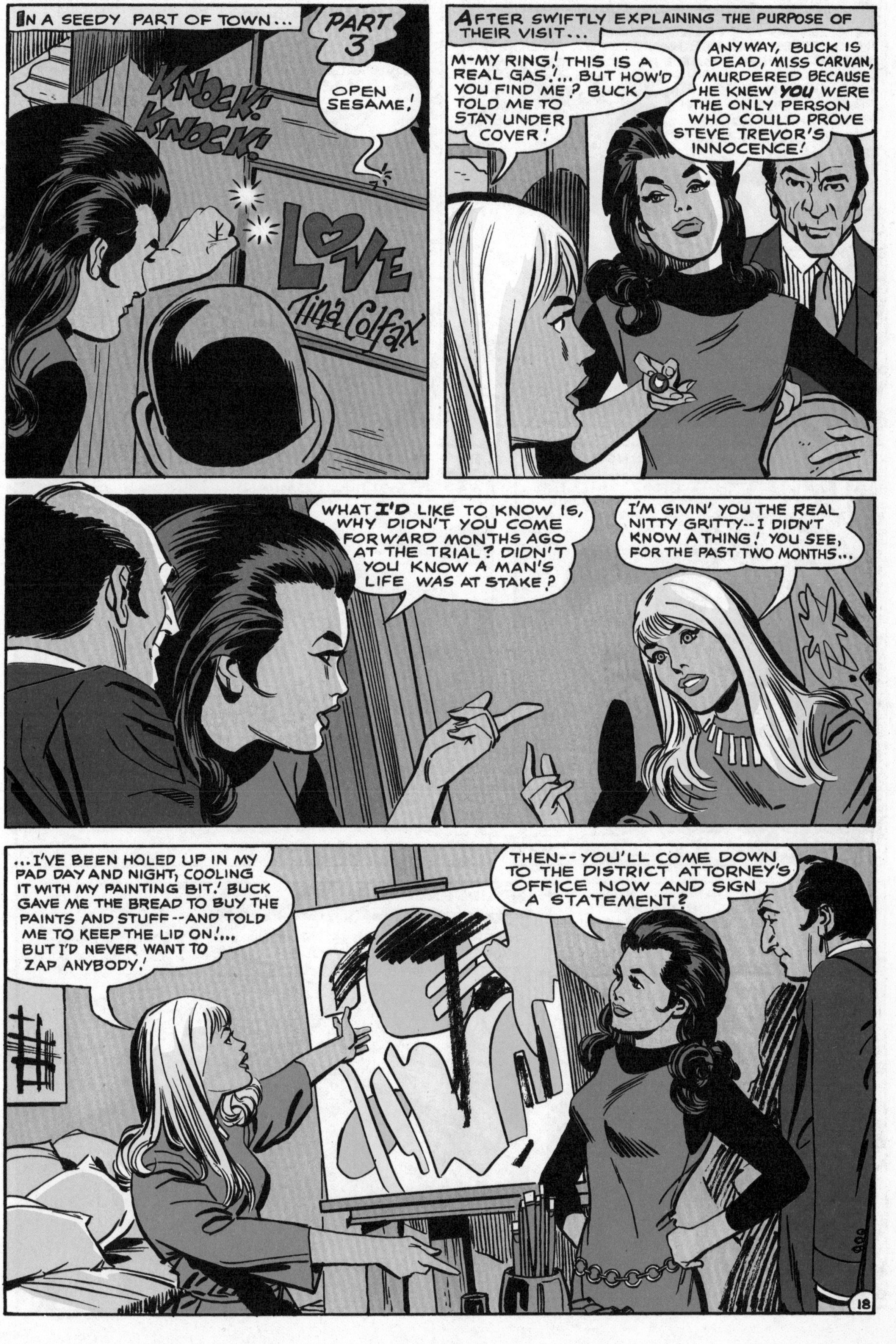
IN A SEEDY PART OF TOWN...
PART 3
KNOCK! KNOCK!
OPEN SESAME!
LOVE Tina Colfax
AFTER SWIFTLY EXPLAINING THE PURPOSE OF THEIR VISIT...
M-MY RING! THIS IS A REAL GAS!... BUT HOW'D YOU FIND ME? BUCK TOLD ME TO STAY UNDER COVER!
ANYWAY, BUCK IS DEAD, MISS CARVAN, MURDERED BECAUSE HE KNEW YOU WERE THE ONLY PERSON WHO COULD PROVE STEVE TREVOR'S INNOCENCE!
WHAT I'D LIKE TO KNOW IS, WHY DIDN'T YOU COME FORWARD MONTHS AGO AT THE TRIAL? DIDN'T YOU KNOW A MAN'S LIFE WAS AT STAKE?
I'M GIVIN' YOU THE REAL NITTY GRITTY--I DIDN'T KNOW A THING! YOU SEE, FOR THE PAST TWO MONTHS...
...I'VE BEEN HOLED UP IN MY PAD DAY AND NIGHT, COOLING IT WITH MY PAINTING BIT! BUCK GAVE ME THE BREAD TO BUY THE PAINTS AND STUFF--AND TOLD ME TO KEEP THE LID ON!... BUT I'D NEVER WANT TO ZAP ANYBODY!
THEN--YOU'LL COME DOWN TO THE DISTRICT ATTORNEY'S OFFICE NOW AND SIGN A STATEMENT?
18

SHORTLY...

AS SOON AS THE POLICE REALIZE STEVE IS INNOCENT--THEY'LL HAVE ALEX BLOCK'S KILLER BEHIND BARS IN NO TIME!

YOU MAY THINK SO, MISS PRINCE...BUT I DON'T THINK THOSE FOOLS WILL EVER FIND HIM!

NO...THEY'LL NEVER BE ABLE TO FIND ME...ONCE THE ONLY TWO PEOPLE WHO CAN PROVE STEVE INNOCENT ARE... DEAD!

KEEP DRIVING STRAIGHT ON TO CANYON HILLS, MISS PRINCE! TOO BAD-- FOR YOU-- YOU HAD TO GO SNOOPING AROUND!

I--I DARE NOT MAKE A MOVE AGAINST THAT CRAZY KILLER N-NOT--NOT AS LONG AS HE KEEPS THAT GUN ON HER...

I HAD A FEELING I COULDN'T TRUST BUCK...NEVER COULD TRUST ANYONE... TAKE THAT FOOL, ALEX BLOCK...

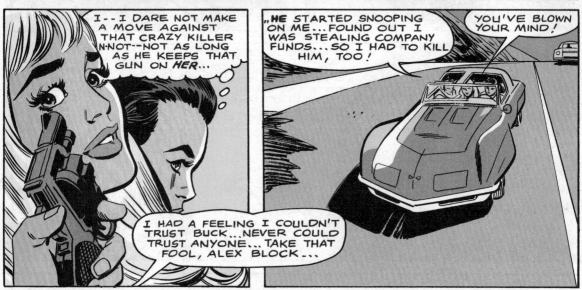

"HE STARTED SNOOPING ON ME...FOUND OUT I WAS STEALING COMPANY FUNDS...SO I HAD TO KILL HIM, TOO!

YOU'VE BLOWN YOUR MIND!

MAD, AM I? HA, HA! I FOOLED EVERYONE! NO ONE SUSPECTED I HIRED AN ACTOR TO MAKE HIMSELF UP TO LOOK LIKE ME AND TAKE MY PLACE ON THAT FLIGHT...

...SO I COULD STAY HERE AND STOP ALEX FROM TURNING ME IN! HA, HA! HE SAID I WAS CRAZY, TOO! BUT I SHOWED 'IM!

SUDDENLY...

KEEP DRIVING, MISS PRINCE! DON'T STOP! RIGHT OVER THE CLIFF!

19

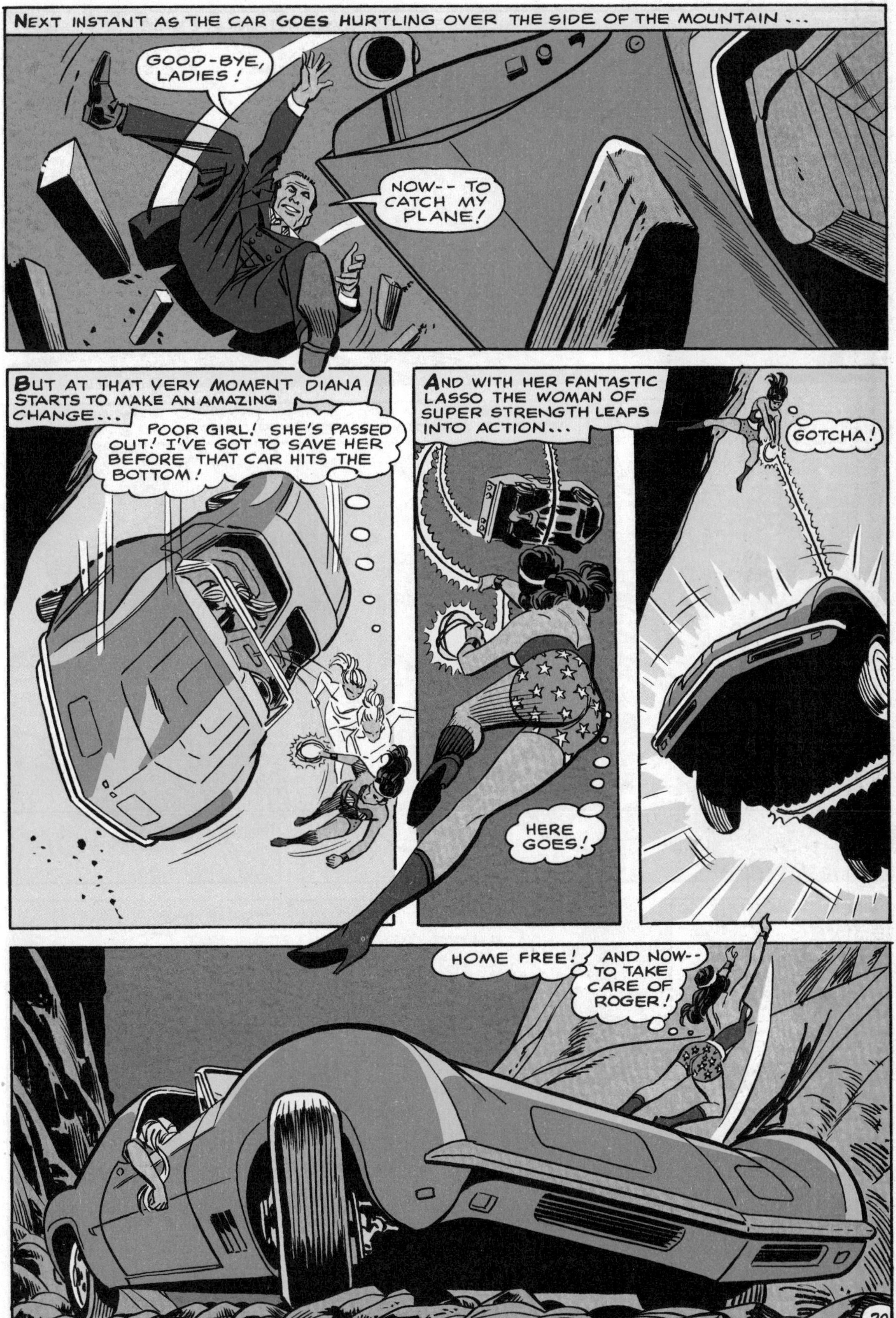
NEXT INSTANT AS THE CAR GOES HURTLING OVER THE SIDE OF THE MOUNTAIN ...
GOOD-BYE, LADIES!
NOW-- TO CATCH MY PLANE!
BUT AT THAT VERY MOMENT DIANA STARTS TO MAKE AN AMAZING CHANGE...
POOR GIRL! SHE'S PASSED OUT! I'VE GOT TO SAVE HER BEFORE THAT CAR HITS THE BOTTOM!
AND WITH HER FANTASTIC LASSO THE WOMAN OF SUPER STRENGTH LEAPS INTO ACTION...
HERE GOES!
GOTCHA!
HOME FREE!
AND NOW-- TO TAKE CARE OF ROGER!
20

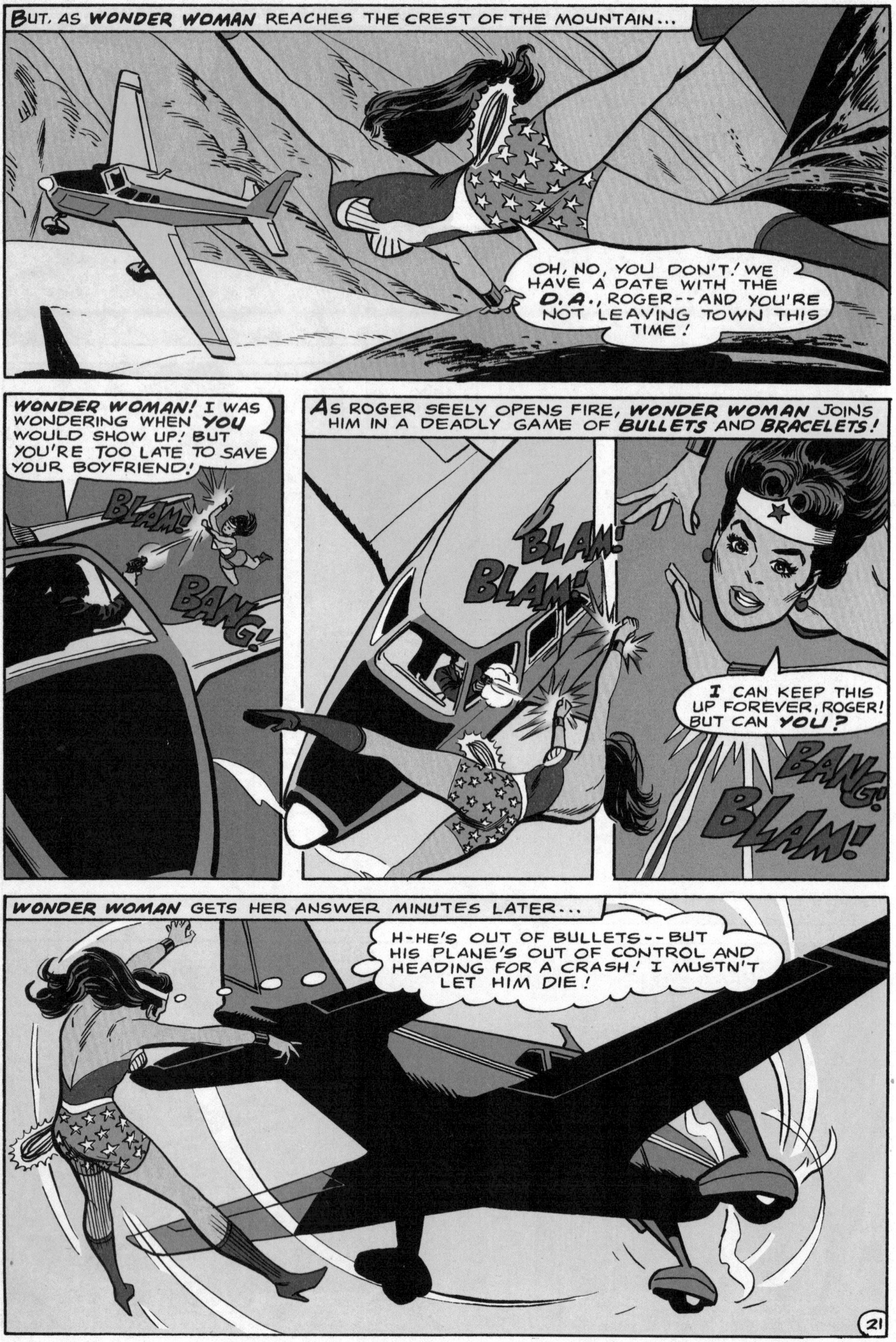
BUT, AS WONDER WOMAN REACHES THE CREST OF THE MOUNTAIN...
OH, NO, YOU DON'T! WE HAVE A DATE WITH THE D.A., ROGER--AND YOU'RE NOT LEAVING TOWN THIS TIME!
WONDER WOMAN! I WAS WONDERING WHEN YOU WOULD SHOW UP! BUT YOU'RE TOO LATE TO SAVE YOUR BOYFRIEND!
BLAM!
BANG!
AS ROGER SEELY OPENS FIRE, WONDER WOMAN JOINS HIM IN A DEADLY GAME OF BULLETS AND BRACELETS!
BLAM!
BLAM!
I CAN KEEP THIS UP FOREVER, ROGER! BUT CAN YOU?
BANG!
BLAM!
WONDER WOMAN GETS HER ANSWER MINUTES LATER...
H-HE'S OUT OF BULLETS--BUT HIS PLANE'S OUT OF CONTROL AND HEADING FOR A CRASH! I MUSTN'T LET HIM DIE!
21

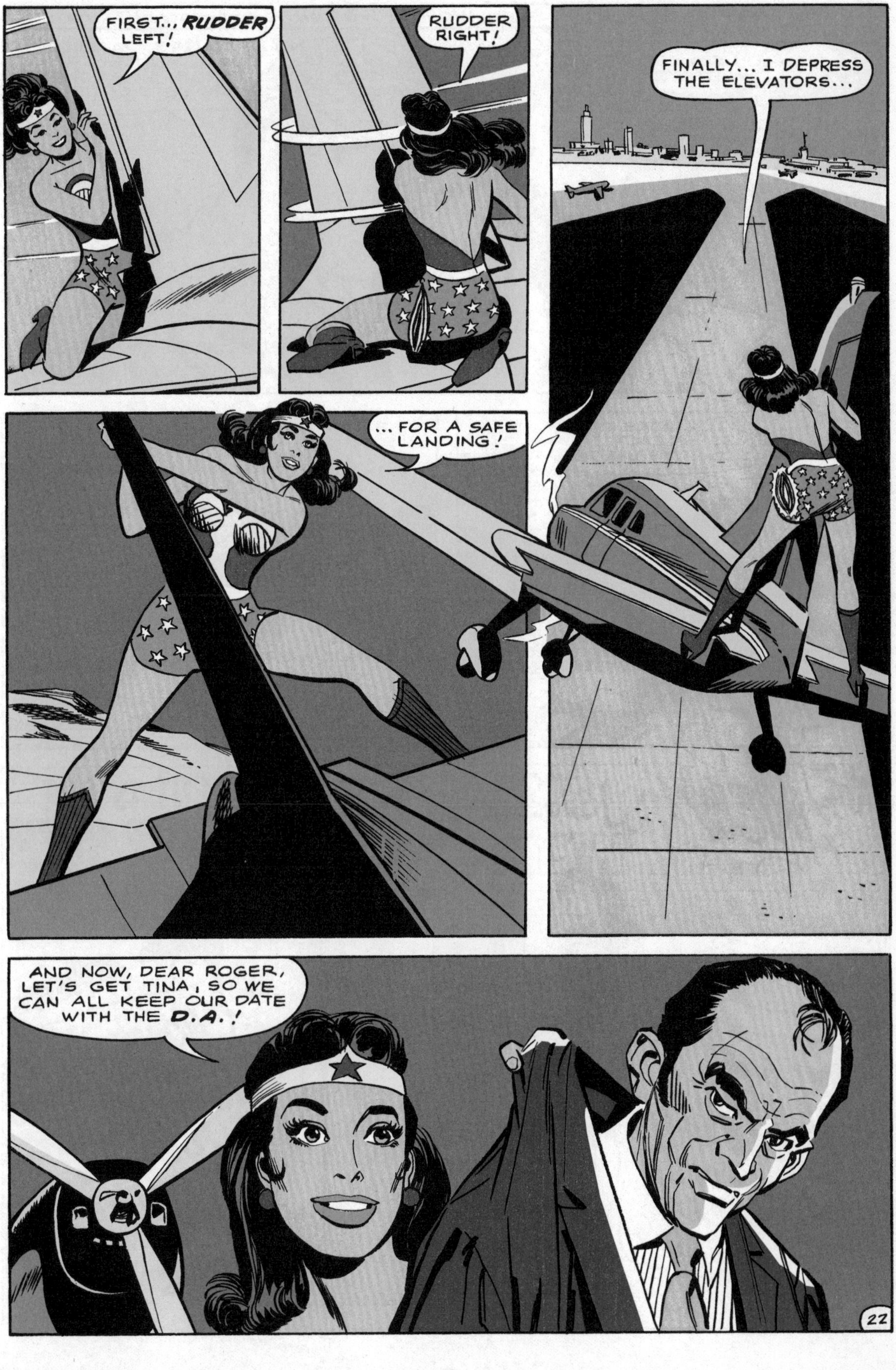
FIRST.., RUDDER LEFT!
RUDDER RIGHT!
FINALLY... I DEPRESS THE ELEVATORS...
...FOR A SAFE LANDING!
AND NOW, DEAR ROGER, LET'S GET TINA, SO WE CAN ALL KEEP OUR DATE WITH THE D.A.!
22

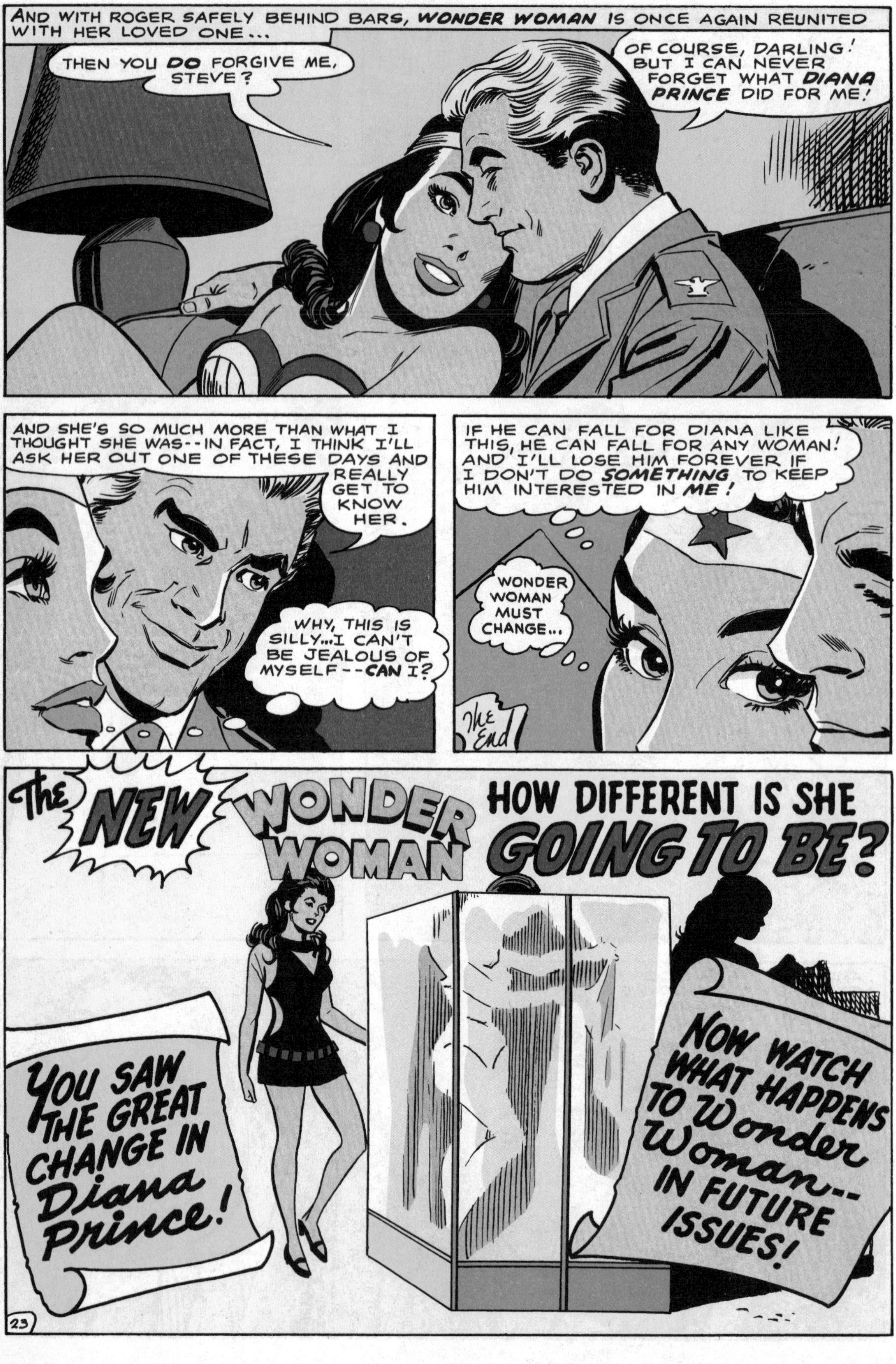
AND WITH ROGER SAFELY BEHIND BARS, WONDER WOMAN IS ONCE AGAIN REUNITED WITH HER LOVED ONE...
THEN YOU DO FORGIVE ME, STEVE?
OF COURSE, DARLING! BUT I CAN NEVER FORGET WHAT DIANA PRINCE DID FOR ME!
AND SHE'S SO MUCH MORE THAN WHAT I THOUGHT SHE WAS--IN FACT, I THINK I'LL ASK HER OUT ONE OF THESE DAYS AND REALLY GET TO KNOW HER.
WHY, THIS IS SILLY...I CAN'T BE JEALOUS OF MYSELF--CAN I?
IF HE CAN FALL FOR DIANA LIKE THIS, HE CAN FALL FOR ANY WOMAN! AND I'LL LOSE HIM FOREVER IF I DON'T DO SOMETHING TO KEEP HIM INTERESTED IN ME!
WONDER WOMAN MUST CHANGE...
The End
The NEW WONDER WOMAN
HOW DIFFERENT IS SHE GOING TO BE?
You saw the great change in Diana Prince!
Now watch what happens to Wonder Woman-- in future issues!
23

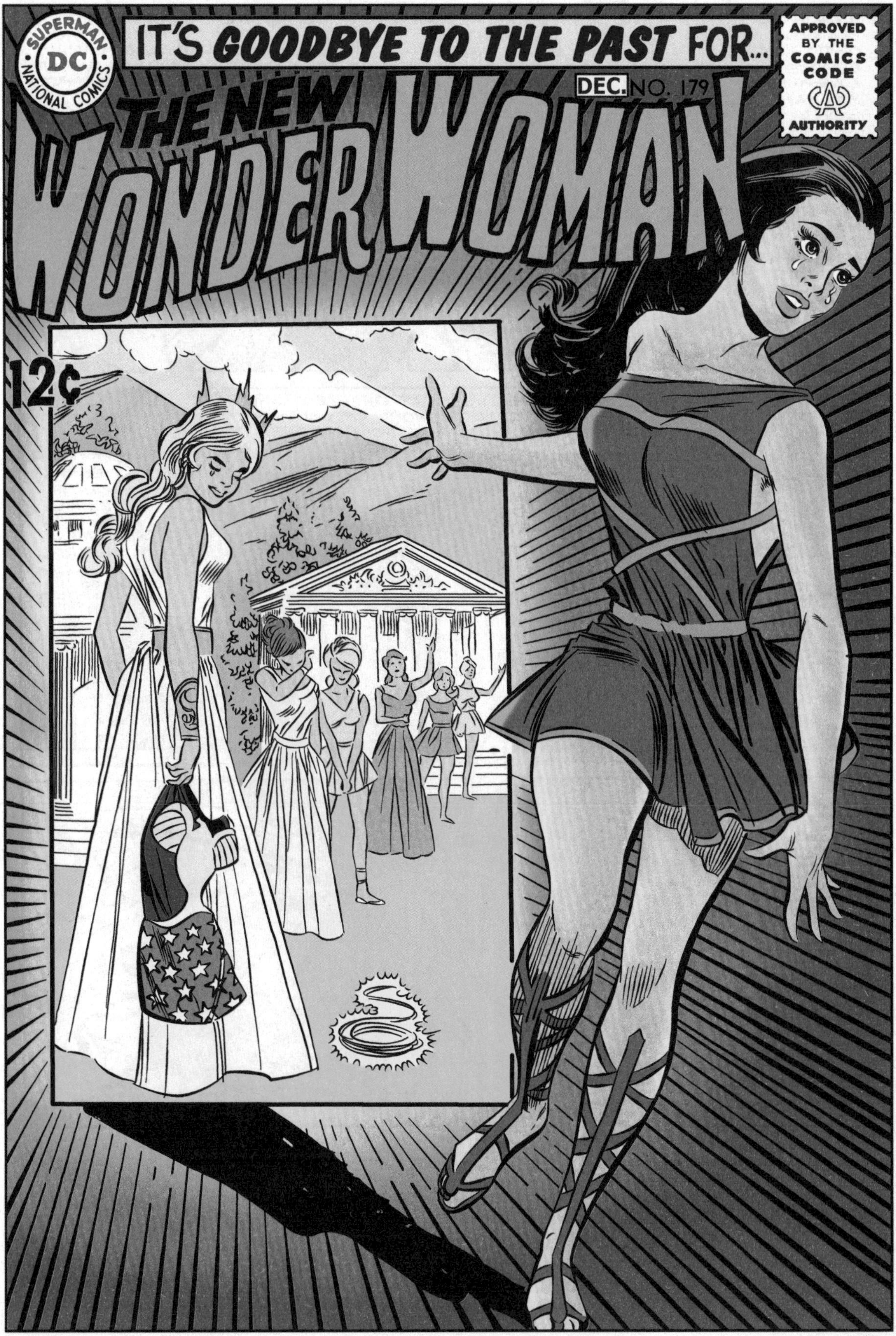
SUPERMAN DC NATIONAL COMICS
IT'S GOODBYE TO THE PAST FOR...
APPROVED BY THE COMICS CODE AUTHORITY
DEC. NO. 179
THE NEW WONDER WOMAN
12¢

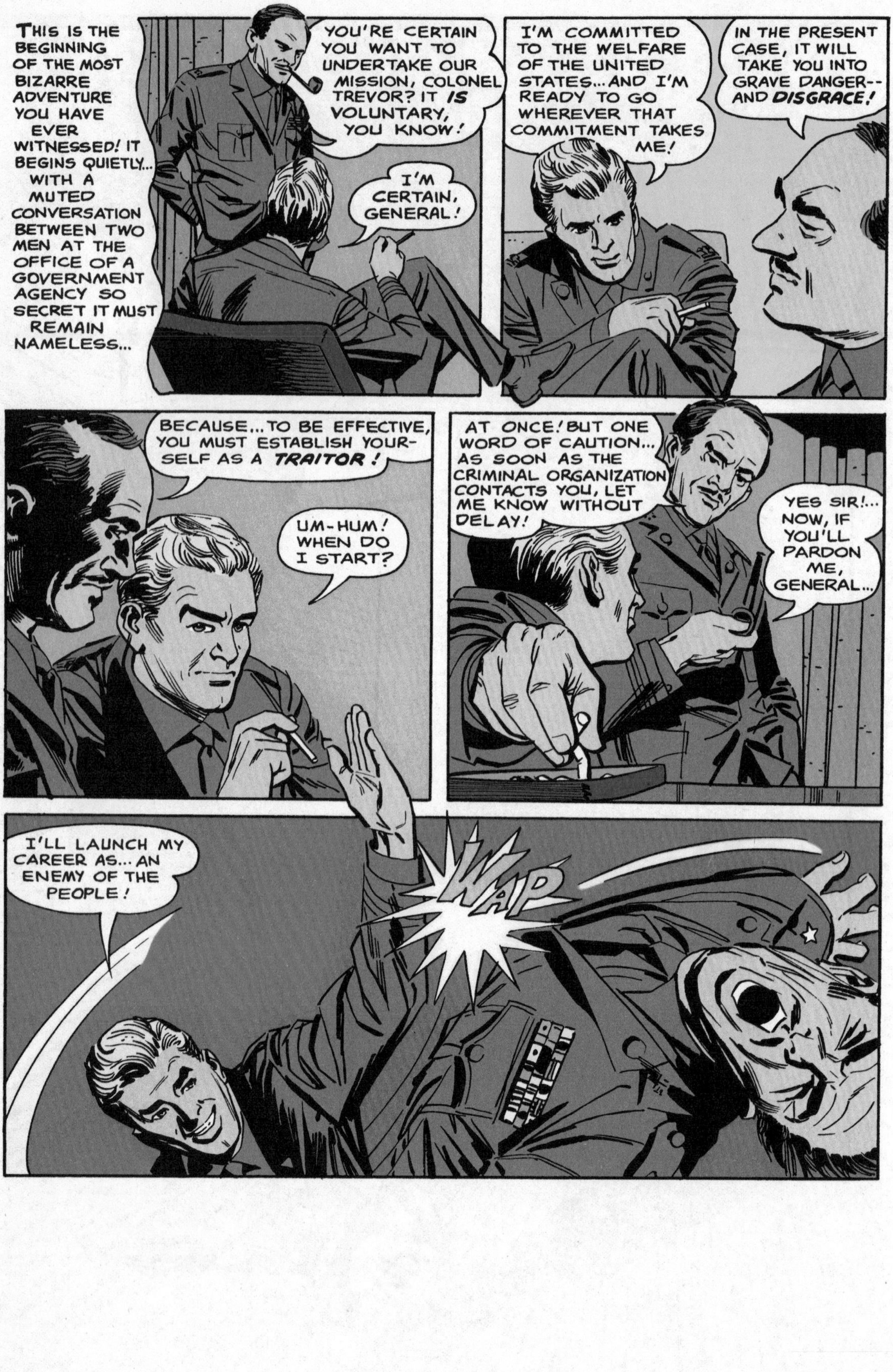
THIS IS THE BEGINNING OF THE MOST BIZARRE ADVENTURE YOU HAVE EVER WITNESSED! IT BEGINS QUIETLY... WITH A MUTED CONVERSATION BETWEEN TWO MEN AT THE OFFICE OF A GOVERNMENT AGENCY SO SECRET IT MUST REMAIN NAMELESS...
YOU'RE CERTAIN YOU WANT TO UNDERTAKE OUR MISSION, COLONEL TREVOR? IT IS VOLUNTARY, YOU KNOW!
I'M CERTAIN, GENERAL!
I'M COMMITTED TO THE WELFARE OF THE UNITED STATES...AND I'M READY TO GO WHEREVER THAT COMMITMENT TAKES ME!
IN THE PRESENT CASE, IT WILL TAKE YOU INTO GRAVE DANGER-- AND DISGRACE!
BECAUSE...TO BE EFFECTIVE, YOU MUST ESTABLISH YOURSELF AS A TRAITOR!
UM-HUM! WHEN DO I START?
AT ONCE! BUT ONE WORD OF CAUTION... AS SOON AS THE CRIMINAL ORGANIZATION CONTACTS YOU, LET ME KNOW WITHOUT DELAY!
YES SIR!... NOW, IF YOU'LL PARDON ME, GENERAL...
I'LL LAUNCH MY CAREER AS... AN ENEMY OF THE PEOPLE!
WAP

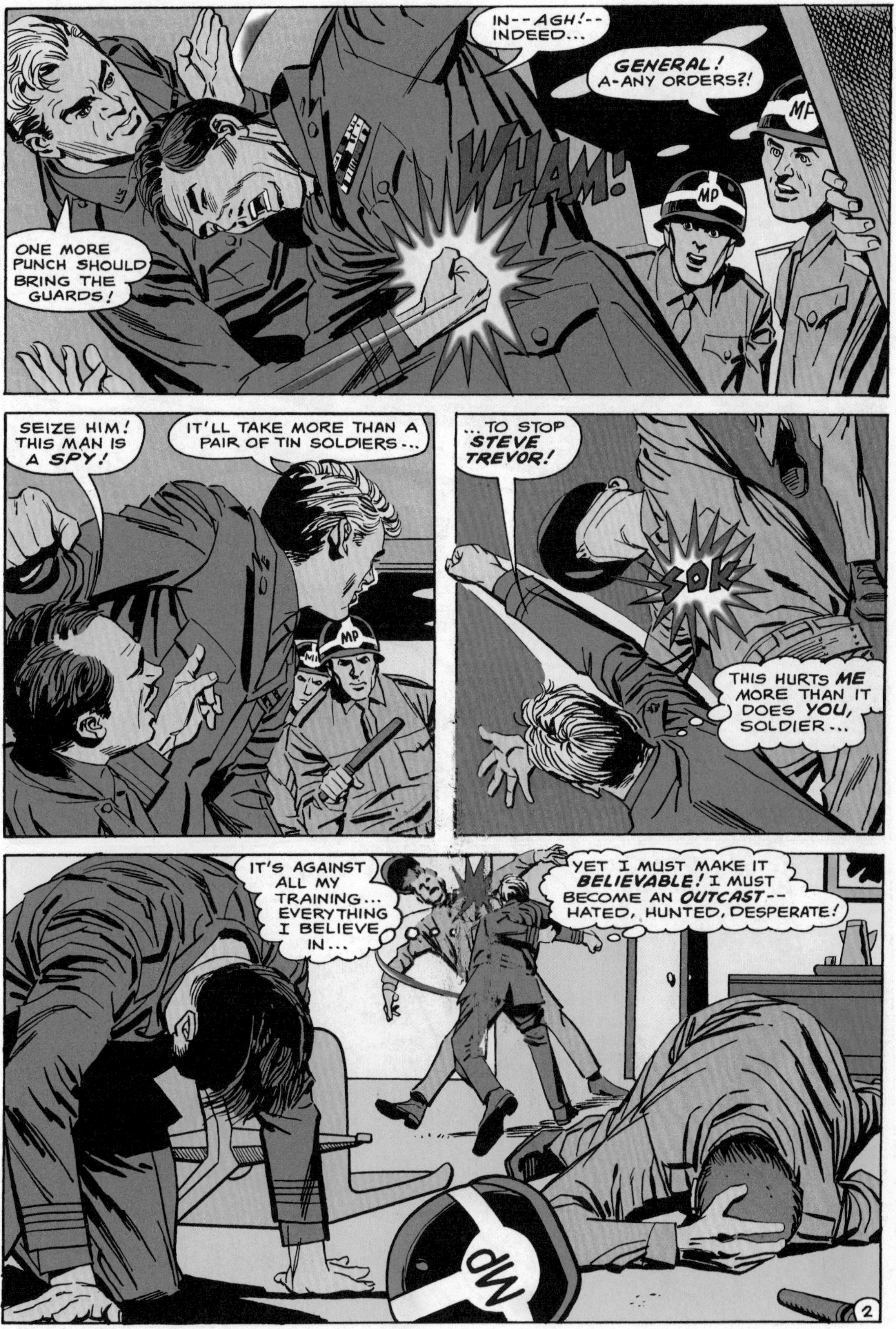
IN--AGH!--
INDEED...
GENERAL!
A-ANY ORDERS?!
WHAM!
ONE MORE PUNCH SHOULD BRING THE GUARDS!
SEIZE HIM! THIS MAN IS A SPY!
IT'LL TAKE MORE THAN A PAIR OF TIN SOLDIERS...
...TO STOP STEVE TREVOR!
SOK!
THIS HURTS ME MORE THAN IT DOES YOU, SOLDIER...
IT'S AGAINST ALL MY TRAINING... EVERYTHING I BELIEVE IN...
YET I MUST MAKE IT BELIEVABLE! I MUST BECOME AN OUTCAST--HATED, HUNTED, DESPERATE!
2

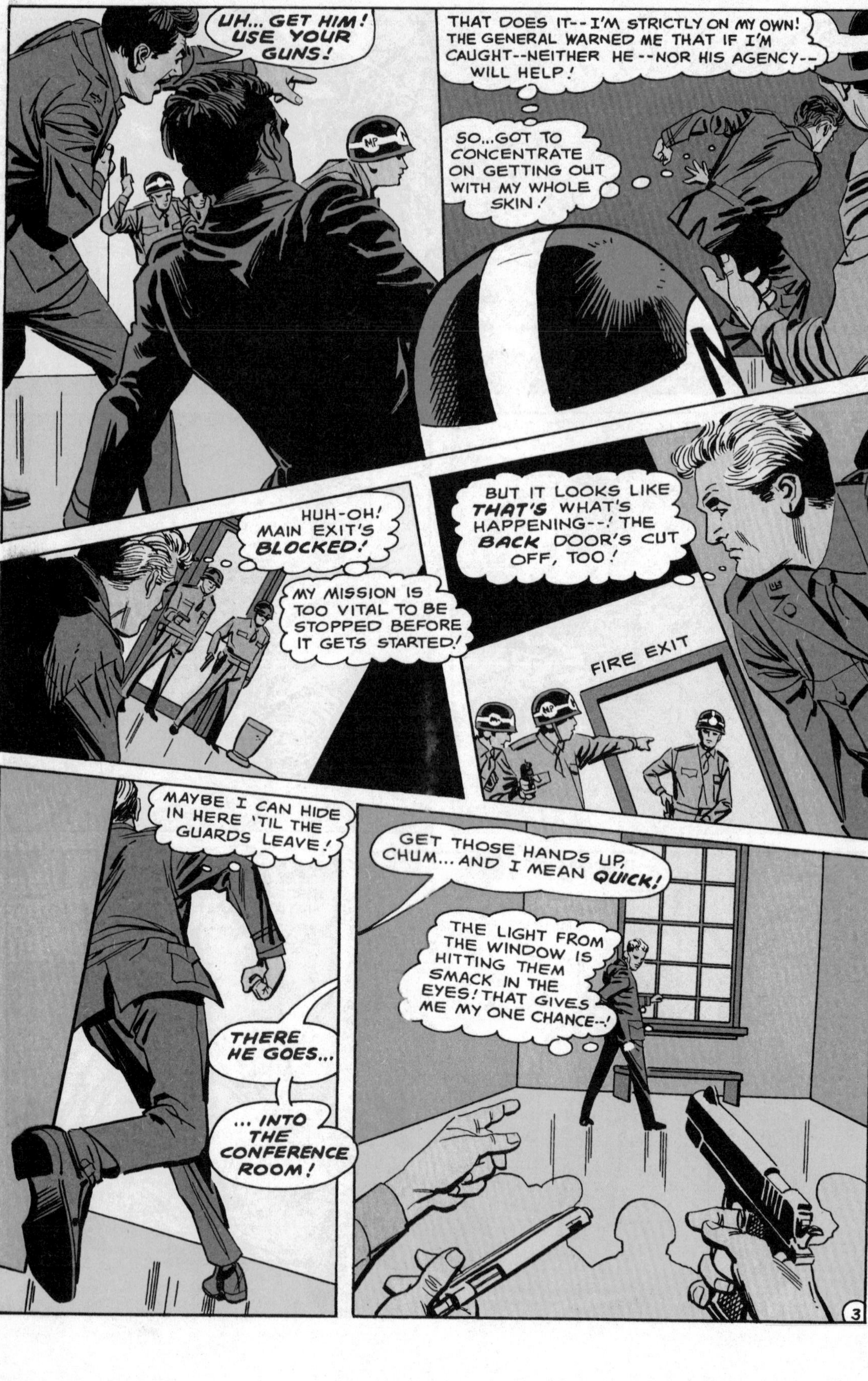
UH... GET HIM! USE YOUR GUNS!
THAT DOES IT-- I'M STRICTLY ON MY OWN! THE GENERAL WARNED ME THAT IF I'M CAUGHT--NEITHER HE --NOR HIS AGENCY-- WILL HELP!
SO...GOT TO CONCENTRATE ON GETTING OUT WITH MY WHOLE SKIN!
HUH-OH! MAIN EXIT'S BLOCKED!
MY MISSION IS TOO VITAL TO BE STOPPED BEFORE IT GETS STARTED!
BUT IT LOOKS LIKE THAT'S WHAT'S HAPPENING--! THE BACK DOOR'S CUT OFF, TOO!
FIRE EXIT
MAYBE I CAN HIDE IN HERE 'TIL THE GUARDS LEAVE!
THERE HE GOES...
... INTO THE CONFERENCE ROOM!
GET THOSE HANDS UP, CHUM... AND I MEAN QUICK!
THE LIGHT FROM THE WINDOW IS HITTING THEM SMACK IN THE EYES! THAT GIVES ME MY ONE CHANCE--!
3

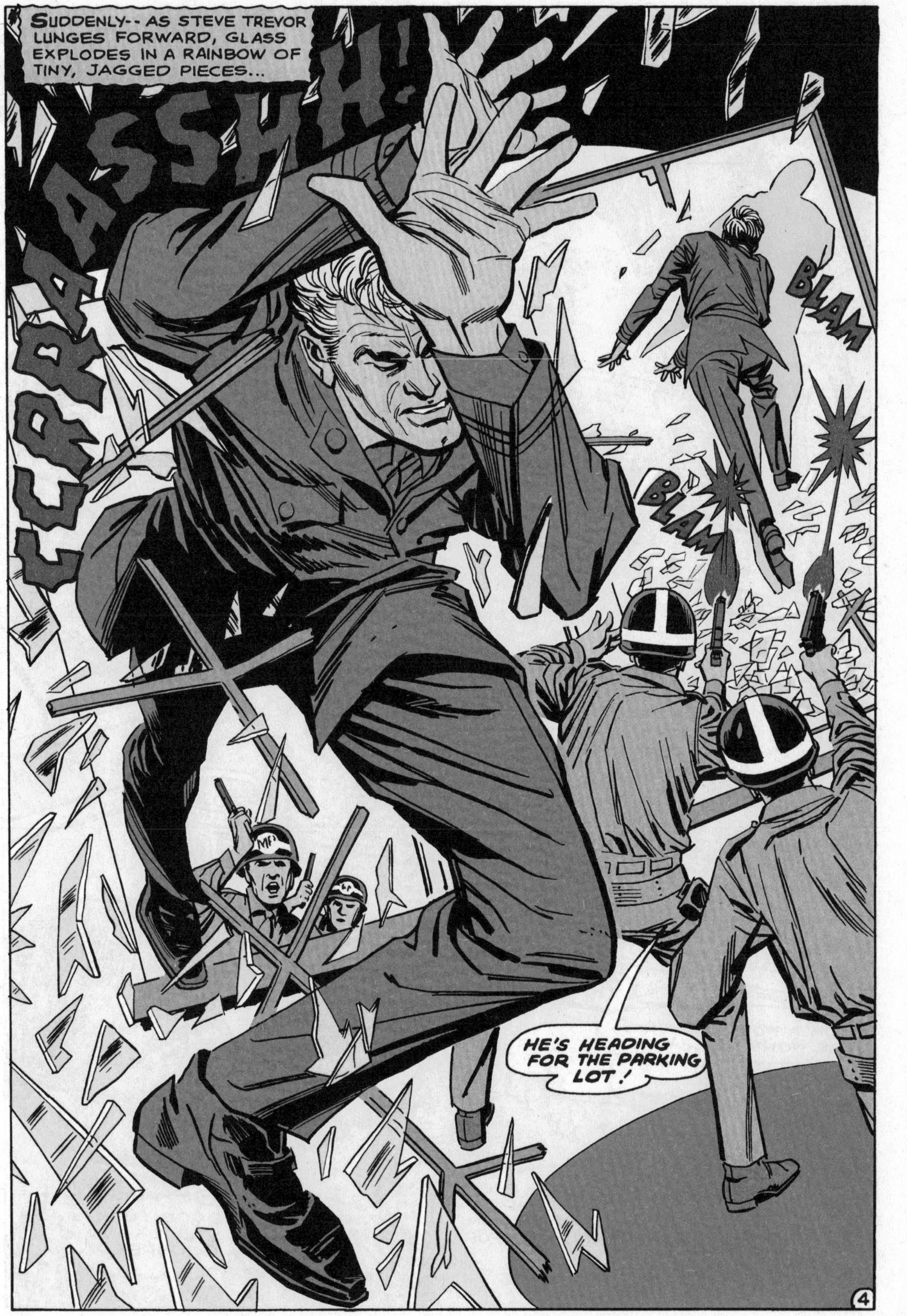
SUDDENLY-- AS STEVE TREVOR LUNGES FORWARD, GLASS EXPLODES IN A RAINBOW OF TINY, JAGGED PIECES...
CCRRASSHH!
BLAM
BLAM
BLAM
HE'S HEADING FOR THE PARKING LOT!
4

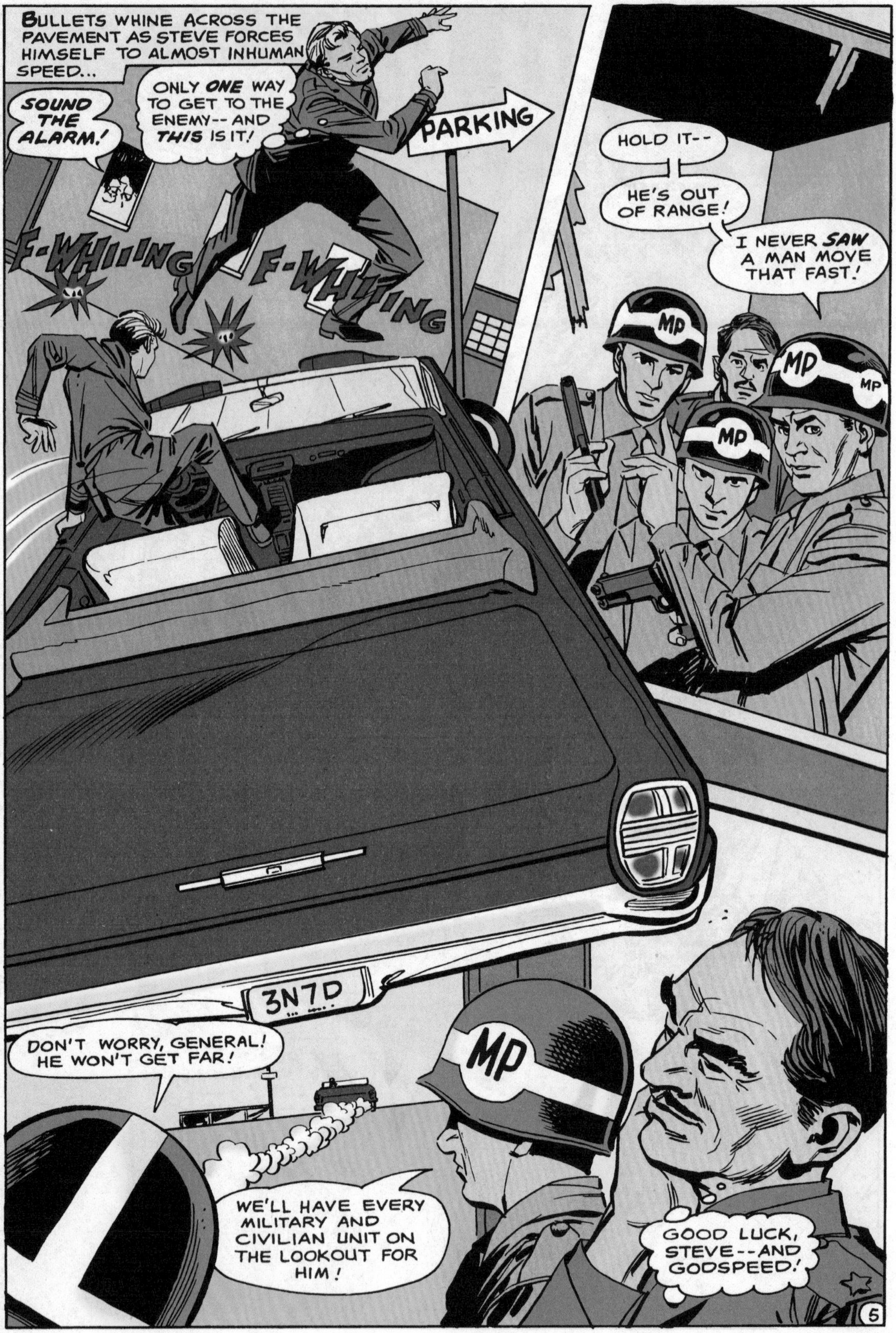
BULLETS WHINE ACROSS THE PAVEMENT AS STEVE FORCES HIMSELF TO ALMOST INHUMAN SPEED...
SOUND THE ALARM!
ONLY ONE WAY TO GET TO THE ENEMY-- AND THIS IS IT!
PARKING
F-WHIIING
F-WHIIING
HOLD IT--
HE'S OUT OF RANGE!
I NEVER SAW A MAN MOVE THAT FAST!
MP
MP
MP
MP
3N7D
DON'T WORRY, GENERAL! HE WON'T GET FAR!
MP
WE'LL HAVE EVERY MILITARY AND CIVILIAN UNIT ON THE LOOKOUT FOR HIM!
GOOD LUCK, STEVE--AND GODSPEED!
5

RETURN TO YOUR POSTS, MEN!

SO FAR, SO GOOD! COLONEL TREVOR, THE MOST LOYAL OFFICER I'VE EVER KNOWN, IS BRANDED A TRAITOR!

6

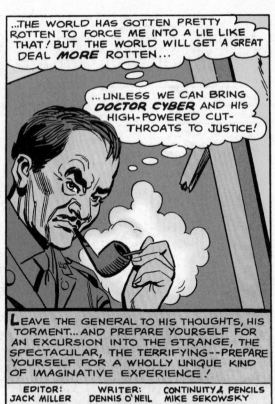

...THE WORLD HAS GOTTEN PRETTY ROTTEN TO FORCE ME INTO A LIE LIKE THAT! BUT THE WORLD WILL GET A GREAT DEAL *MORE* ROTTEN...

...UNLESS WE CAN BRING *DOCTOR CYBER* AND HIS HIGH-POWERED CUT-THROATS TO JUSTICE!

LEAVE THE GENERAL TO HIS THOUGHTS, HIS TORMENT...AND PREPARE YOURSELF FOR AN EXCURSION INTO THE STRANGE, THE SPECTACULAR, THE TERRIFYING--PREPARE YOURSELF FOR A WHOLLY UNIQUE KIND OF IMAGINATIVE EXPERIENCE!

| EDITOR: JACK MILLER | WRITER: DENNIS O'NEIL | CONTINUITY & PENCILS MIKE SEKOWSKY |

INKS: DICK GIORDANO

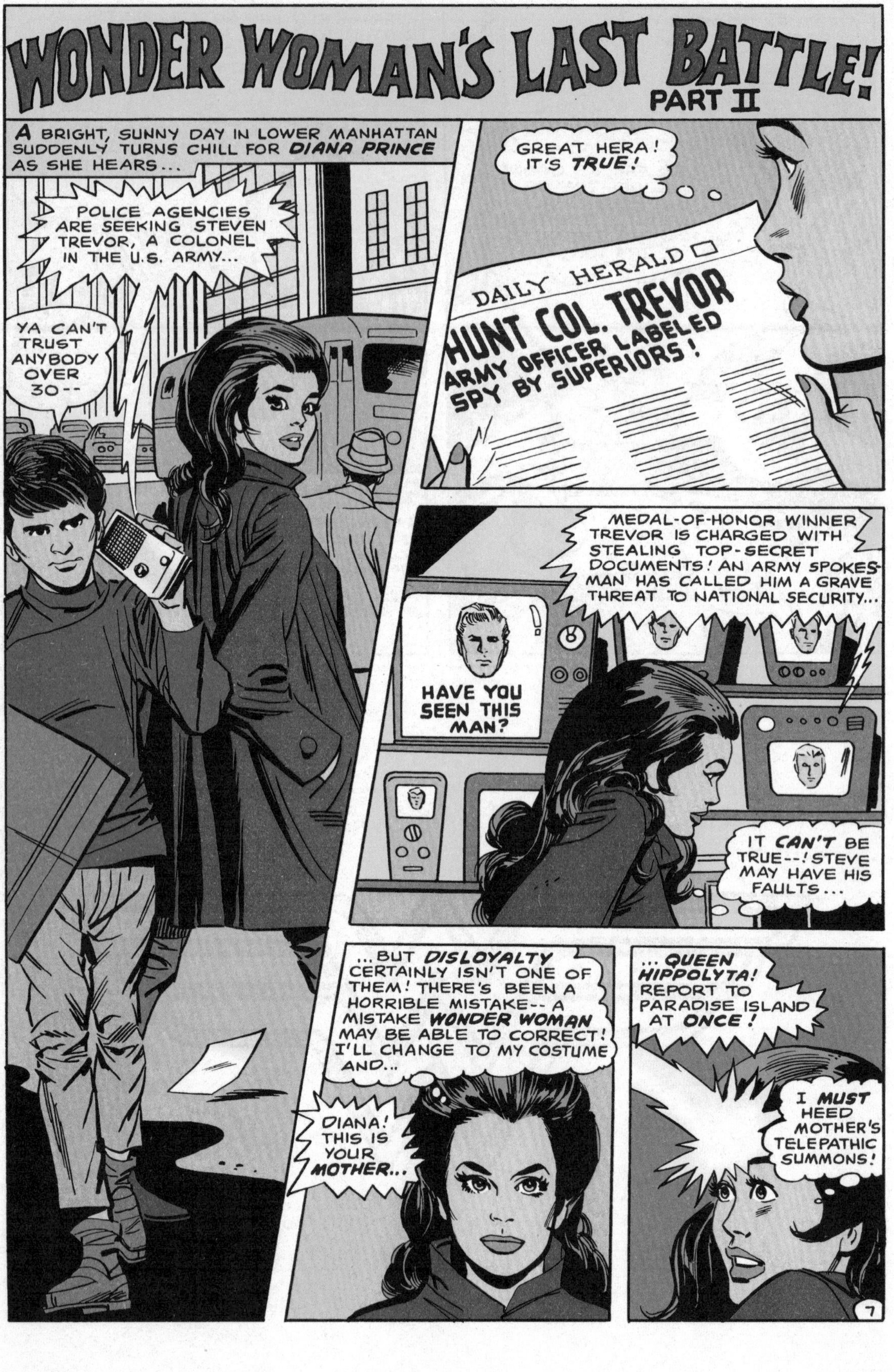
WONDER WOMAN'S LAST BATTLE!
PART II
A BRIGHT, SUNNY DAY IN LOWER MANHATTAN SUDDENLY TURNS CHILL FOR DIANA PRINCE AS SHE HEARS...
POLICE AGENCIES ARE SEEKING STEVEN TREVOR, A COLONEL IN THE U.S. ARMY...
YA CAN'T TRUST ANYBODY OVER 30--
GREAT HERA! IT'S TRUE!
DAILY HERALD
HUNT COL. TREVOR
ARMY OFFICER LABELED SPY BY SUPERIORS!
MEDAL-OF-HONOR WINNER TREVOR IS CHARGED WITH STEALING TOP-SECRET DOCUMENTS! AN ARMY SPOKESMAN HAS CALLED HIM A GRAVE THREAT TO NATIONAL SECURITY...
HAVE YOU SEEN THIS MAN?
IT CAN'T BE TRUE--! STEVE MAY HAVE HIS FAULTS...
...BUT DISLOYALTY CERTAINLY ISN'T ONE OF THEM! THERE'S BEEN A HORRIBLE MISTAKE-- A MISTAKE WONDER WOMAN MAY BE ABLE TO CORRECT! I'LL CHANGE TO MY COSTUME AND...
DIANA! THIS IS YOUR MOTHER...
...QUEEN HIPPOLYTA! REPORT TO PARADISE ISLAND AT ONCE!
I MUST HEED MOTHER'S TELEPATHIC SUMMONS!
7

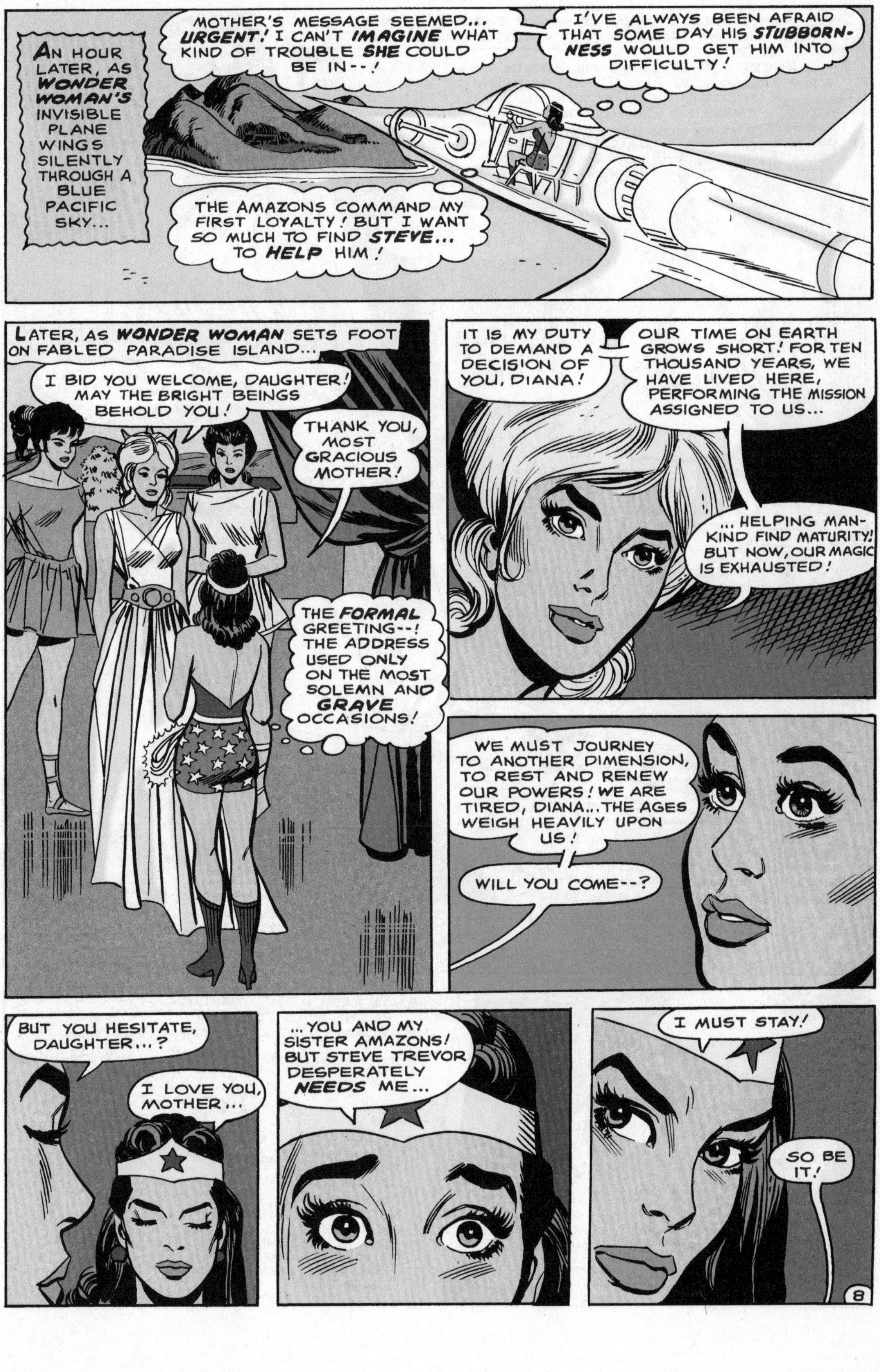
AN HOUR LATER, AS WONDER WOMAN'S INVISIBLE PLANE WINGS SILENTLY THROUGH A BLUE PACIFIC SKY...
MOTHER'S MESSAGE SEEMED... URGENT! I CAN'T IMAGINE WHAT KIND OF TROUBLE SHE COULD BE IN--!
I'VE ALWAYS BEEN AFRAID THAT SOME DAY HIS STUBBORNNESS WOULD GET HIM INTO DIFFICULTY!
THE AMAZONS COMMAND MY FIRST LOYALTY! BUT I WANT SO MUCH TO FIND STEVE... TO HELP HIM!
LATER, AS WONDER WOMAN SETS FOOT ON FABLED PARADISE ISLAND...
I BID YOU WELCOME, DAUGHTER! MAY THE BRIGHT BEINGS BEHOLD YOU!
THANK YOU, MOST GRACIOUS MOTHER!
THE FORMAL GREETING--! THE ADDRESS USED ONLY ON THE MOST SOLEMN AND GRAVE OCCASIONS!
IT IS MY DUTY TO DEMAND A DECISION OF YOU, DIANA!
OUR TIME ON EARTH GROWS SHORT! FOR TEN THOUSAND YEARS, WE HAVE LIVED HERE, PERFORMING THE MISSION ASSIGNED TO US...
... HELPING MANKIND FIND MATURITY! BUT NOW, OUR MAGIC IS EXHAUSTED!
WE MUST JOURNEY TO ANOTHER DIMENSION, TO REST AND RENEW OUR POWERS! WE ARE TIRED, DIANA... THE AGES WEIGH HEAVILY UPON US!
WILL YOU COME--?
BUT YOU HESITATE, DAUGHTER...?
I LOVE YOU, MOTHER...
...YOU AND MY SISTER AMAZONS! BUT STEVE TREVOR DESPERATELY NEEDS ME...
I MUST STAY!
SO BE IT!
8

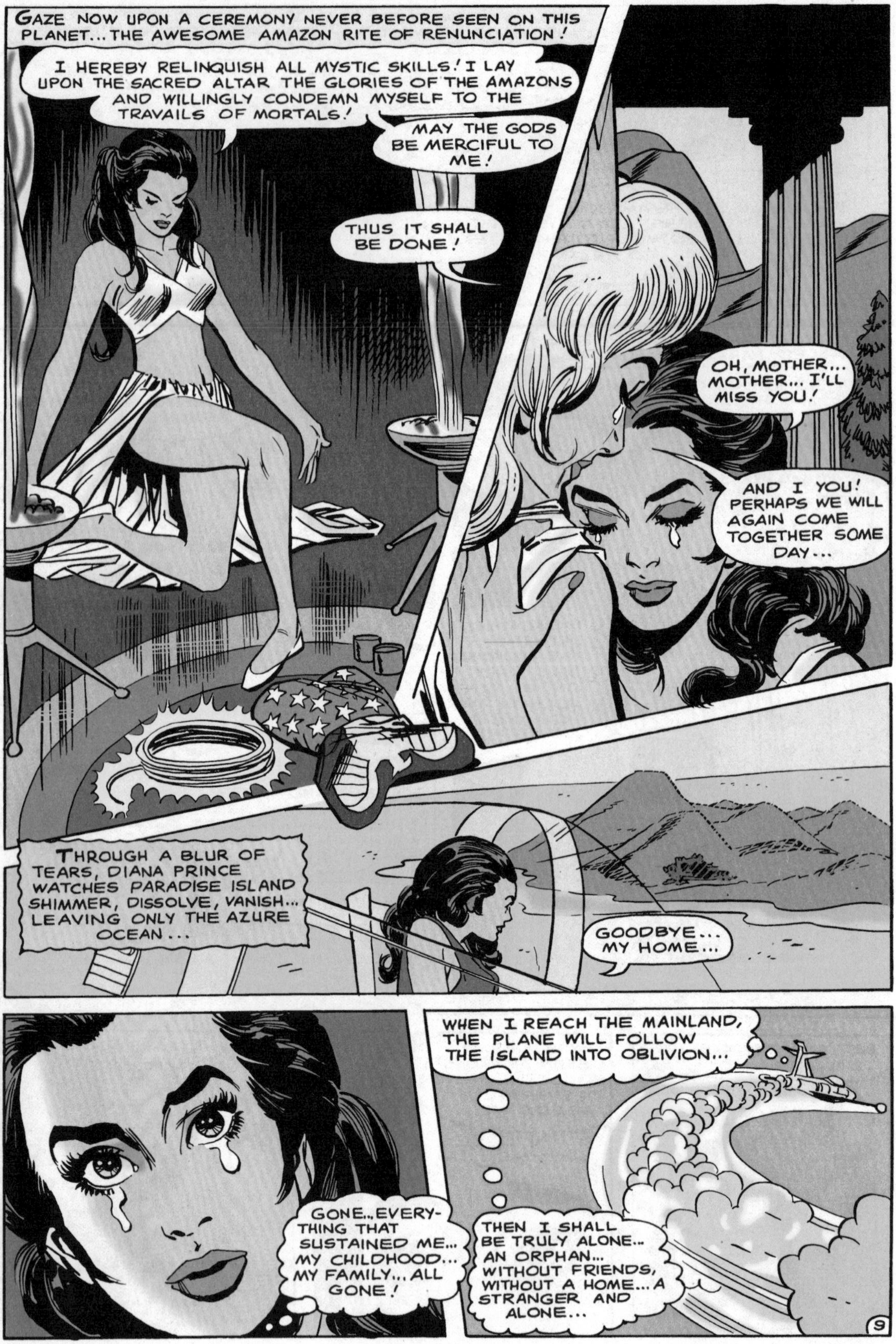

GAZE NOW UPON A CEREMONY NEVER BEFORE SEEN ON THIS PLANET... THE AWESOME AMAZON RITE OF RENUNCIATION!
I HEREBY RELINQUISH ALL MYSTIC SKILLS! I LAY UPON THE SACRED ALTAR THE GLORIES OF THE AMAZONS AND WILLINGLY CONDEMN MYSELF TO THE TRAVAILS OF MORTALS!
MAY THE GODS BE MERCIFUL TO ME!
THUS IT SHALL BE DONE!
OH, MOTHER... MOTHER... I'LL MISS YOU!
AND I YOU! PERHAPS WE WILL AGAIN COME TOGETHER SOME DAY...
THROUGH A BLUR OF TEARS, DIANA PRINCE WATCHES PARADISE ISLAND SHIMMER, DISSOLVE, VANISH... LEAVING ONLY THE AZURE OCEAN...
GOODBYE... MY HOME...
GONE... EVERYTHING THAT SUSTAINED ME... MY CHILDHOOD... MY FAMILY... ALL GONE!
WHEN I REACH THE MAINLAND, THE PLANE WILL FOLLOW THE ISLAND INTO OBLIVION...
THEN I SHALL BE TRULY ALONE... AN ORPHAN... WITHOUT FRIENDS, WITHOUT A HOME... A STRANGER AND ALONE...
9

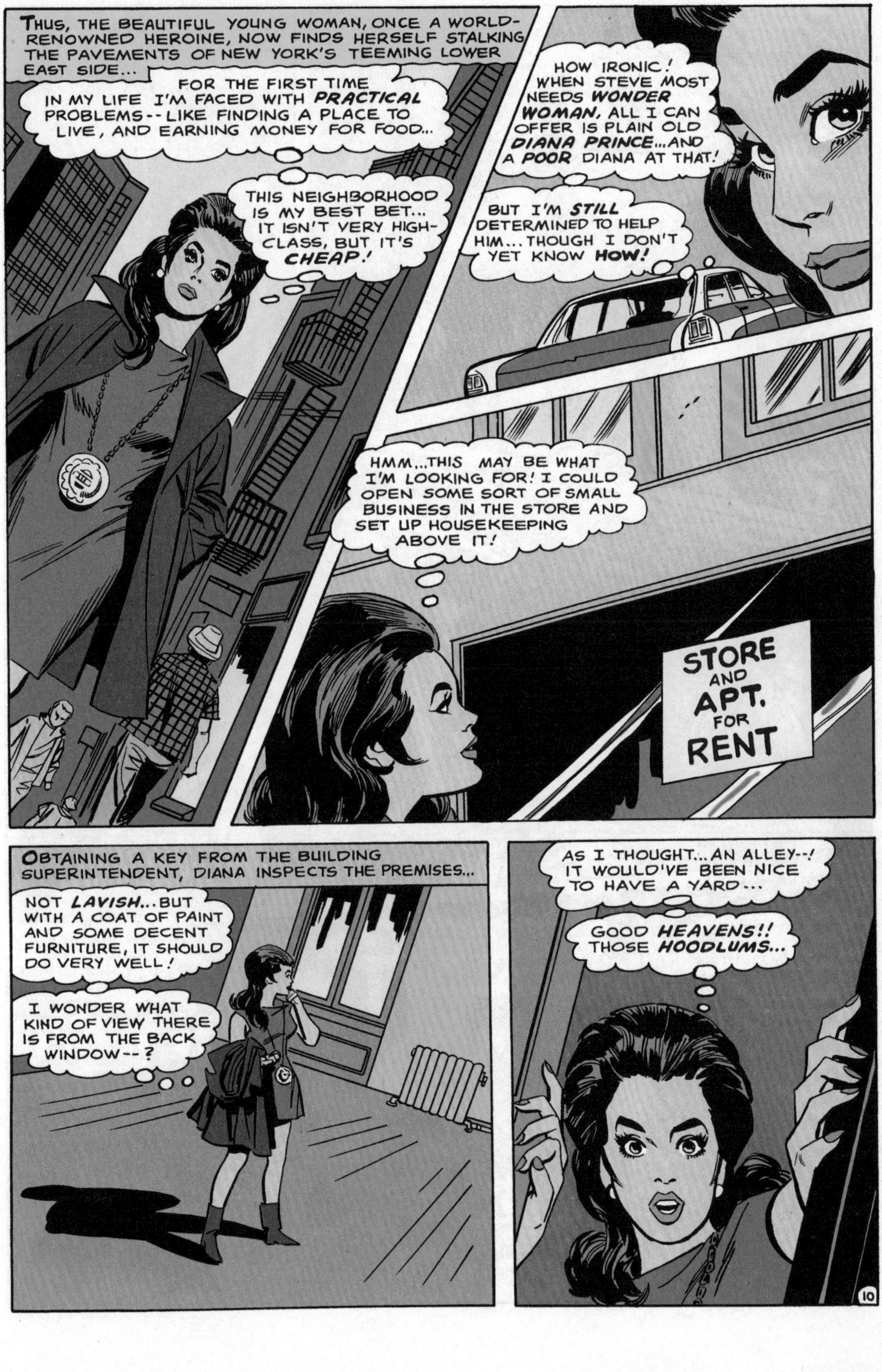
THUS, THE BEAUTIFUL YOUNG WOMAN, ONCE A WORLD-RENOWNED HEROINE, NOW FINDS HERSELF STALKING THE PAVEMENTS OF NEW YORK'S TEEMING LOWER EAST SIDE...
FOR THE FIRST TIME IN MY LIFE I'M FACED WITH PRACTICAL PROBLEMS--LIKE FINDING A PLACE TO LIVE, AND EARNING MONEY FOR FOOD...
THIS NEIGHBORHOOD IS MY BEST BET... IT ISN'T VERY HIGH-CLASS, BUT IT'S CHEAP!
HOW IRONIC! WHEN STEVE MOST NEEDS WONDER WOMAN, ALL I CAN OFFER IS PLAIN OLD DIANA PRINCE...AND A POOR DIANA AT THAT!
BUT I'M STILL DETERMINED TO HELP HIM... THOUGH I DON'T YET KNOW HOW!
HMM...THIS MAY BE WHAT I'M LOOKING FOR! I COULD OPEN SOME SORT OF SMALL BUSINESS IN THE STORE AND SET UP HOUSEKEEPING ABOVE IT!
STORE AND APT. FOR RENT
OBTAINING A KEY FROM THE BUILDING SUPERINTENDENT, DIANA INSPECTS THE PREMISES...
NOT LAVISH...BUT WITH A COAT OF PAINT AND SOME DECENT FURNITURE, IT SHOULD DO VERY WELL!
I WONDER WHAT KIND OF VIEW THERE IS FROM THE BACK WINDOW--?
AS I THOUGHT...AN ALLEY--! IT WOULD'VE BEEN NICE TO HAVE A YARD...
GOOD HEAVENS!! THOSE HOODLUMS...
10

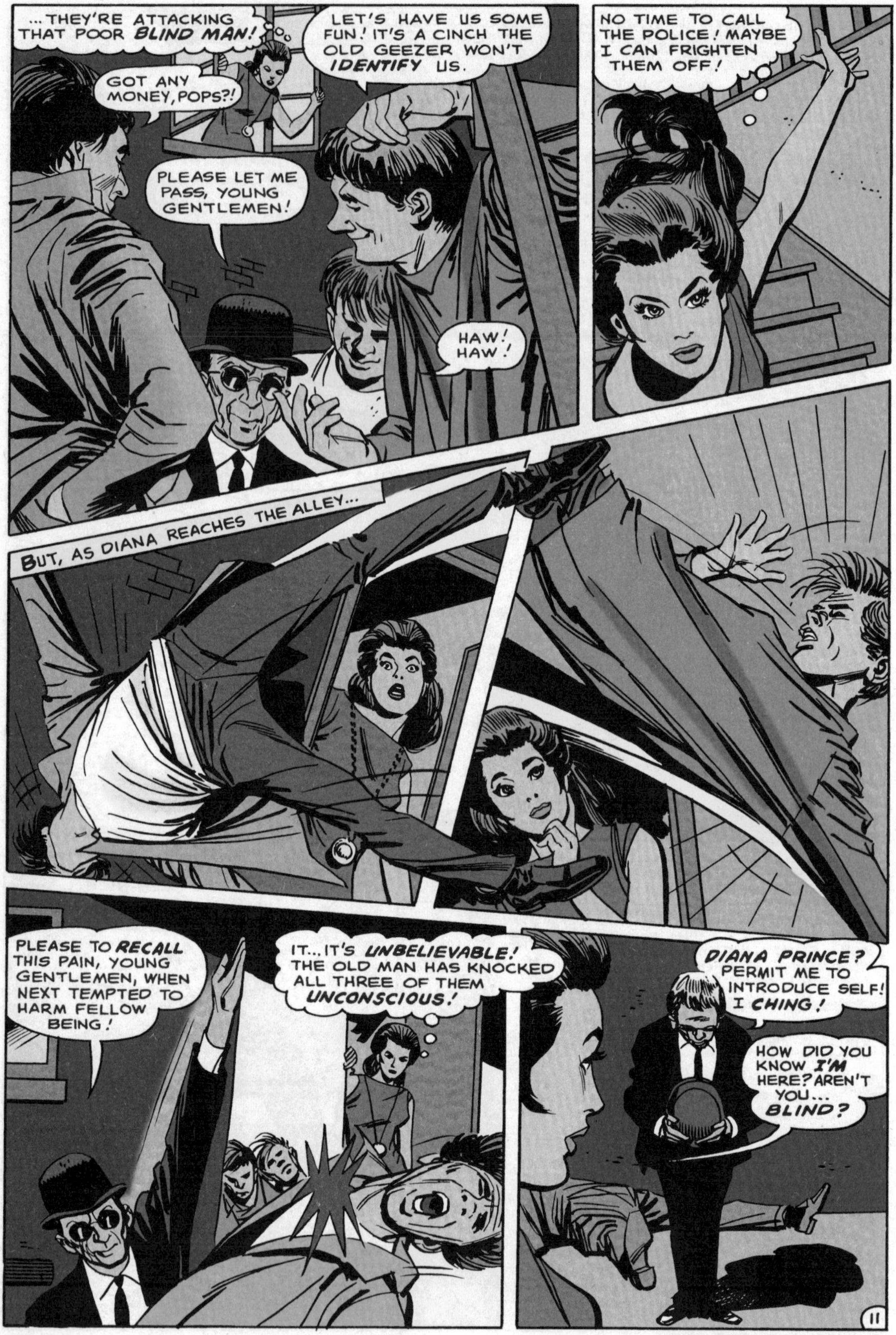
...THEY'RE ATTACKING THAT POOR BLIND MAN!
LET'S HAVE US SOME FUN! IT'S A CINCH THE OLD GEEZER WON'T IDENTIFY US.
GOT ANY MONEY, POPS?!
PLEASE LET ME PASS, YOUNG GENTLEMEN!
HAW! HAW!
NO TIME TO CALL THE POLICE! MAYBE I CAN FRIGHTEN THEM OFF!
BUT, AS DIANA REACHES THE ALLEY...
PLEASE TO RECALL THIS PAIN, YOUNG GENTLEMEN, WHEN NEXT TEMPTED TO HARM FELLOW BEING!
IT...IT'S UNBELIEVABLE! THE OLD MAN HAS KNOCKED ALL THREE OF THEM UNCONSCIOUS!
DIANA PRINCE? PERMIT ME TO INTRODUCE SELF! I CHING!
HOW DID YOU KNOW I'M HERE? AREN'T YOU... BLIND?
11

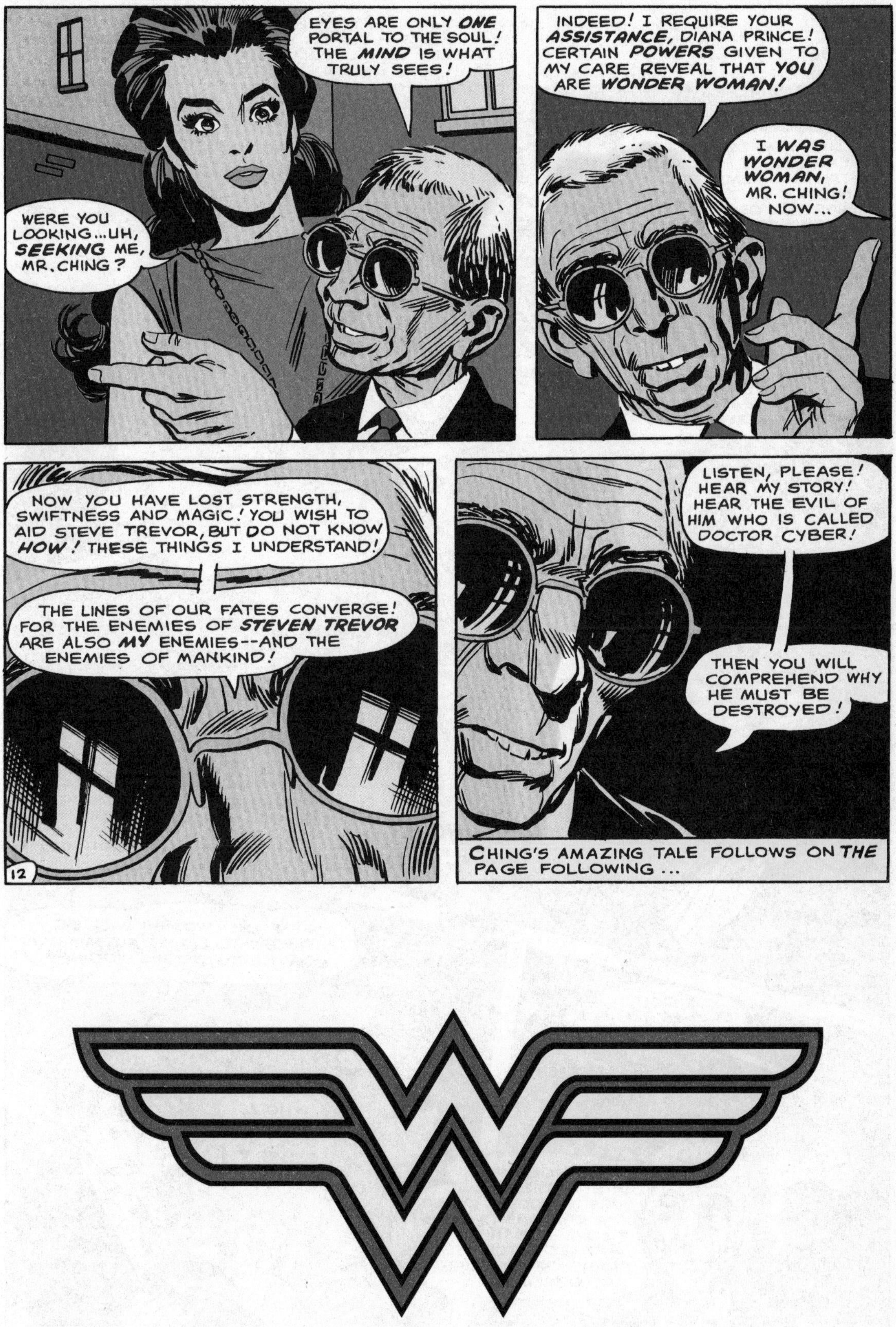
WERE YOU LOOKING...UH, SEEKING ME, MR. CHING?
EYES ARE ONLY ONE PORTAL TO THE SOUL! THE MIND IS WHAT TRULY SEES!
INDEED! I REQUIRE YOUR ASSISTANCE, DIANA PRINCE! CERTAIN POWERS GIVEN TO MY CARE REVEAL THAT YOU ARE WONDER WOMAN!
I WAS WONDER WOMAN, MR. CHING! NOW...
NOW YOU HAVE LOST STRENGTH, SWIFTNESS AND MAGIC! YOU WISH TO AID STEVE TREVOR, BUT DO NOT KNOW HOW! THESE THINGS I UNDERSTAND!
THE LINES OF OUR FATES CONVERGE! FOR THE ENEMIES OF STEVEN TREVOR ARE ALSO MY ENEMIES--AND THE ENEMIES OF MANKIND!
12
LISTEN, PLEASE! HEAR MY STORY! HEAR THE EVIL OF HIM WHO IS CALLED DOCTOR CYBER!
THEN YOU WILL COMPREHEND WHY HE MUST BE DESTROYED!
CHING'S AMAZING TALE FOLLOWS ON THE PAGE FOLLOWING ...

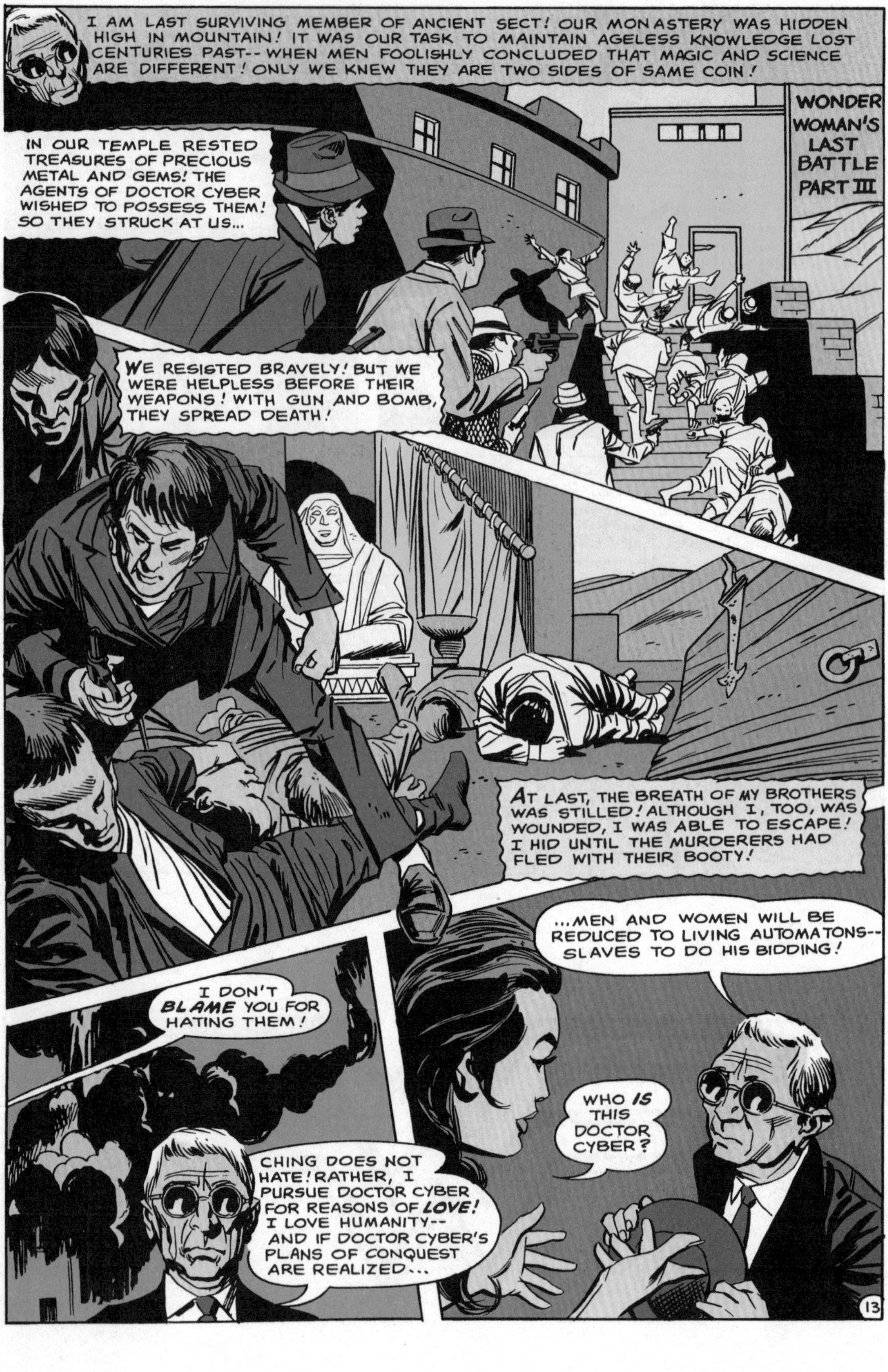
I AM LAST SURVIVING MEMBER OF ANCIENT SECT! OUR MONASTERY WAS HIDDEN HIGH IN MOUNTAIN! IT WAS OUR TASK TO MAINTAIN AGELESS KNOWLEDGE LOST CENTURIES PAST-- WHEN MEN FOOLISHLY CONCLUDED THAT MAGIC AND SCIENCE ARE DIFFERENT! ONLY WE KNEW THEY ARE TWO SIDES OF SAME COIN!
WONDER WOMAN'S LAST BATTLE PART III
IN OUR TEMPLE RESTED TREASURES OF PRECIOUS METAL AND GEMS! THE AGENTS OF DOCTOR CYBER WISHED TO POSSESS THEM! SO THEY STRUCK AT US...
WE RESISTED BRAVELY! BUT WE WERE HELPLESS BEFORE THEIR WEAPONS! WITH GUN AND BOMB, THEY SPREAD DEATH!
AT LAST, THE BREATH OF MY BROTHERS WAS STILLED! ALTHOUGH I, TOO, WAS WOUNDED, I WAS ABLE TO ESCAPE! I HID UNTIL THE MURDERERS HAD FLED WITH THEIR BOOTY!
I DON'T BLAME YOU FOR HATING THEM!
CHING DOES NOT HATE! RATHER, I PURSUE DOCTOR CYBER FOR REASONS OF LOVE! I LOVE HUMANITY-- AND IF DOCTOR CYBER'S PLANS OF CONQUEST ARE REALIZED...
...MEN AND WOMEN WILL BE REDUCED TO LIVING AUTOMATONS-- SLAVES TO DO HIS BIDDING!
WHO IS THIS DOCTOR CYBER?
13

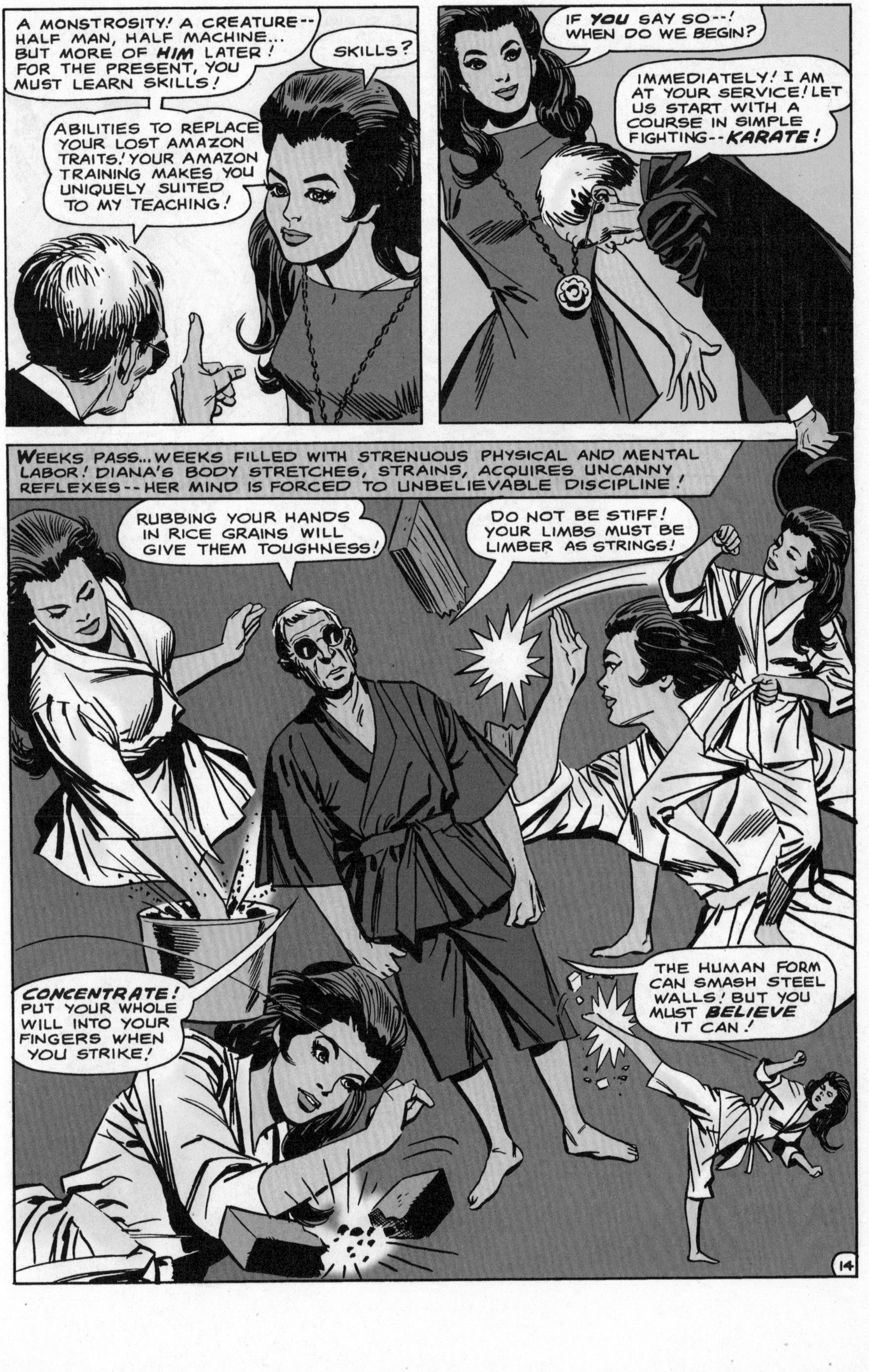

A MONSTROSITY! A CREATURE-- HALF MAN, HALF MACHINE... BUT MORE OF **HIM** LATER! FOR THE PRESENT, YOU MUST LEARN SKILLS!
SKILLS?
ABILITIES TO REPLACE YOUR LOST AMAZON TRAITS! YOUR AMAZON TRAINING MAKES YOU UNIQUELY SUITED TO MY TEACHING!
IF **YOU** SAY SO--! WHEN DO WE BEGIN?
IMMEDIATELY! I AM AT YOUR SERVICE! LET US START WITH A COURSE IN SIMPLE FIGHTING--**KARATE**!
WEEKS PASS...WEEKS FILLED WITH STRENUOUS PHYSICAL AND MENTAL LABOR! DIANA'S BODY STRETCHES, STRAINS, ACQUIRES UNCANNY REFLEXES--HER MIND IS FORCED TO UNBELIEVABLE DISCIPLINE!
RUBBING YOUR HANDS IN RICE GRAINS WILL GIVE THEM TOUGHNESS!
DO NOT BE STIFF! YOUR LIMBS MUST BE LIMBER AS STRINGS!
CONCENTRATE! PUT YOUR WHOLE WILL INTO YOUR FINGERS WHEN YOU STRIKE!
THE HUMAN FORM CAN SMASH STEEL WALLS! BUT YOU MUST **BELIEVE** IT CAN!
14

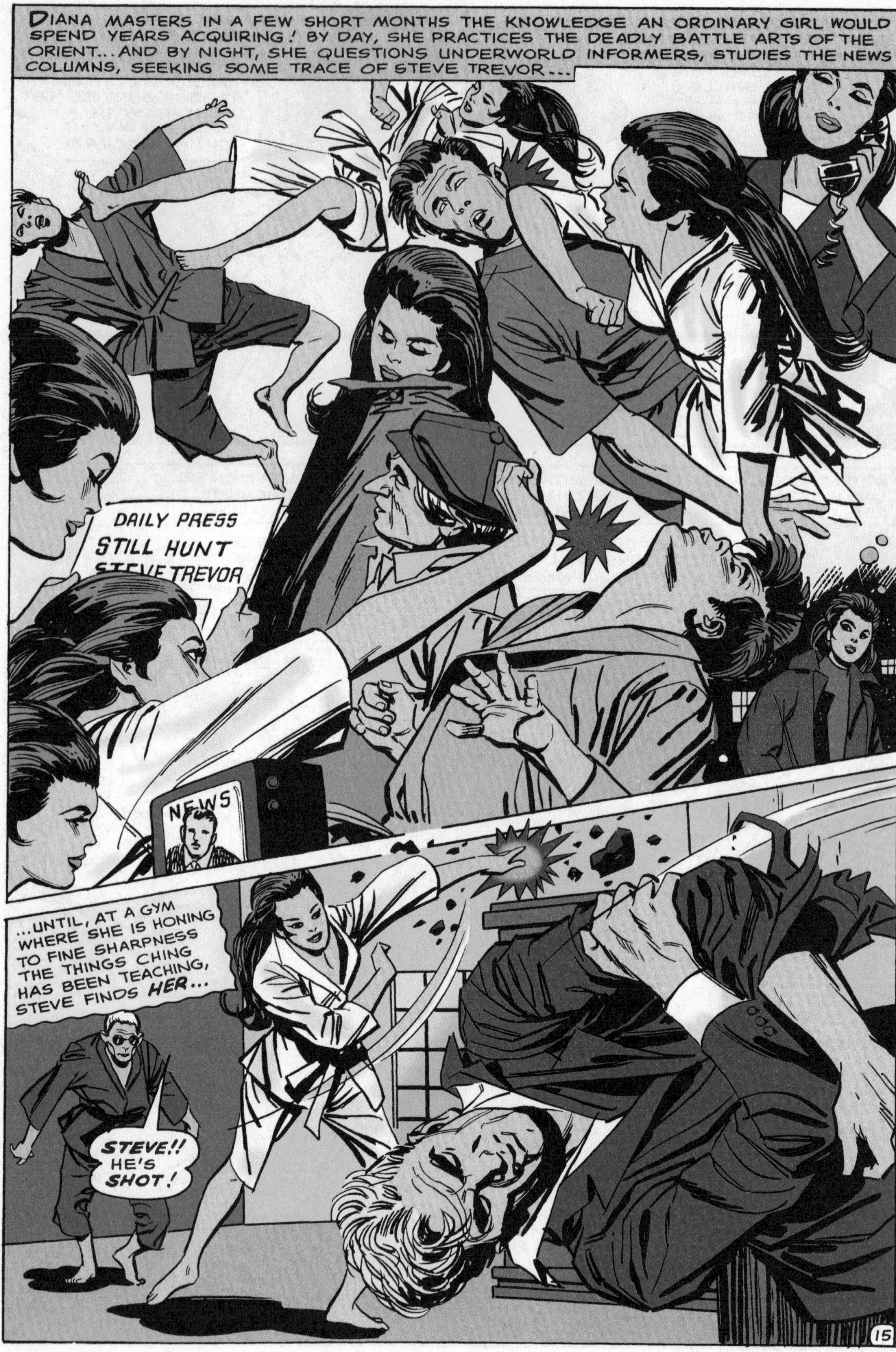
DIANA MASTERS IN A FEW SHORT MONTHS THE KNOWLEDGE AN ORDINARY GIRL WOULD SPEND YEARS ACQUIRING! BY DAY, SHE PRACTICES THE DEADLY BATTLE ARTS OF THE ORIENT... AND BY NIGHT, SHE QUESTIONS UNDERWORLD INFORMERS, STUDIES THE NEWS COLUMNS, SEEKING SOME TRACE OF STEVE TREVOR...
DAILY PRESS
STILL HUNT
NEWS
...UNTIL, AT A GYM WHERE SHE IS HONING TO FINE SHARPNESS THE THINGS CHING HAS BEEN TEACHING, STEVE FINDS HER...
STEVE!! HE'S SHOT!
15

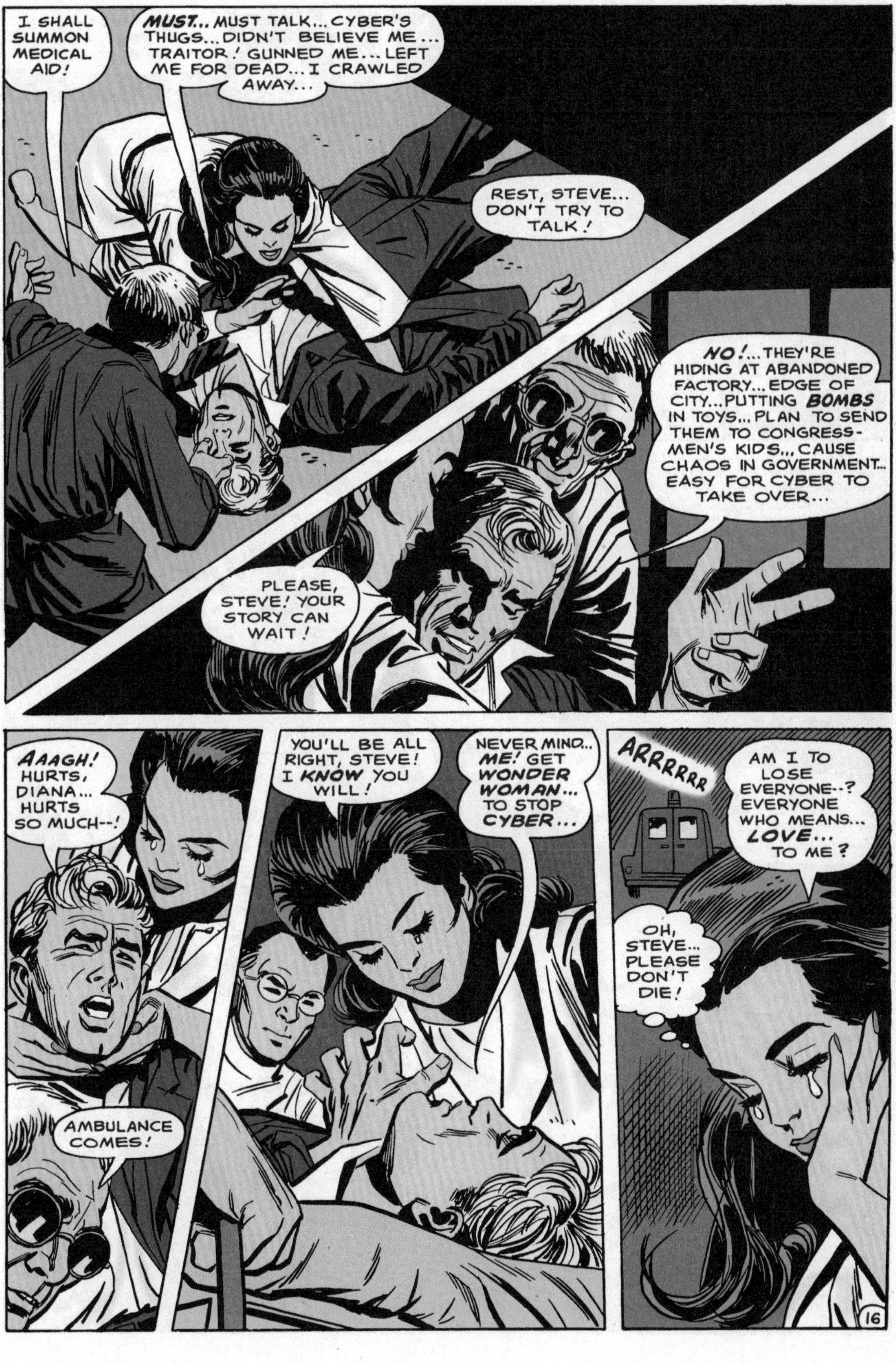
I SHALL SUMMON MEDICAL AID!
MUST... MUST TALK... CYBER'S THUGS... DIDN'T BELIEVE ME... TRAITOR! GUNNED ME... LEFT ME FOR DEAD... I CRAWLED AWAY...
REST, STEVE... DON'T TRY TO TALK!
NO!... THEY'RE HIDING AT ABANDONED FACTORY... EDGE OF CITY... PUTTING BOMBS IN TOYS... PLAN TO SEND THEM TO CONGRESS-MEN'S KIDS... CAUSE CHAOS IN GOVERNMENT... EASY FOR CYBER TO TAKE OVER...
PLEASE, STEVE! YOUR STORY CAN WAIT!
AAAGH! HURTS, DIANA... HURTS SO MUCH--!
AMBULANCE COMES!
YOU'LL BE ALL RIGHT, STEVE! I KNOW YOU WILL!
NEVER MIND.. ME! GET WONDER WOMAN... TO STOP CYBER...
ARRRRRR
AM I TO LOSE EVERYONE--? EVERYONE WHO MEANS... LOVE... TO ME?
OH, STEVE... PLEASE DON'T DIE!
16

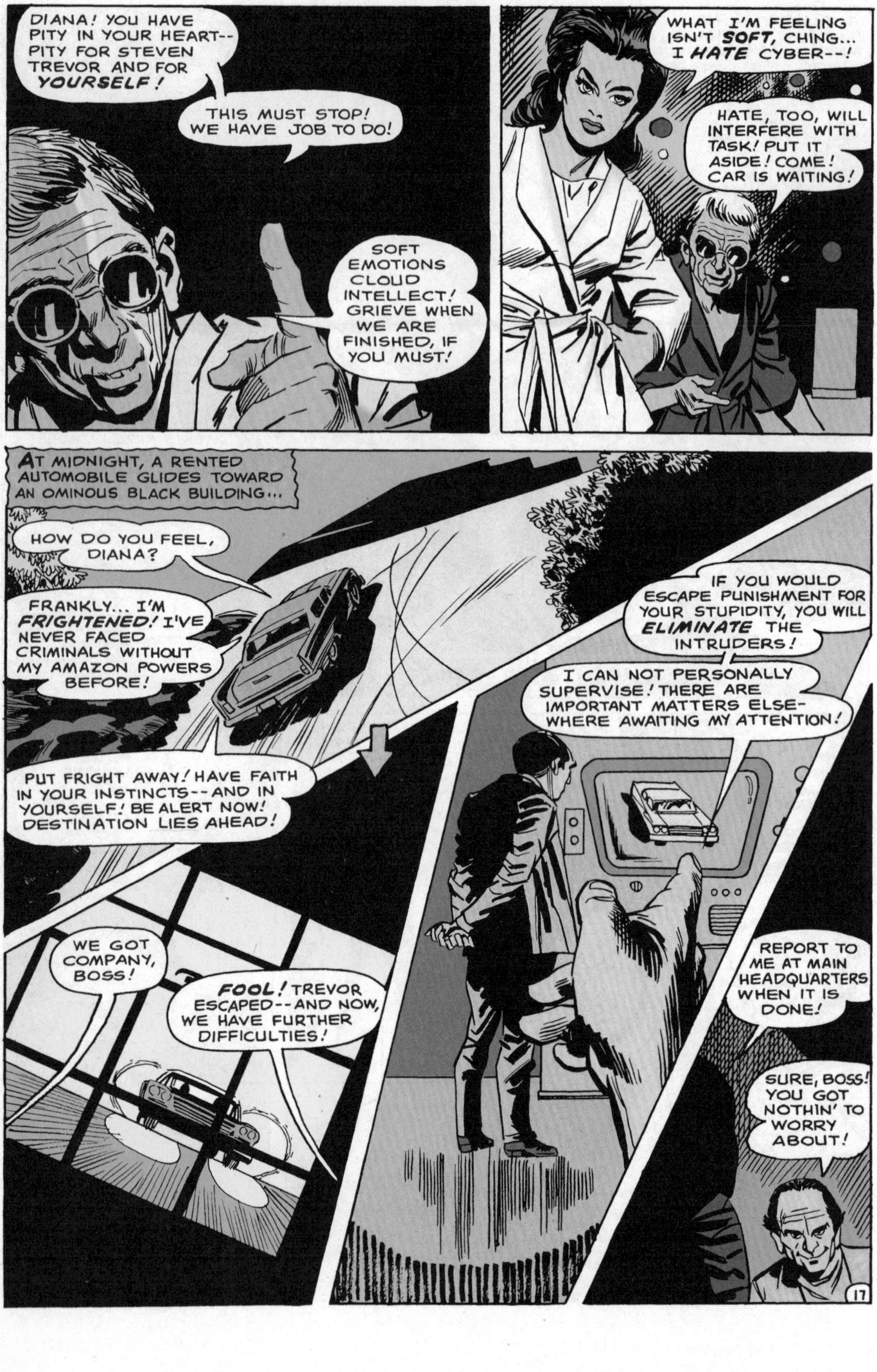
DIANA! YOU HAVE PITY IN YOUR HEART-- PITY FOR STEVEN TREVOR AND FOR YOURSELF!
THIS MUST STOP! WE HAVE JOB TO DO!
SOFT EMOTIONS CLOUD INTELLECT! GRIEVE WHEN WE ARE FINISHED, IF YOU MUST!
WHAT I'M FEELING ISN'T SOFT, CHING... I HATE CYBER--!
HATE, TOO, WILL INTERFERE WITH TASK! PUT IT ASIDE! COME! CAR IS WAITING!
AT MIDNIGHT, A RENTED AUTOMOBILE GLIDES TOWARD AN OMINOUS BLACK BUILDING...
HOW DO YOU FEEL, DIANA?
FRANKLY... I'M FRIGHTENED! I'VE NEVER FACED CRIMINALS WITHOUT MY AMAZON POWERS BEFORE!
PUT FRIGHT AWAY! HAVE FAITH IN YOUR INSTINCTS--AND IN YOURSELF! BE ALERT NOW! DESTINATION LIES AHEAD!
WE GOT COMPANY, BOSS!
FOOL! TREVOR ESCAPED--AND NOW, WE HAVE FURTHER DIFFICULTIES!
IF YOU WOULD ESCAPE PUNISHMENT FOR YOUR STUPIDITY, YOU WILL ELIMINATE THE INTRUDERS!
I CAN NOT PERSONALLY SUPERVISE! THERE ARE IMPORTANT MATTERS ELSE-WHERE AWAITING MY ATTENTION!
REPORT TO ME AT MAIN HEADQUARTERS WHEN IT IS DONE!
SURE, BOSS! YOU GOT NOTHIN' TO WORRY ABOUT!
17

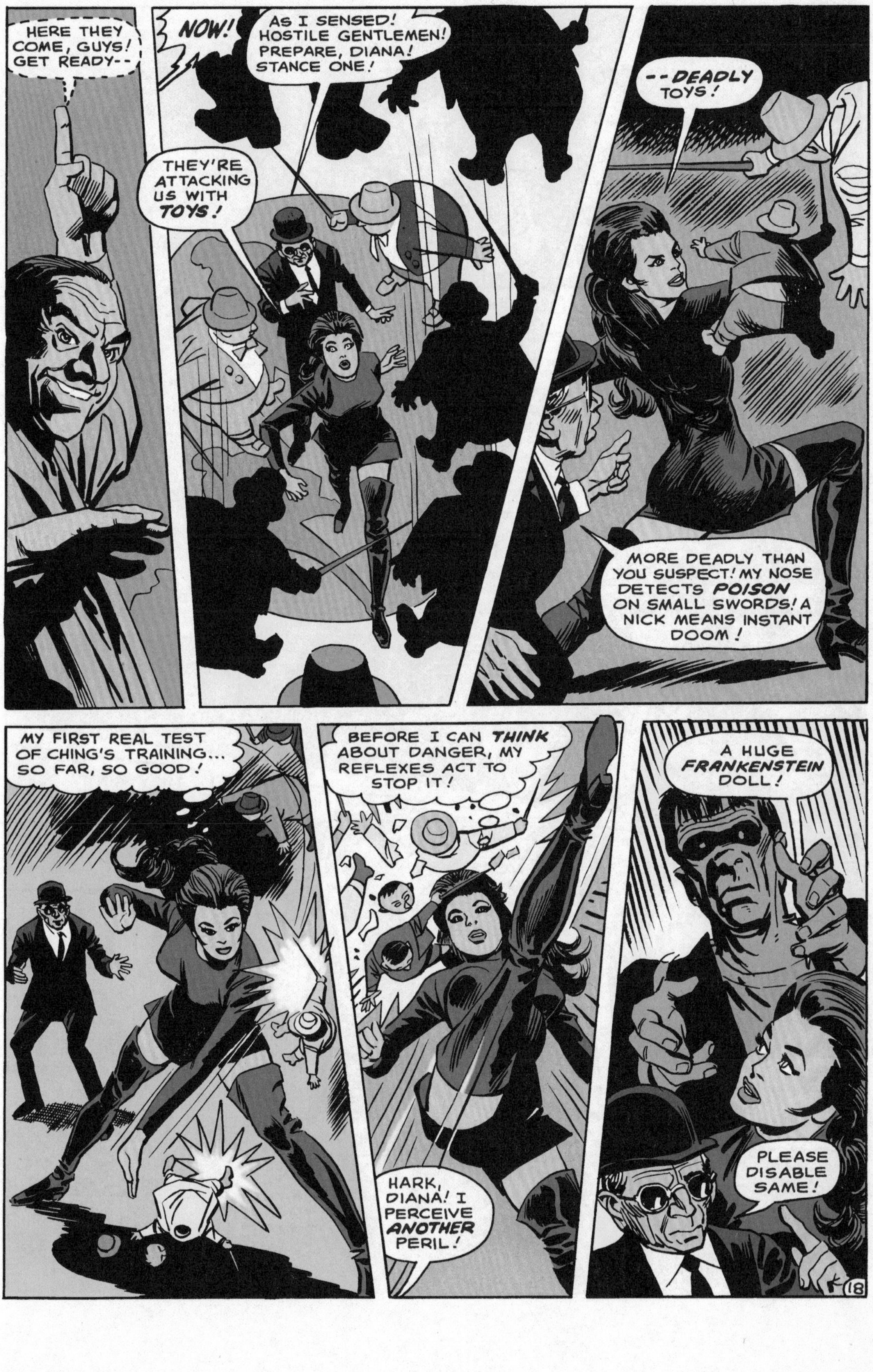
HERE THEY COME, GUYS! GET READY--
NOW!
AS I SENSED! HOSTILE GENTLEMEN! PREPARE, DIANA! STANCE ONE!
THEY'RE ATTACKING US WITH TOYS!
--DEADLY TOYS!
MORE DEADLY THAN YOU SUSPECT! MY NOSE DETECTS POISON ON SMALL SWORDS! A NICK MEANS INSTANT DOOM!
MY FIRST REAL TEST OF CHING'S TRAINING... SO FAR, SO GOOD!
BEFORE I CAN THINK ABOUT DANGER, MY REFLEXES ACT TO STOP IT!
HARK, DIANA! I PERCEIVE ANOTHER PERIL!
A HUGE FRANKENSTEIN DOLL!
PLEASE DISABLE SAME!
18

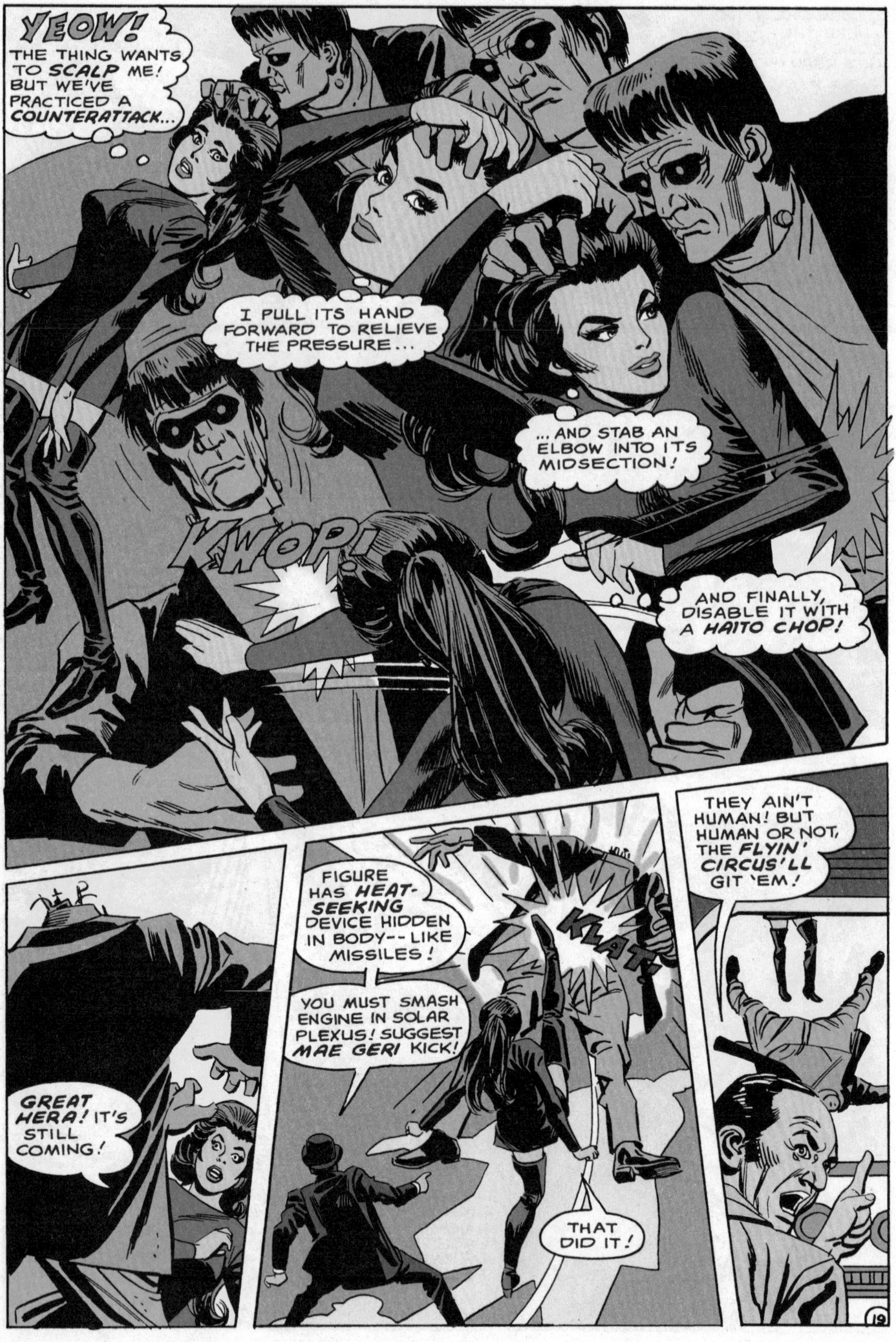
YEOW! THE THING WANTS TO SCALP ME! BUT WE'VE PRACTICED A COUNTERATTACK...
I PULL ITS HAND FORWARD TO RELIEVE THE PRESSURE...
...AND STAB AN ELBOW INTO ITS MIDSECTION!
KWOP!
AND FINALLY, DISABLE IT WITH A HAITO CHOP!
GREAT HERA! IT'S STILL COMING!
FIGURE HAS HEAT-SEEKING DEVICE HIDDEN IN BODY-- LIKE MISSILES!
YOU MUST SMASH ENGINE IN SOLAR PLEXUS! SUGGEST MAE GERI KICK!
KLAT!
THAT DID IT!
THEY AIN'T HUMAN! BUT HUMAN OR NOT, THE FLYIN' CIRCUS'LL GIT 'EM!
19

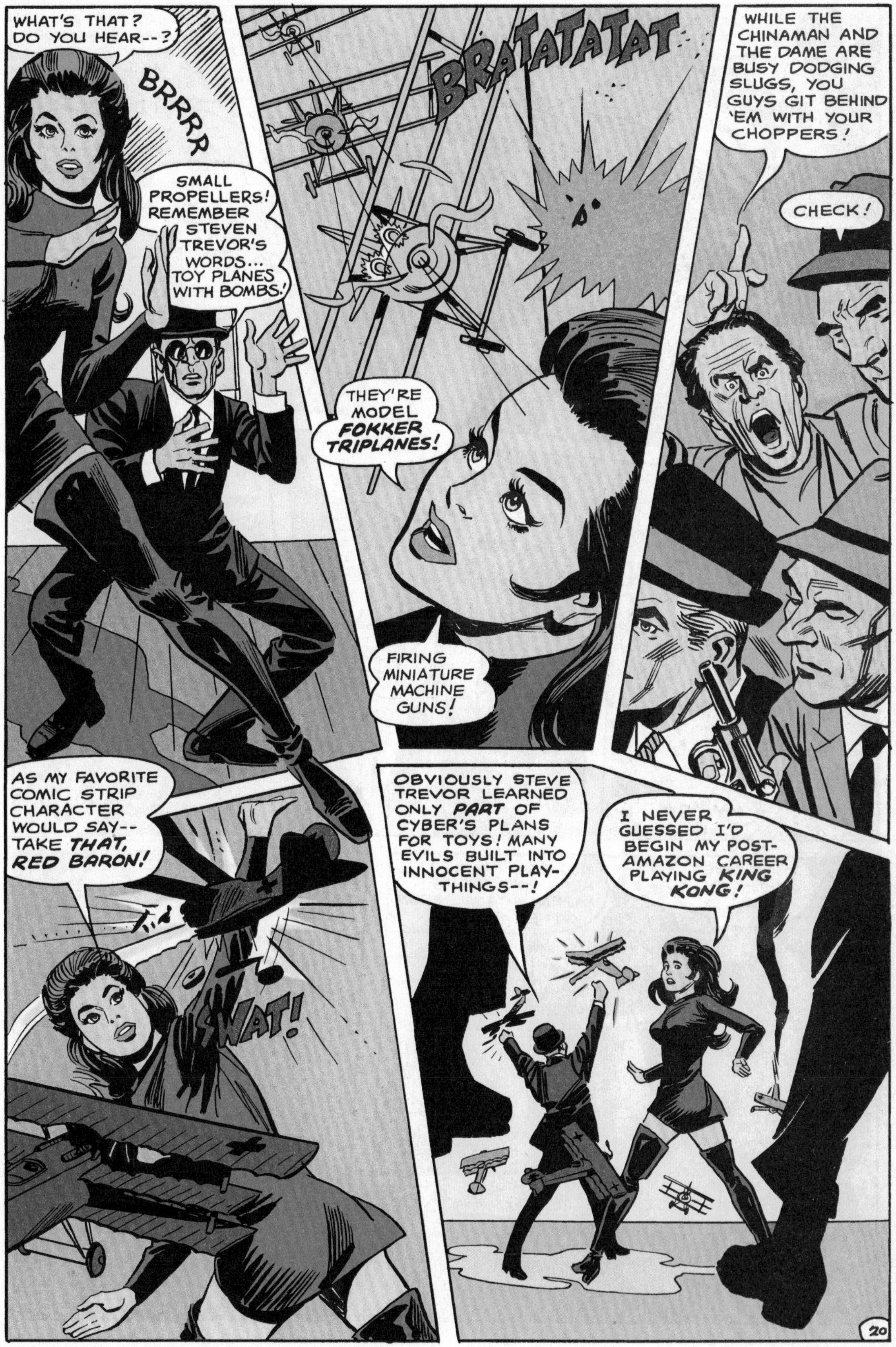
WHAT'S THAT? DO YOU HEAR--?
BRRRRR
SMALL PROPELLERS! REMEMBER STEVEN TREVOR'S WORDS... TOY PLANES WITH BOMBS!
BRATATATAT
THEY'RE MODEL FOKKER TRIPLANES!
FIRING MINIATURE MACHINE GUNS!
WHILE THE CHINAMAN AND THE DAME ARE BUSY DODGING SLUGS, YOU GUYS GIT BEHIND 'EM WITH YOUR CHOPPERS!
CHECK!
AS MY FAVORITE COMIC STRIP CHARACTER WOULD SAY-- TAKE THAT, RED BARON!
SWAT!
OBVIOUSLY STEVE TREVOR LEARNED ONLY PART OF CYBER'S PLANS FOR TOYS! MANY EVILS BUILT INTO INNOCENT PLAY-THINGS--!
I NEVER GUESSED I'D BEGIN MY POST-AMAZON CAREER PLAYING KING KONG!
20

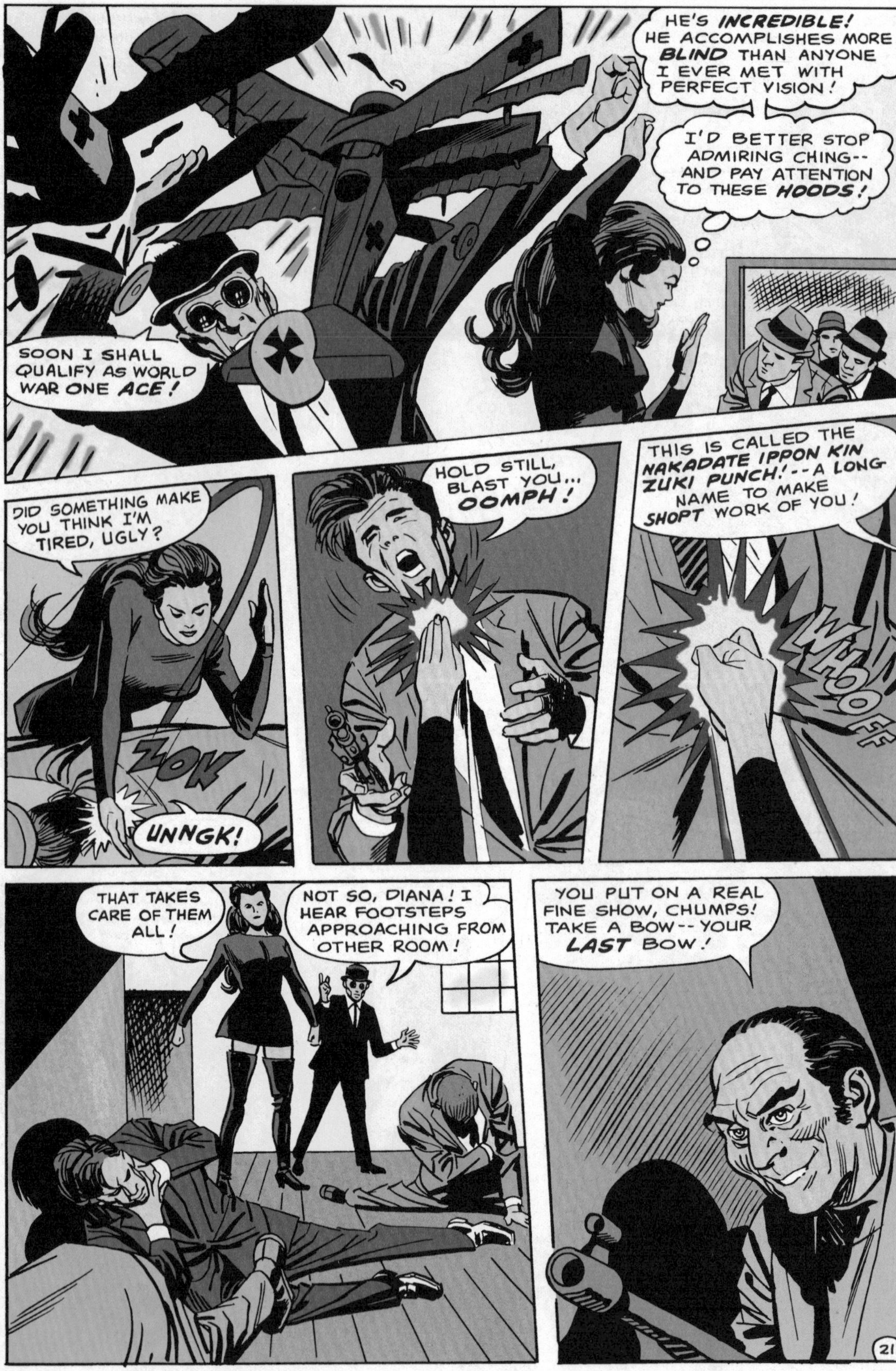
HE'S INCREDIBLE! HE ACCOMPLISHES MORE BLIND THAN ANYONE I EVER MET WITH PERFECT VISION!
I'D BETTER STOP ADMIRING CHING-- AND PAY ATTENTION TO THESE HOODS!
SOON I SHALL QUALIFY AS WORLD WAR ONE ACE!
DID SOMETHING MAKE YOU THINK I'M TIRED, UGLY?
ZOK
UNNGK!
HOLD STILL, BLAST YOU... OOMPH!
THIS IS CALLED THE NAKADATE IPPON KIN ZUKI PUNCH!--A LONG NAME TO MAKE SHORT WORK OF YOU!
WHOOFF
THAT TAKES CARE OF THEM ALL!
NOT SO, DIANA! I HEAR FOOTSTEPS APPROACHING FROM OTHER ROOM!
YOU PUT ON A REAL FINE SHOW, CHUMPS! TAKE A BOW-- YOUR LAST BOW!
21

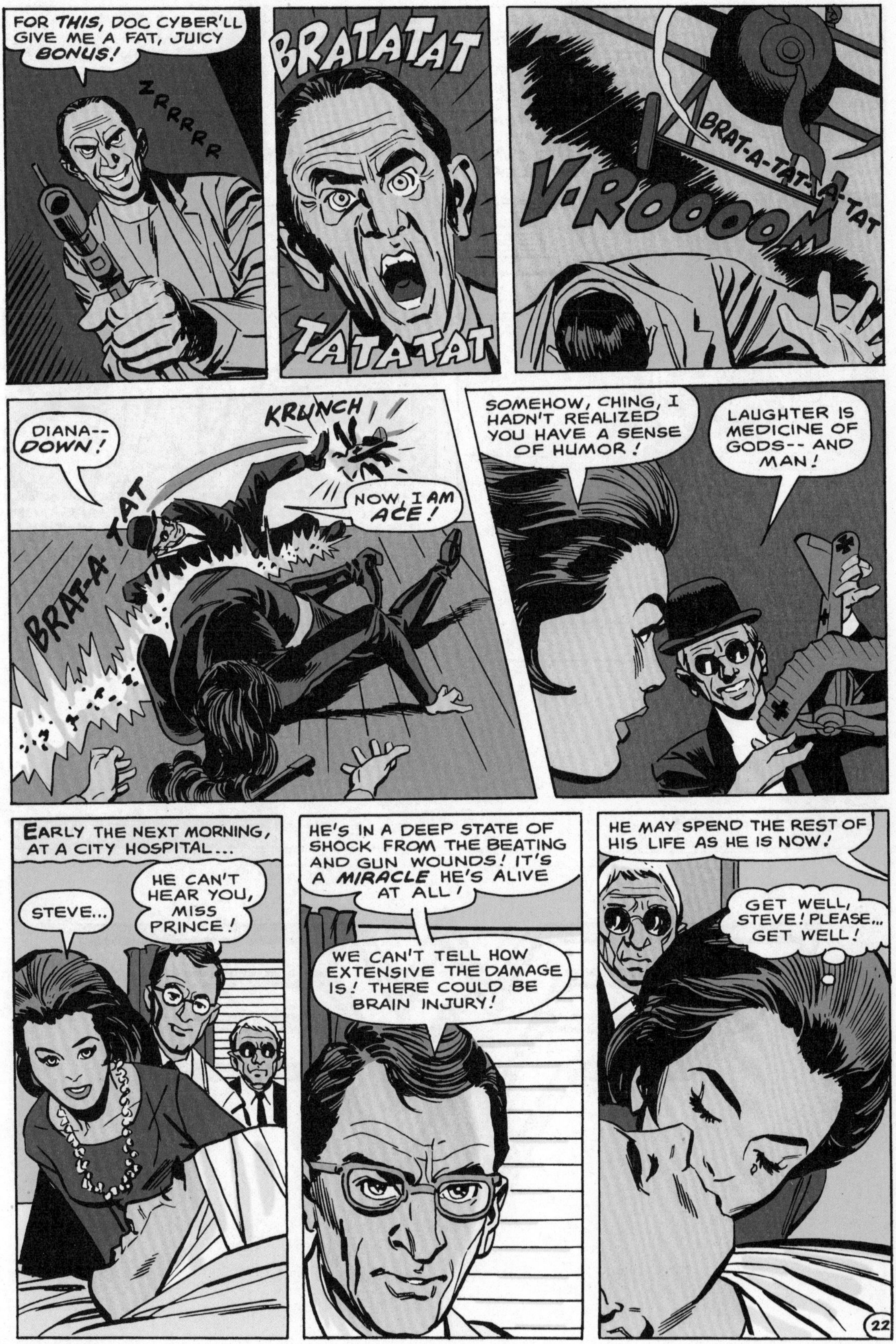
FOR THIS, DOC CYBER'LL GIVE ME A FAT, JUICY BONUS!
ZRRRRRR
BRATATAT
TATATAT
BRAT-A-TAT-A-TAT
V-ROOOOOM
DIANA-- DOWN!
KRUNCH
NOW, I AM ACE!
BRAT-A-TAT
SOMEHOW, CHING, I HADN'T REALIZED YOU HAVE A SENSE OF HUMOR!
LAUGHTER IS MEDICINE OF GODS-- AND MAN!
EARLY THE NEXT MORNING, AT A CITY HOSPITAL...
STEVE...
HE CAN'T HEAR YOU, MISS PRINCE!
HE'S IN A DEEP STATE OF SHOCK FROM THE BEATING AND GUN WOUNDS! IT'S A MIRACLE HE'S ALIVE AT ALL!
WE CAN'T TELL HOW EXTENSIVE THE DAMAGE IS! THERE COULD BE BRAIN INJURY!
HE MAY SPEND THE REST OF HIS LIFE AS HE IS NOW!
GET WELL, STEVE! PLEASE... GET WELL!
22

THEN, OUTSIDE, IN THE COOL DAWN AIR...

I'M EXHAUSTED... AND A BIT *NUMB!* MY LIFE HAS CHANGED SO MUCH...

NO! WE HAVE BARELY *STARTED!* DOCTOR CYBER IS STILL FREE! HE IS LIKE AN *INFECTION* IN HUMAN STRAIN! OUR TASK IS TO *CURE* DISEASE--BY CRUSHING HIM!

23

AS FOR *CHANGES*-- THEY HAVE JUST BEGUN!

A GOOD-LOOKING DAME AND A BLIND CHINESE... THOSE THE PEOPLE I'M AFTER, ALL RIGHT!

THUS, THE FIRST CHAPTER IN THE SAGA OF THE *NEW WONDER WOMAN* ENDS... WITH DIANA AND HER AGED MENTOR BEING OBSERVED BY A SINISTER FIGURE HIDDEN IN THE SHADOWS! MORE DANGER--MORE HIGH-VOLTAGE EXCITEMENT--MORE HEARTBREAK-- AWAIT DIANA PRINCE AS SHE AND CHING CONTINUE THEIR PURSUIT OF THE SUPREMELY DEPRAVED *DOCTOR CYBER!*

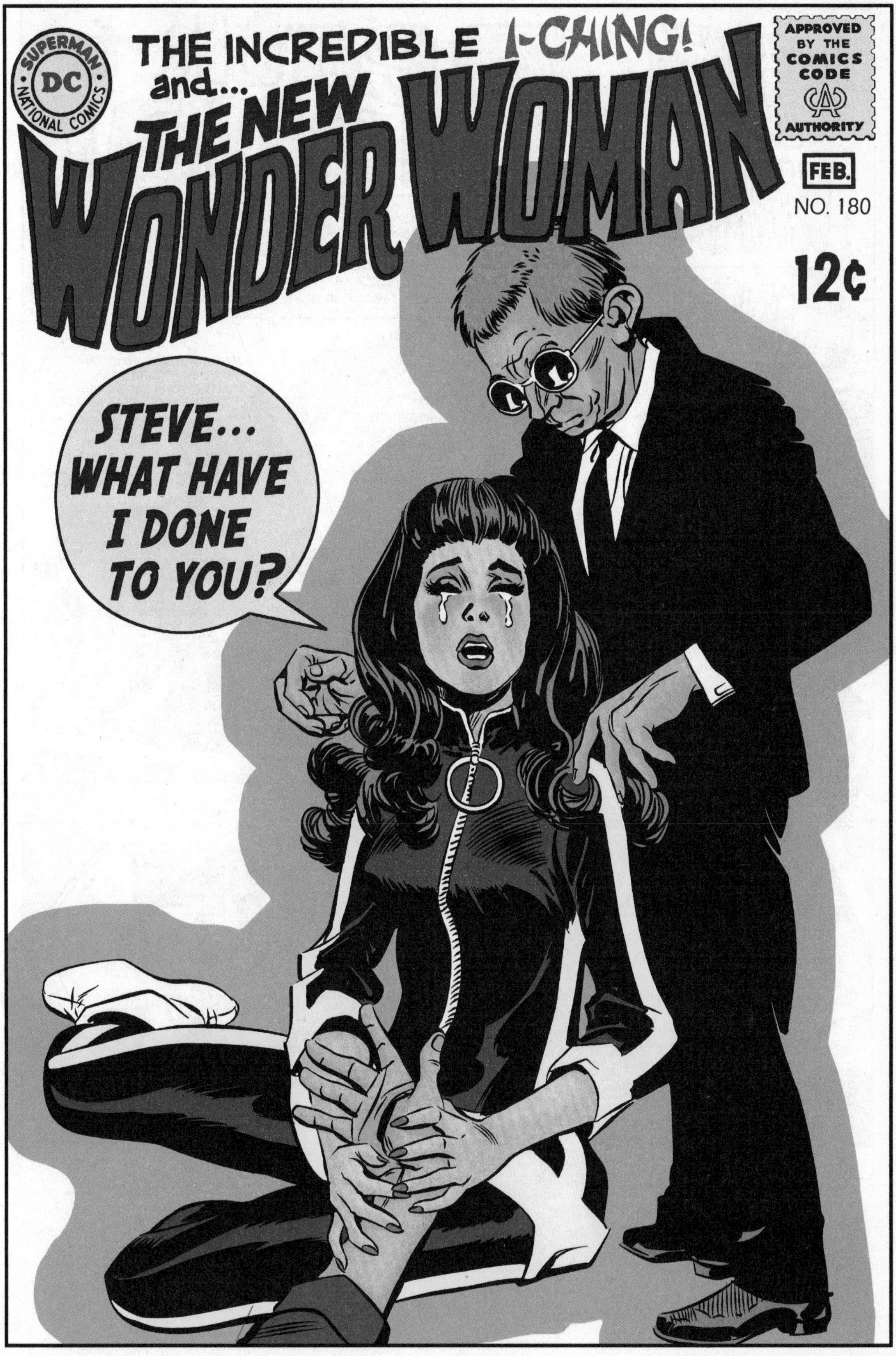

THE INCREDIBLE I-CHING!
and...
THE NEW
WONDER WOMAN
SUPERMAN DC NATIONAL COMICS
APPROVED BY THE COMICS CODE AUTHORITY
FEB.
NO. 180
12¢
STEVE... WHAT HAVE I DONE TO YOU?

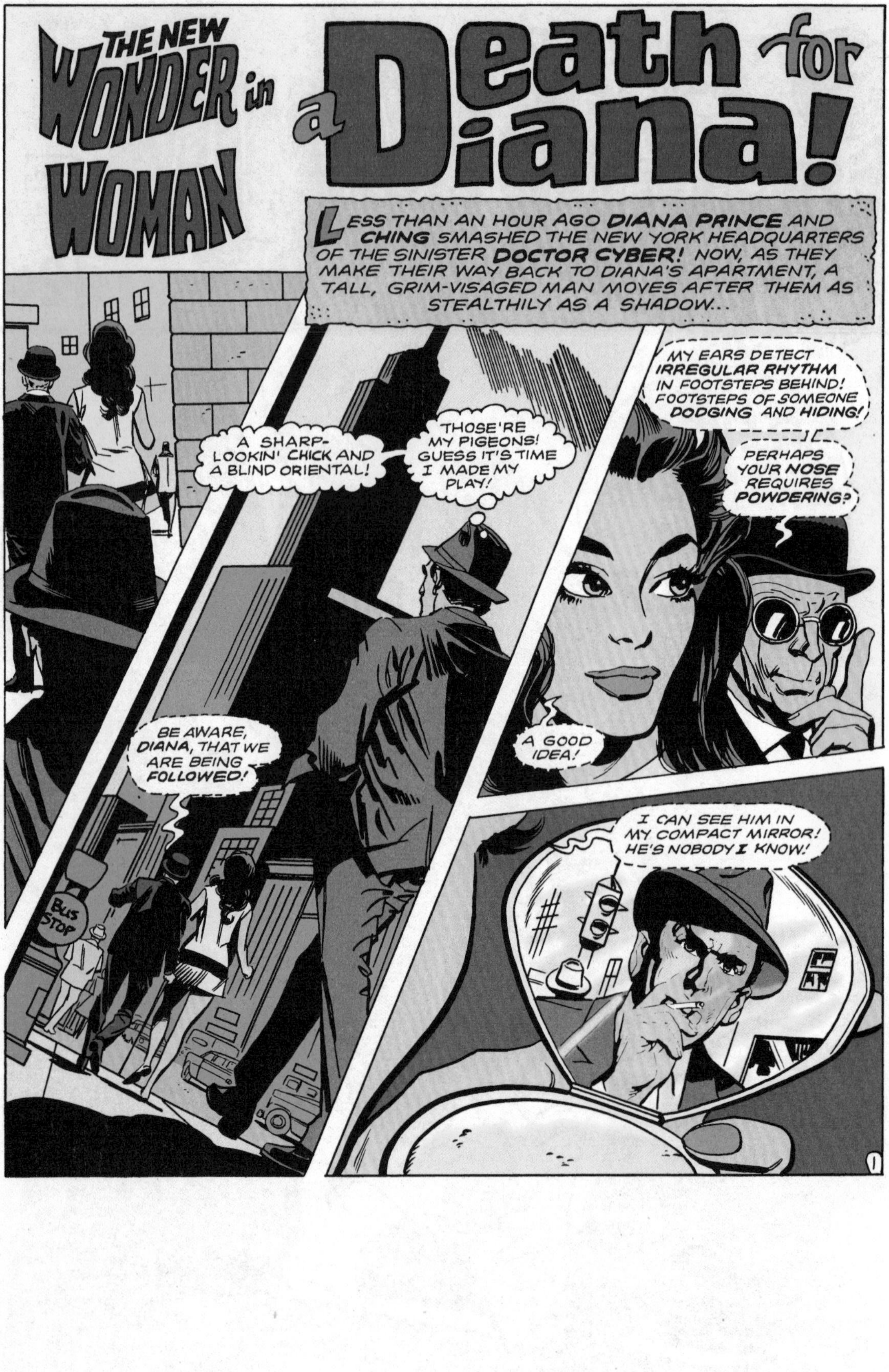
THE NEW WONDER WOMAN in
a Death for Diana!
LESS THAN AN HOUR AGO DIANA PRINCE AND CHING SMASHED THE NEW YORK HEADQUARTERS OF THE SINISTER DOCTOR CYBER! NOW, AS THEY MAKE THEIR WAY BACK TO DIANA'S APARTMENT, A TALL, GRIM-VISAGED MAN MOVES AFTER THEM AS STEALTHILY AS A SHADOW...
A SHARP-LOOKIN' CHICK AND A BLIND ORIENTAL!
THOSE'RE MY PIGEONS! GUESS IT'S TIME I MADE MY PLAY!
BE AWARE, DIANA, THAT WE ARE BEING FOLLOWED!
BUS STOP
MY EARS DETECT IRREGULAR RHYTHM IN FOOTSTEPS BEHIND! FOOTSTEPS OF SOMEONE DODGING AND HIDING!
PERHAPS YOUR NOSE REQUIRES POWDERING?
A GOOD IDEA!
I CAN SEE HIM IN MY COMPACT MIRROR! HE'S NOBODY I KNOW!
1

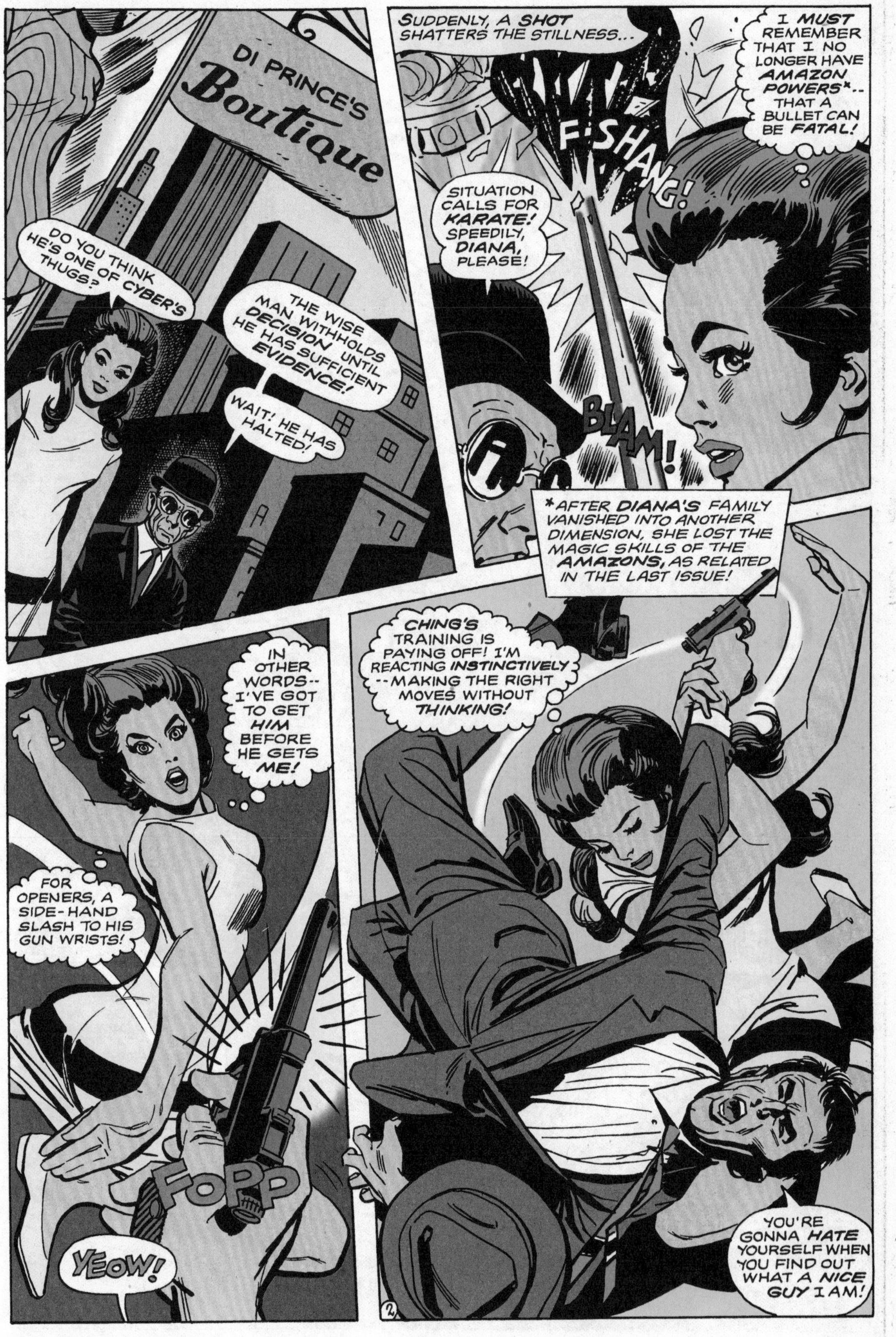
DI PRINCE'S Boutique
DO YOU THINK HE'S ONE OF CYBER'S THUGS?
THE WISE MAN WITHHOLDS DECISION UNTIL HE HAS SUFFICIENT EVIDENCE!
WAIT! HE HAS HALTED!
SUDDENLY, A SHOT SHATTERS THE STILLNESS...
F-SHANG!
SITUATION CALLS FOR KARATE! SPEEDILY, DIANA, PLEASE!
I MUST REMEMBER THAT I NO LONGER HAVE AMAZON POWERS*-- THAT A BULLET CAN BE FATAL!
BLAM!
*AFTER DIANA'S FAMILY VANISHED INTO ANOTHER DIMENSION, SHE LOST THE MAGIC SKILLS OF THE AMAZONS, AS RELATED IN THE LAST ISSUE!
IN OTHER WORDS-- I'VE GOT TO GET HIM BEFORE HE GETS ME!
FOR OPENERS, A SIDE-HAND SLASH TO HIS GUN WRISTS!
FOPP
YEOW!
CHING'S TRAINING IS PAYING OFF! I'M REACTING INSTINCTIVELY --MAKING THE RIGHT MOVES WITHOUT THINKING!
YOU'RE GONNA HATE YOURSELF WHEN YOU FIND OUT WHAT A NICE GUY I AM!
2

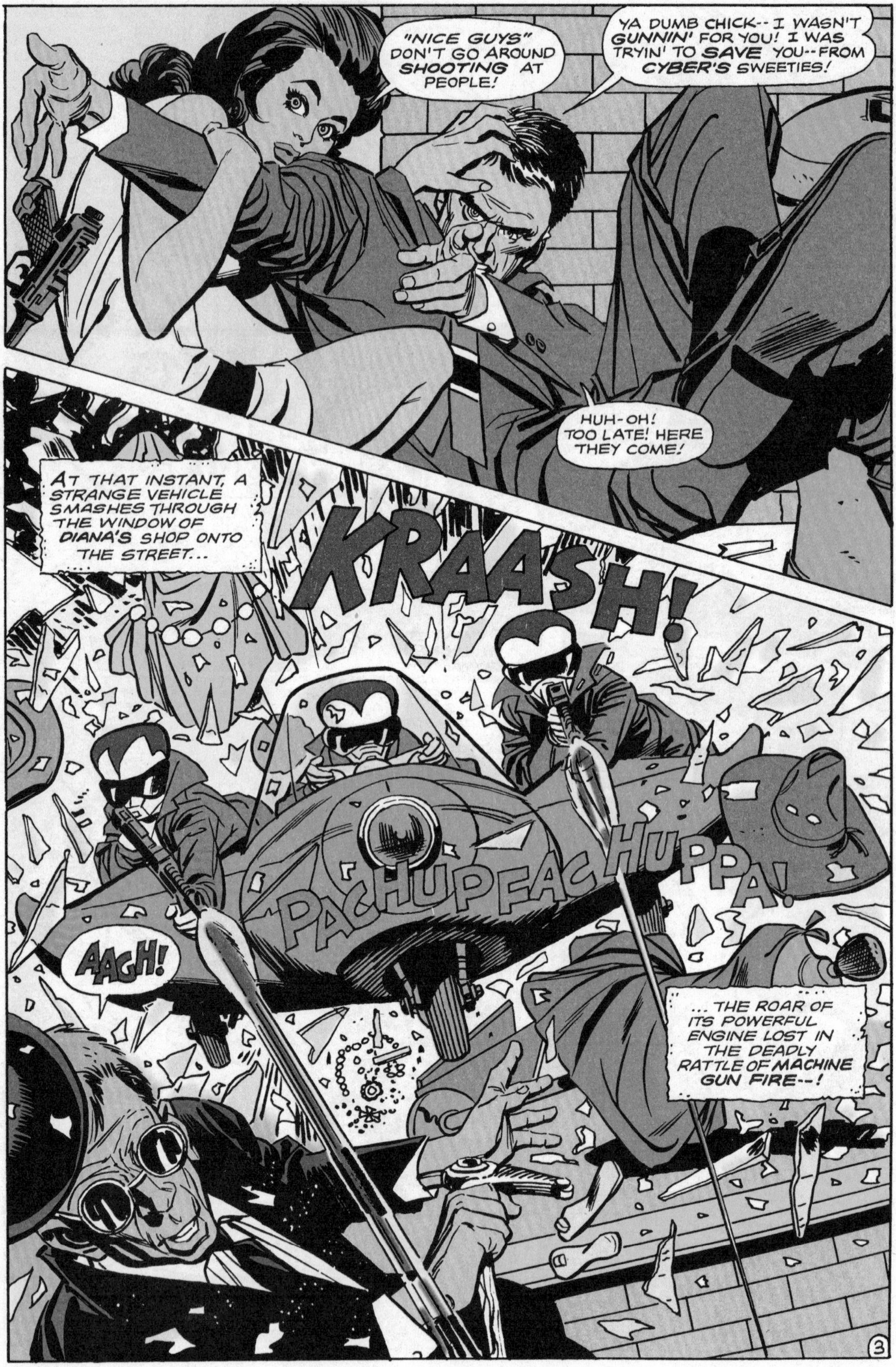
"NICE GUYS" DON'T GO AROUND SHOOTING AT PEOPLE!
YA DUMB CHICK-- I WASN'T GUNNIN' FOR YOU! I WAS TRYIN' TO SAVE YOU--FROM CYBER'S SWEETIES!
HUH-OH! TOO LATE! HERE THEY COME!
AT THAT INSTANT, A STRANGE VEHICLE SMASHES THROUGH THE WINDOW OF DIANA'S SHOP ONTO THE STREET...
KRAASH!
PACHUPFACHUPPA!
AAGH!
... THE ROAR OF ITS POWERFUL ENGINE LOST IN THE DEADLY RATTLE OF MACHINE GUN FIRE--!
3

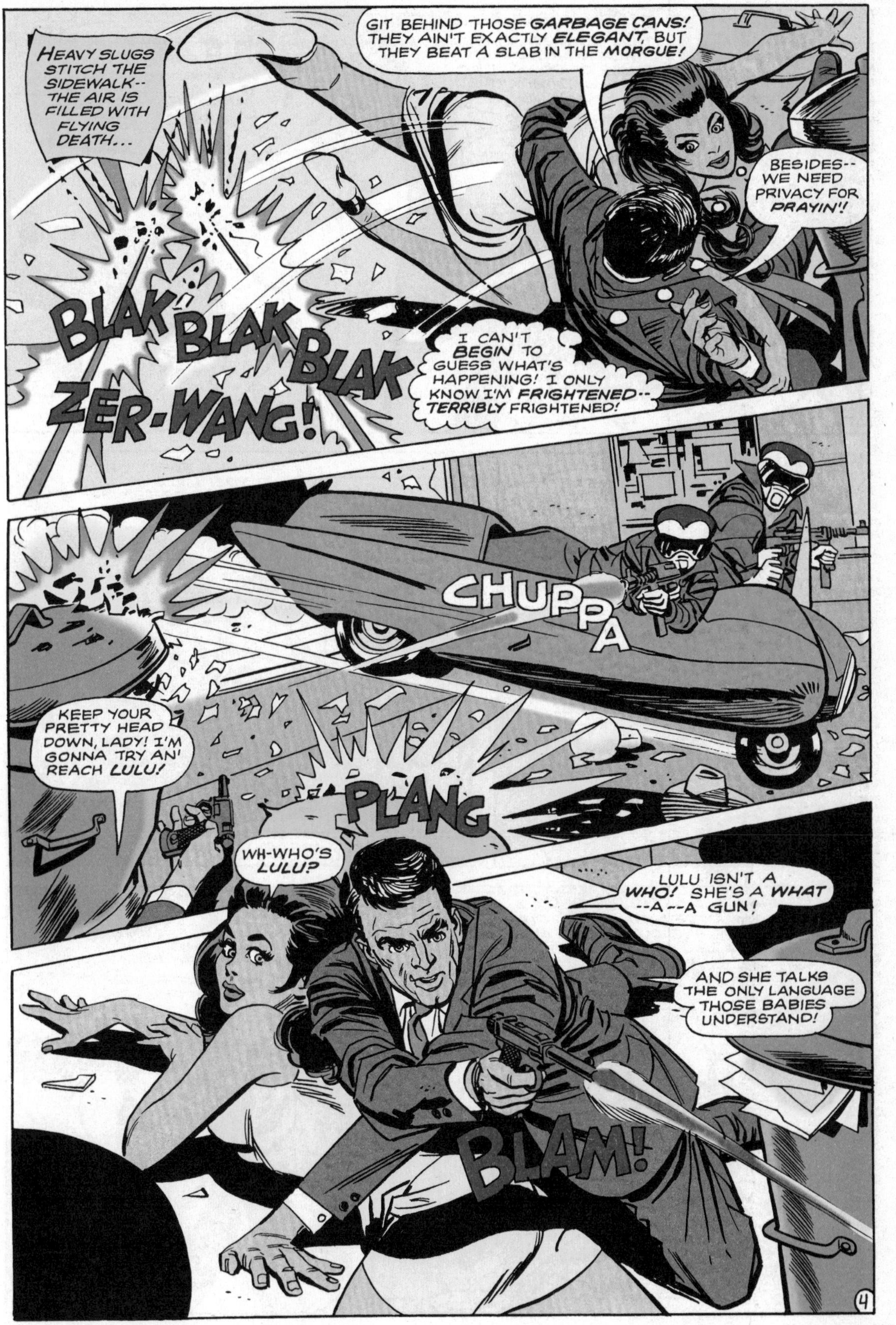
HEAVY SLUGS STITCH THE SIDEWALK-- THE AIR IS FILLED WITH FLYING DEATH...
GIT BEHIND THOSE GARBAGE CANS! THEY AIN'T EXACTLY ELEGANT, BUT THEY BEAT A SLAB IN THE MORGUE!
BESIDES-- WE NEED PRIVACY FOR PRAYIN'!
BLAK BLAK BLAK
ZER-WANG!
I CAN'T BEGIN TO GUESS WHAT'S HAPPENING! I ONLY KNOW I'M FRIGHTENED-- TERRIBLY FRIGHTENED!
CHUPPA
KEEP YOUR PRETTY HEAD DOWN, LADY! I'M GONNA TRY AN' REACH LULU!
PLANG
WH-WHO'S LULU?
LULU ISN'T A WHO! SHE'S A WHAT --A --A GUN!
AND SHE TALKS THE ONLY LANGUAGE THOSE BABIES UNDERSTAND!
BLAM!
4

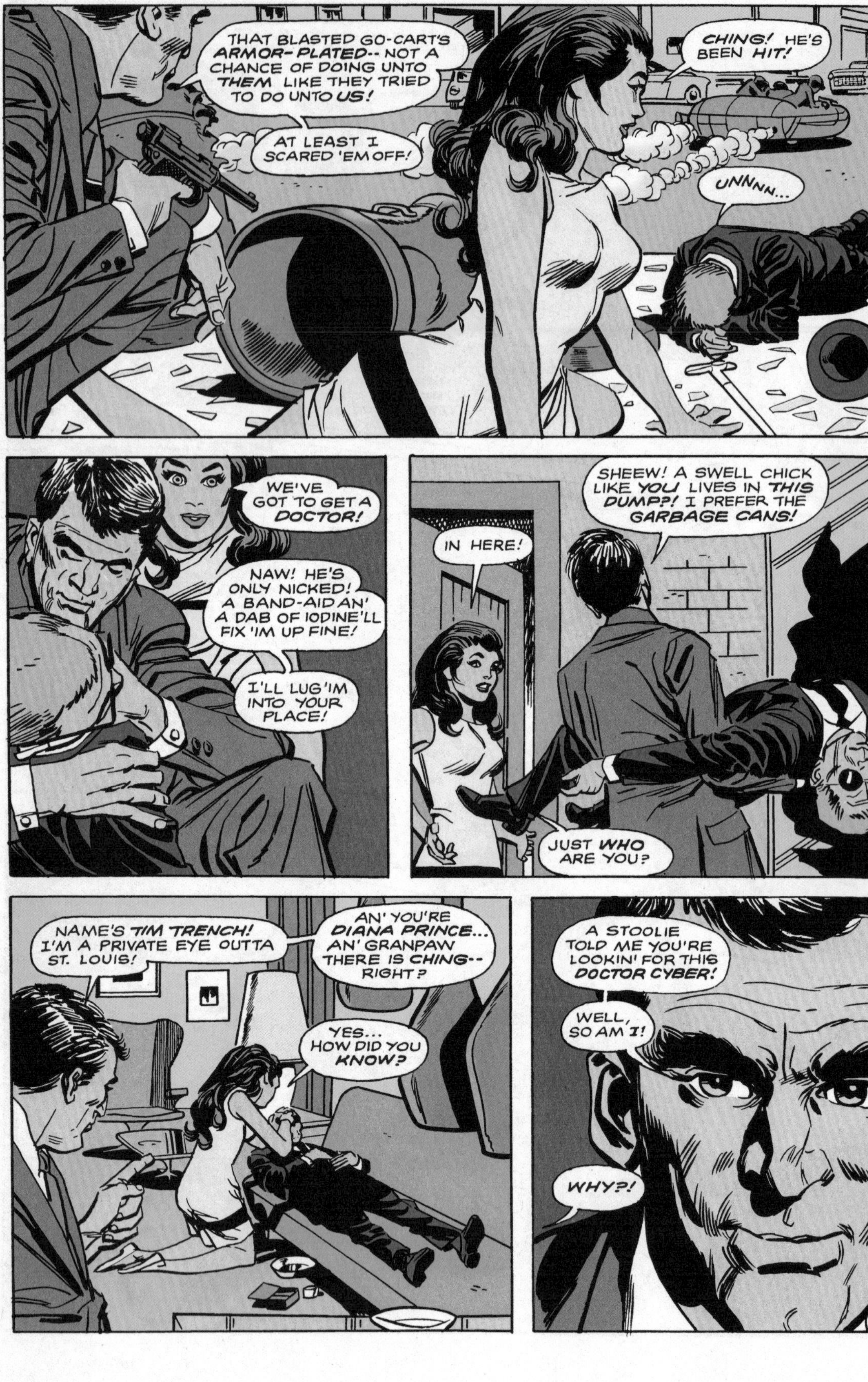
THAT BLASTED GO-CART'S ARMOR-PLATED-- NOT A CHANCE OF DOING UNTO THEM LIKE THEY TRIED TO DO UNTO US!
AT LEAST I SCARED 'EM OFF!
CHING! HE'S BEEN HIT!
UNNNN...
WE'VE GOT TO GET A DOCTOR!
NAW! HE'S ONLY NICKED! A BAND-AID AN' A DAB OF IODINE'LL FIX 'IM UP FINE!
I'LL LUG 'IM INTO YOUR PLACE!
SHEEW! A SWELL CHICK LIKE YOU LIVES IN THIS DUMP?! I PREFER THE GARBAGE CANS!
IN HERE!
JUST WHO ARE YOU?
NAME'S TIM TRENCH! I'M A PRIVATE EYE OUTTA ST. LOUIS!
AN' YOU'RE DIANA PRINCE... AN' GRANPAW THERE IS CHING-- RIGHT?
YES... HOW DID YOU KNOW?
A STOOLIE TOLD ME YOU'RE LOOKIN' FOR THIS DOCTOR CYBER!
WELL, SO AM I!
WHY?!
5

ONE OF *CYBER'S* GUNSELS NAILED MY PARTNER, *ARCHY MILES!* IN MY BUSINESS, YOU DON'T LET *ANYBODY* GET AWAY WITH KILLIN' A PAL...

...'CAUSE THEY MIGHT MAKE IT A *HABIT!* WHAT'S *YOUR* INTEREST IN *CYBER?*

ALMOST THE SAME AS YOURS! *DOCTOR CYBER* SHOT MY ...MY FRIEND, *STEVE TREVOR!*

STEVE'S IN THE *HOSPITAL!* HE MAY... *DIE!*

SAVE THE HEARTS-AN'-FLOWERS! I LEFT MY CRYIN' TOWEL AT HOME!

YOU WISH TO *JOIN US,* MR. TRENCH?

YEAH! THAT'S KINDA WHAT I HAD IN MIND!

WE *WELCOME* YOUR AID!

SO! MY ENEMIES POOL THEIR RESOURCES-- THE PITIFUL *FOOLS!*

THUS THE SUPREMELY EVIL DOCTOR CYBER WATCHES...SCHEMES ...AND PREPARES A DEATH TRAP MORE SURPRISES FOLLOW!

6

CHAPTER 2 WONDER WOMAN in a DEATH FOR DIANA!

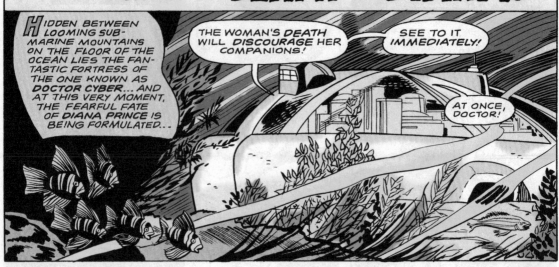

HIDDEN BETWEEN LOOMING SUBMARINE MOUNTAINS ON THE FLOOR OF THE OCEAN LIES THE FANTASTIC FORTRESS OF THE ONE KNOWN AS *DOCTOR CYBER*... AND AT THIS VERY MOMENT, THE FEARFUL FATE OF *DIANA PRINCE* IS BEING FORMULATED...

THE WOMAN'S *DEATH* WILL *DISCOURAGE* HER COMPANIONS!

SEE TO IT *IMMEDIATELY!*

AT ONCE, DOCTOR!

UNAWARE OF HER IMMINENT PERIL, *DIANA* CONTINUES HER CONVERSATION WITH PRIVATE DETECTIVE *TIM TRENCH*, AND ORIENTAL MASTER *I CHING*...

WE HAVE NO *IDEA* JUST *WHO* THIS BIRD *CYBER* IS... *WHERE* IN BLAZES TO *BEGIN* SEARCHIN' FOR 'IM!

CHING... DIDN'T YOU SAY CYBER'S *HOODS* STOLE A LOT OF *RARE GEMS* WHEN THEY ATTACKED YOUR *MONASTERY?*

SO?

SURELY SOME OF THOSE GEMS WILL BEGIN TO *TURN UP!*

YEAH... ALL WE GOTTA DO IS WATCH FOR *HOT ICE!* HEY, CHICK, YOU AIN'T SO DUMB!

INTELLIGENT, *DIANA* IS! BUT, LIKE THE CLAY OF THE *SCULPTOR*, *UNFORMED!* COME, DIANA, WE MUST RESUME YOUR *TRAINING!*

⑦

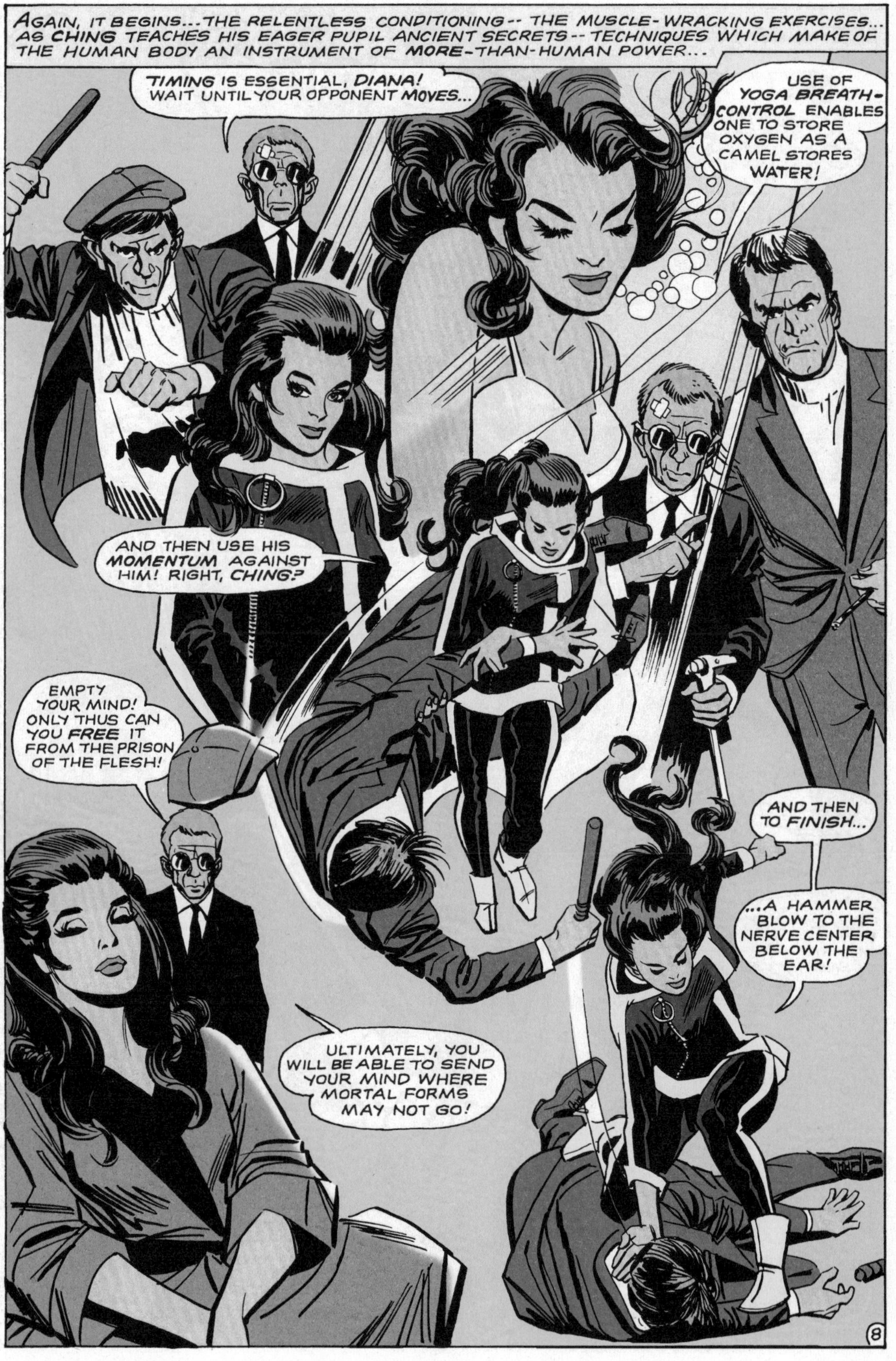
AGAIN, IT BEGINS...THE RELENTLESS CONDITIONING-- THE MUSCLE-WRACKING EXERCISES... AS CHING TEACHES HIS EAGER PUPIL ANCIENT SECRETS-- TECHNIQUES WHICH MAKE OF THE HUMAN BODY AN INSTRUMENT OF MORE-THAN-HUMAN POWER...
TIMING IS ESSENTIAL, DIANA! WAIT UNTIL YOUR OPPONENT MOVES...
AND THEN USE HIS MOMENTUM AGAINST HIM! RIGHT, CHING?
USE OF YOGA BREATH-CONTROL ENABLES ONE TO STORE OXYGEN AS A CAMEL STORES WATER!
EMPTY YOUR MIND! ONLY THUS CAN YOU FREE IT FROM THE PRISON OF THE FLESH!
ULTIMATELY, YOU WILL BE ABLE TO SEND YOUR MIND WHERE MORTAL FORMS MAY NOT GO!
AND THEN TO FINISH...
...A HAMMER BLOW TO THE NERVE CENTER BELOW THE EAR!
8

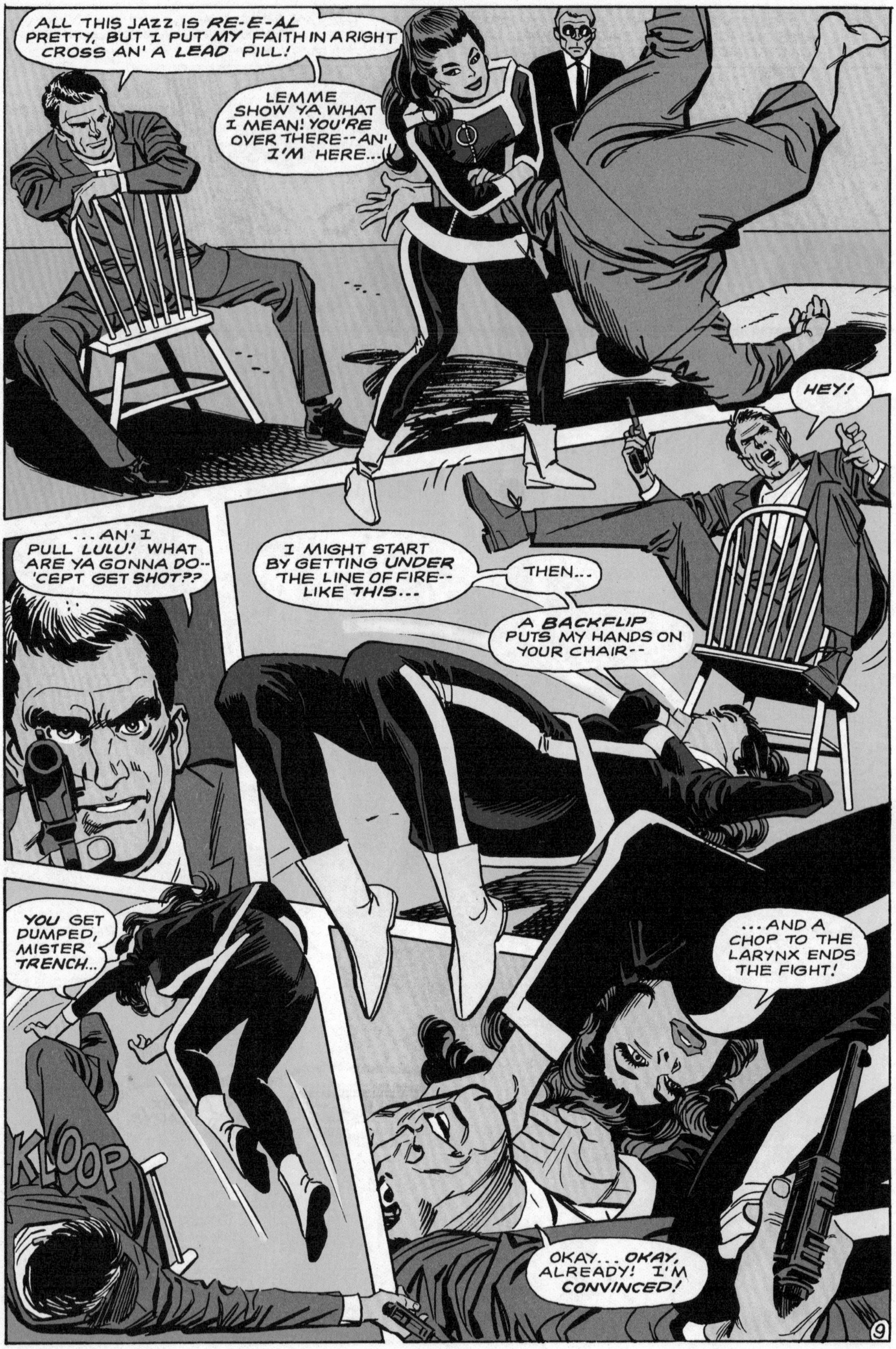
ALL THIS JAZZ IS RE-E-AL PRETTY, BUT I PUT MY FAITH IN A RIGHT CROSS AN' A LEAD PILL!
LEMME SHOW YA WHAT I MEAN! YOU'RE OVER THERE--AN' I'M HERE...
HEY!
...AN' I PULL LULU! WHAT ARE YA GONNA DO--'CEPT GET SHOT??
I MIGHT START BY GETTING UNDER THE LINE OF FIRE--LIKE THIS...
THEN...
A BACKFLIP PUTS MY HANDS ON YOUR CHAIR--
YOU GET DUMPED, MISTER TRENCH...
KLOOP
...AND A CHOP TO THE LARYNX ENDS THE FIGHT!
OKAY... OKAY, ALREADY! I'M CONVINCED!
9

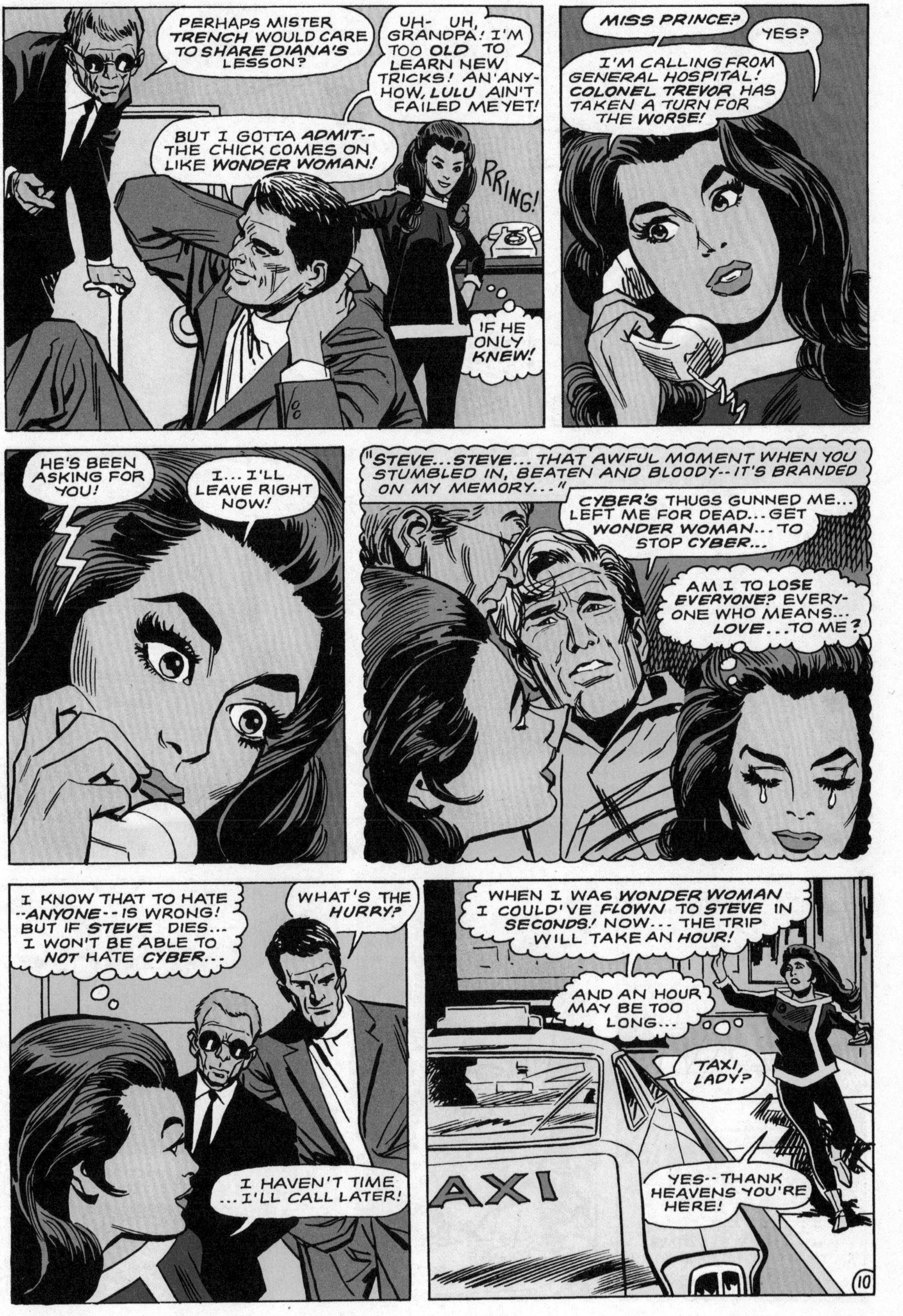
PERHAPS MISTER TRENCH WOULD CARE TO SHARE DIANA'S LESSON?
UH- UH, GRANDPA! I'M TOO OLD TO LEARN NEW TRICKS! AN' ANY-HOW, LULU AIN'T FAILED ME YET!
BUT I GOTTA ADMIT-- THE CHICK COMES ON LIKE WONDER WOMAN!
RRING!
IF HE ONLY KNEW!
MISS PRINCE?
YES?
I'M CALLING FROM GENERAL HOSPITAL! COLONEL TREVOR HAS TAKEN A TURN FOR THE WORSE!
HE'S BEEN ASKING FOR YOU!
I... I'LL LEAVE RIGHT NOW!
"STEVE... STEVE... THAT AWFUL MOMENT WHEN YOU STUMBLED IN, BEATEN AND BLOODY-- IT'S BRANDED ON MY MEMORY..."
CYBER'S THUGS GUNNED ME... LEFT ME FOR DEAD... GET WONDER WOMAN... TO STOP CYBER...
AM I TO LOSE EVERYONE? EVERY-ONE WHO MEANS... LOVE... TO ME?
I KNOW THAT TO HATE --ANYONE-- IS WRONG! BUT IF STEVE DIES... I WON'T BE ABLE TO NOT HATE CYBER...
WHAT'S THE HURRY?
I HAVEN'T TIME ...I'LL CALL LATER!
WHEN I WAS WONDER WOMAN I COULD'VE FLOWN TO STEVE IN SECONDS! NOW... THE TRIP WILL TAKE AN HOUR!
AND AN HOUR MAY BE TOO LONG...
TAXI, LADY?
YES-- THANK HEAVENS YOU'RE HERE!
AXI
10

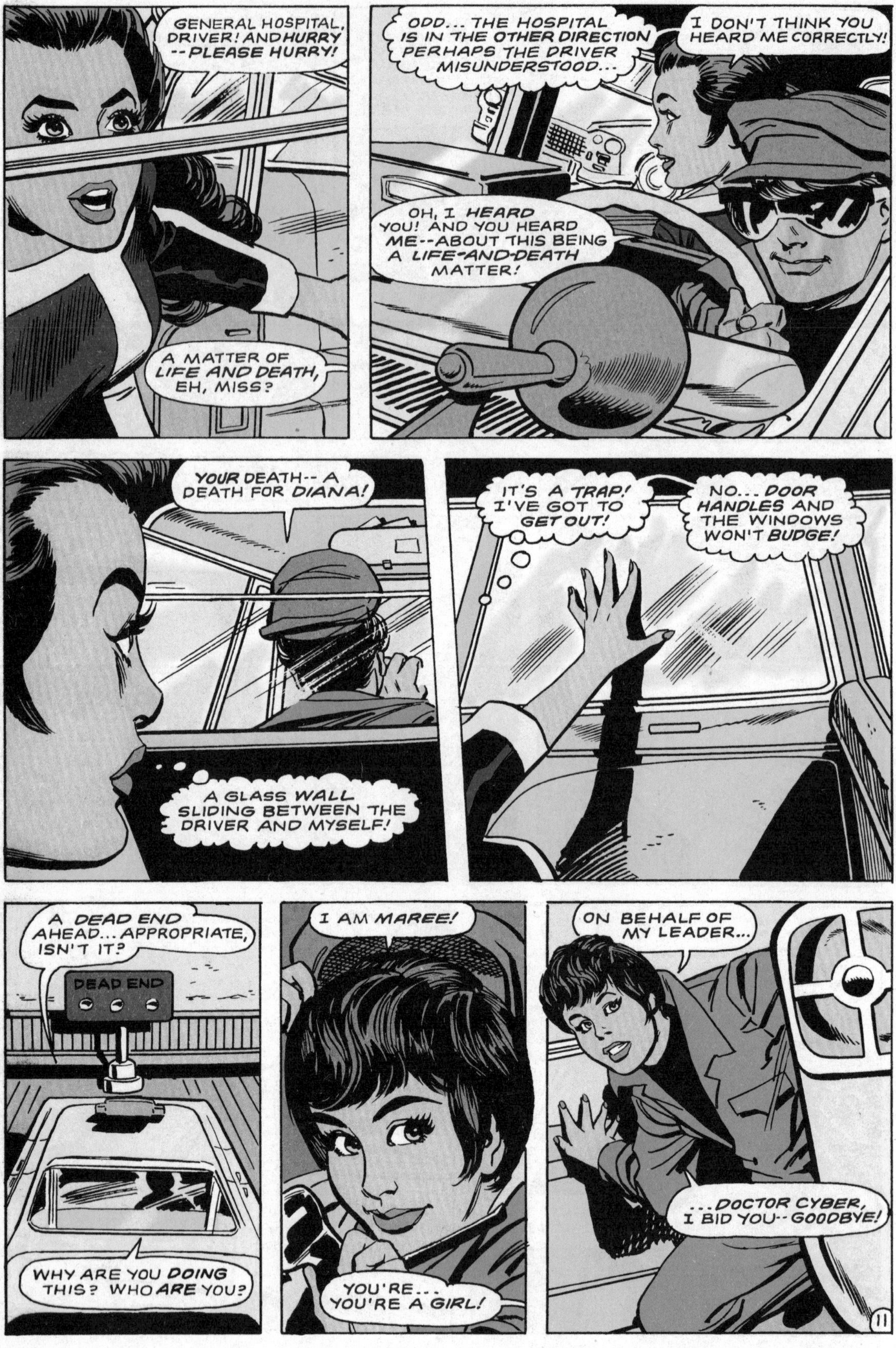
GENERAL HOSPITAL, DRIVER! AND HURRY --PLEASE HURRY!
A MATTER OF LIFE AND DEATH, EH, MISS?
ODD... THE HOSPITAL IS IN THE OTHER DIRECTION PERHAPS THE DRIVER MISUNDERSTOOD...
I DON'T THINK YOU HEARD ME CORRECTLY!
OH, I HEARD YOU! AND YOU HEARD ME--ABOUT THIS BEING A LIFE-AND-DEATH MATTER!
YOUR DEATH-- A DEATH FOR DIANA!
A GLASS WALL SLIDING BETWEEN THE DRIVER AND MYSELF!
IT'S A TRAP! I'VE GOT TO GET OUT!
NO... DOOR HANDLES AND THE WINDOWS WON'T BUDGE!
A DEAD END AHEAD... APPROPRIATE, ISN'T IT?
DEAD END
WHY ARE YOU DOING THIS? WHO ARE YOU?
I AM MAREE!
YOU'RE... YOU'RE A GIRL!
ON BEHALF OF MY LEADER...
...DOCTOR CYBER, I BID YOU-- GOODBYE!
11

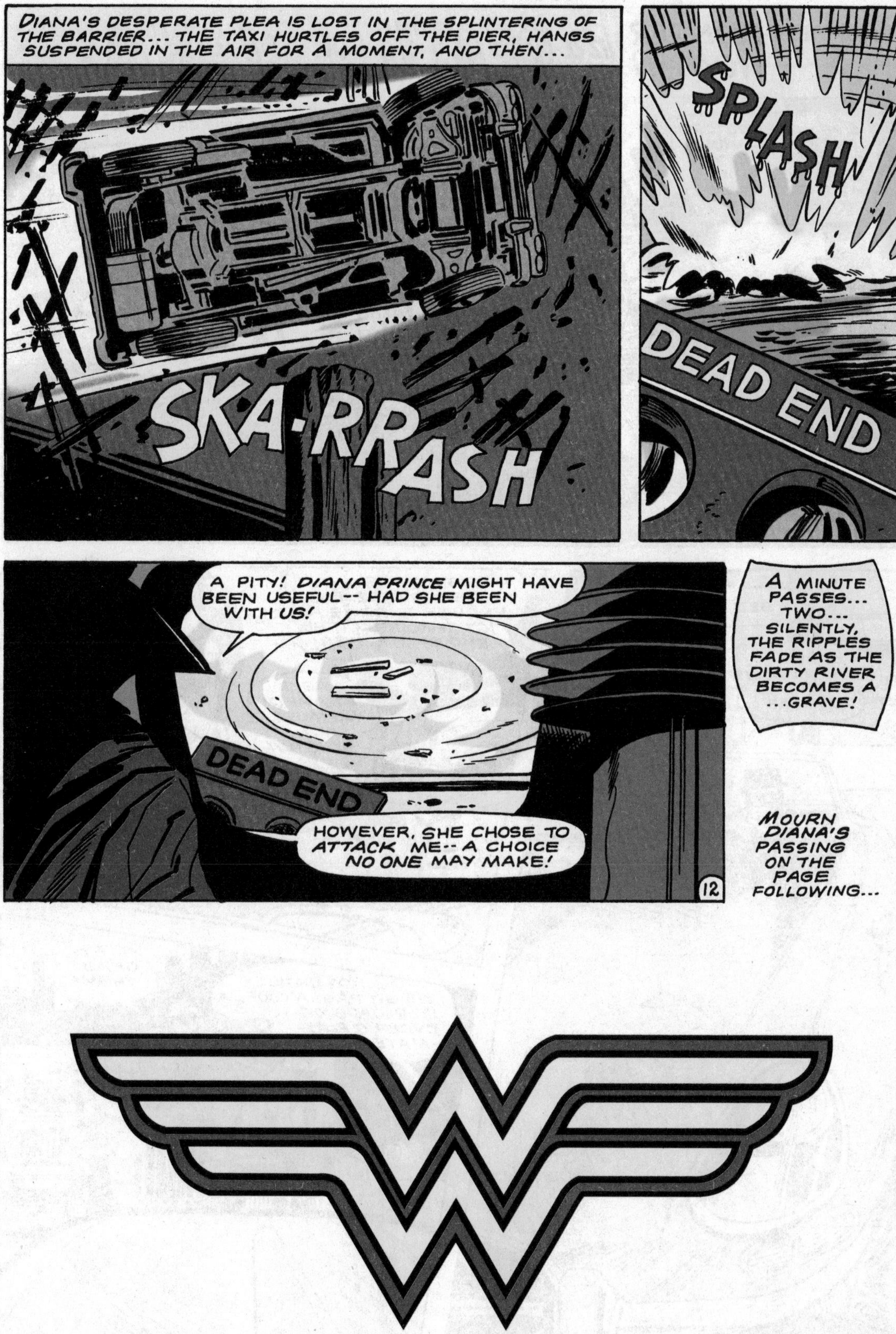
DIANA'S DESPERATE PLEA IS LOST IN THE SPLINTERING OF THE BARRIER... THE TAXI HURTLES OFF THE PIER, HANGS SUSPENDED IN THE AIR FOR A MOMENT, AND THEN...
SKA-RRASH
SPLASH
DEAD END
A PITY! DIANA PRINCE MIGHT HAVE BEEN USEFUL-- HAD SHE BEEN WITH US!
DEAD END
HOWEVER, SHE CHOSE TO ATTACK ME-- A CHOICE NO ONE MAY MAKE!
12
A MINUTE PASSES... TWO... SILENTLY, THE RIPPLES FADE AS THE DIRTY RIVER BECOMES A ...GRAVE!
MOURN DIANA'S PASSING ON THE PAGE FOLLOWING...

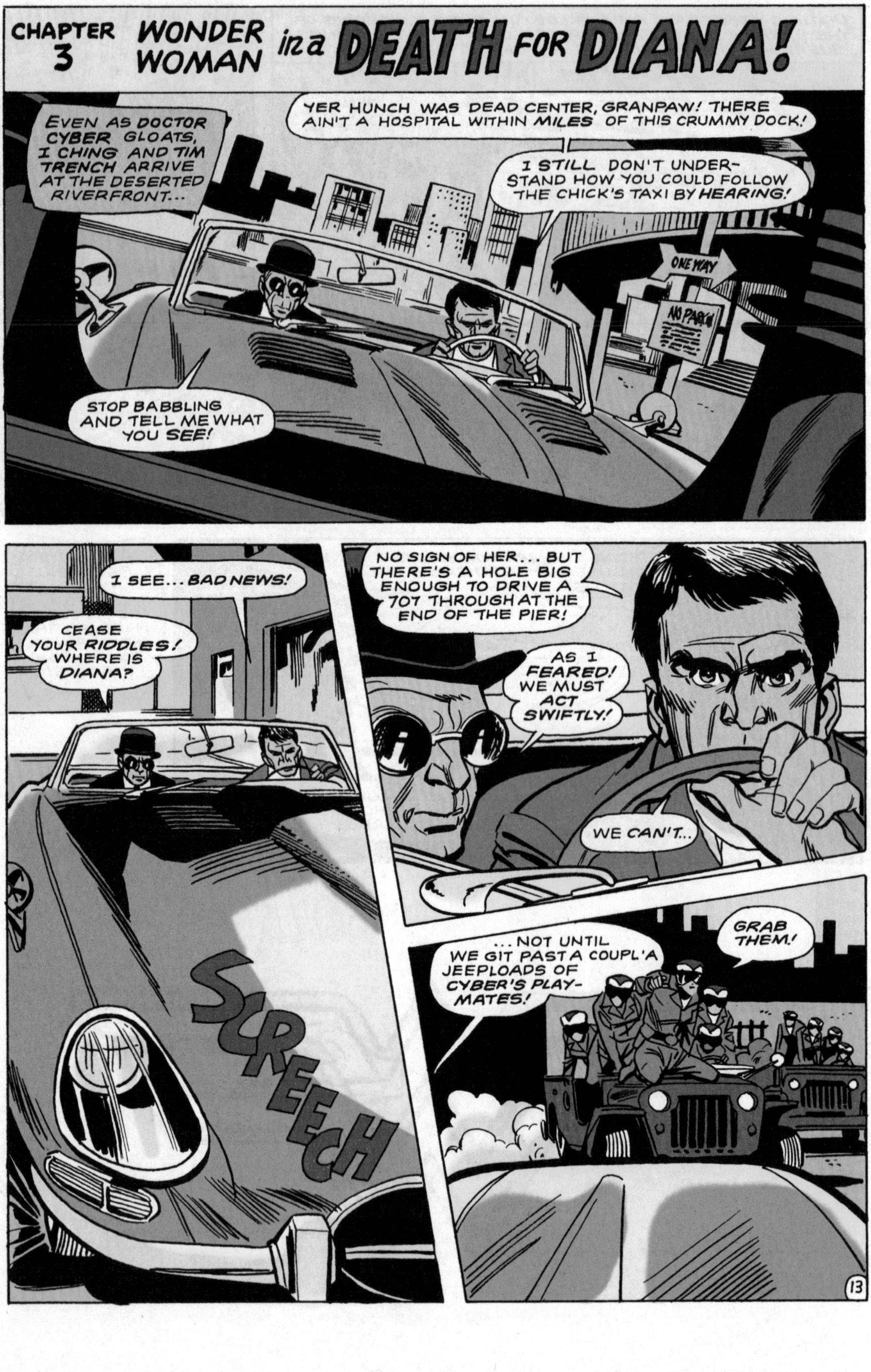
CHAPTER 3
WONDER WOMAN in a DEATH FOR DIANA!
EVEN AS DOCTOR CYBER GLOATS, I CHING AND TIM TRENCH ARRIVE AT THE DESERTED RIVERFRONT...
YER HUNCH WAS DEAD CENTER, GRANPAW! THERE AIN'T A HOSPITAL WITHIN MILES OF THIS CRUMMY DOCK!
I STILL DON'T UNDER-STAND HOW YOU COULD FOLLOW THE CHICK'S TAXI BY HEARING!
STOP BABBLING AND TELL ME WHAT YOU SEE!
ONE WAY
I SEE... BAD NEWS!
CEASE YOUR RIDDLES! WHERE IS DIANA?
SCREECH
NO SIGN OF HER... BUT THERE'S A HOLE BIG ENOUGH TO DRIVE A 707 THROUGH AT THE END OF THE PIER!
AS I FEARED! WE MUST ACT SWIFTLY!
WE CAN'T...
... NOT UNTIL WE GIT PAST A COUPL'A JEEPLOADS OF CYBER'S PLAY-MATES!
GRAB THEM!
13

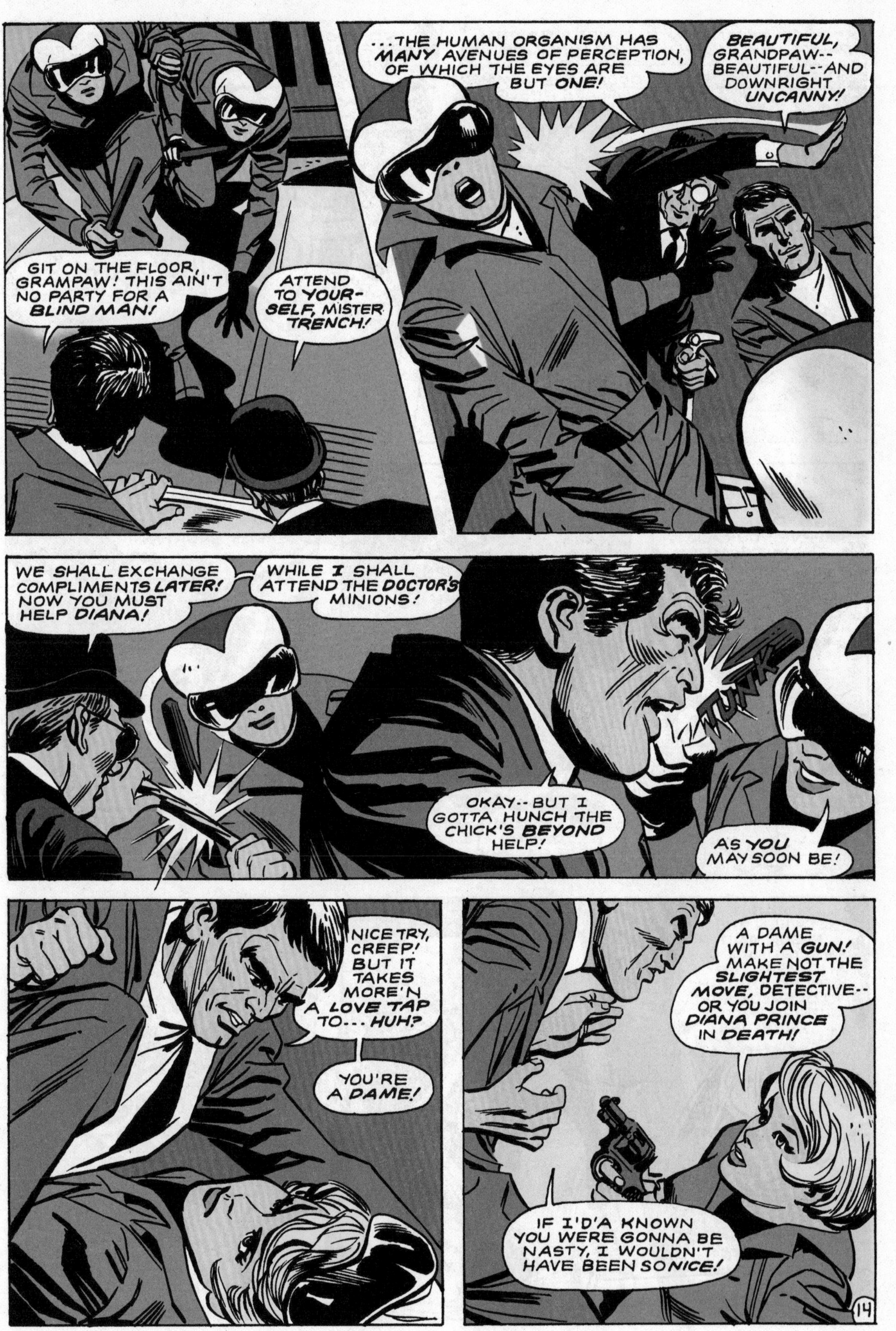
GIT ON THE FLOOR, GRAMPAW! THIS AIN'T NO PARTY FOR A BLIND MAN!
ATTEND TO YOURSELF, MISTER TRENCH!
...THE HUMAN ORGANISM HAS MANY AVENUES OF PERCEPTION, OF WHICH THE EYES ARE BUT ONE!
BEAUTIFUL, GRANDPAW-- BEAUTIFUL--AND DOWNRIGHT UNCANNY!
WE SHALL EXCHANGE COMPLIMENTS LATER! NOW YOU MUST HELP DIANA!
WHILE I SHALL ATTEND THE DOCTOR'S MINIONS!
TUNK
OKAY-- BUT I GOTTA HUNCH THE CHICK'S BEYOND HELP!
AS YOU MAY SOON BE!
NICE TRY, CREEP! BUT IT TAKES MORE'N A LOVE TAP TO... HUH?
YOU'RE A DAME!
A DAME WITH A GUN! MAKE NOT THE SLIGHTEST MOVE, DETECTIVE-- OR YOU JOIN DIANA PRINCE IN DEATH!
IF I'D'A KNOWN YOU WERE GONNA BE NASTY, I WOULDN'T HAVE BEEN SO NICE!
14

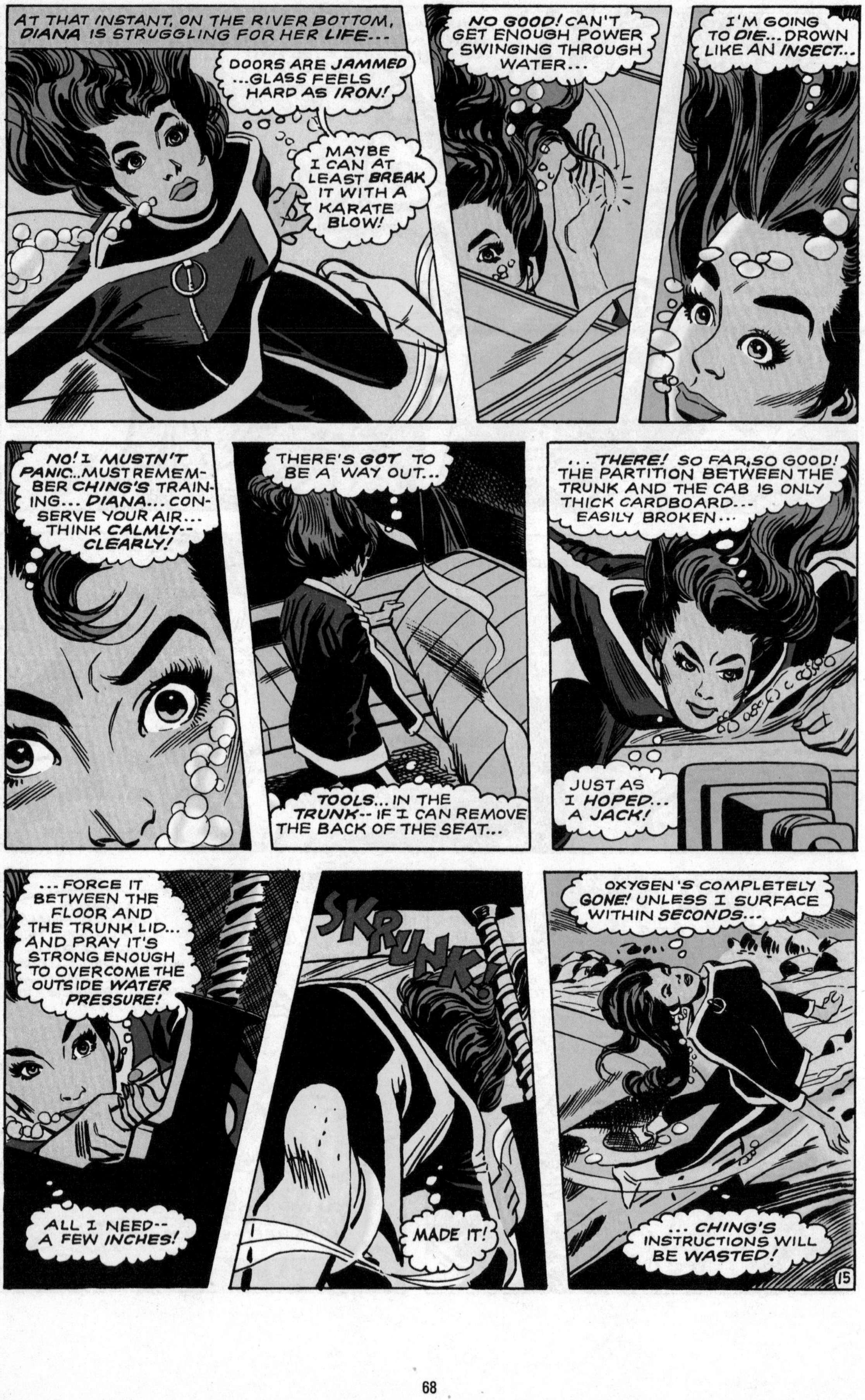
AT THAT INSTANT, ON THE RIVER BOTTOM, DIANA IS STRUGGLING FOR HER LIFE...
DOORS ARE JAMMED ...GLASS FEELS HARD AS IRON!
MAYBE I CAN AT LEAST BREAK IT WITH A KARATE BLOW!
NO GOOD! CAN'T GET ENOUGH POWER SWINGING THROUGH WATER...
I'M GOING TO DIE... DROWN LIKE AN INSECT...
NO! I MUSTN'T PANIC...MUST REMEMBER CHING'S TRAINING... DIANA... CONSERVE YOUR AIR... THINK CALMLY-- CLEARLY!
THERE'S GOT TO BE A WAY OUT...
TOOLS... IN THE TRUNK-- IF I CAN REMOVE THE BACK OF THE SEAT...
... THERE! SO FAR, SO GOOD! THE PARTITION BETWEEN THE TRUNK AND THE CAB IS ONLY THICK CARDBOARD... EASILY BROKEN...
JUST AS I HOPED... A JACK!
... FORCE IT BETWEEN THE FLOOR AND THE TRUNK LID... AND PRAY IT'S STRONG ENOUGH TO OVERCOME THE OUTSIDE WATER PRESSURE!
ALL I NEED-- A FEW INCHES!
SKRUNK!
MADE IT!
OXYGEN'S COMPLETELY GONE! UNLESS I SURFACE WITHIN SECONDS...
... CHING'S INSTRUCTIONS WILL BE WASTED!
15

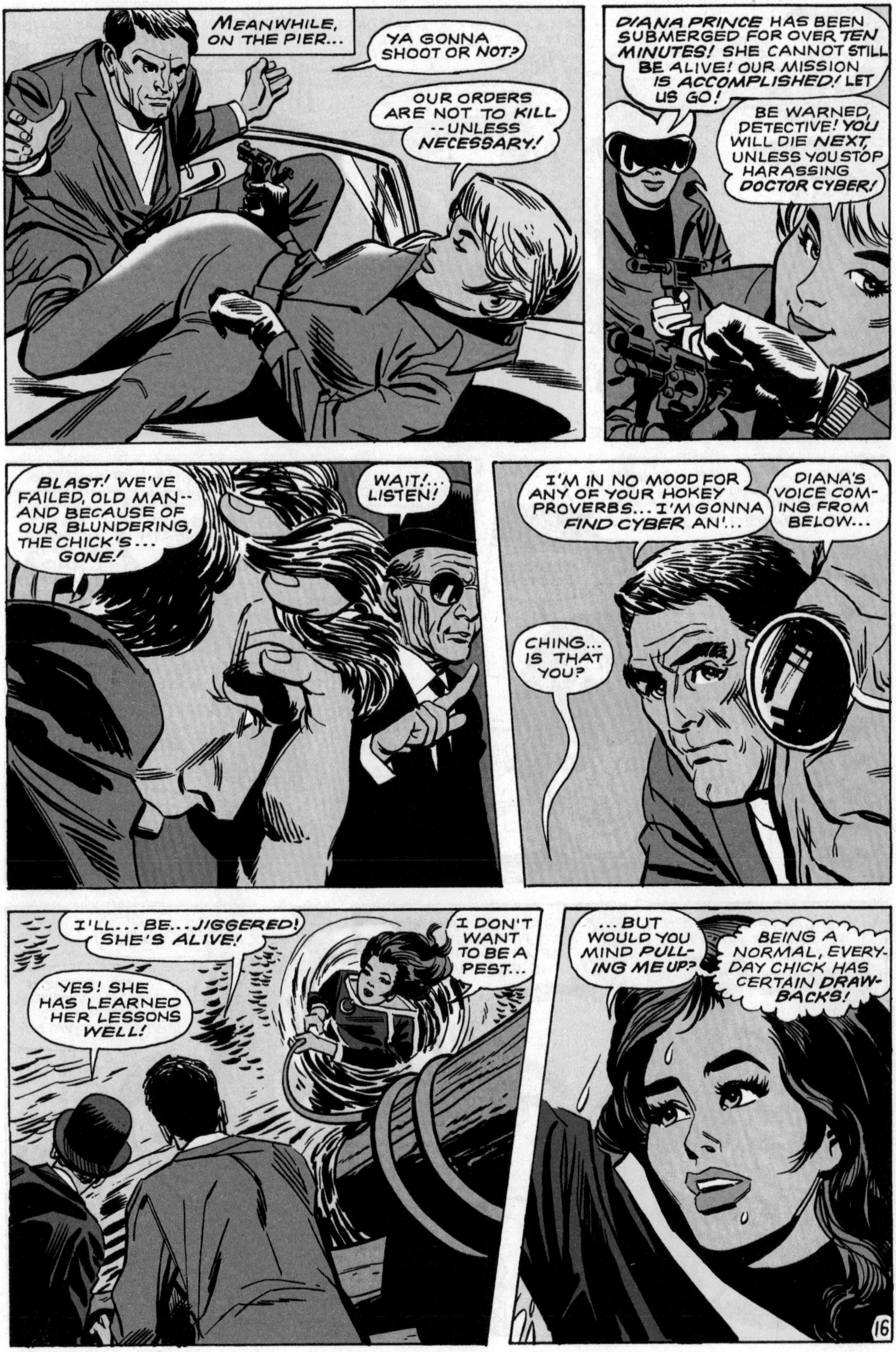
MEANWHILE, ON THE PIER...
YA GONNA SHOOT OR NOT?
OUR ORDERS ARE NOT TO KILL --UNLESS NECESSARY!
DIANA PRINCE HAS BEEN SUBMERGED FOR OVER TEN MINUTES! SHE CANNOT STILL BE ALIVE! OUR MISSION IS ACCOMPLISHED! LET US GO!
BE WARNED, DETECTIVE! YOU WILL DIE NEXT, UNLESS YOU STOP HARASSING DOCTOR CYBER!
BLAST! WE'VE FAILED, OLD MAN-- AND BECAUSE OF OUR BLUNDERING, THE CHICK'S... GONE!
WAIT!... LISTEN!
I'M IN NO MOOD FOR ANY OF YOUR HOKEY PROVERBS... I'M GONNA FIND CYBER AN'...
DIANA'S VOICE COMING FROM BELOW...
CHING... IS THAT YOU?
I'LL... BE... JIGGERED! SHE'S ALIVE!
YES! SHE HAS LEARNED HER LESSONS WELL!
I DON'T WANT TO BE A PEST...
...BUT WOULD YOU MIND PULLING ME UP?
BEING A NORMAL, EVERYDAY CHICK HAS CERTAIN DRAWBACKS!
16

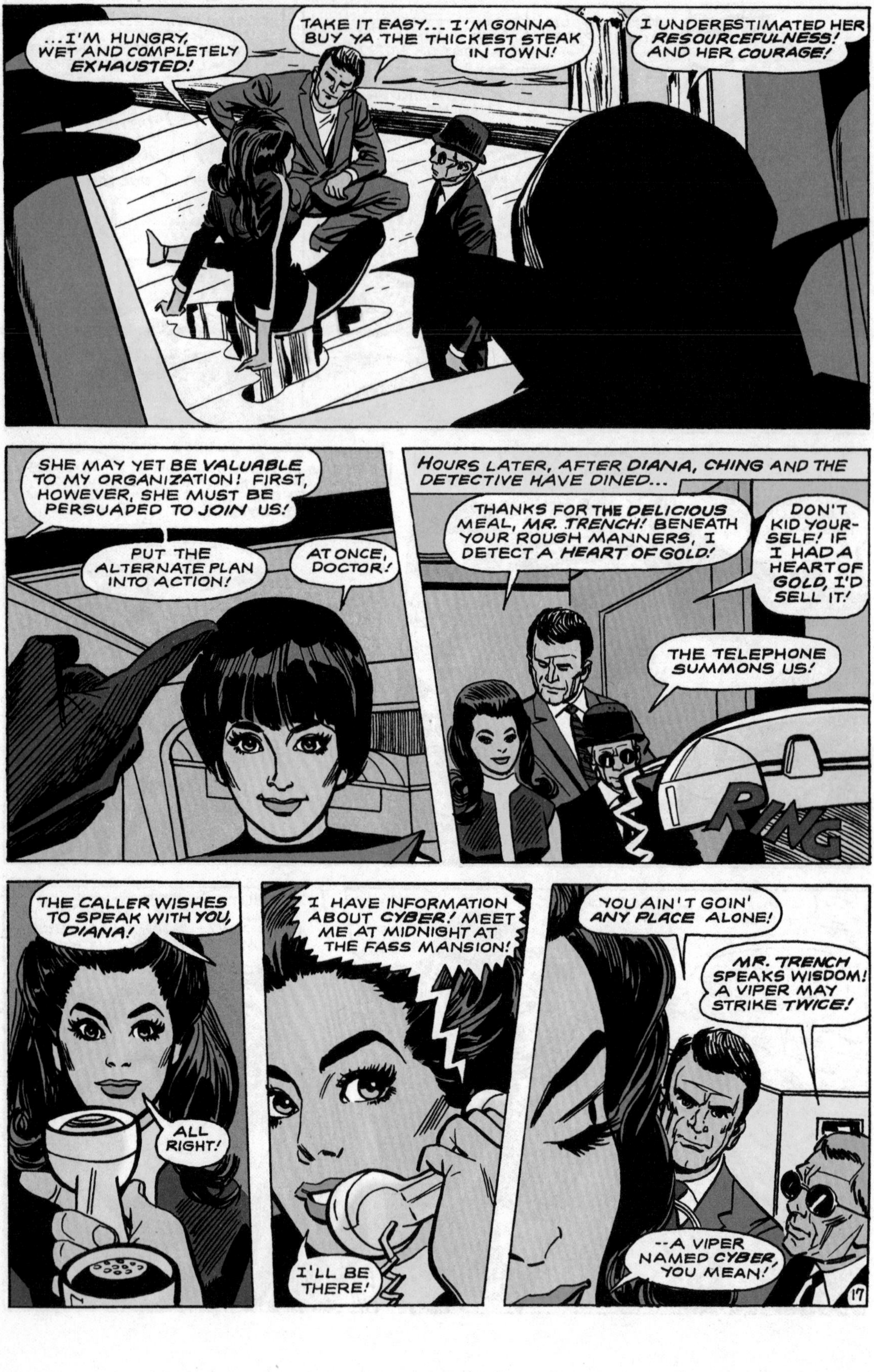
...I'M HUNGRY, WET AND COMPLETELY EXHAUSTED!
TAKE IT EASY... I'M GONNA BUY YA THE THICKEST STEAK IN TOWN!
I UNDERESTIMATED HER RESOURCEFULNESS! AND HER COURAGE!
SHE MAY YET BE VALUABLE TO MY ORGANIZATION! FIRST, HOWEVER, SHE MUST BE PERSUADED TO JOIN US!
PUT THE ALTERNATE PLAN INTO ACTION!
AT ONCE, DOCTOR!
HOURS LATER, AFTER DIANA, CHING AND THE DETECTIVE HAVE DINED...
THANKS FOR THE DELICIOUS MEAL, MR. TRENCH! BENEATH YOUR ROUGH MANNERS, I DETECT A HEART OF GOLD!
DON'T KID YOURSELF! IF I HAD A HEART OF GOLD, I'D SELL IT!
THE TELEPHONE SUMMONS US!
RING
THE CALLER WISHES TO SPEAK WITH YOU, DIANA!
ALL RIGHT!
I HAVE INFORMATION ABOUT CYBER! MEET ME AT MIDNIGHT AT THE FASS MANSION!
I'LL BE THERE!
YOU AIN'T GOIN' ANY PLACE ALONE!
MR. TRENCH SPEAKS WISDOM! A VIPER MAY STRIKE TWICE!
--A VIPER NAMED CYBER, YOU MEAN!
17

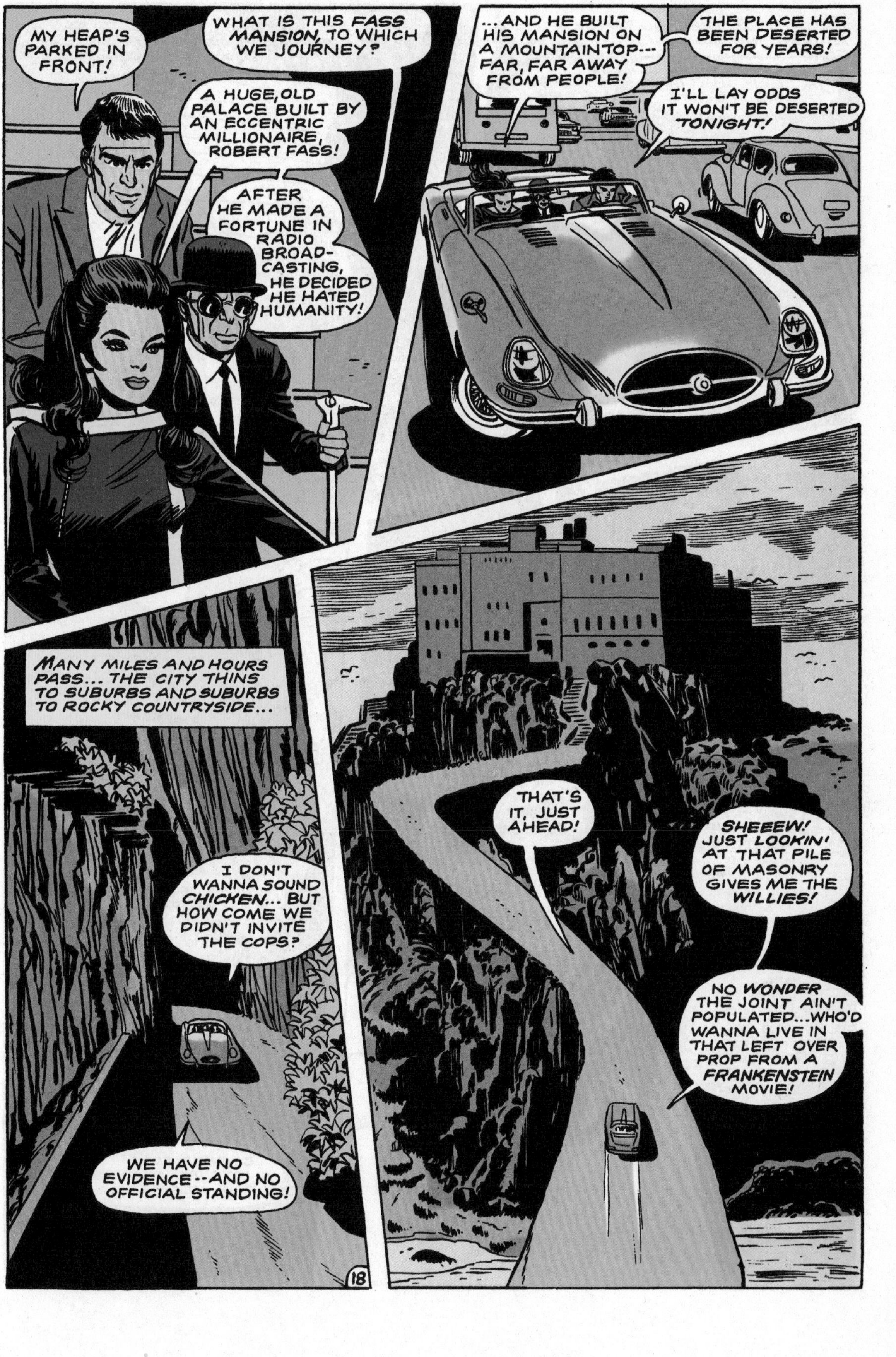

MY HEAP'S PARKED IN FRONT!
WHAT IS THIS FASS MANSION, TO WHICH WE JOURNEY?
A HUGE, OLD PALACE BUILT BY AN ECCENTRIC MILLIONAIRE, ROBERT FASS!
AFTER HE MADE A FORTUNE IN RADIO BROADCASTING, HE DECIDED HE HATED HUMANITY!
...AND HE BUILT HIS MANSION ON A MOUNTAINTOP--- FAR, FAR AWAY FROM PEOPLE!
THE PLACE HAS BEEN DESERTED FOR YEARS!
I'LL LAY ODDS IT WON'T BE DESERTED TONIGHT!
MANY MILES AND HOURS PASS... THE CITY THINS TO SUBURBS AND SUBURBS TO ROCKY COUNTRYSIDE...
I DON'T WANNA SOUND CHICKEN... BUT HOW COME WE DIDN'T INVITE THE COPS?
WE HAVE NO EVIDENCE--AND NO OFFICIAL STANDING!
18
THAT'S IT, JUST AHEAD!
SHEEEW! JUST LOOKIN' AT THAT PILE OF MASONRY GIVES ME THE WILLIES!
NO WONDER THE JOINT AIN'T POPULATED...WHO'D WANNA LIVE IN THAT LEFT OVER PROP FROM A FRANKENSTEIN MOVIE!

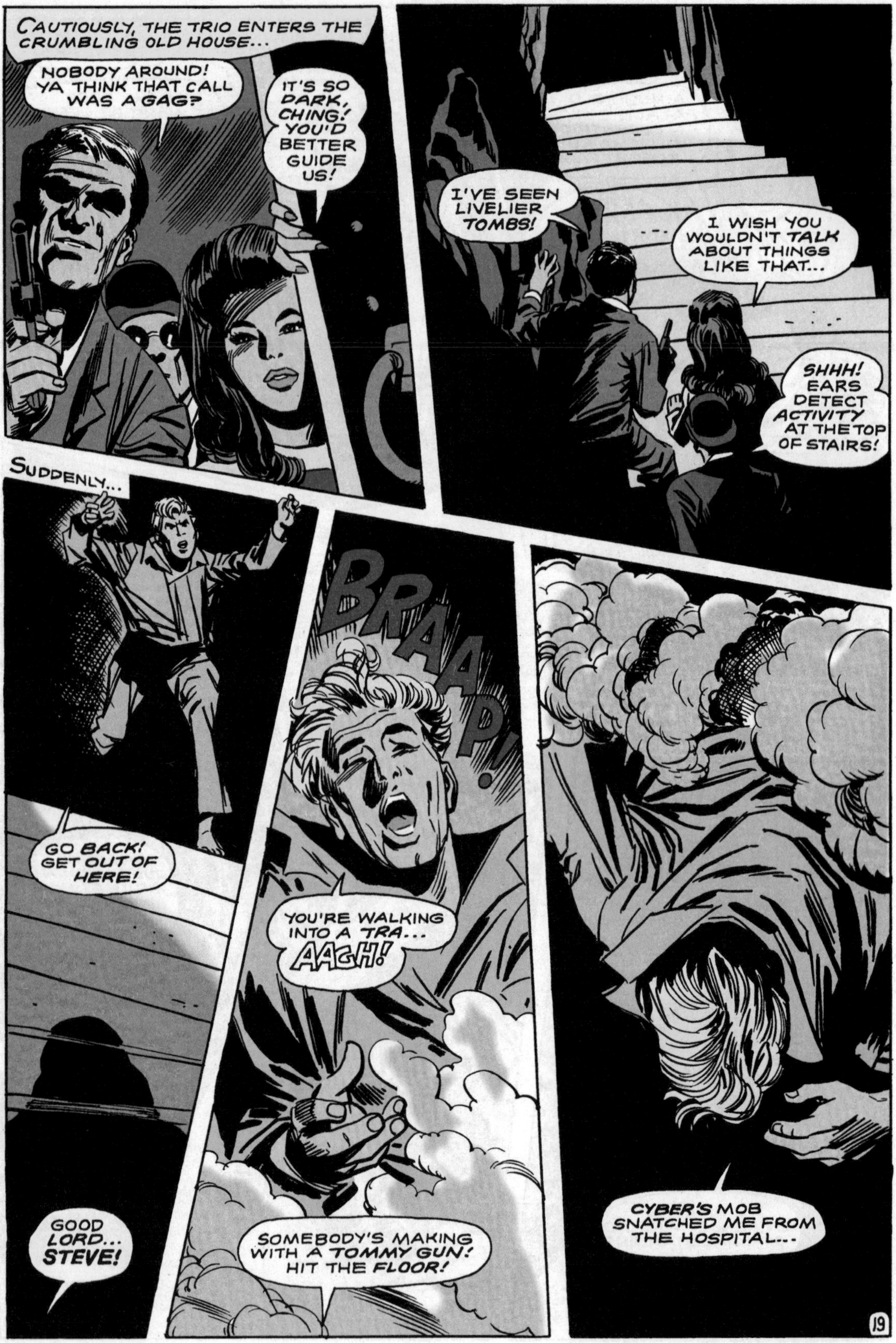
CAUTIOUSLY, THE TRIO ENTERS THE CRUMBLING OLD HOUSE...
NOBODY AROUND! YA THINK THAT CALL WAS A GAG?
IT'S SO DARK, CHING! YOU'D BETTER GUIDE US!
I'VE SEEN LIVELIER TOMBS!
I WISH YOU WOULDN'T TALK ABOUT THINGS LIKE THAT...
SHHH! EARS DETECT ACTIVITY AT THE TOP OF STAIRS!
SUDDENLY...
GO BACK! GET OUT OF HERE!
GOOD LORD... STEVE!
BRAAAP!
YOU'RE WALKING INTO A TRA... AAGH!
SOMEBODY'S MAKING WITH A TOMMY GUN! HIT THE FLOOR!
CYBER'S MOB SNATCHED ME FROM THE HOSPITAL...
19

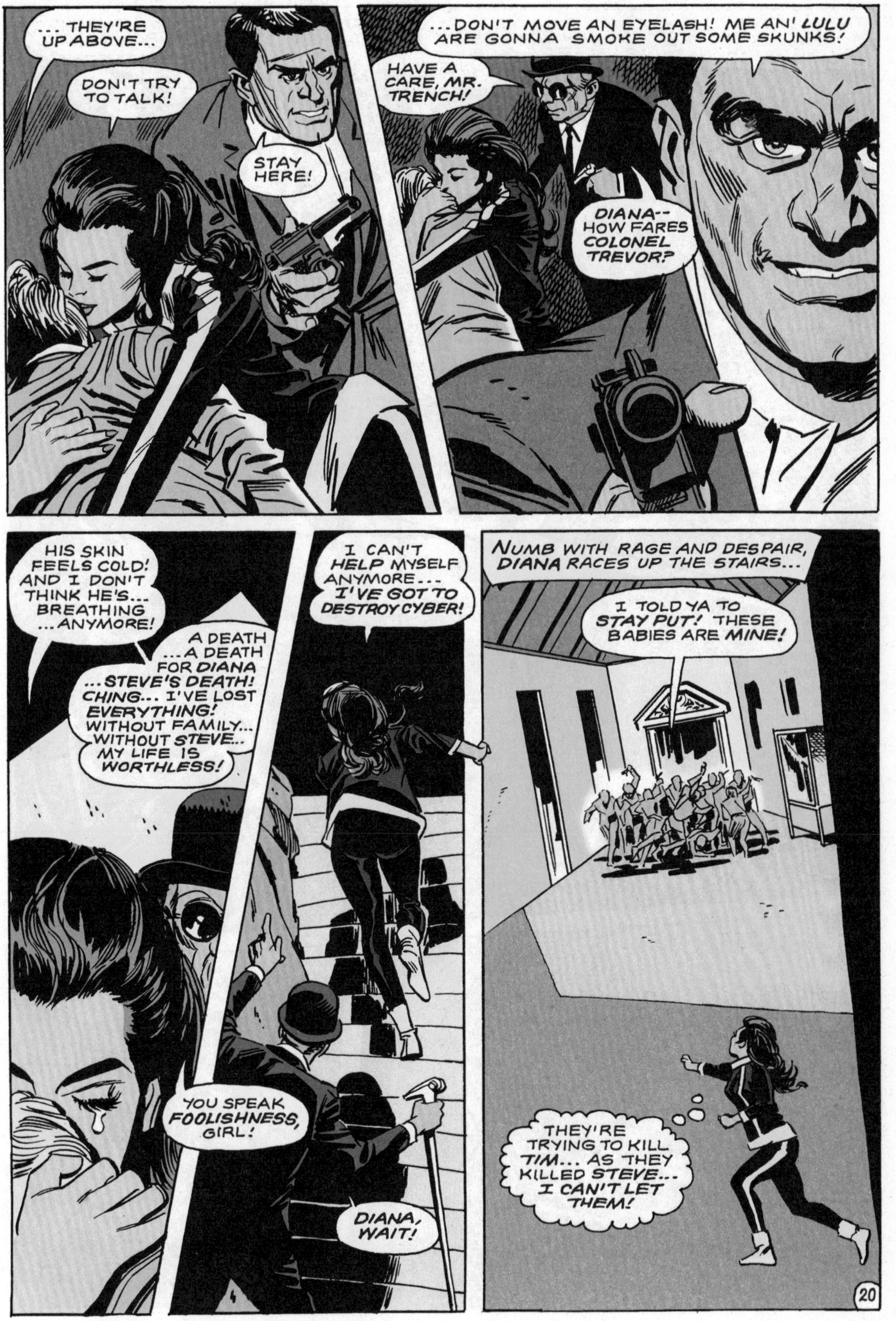
... THEY'RE UP ABOVE...
DON'T TRY TO TALK!
STAY HERE!
...DON'T MOVE AN EYELASH! ME AN' LULU ARE GONNA SMOKE OUT SOME SKUNKS!
HAVE A CARE, MR. TRENCH!
DIANA-- HOW FARES COLONEL TREVOR?
HIS SKIN FEELS COLD! AND I DON'T THINK HE'S... BREATHING ...ANYMORE!
A DEATH ...A DEATH FOR DIANA ...STEVE'S DEATH! CHING... I'VE LOST EVERYTHING! WITHOUT FAMILY... WITHOUT STEVE... MY LIFE IS WORTHLESS!
YOU SPEAK FOOLISHNESS, GIRL!
I CAN'T HELP MYSELF ANYMORE... I'VE GOT TO DESTROY CYBER!
DIANA, WAIT!
NUMB WITH RAGE AND DESPAIR, DIANA RACES UP THE STAIRS...
I TOLD YA TO STAY PUT! THESE BABIES ARE MINE!
THEY'RE TRYING TO KILL TIM... AS THEY KILLED STEVE... I CAN'T LET THEM!
20

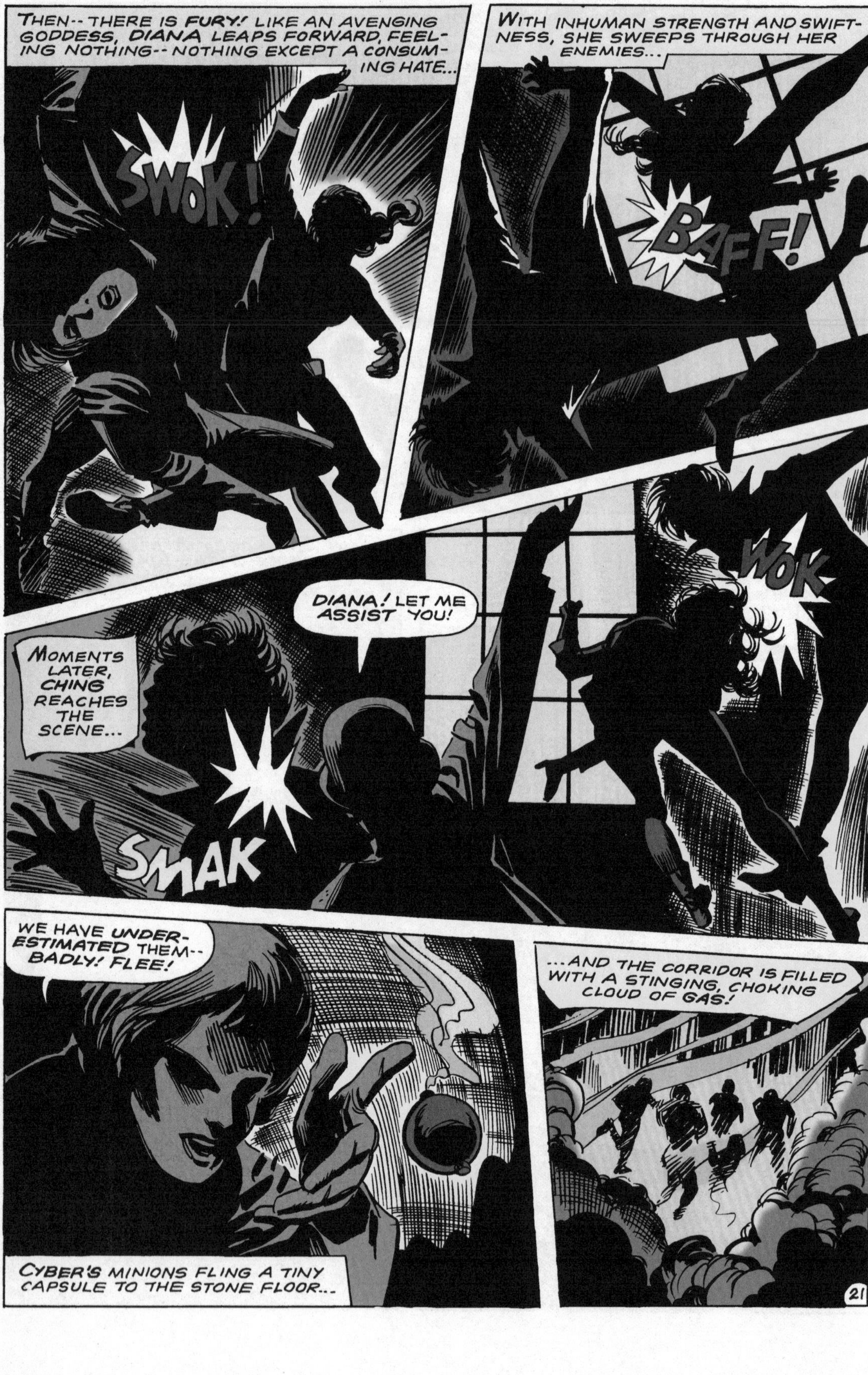
THEN-- THERE IS FURY! LIKE AN AVENGING GODDESS, DIANA LEAPS FORWARD, FEELING NOTHING-- NOTHING EXCEPT A CONSUMING HATE...
SWOK!
WITH INHUMAN STRENGTH AND SWIFTNESS, SHE SWEEPS THROUGH HER ENEMIES...
BAFF!
MOMENTS LATER, CHING REACHES THE SCENE...
DIANA! LET ME ASSIST YOU!
WOK
SMAK
WE HAVE UNDERESTIMATED THEM-- BADLY! FLEE!
CYBER'S MINIONS FLING A TINY CAPSULE TO THE STONE FLOOR...
...AND THE CORRIDOR IS FILLED WITH A STINGING, CHOKING CLOUD OF GAS!
21

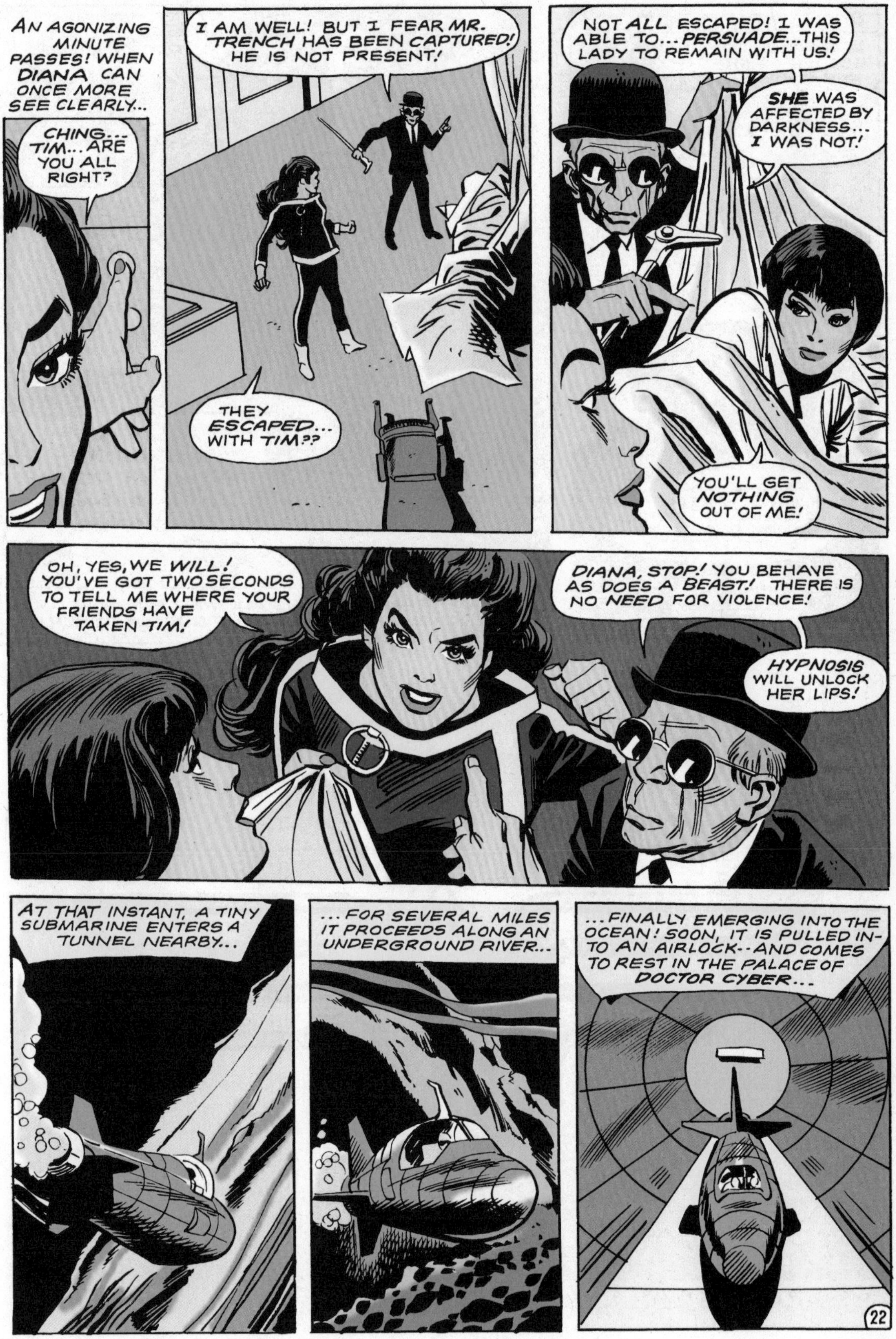
AN AGONIZING MINUTE PASSES! WHEN DIANA CAN ONCE MORE SEE CLEARLY...
CHING... TIM... ARE YOU ALL RIGHT?
I AM WELL! BUT I FEAR MR. TRENCH HAS BEEN CAPTURED! HE IS NOT PRESENT!
THEY ESCAPED... WITH TIM??
NOT ALL ESCAPED! I WAS ABLE TO... PERSUADE... THIS LADY TO REMAIN WITH US!
SHE WAS AFFECTED BY DARKNESS... I WAS NOT!
YOU'LL GET NOTHING OUT OF ME!
OH, YES, WE WILL! YOU'VE GOT TWO SECONDS TO TELL ME WHERE YOUR FRIENDS HAVE TAKEN TIM!
DIANA, STOP! YOU BEHAVE AS DOES A BEAST! THERE IS NO NEED FOR VIOLENCE!
HYPNOSIS WILL UNLOCK HER LIPS!
AT THAT INSTANT, A TINY SUBMARINE ENTERS A TUNNEL NEARBY...
... FOR SEVERAL MILES IT PROCEEDS ALONG AN UNDERGROUND RIVER...
... FINALLY EMERGING INTO THE OCEAN! SOON, IT IS PULLED INTO AN AIRLOCK--AND COMES TO REST IN THE PALACE OF DOCTOR CYBER...
22

SOON... DIANA PRINCE ELUDED US, DOCTOR! BUT WE SNARED HER COMPANION!

ONE OF US WAS CAPTURED ALSO!

ANYONE WHO ALLOWS HERSELF TO FALL INTO HOSTILE HANDS DESERVES HER FATE!

BRING THE DETECTIVE HERE!

WELCOME, MR. TRENCH! I AM... DOCTOR CYBER!

STUNNED, TIM TRENCH STARES UP INTO THE GLITTERING EYES OF A STRANGELY BEAUTIFUL, WHOLLY MERCILESS WOMAN...

ART & CONTINUITY—MIKE SEKOWSKY—inking—DICK GIORDANO plot & dialogue... DENNY O'NEIL

23

NEXT -- DIANA AND CHING PIT THEIR EXTRAORDINARY SKILLS AGAINST-- **THE WRATH OF DOCTOR CYBER!**

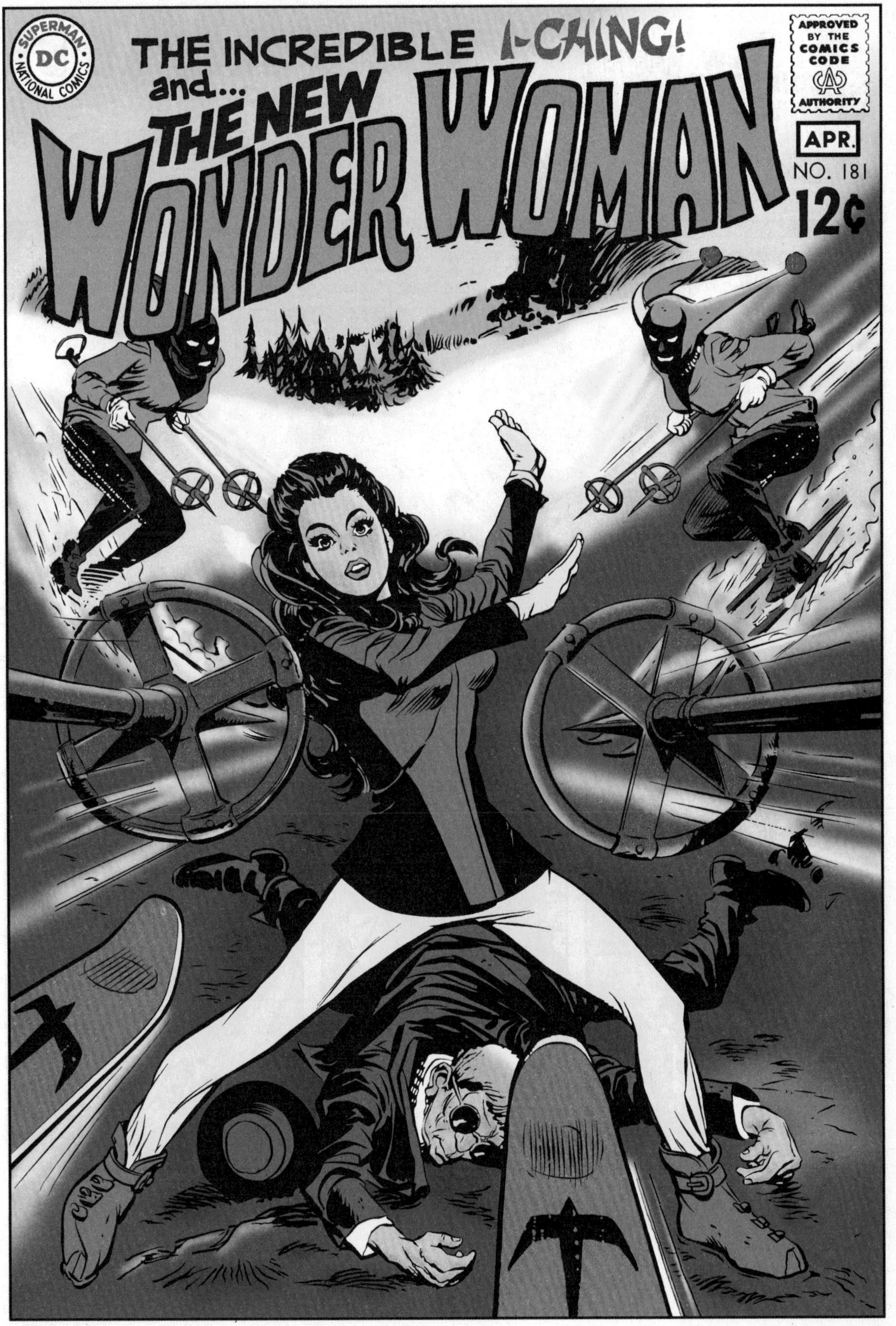
SUPERMAN DC NATIONAL COMICS
THE INCREDIBLE I-CHING!
and... THE NEW WONDER WOMAN
APPROVED BY THE COMICS CODE AUTHORITY
APR.
NO. 181
12¢

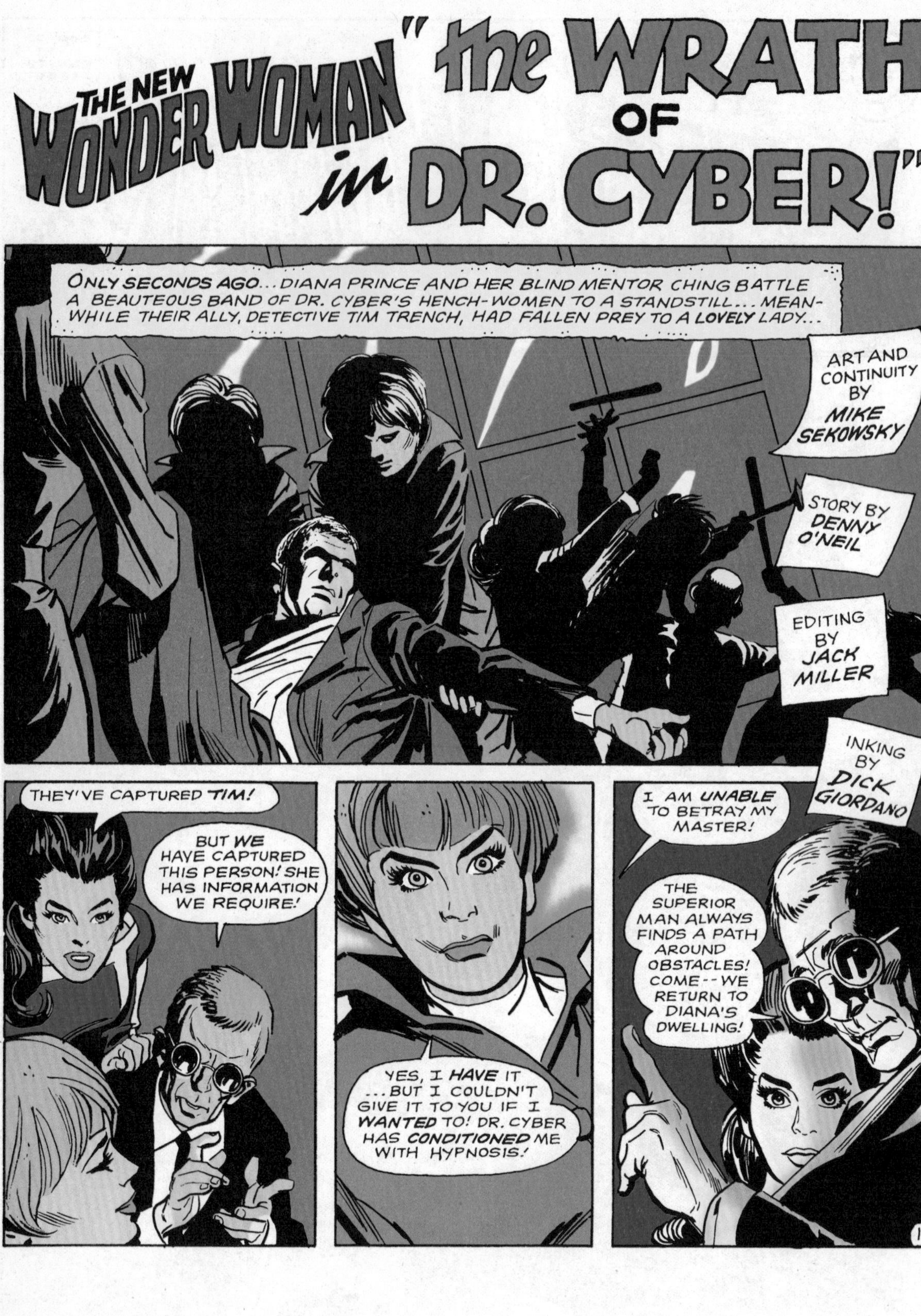
THE NEW WONDER WOMAN in "the WRATH OF DR. CYBER!"
ONLY SECONDS AGO... DIANA PRINCE AND HER BLIND MENTOR CHING BATTLE A BEAUTEOUS BAND OF DR. CYBER'S HENCH-WOMEN TO A STANDSTILL... MEANWHILE THEIR ALLY, DETECTIVE TIM TRENCH, HAD FALLEN PREY TO A LOVELY LADY...
ART AND CONTINUITY BY MIKE SEKOWSKY
STORY BY DENNY O'NEIL
EDITING BY JACK MILLER
INKING BY DICK GIORDANO
THEY'VE CAPTURED TIM!
BUT WE HAVE CAPTURED THIS PERSON! SHE HAS INFORMATION WE REQUIRE!
YES, I HAVE IT ...BUT I COULDN'T GIVE IT TO YOU IF I WANTED TO! DR. CYBER HAS CONDITIONED ME WITH HYPNOSIS!
I AM UNABLE TO BETRAY MY MASTER!
THE SUPERIOR MAN ALWAYS FINDS A PATH AROUND OBSTACLES! COME--WE RETURN TO DIANA'S DWELLING!
1

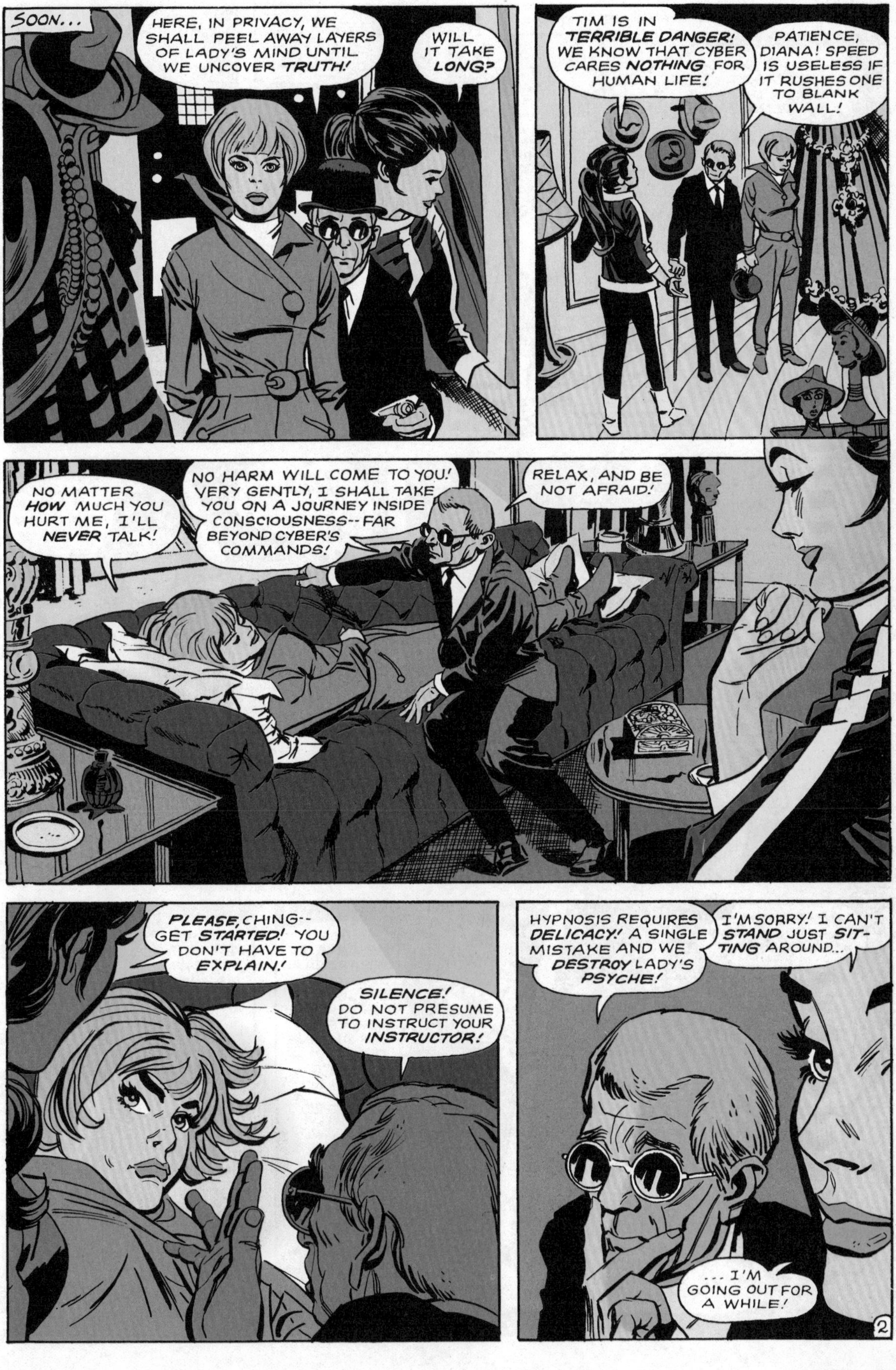
SOON...
HERE, IN PRIVACY, WE SHALL PEEL AWAY LAYERS OF LADY'S MIND UNTIL WE UNCOVER TRUTH!
WILL IT TAKE LONG?
TIM IS IN TERRIBLE DANGER! WE KNOW THAT CYBER CARES NOTHING FOR HUMAN LIFE!
PATIENCE, DIANA! SPEED IS USELESS IF IT RUSHES ONE TO BLANK WALL!
NO MATTER HOW MUCH YOU HURT ME, I'LL NEVER TALK!
NO HARM WILL COME TO YOU! VERY GENTLY, I SHALL TAKE YOU ON A JOURNEY INSIDE CONSCIOUSNESS-- FAR BEYOND CYBER'S COMMANDS!
RELAX, AND BE NOT AFRAID!
PLEASE, CHING-- GET STARTED! YOU DON'T HAVE TO EXPLAIN!
SILENCE! DO NOT PRESUME TO INSTRUCT YOUR INSTRUCTOR!
HYPNOSIS REQUIRES DELICACY! A SINGLE MISTAKE AND WE DESTROY LADY'S PSYCHE!
I'M SORRY! I CAN'T STAND JUST SITTING AROUND...
... I'M GOING OUT FOR A WHILE!
2

THEN IN A RUN-DOWN NEIGHBORHOOD...

CHING IS SO *OLD*... SOMETIMES I THINK HE JUST DOESN'T *UNDERSTAND!*

I NEED SOME *INSURANCE*--IN CASE HIS METHODS *FAIL!*

HMM...*RAPHAEL* USED TO LIVE AROUND THE CORNER! HERE'S HOPING HE HASN'T *MOVED!*

ARRIVING AT A SHABBY TENEMENT DOOR, DIANA RAPS OUT A *CODED* KNOCK AND...

NOK NOK

TAPETY TAP

AH, *DIANA,* ME DARLIN'-- COME IN!

HELLO, RAPHAEL!

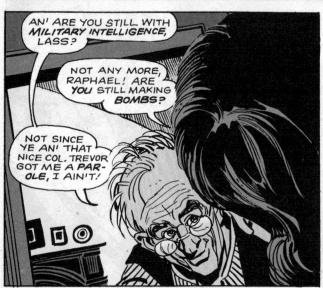

AN' ARE YOU STILL WITH *MILITARY INTELLIGENCE,* LASS?

NOT ANY MORE, RAPHAEL! ARE *YOU* STILL MAKING *BOMBS?*

NOT SINCE YE AN' THAT NICE COL. TREVOR GOT ME A *PAROLE,* I AIN'T!

NOT AS A *BUSINESS,* THAT IS! BUT WHY D'YA *ASK?*

I NEED HELP-- THE KIND OF HELP ONLY *YOU* CAN GIVE ME!

SURE YE MUST BE REFERRIN' T'ME *JEWELRY!* ME LOVELY GAS-BOMB PEARLS, GRENADE EARRINGS!

THOSE ARE EXACTLY WHAT I MEAN, RAPHAEL!

IT SO HAPPENS I *DO* HAVE A FEW TRINKETS-- MADE 'EM PURELY AS A *HOBBY,* YA UNNERSTAND!

THIS'S ME *LATEST* CREATION! A *CHARMIN'* BRACELET THAT BECOMES A *GRAPPLIN'* HOOK AN' LINE QUICK AS A FLIRT'S SMILE!

HERE'S *ANOTHER* DELIGHT-- PUSH THE EDGE OF THIS BUTTON AN' IT TURNS IN- TO A PELLET OF *HIGH EXPLOSIVES!* CLEVER, AIN'T IT?

A WORK OF *GENIUS!*

3

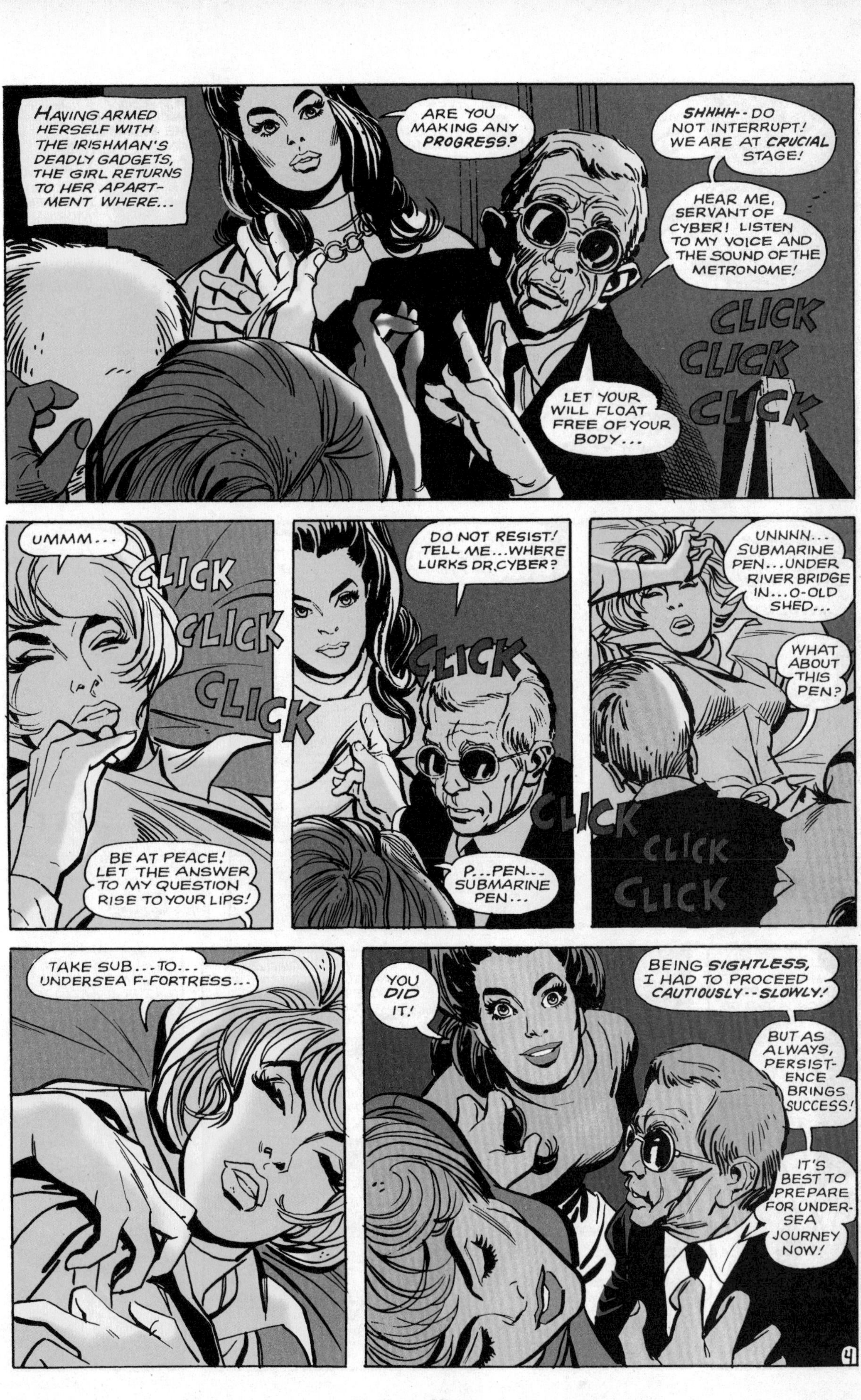

HAVING ARMED HERSELF WITH THE IRISHMAN'S DEADLY GADGETS, THE GIRL RETURNS TO HER APARTMENT WHERE...
ARE YOU MAKING ANY PROGRESS?
SHHHH-- DO NOT INTERRUPT! WE ARE AT CRUCIAL STAGE!
HEAR ME, SERVANT OF CYBER! LISTEN TO MY VOICE AND THE SOUND OF THE METRONOME!
CLICK CLICK CLICK
LET YOUR WILL FLOAT FREE OF YOUR BODY...
UMMM...
CLICK CLICK CLICK
BE AT PEACE! LET THE ANSWER TO MY QUESTION RISE TO YOUR LIPS!
DO NOT RESIST! TELL ME...WHERE LURKS DR.CYBER?
CLICK
P...PEN... SUBMARINE PEN...
CLICK CLICK CLICK
UNNNN... SUBMARINE PEN...UNDER RIVER BRIDGE IN...O-OLD SHED...
WHAT ABOUT THIS PEN?
TAKE SUB...TO... UNDERSEA F-FORTRESS...
YOU DID IT!
BEING SIGHTLESS, I HAD TO PROCEED CAUTIOUSLY--SLOWLY!
BUT AS ALWAYS, PERSISTENCE BRINGS SUCCESS!
IT'S BEST TO PREPARE FOR UNDERSEA JOURNEY NOW!
4

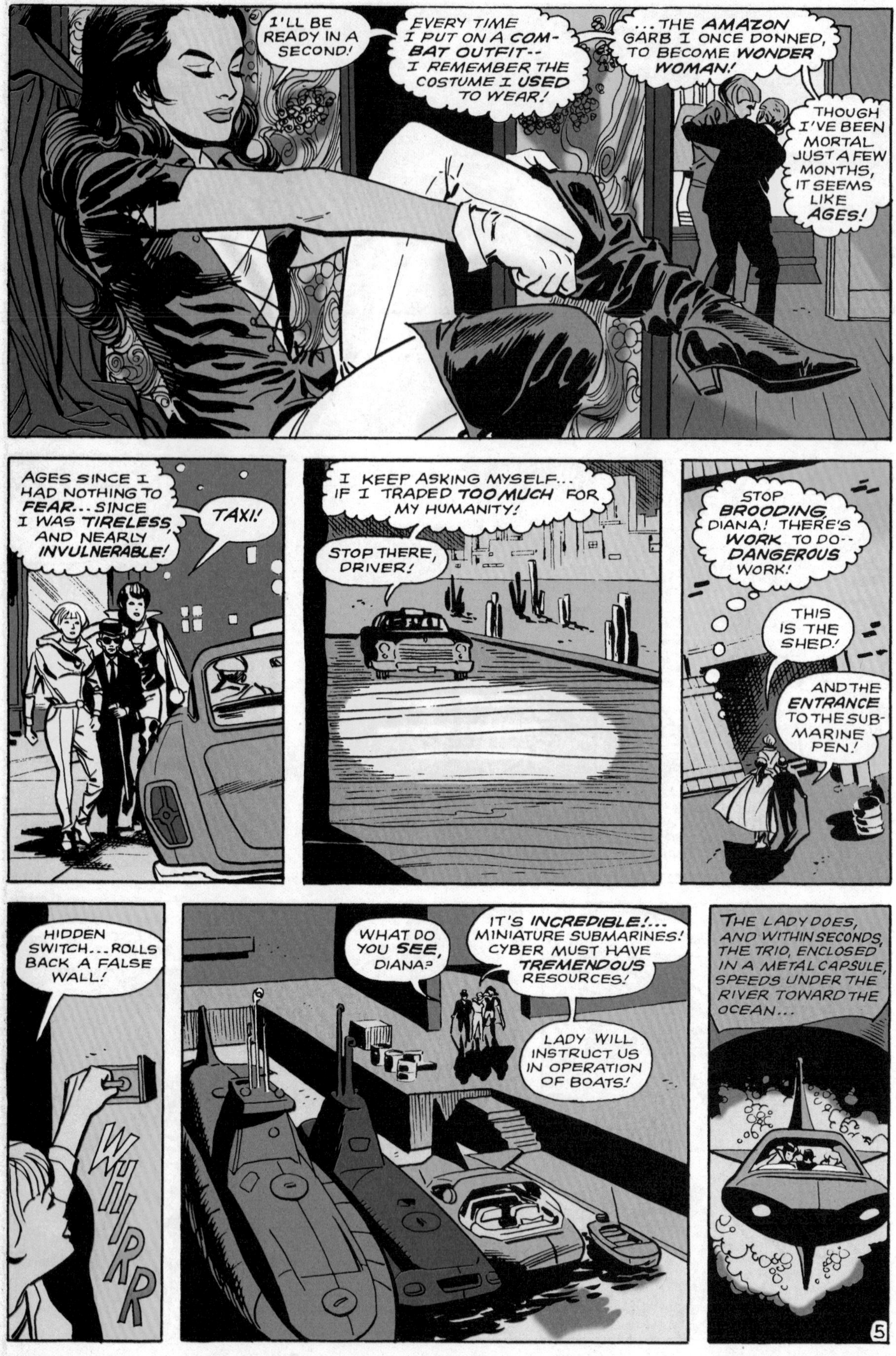
I'LL BE READY IN A SECOND!
EVERY TIME I PUT ON A COMBAT OUTFIT-- I REMEMBER THE COSTUME I USED TO WEAR!
...THE AMAZON GARB I ONCE DONNED, TO BECOME WONDER WOMAN!
THOUGH I'VE BEEN MORTAL JUST A FEW MONTHS, IT SEEMS LIKE AGES!
AGES SINCE I HAD NOTHING TO FEAR... SINCE I WAS TIRELESS, AND NEARLY INVULNERABLE!
TAXI!
I KEEP ASKING MYSELF... IF I TRADED TOO MUCH FOR MY HUMANITY!
STOP THERE, DRIVER!
STOP BROODING, DIANA! THERE'S WORK TO DO-- DANGEROUS WORK!
THIS IS THE SHED!
AND THE ENTRANCE TO THE SUB-MARINE PEN!
HIDDEN SWITCH... ROLLS BACK A FALSE WALL!
WHIRR
WHAT DO YOU SEE, DIANA?
IT'S INCREDIBLE!... MINIATURE SUBMARINES! CYBER MUST HAVE TREMENDOUS RESOURCES!
LADY WILL INSTRUCT US IN OPERATION OF BOATS!
THE LADY DOES, AND WITHIN SECONDS, THE TRIO, ENCLOSED IN A METAL CAPSULE, SPEEDS UNDER THE RIVER TOWARD THE OCEAN...
5

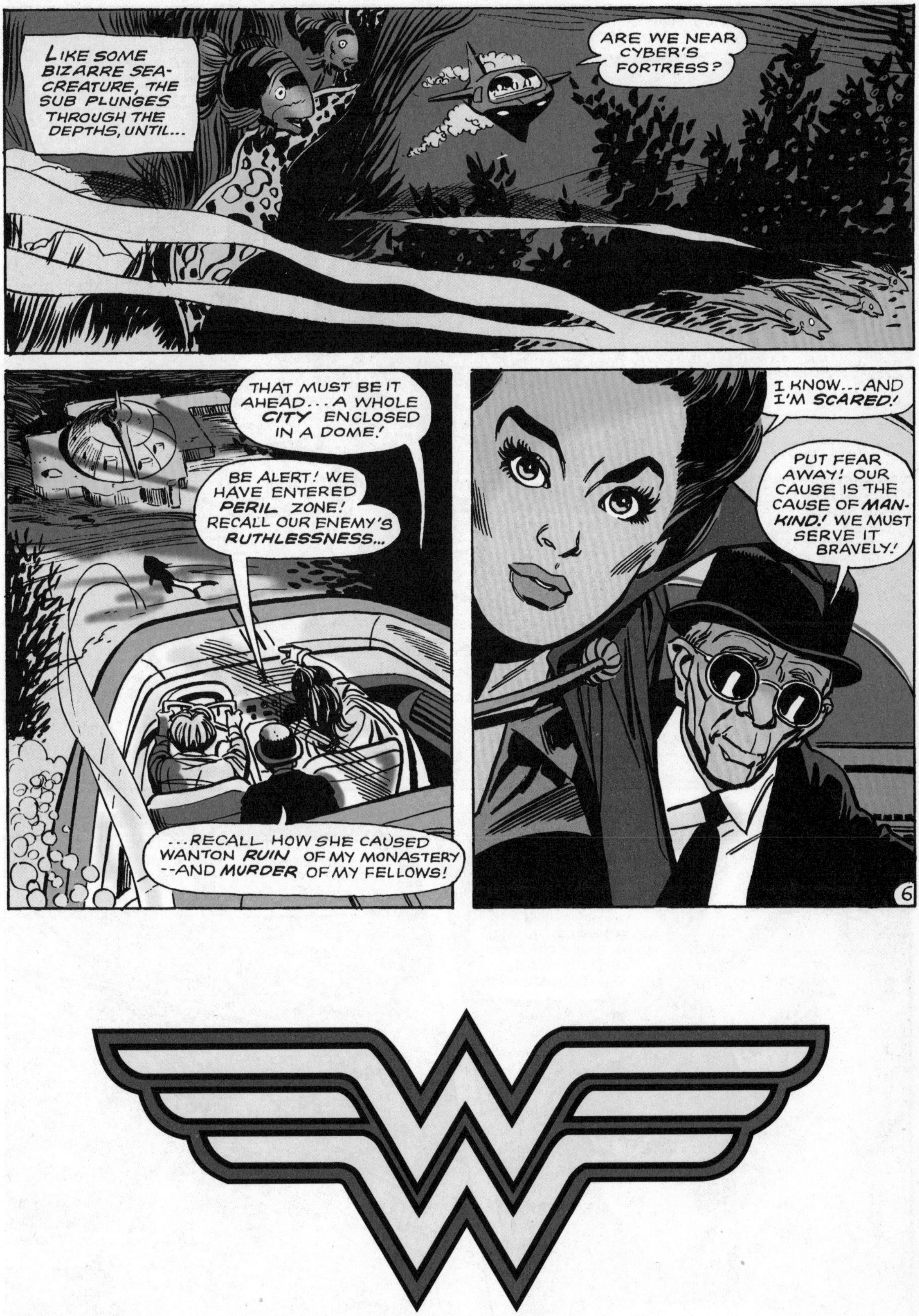
LIKE SOME BIZARRE SEA-CREATURE, THE SUB PLUNGES THROUGH THE DEPTHS, UNTIL...
ARE WE NEAR CYBER'S FORTRESS?
THAT MUST BE IT AHEAD... A WHOLE CITY ENCLOSED IN A DOME!
BE ALERT! WE HAVE ENTERED PERIL ZONE! RECALL OUR ENEMY'S RUTHLESSNESS...
...RECALL HOW SHE CAUSED WANTON RUIN OF MY MONASTERY --AND MURDER OF MY FELLOWS!
I KNOW... AND I'M SCARED!
PUT FEAR AWAY! OUR CAUSE IS THE CAUSE OF MAN-KIND! WE MUST SERVE IT BRAVELY!
6

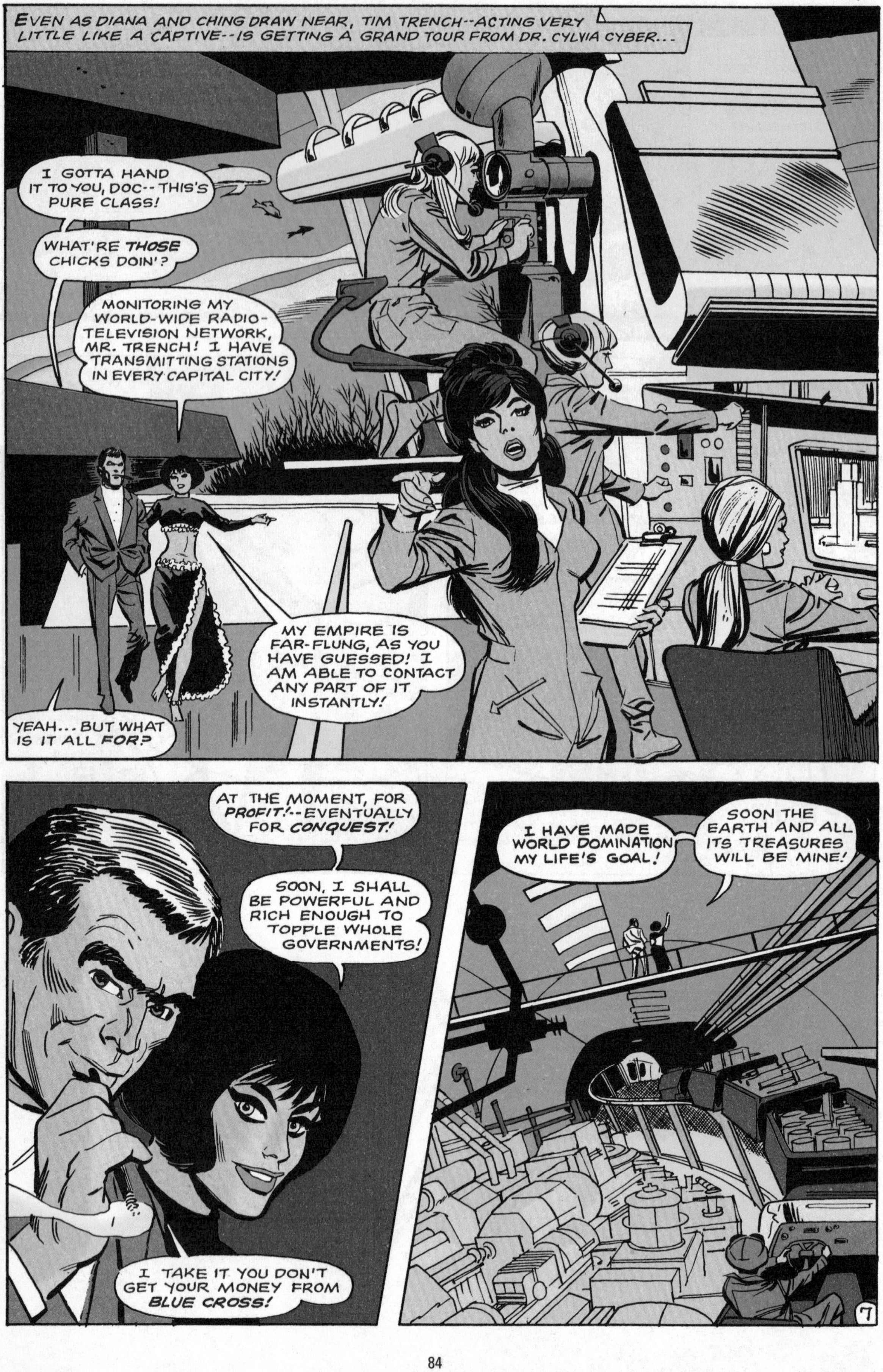
EVEN AS DIANA AND CHING DRAW NEAR, TIM TRENCH--ACTING VERY LITTLE LIKE A CAPTIVE--IS GETTING A GRAND TOUR FROM DR. CYLVIA CYBER...
I GOTTA HAND IT TO YOU, DOC--THIS'S PURE CLASS!
WHAT'RE THOSE CHICKS DOIN'?
MONITORING MY WORLD-WIDE RADIO-TELEVISION NETWORK, MR. TRENCH! I HAVE TRANSMITTING STATIONS IN EVERY CAPITAL CITY!
MY EMPIRE IS FAR-FLUNG, AS YOU HAVE GUESSED! I AM ABLE TO CONTACT ANY PART OF IT INSTANTLY!
YEAH... BUT WHAT IS IT ALL FOR?
AT THE MOMENT, FOR PROFIT!--EVENTUALLY FOR CONQUEST!
SOON, I SHALL BE POWERFUL AND RICH ENOUGH TO TOPPLE WHOLE GOVERNMENTS!
I TAKE IT YOU DON'T GET YOUR MONEY FROM BLUE CROSS!
I HAVE MADE WORLD DOMINATION MY LIFE'S GOAL!
SOON THE EARTH AND ALL ITS TREASURES WILL BE MINE!
7

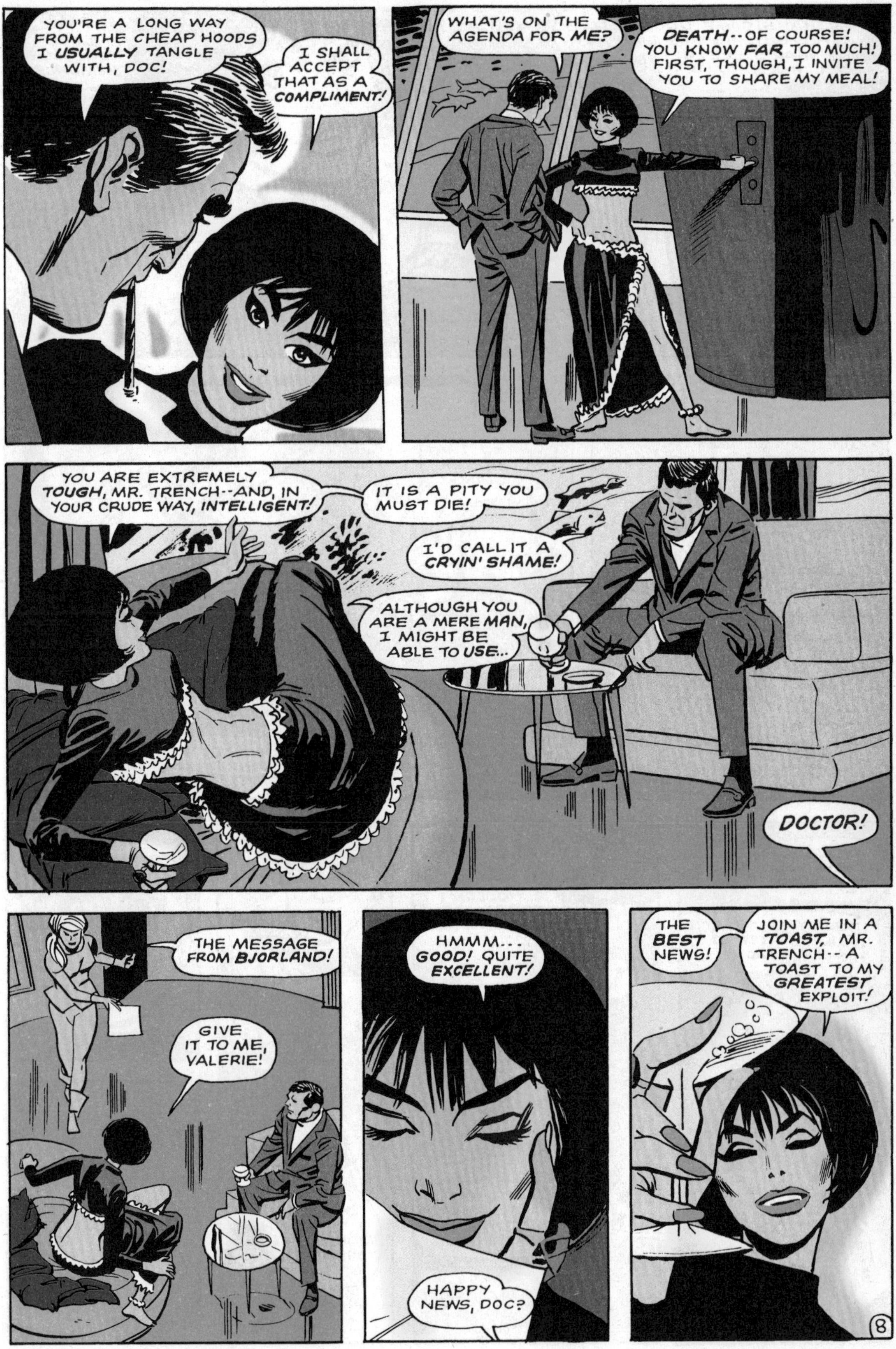
YOU'RE A LONG WAY FROM THE CHEAP HOODS I USUALLY TANGLE WITH, DOC!
I SHALL ACCEPT THAT AS A COMPLIMENT!
WHAT'S ON THE AGENDA FOR ME?
DEATH--OF COURSE! YOU KNOW FAR TOO MUCH! FIRST, THOUGH, I INVITE YOU TO SHARE MY MEAL!
YOU ARE EXTREMELY TOUGH, MR. TRENCH--AND, IN YOUR CRUDE WAY, INTELLIGENT!
IT IS A PITY YOU MUST DIE!
I'D CALL IT A CRYIN' SHAME!
ALTHOUGH YOU ARE A MERE MAN, I MIGHT BE ABLE TO USE...
DOCTOR!
THE MESSAGE FROM BJORLAND!
GIVE IT TO ME, VALERIE!
HMMM... GOOD! QUITE EXCELLENT!
HAPPY NEWS, DOC?
THE BEST NEWS!
JOIN ME IN A TOAST, MR. TRENCH--A TOAST TO MY GREATEST EXPLOIT!
8

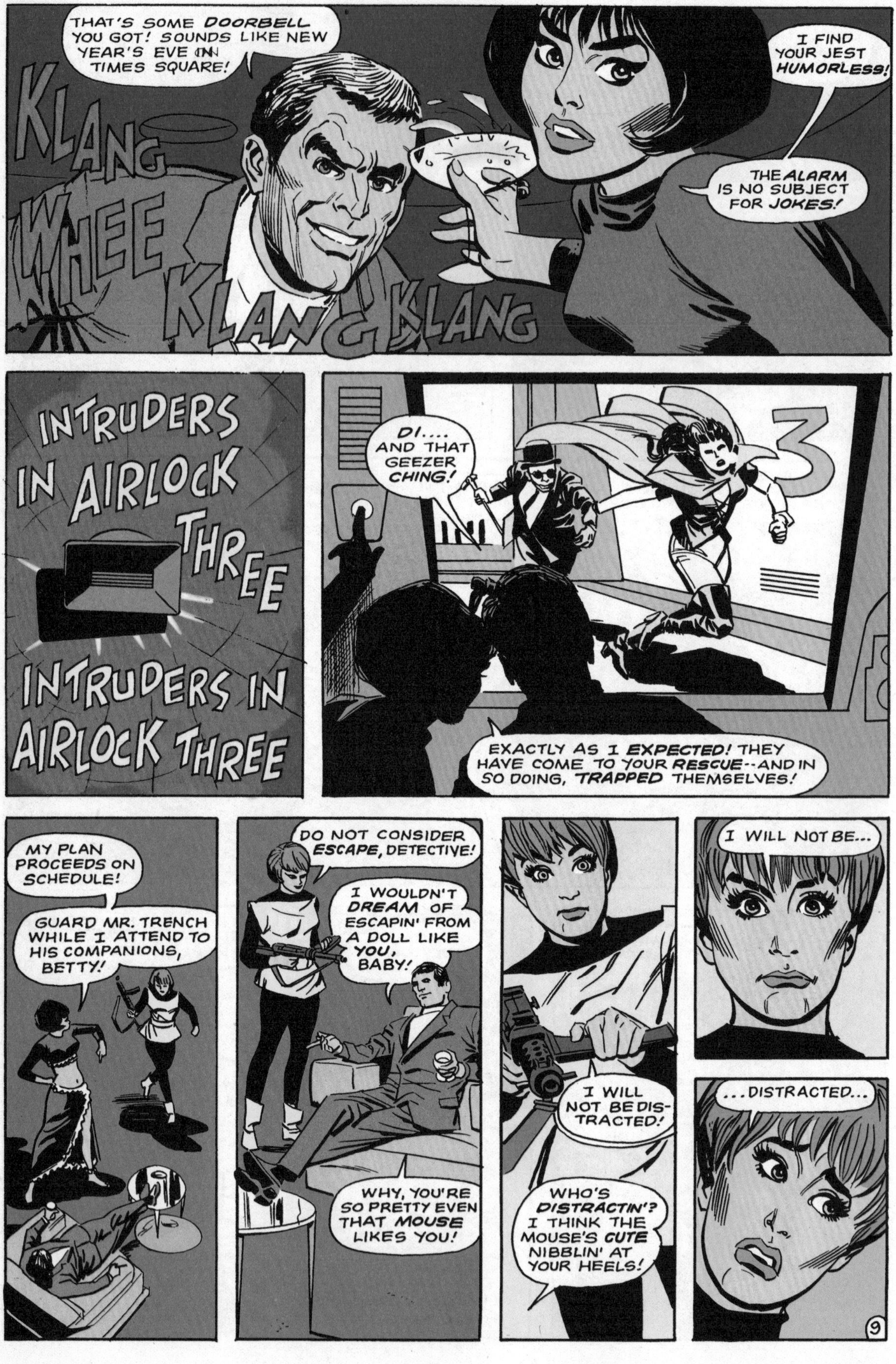
THAT'S SOME DOORBELL YOU GOT! SOUNDS LIKE NEW YEAR'S EVE IN TIMES SQUARE!
I FIND YOUR JEST HUMORLESS!
THE ALARM IS NO SUBJECT FOR JOKES!
KLANG
WHEE
KLANG KLANG KLANG
INTRUDERS IN AIRLOCK THREE
INTRUDERS IN AIRLOCK THREE
DI.... AND THAT GEEZER CHING!
3
EXACTLY AS I EXPECTED! THEY HAVE COME TO YOUR RESCUE--AND IN SO DOING, TRAPPED THEMSELVES!
MY PLAN PROCEEDS ON SCHEDULE!
GUARD MR. TRENCH WHILE I ATTEND TO HIS COMPANIONS, BETTY!
DO NOT CONSIDER ESCAPE, DETECTIVE!
I WOULDN'T DREAM OF ESCAPIN' FROM A DOLL LIKE YOU, BABY!
WHY, YOU'RE SO PRETTY EVEN THAT MOUSE LIKES YOU!
I WILL NOT BE DISTRACTED!
WHO'S DISTRACTIN'? I THINK THE MOUSE'S CUTE NIBBLIN' AT YOUR HEELS!
I WILL NOT BE...
...DISTRACTED...
9

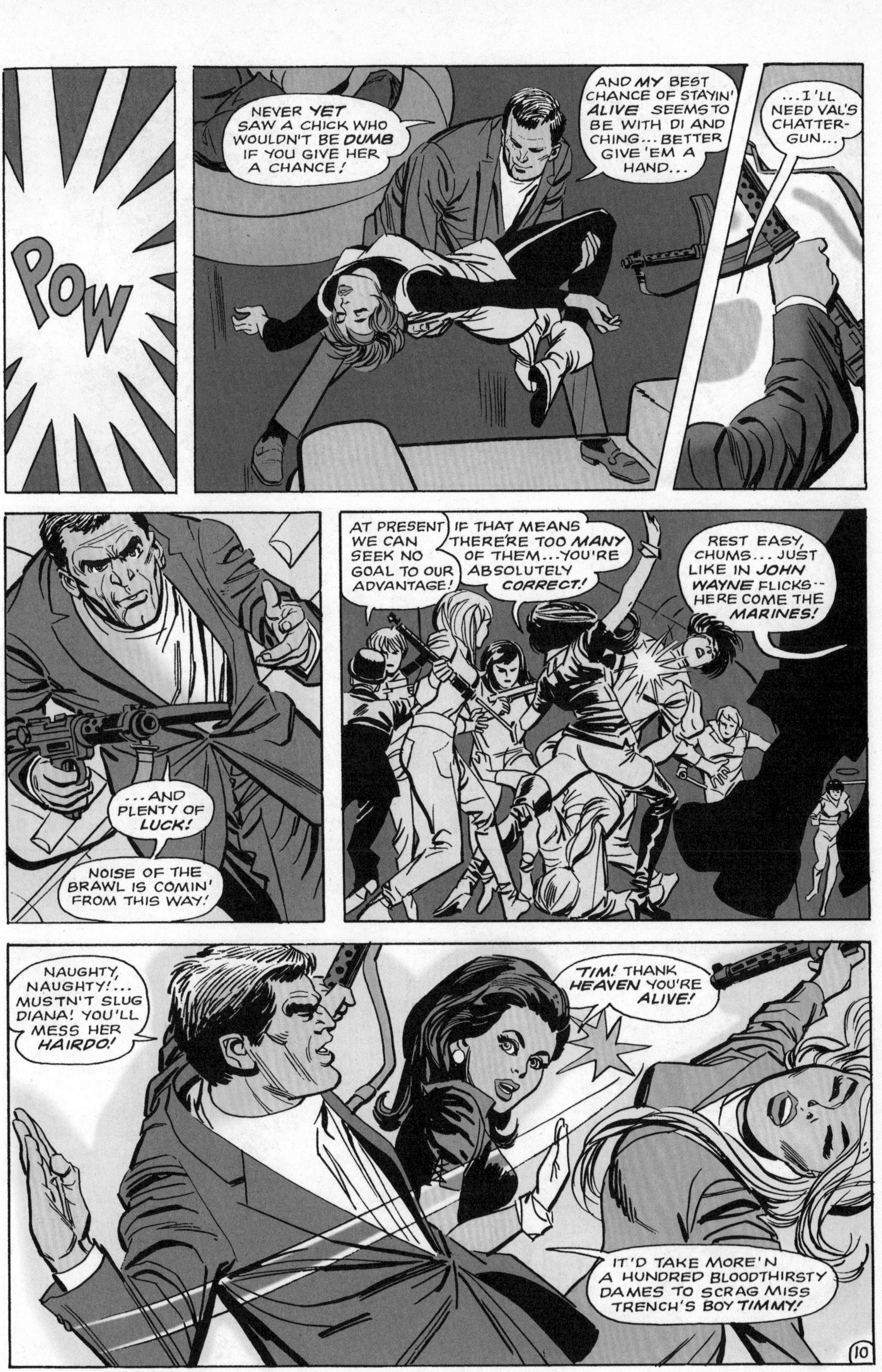
POW
NEVER YET SAW A CHICK WHO WOULDN'T BE DUMB IF YOU GIVE HER A CHANCE!
AND MY BEST CHANCE OF STAYIN' ALIVE SEEMS TO BE WITH DI AND CHING... BETTER GIVE 'EM A HAND...
...I'LL NEED VAL'S CHATTER-GUN...
...AND PLENTY OF LUCK!
NOISE OF THE BRAWL IS COMIN' FROM THIS WAY!
AT PRESENT WE CAN SEEK NO GOAL TO OUR ADVANTAGE!
IF THAT MEANS THERE'RE TOO MANY OF THEM... YOU'RE ABSOLUTELY CORRECT!
REST EASY, CHUMS... JUST LIKE IN JOHN WAYNE FLICKS-- HERE COME THE MARINES!
NAUGHTY, NAUGHTY!... MUSTN'T SLUG DIANA! YOU'LL MESS HER HAIRDO!
TIM! THANK HEAVEN YOU'RE ALIVE!
IT'D TAKE MORE'N A HUNDRED BLOODTHIRSTY DAMES TO SCRAG MISS TRENCH'S BOY TIMMY!
10

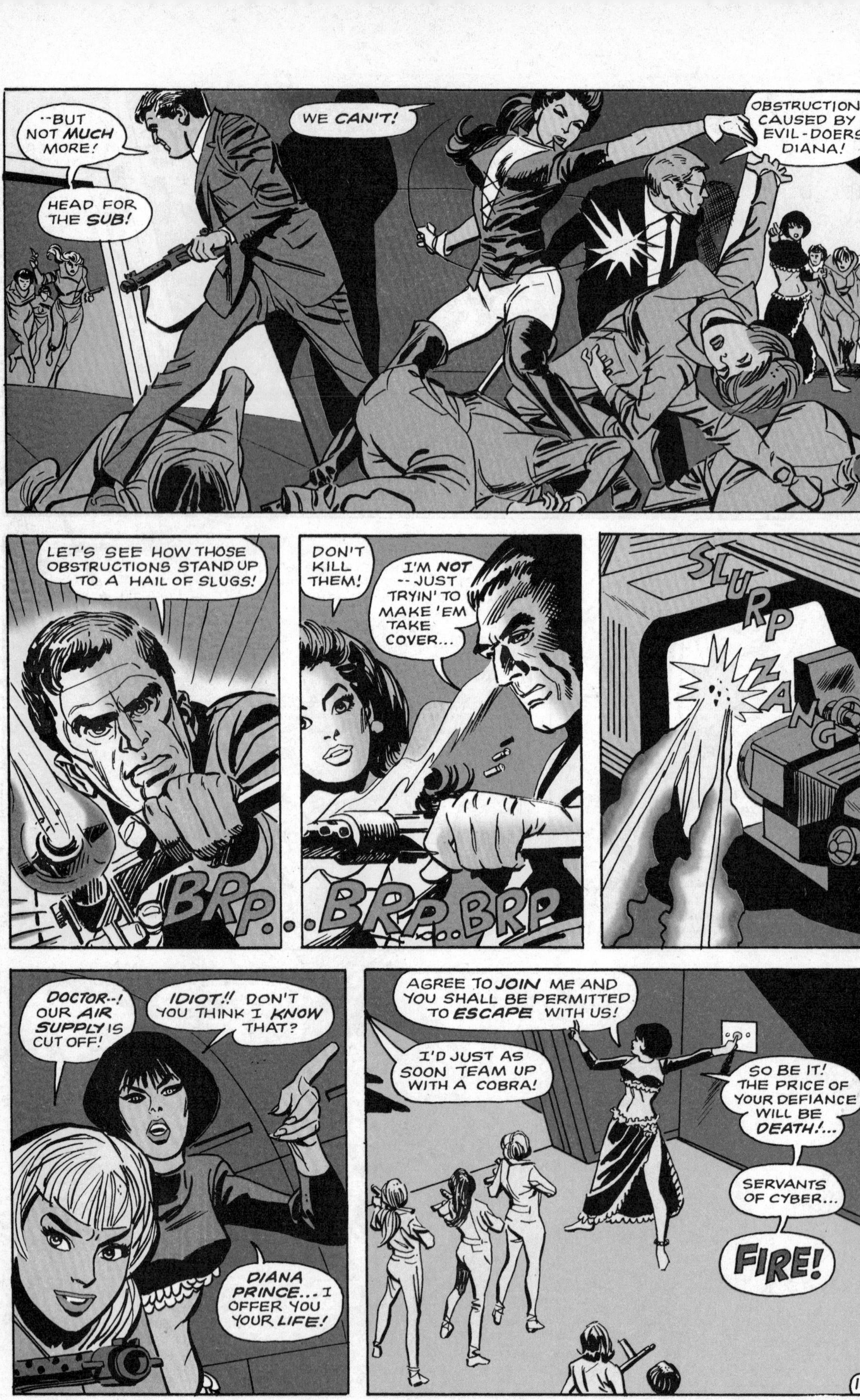
--BUT NOT MUCH MORE!
HEAD FOR THE SUB!
WE CAN'T!
OBSTRUCTION CAUSED BY EVIL-DOERS, DIANA!
LET'S SEE HOW THOSE OBSTRUCTIONS STAND UP TO A HAIL OF SLUGS!
DON'T KILL THEM!
I'M NOT --JUST TRYIN' TO MAKE 'EM TAKE COVER...
BRP...BRP..BRP
SLURP
ZANG
DOCTOR--! OUR AIR SUPPLY IS CUT OFF!
IDIOT!! DON'T YOU THINK I KNOW THAT?
DIANA PRINCE... I OFFER YOU YOUR LIFE!
AGREE TO JOIN ME AND YOU SHALL BE PERMITTED TO ESCAPE WITH US!
I'D JUST AS SOON TEAM UP WITH A COBRA!
SO BE IT! THE PRICE OF YOUR DEFIANCE WILL BE DEATH!...
SERVANTS OF CYBER...
FIRE!
11

CARE TO SHARE MY COZY RETREAT BEHIND THE MACHINERY I STUPIDLY SHOT TO BLAZES?

IT AIN'T THE *RITZ*, BUT IT GROWS ON YOU!

THE WISE MAN DOES NOT QUESTION HIS REFUGE FROM THE STORM!

BRRIIP PTWEEE

ANYPLACE THAT'S AWAY FROM THAT HAIL OF GUNFIRE IS ABSOLUTELY LUXURIOUS!

YOU HAVE ONLY *MINUTES* TO *REGRET* YOUR RASHNESS, DIANA!

...A TOUCH OF A SWITCH LOWERS A BULKHEAD AND *SEALS* YOU WITHIN THIS CHAMBER!

CLANG

THE AIR IS RAPIDLY LEAVING-- AS AM I!

BEFORE I GO, I SHALL TOUCH *ANOTHER* SWITCH-- ONE WHICH ACTIVATES A SMALL NUCLEAR CHARGE BURIED BENEATH THE FORTRESS!

15 MIN

DESTRUCT

...A CHARGE TIMED TO EXPLODE IN EXACTLY *FIFTEEN* MINUTES!

SHOULD YOU SURVIVE THE *AIR-LESSNESS*, YOU WILL BE BLOWN TO BITS!

THOUGH THIS CITY IS NO LONGER OF USE TO ME, IT WILL SERVE YOU-- AS A MOST FITTING *COFFIN!*

SILENTLY, DR. CYBER'S UNDER-SEAS FLEET GLIDES AWAY...

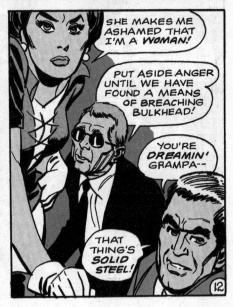

SHE MAKES ME ASHAMED THAT I'M A *WOMAN!*

PUT ASIDE ANGER UNTIL WE HAVE FOUND A MEANS OF BREACHING BULKHEAD!

YOU'RE *DREAMIN'* GRAMPA--

THAT THING'S *SOLID STEEL!*

12

89

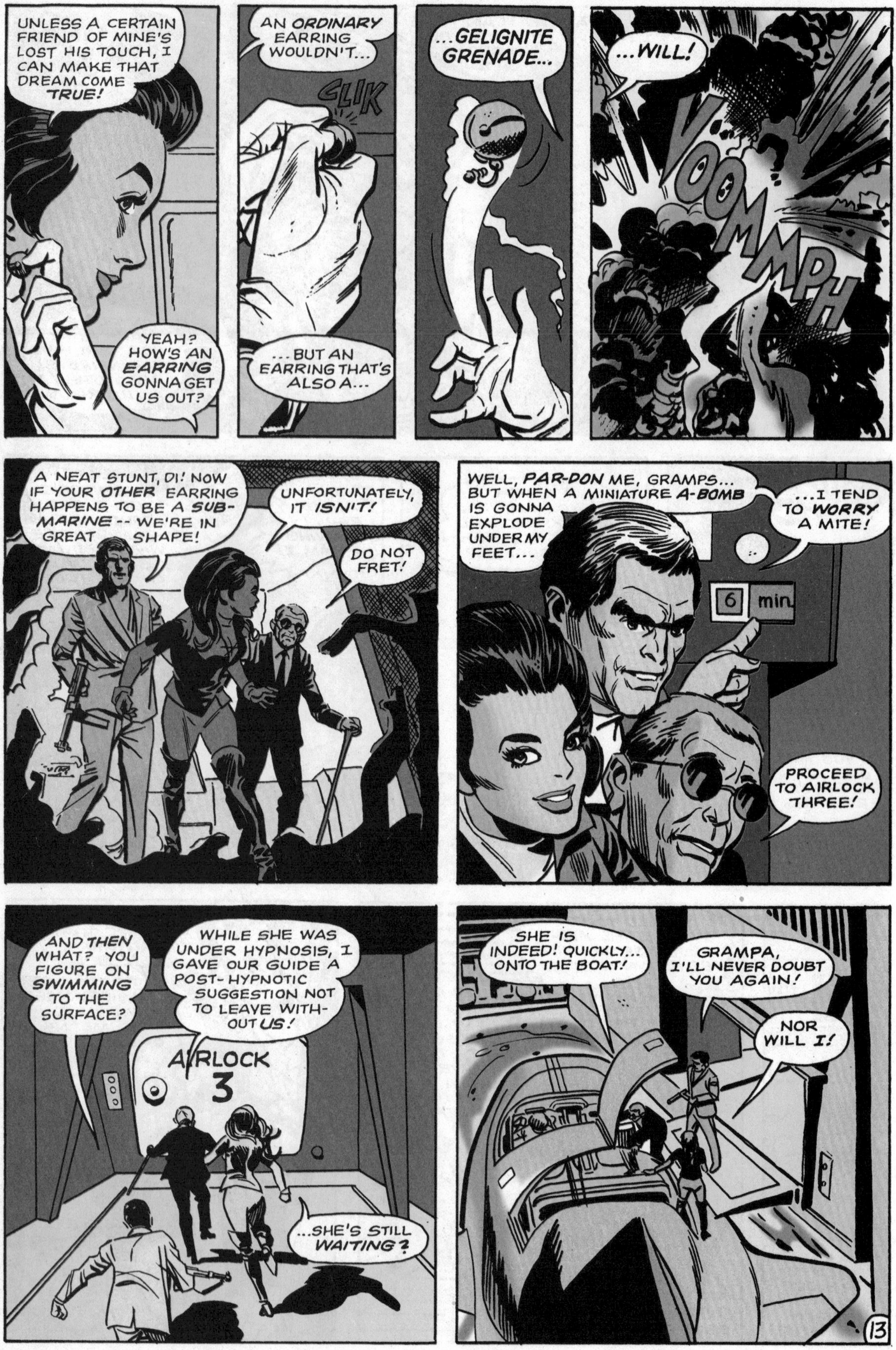

UNLESS A CERTAIN FRIEND OF MINE'S LOST HIS TOUCH, I CAN MAKE THAT DREAM COME TRUE!
YEAH? HOW'S AN EARRING GONNA GET US OUT?
AN ORDINARY EARRING WOULDN'T...
CLIK
...BUT AN EARRING THAT'S ALSO A...
...GELIGNITE GRENADE...
...WILL!
VOOMMPH
A NEAT STUNT, DI! NOW IF YOUR OTHER EARRING HAPPENS TO BE A SUB-MARINE -- WE'RE IN GREAT SHAPE!
UNFORTUNATELY, IT ISN'T!
DO NOT FRET!
WELL, PAR-DON ME, GRAMPS... BUT WHEN A MINIATURE A-BOMB IS GONNA EXPLODE UNDER MY FEET...
...I TEND TO WORRY A MITE!
6 min
PROCEED TO AIRLOCK THREE!
AND THEN WHAT? YOU FIGURE ON SWIMMING TO THE SURFACE?
WHILE SHE WAS UNDER HYPNOSIS, I GAVE OUR GUIDE A POST-HYPNOTIC SUGGESTION NOT TO LEAVE WITH-OUT US!
AIRLOCK 3
...SHE'S STILL WAITING?
SHE IS INDEED! QUICKLY... ONTO THE BOAT!
GRAMPA, I'LL NEVER DOUBT YOU AGAIN!
NOR WILL I!
13

INSTANTS LATER, THE OCEAN BOILS FURIOUSLY AS THE FORTRESS OF DR. CYBER EXPLODES...
THIS CRATE IS SHAKIN' LIKE A DISCOTHEQUE ON SATURDAY NIGHT... BUT IT LOOKS LIKE...
...WE'RE HOME FREE!
WE LIVE-- TO CONTINUE OUR QUEST!
WHOOMP!
THE QUEST IS CONTINUED-- TO A SHOCKING CLIMAX-- ON THE NEXT PAGE
14

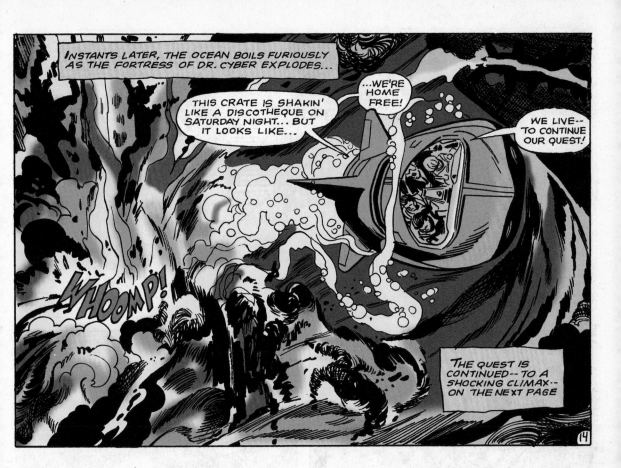

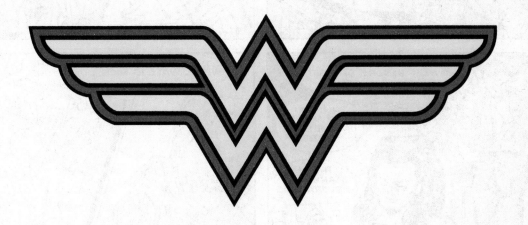

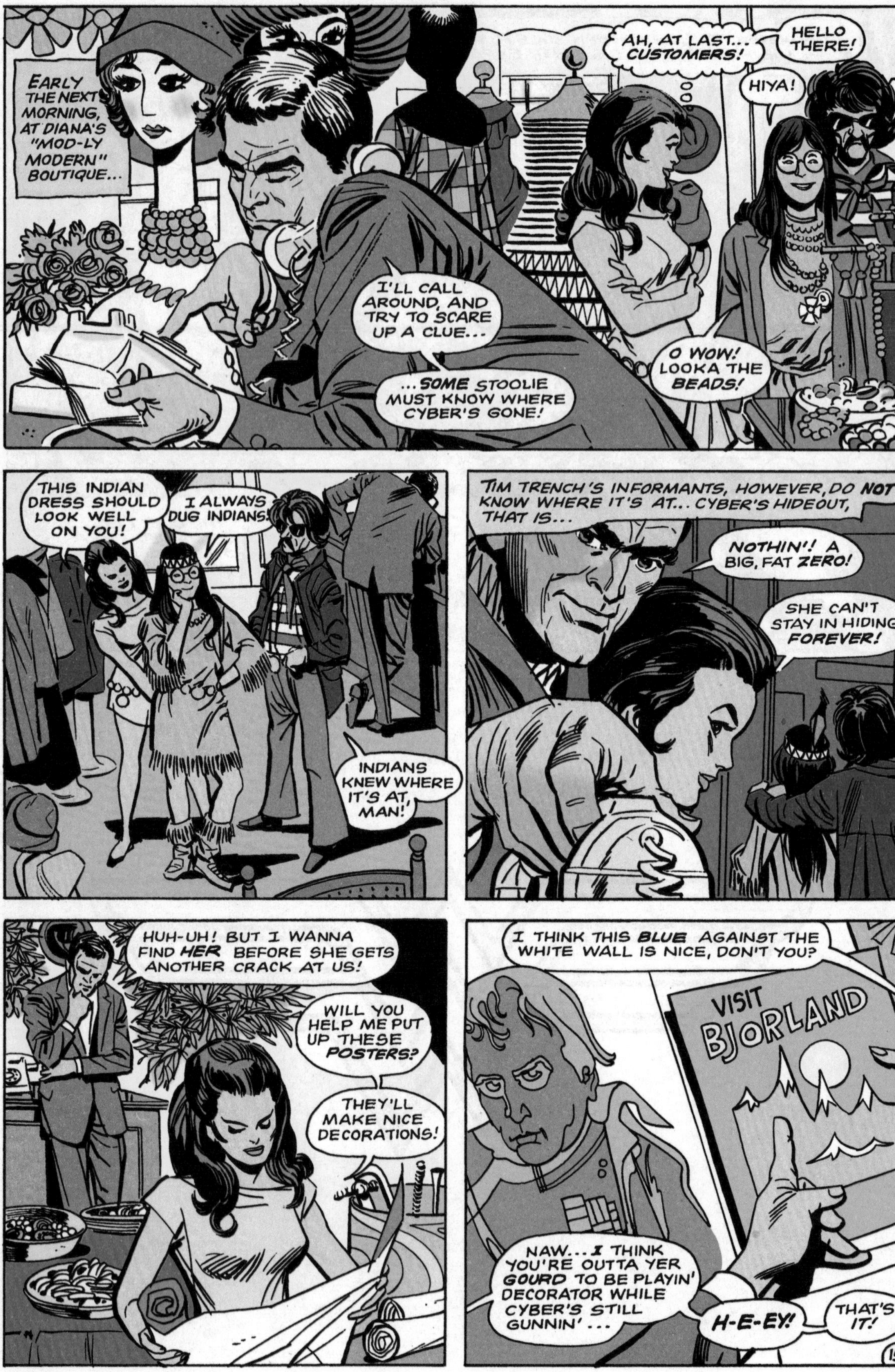
EARLY THE NEXT MORNING, AT DIANA'S "MOD-LY MODERN" BOUTIQUE...
I'LL CALL AROUND, AND TRY TO SCARE UP A CLUE...
...SOME STOOLIE MUST KNOW WHERE CYBER'S GONE!
AH, AT LAST... CUSTOMERS!
HELLO THERE!
HIYA!
O WOW! LOOKA THE BEADS!
THIS INDIAN DRESS SHOULD LOOK WELL ON YOU!
I ALWAYS DUG INDIANS!
INDIANS KNEW WHERE IT'S AT, MAN!
TIM TRENCH'S INFORMANTS, HOWEVER, DO NOT KNOW WHERE IT'S AT... CYBER'S HIDEOUT, THAT IS...
NOTHIN'! A BIG, FAT ZERO!
SHE CAN'T STAY IN HIDING FOREVER!
HUH-UH! BUT I WANNA FIND HER BEFORE SHE GETS ANOTHER CRACK AT US!
WILL YOU HELP ME PUT UP THESE POSTERS?
THEY'LL MAKE NICE DECORATIONS!
I THINK THIS BLUE AGAINST THE WHITE WALL IS NICE, DON'T YOU?
VISIT BJORLAND
NAW... I THINK YOU'RE OUTTA YER GOURD TO BE PLAYIN' DECORATOR WHILE CYBER'S STILL GUNNIN'...
H-E-EY!
THAT'S IT!
15

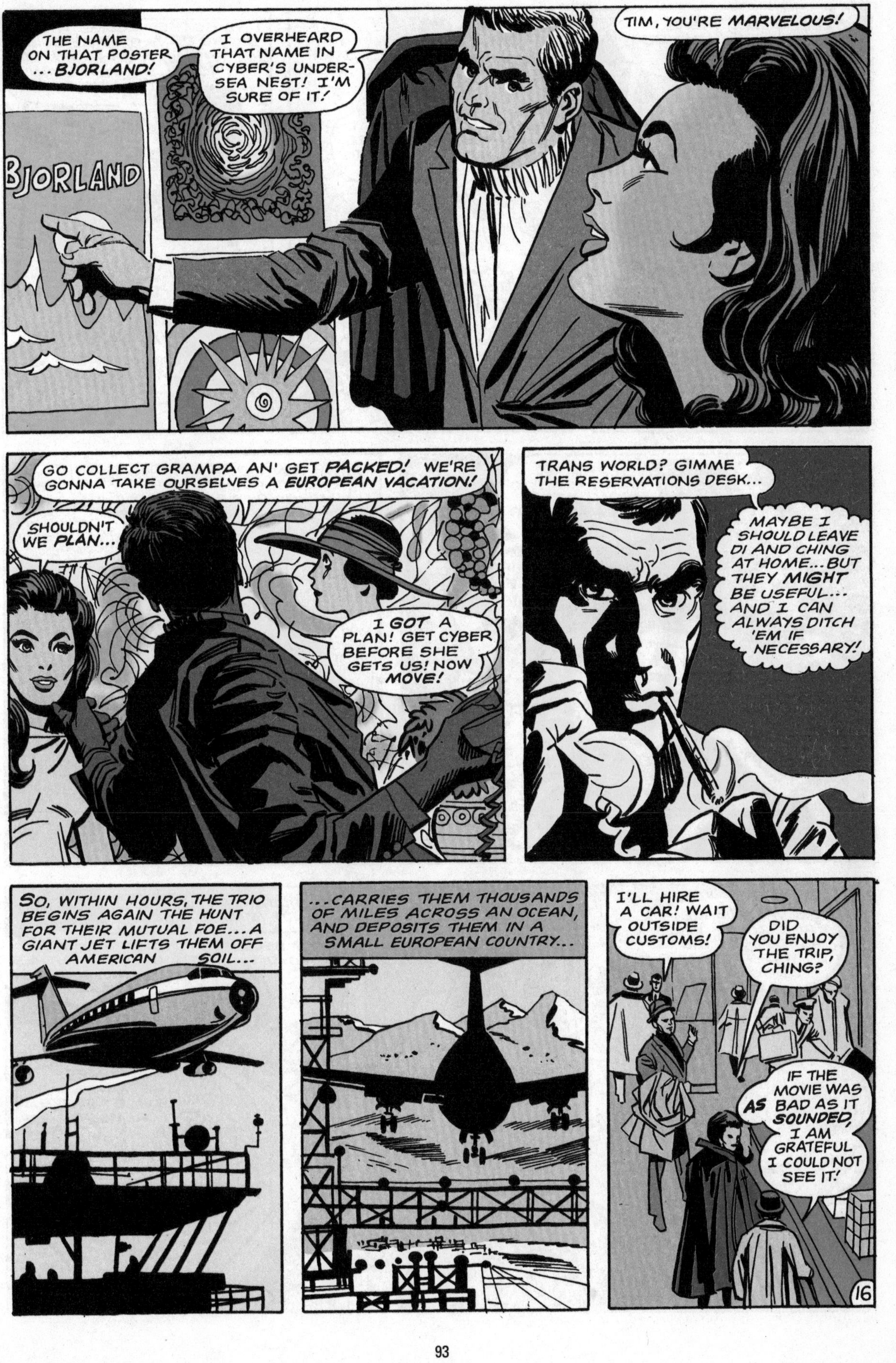
THE NAME ON THAT POSTER ...BJORLAND!
I OVERHEARD THAT NAME IN CYBER'S UNDER-SEA NEST! I'M SURE OF IT!
BJORLAND
TIM, YOU'RE MARVELOUS!
GO COLLECT GRAMPA AN' GET PACKED! WE'RE GONNA TAKE OURSELVES A EUROPEAN VACATION!
SHOULDN'T WE PLAN...
I GOT A PLAN! GET CYBER BEFORE SHE GETS US! NOW MOVE!
TRANS WORLD? GIMME THE RESERVATIONS DESK...
MAYBE I SHOULD LEAVE DI AND CHING AT HOME... BUT THEY MIGHT BE USEFUL... AND I CAN ALWAYS DITCH 'EM IF NECESSARY!
SO, WITHIN HOURS, THE TRIO BEGINS AGAIN THE HUNT FOR THEIR MUTUAL FOE... A GIANT JET LIFTS THEM OFF AMERICAN SOIL...
...CARRIES THEM THOUSANDS OF MILES ACROSS AN OCEAN, AND DEPOSITS THEM IN A SMALL EUROPEAN COUNTRY...
I'LL HIRE A CAR! WAIT OUTSIDE CUSTOMS!
DID YOU ENJOY THE TRIP, CHING?
IF THE MOVIE WAS AS BAD AS IT SOUNDED, I AM GRATEFUL I COULD NOT SEE IT!
16

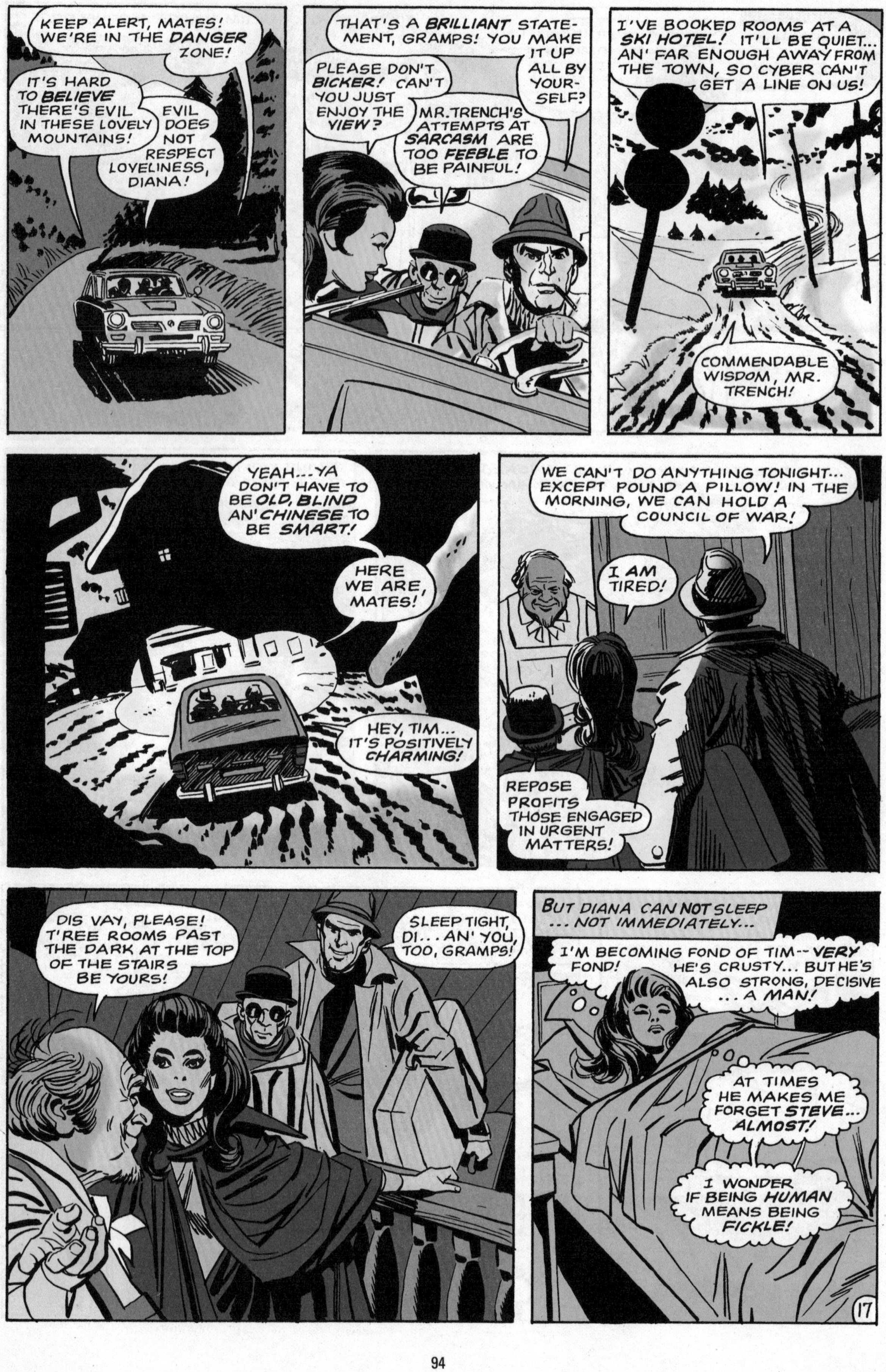
KEEP ALERT, MATES! WE'RE IN THE DANGER ZONE!
IT'S HARD TO BELIEVE THERE'S EVIL IN THESE LOVELY MOUNTAINS!
EVIL DOES NOT RESPECT LOVELINESS, DIANA!
THAT'S A BRILLIANT STATEMENT, GRAMPS! YOU MAKE IT UP ALL BY YOURSELF?
PLEASE DON'T BICKER! CAN'T YOU JUST ENJOY THE VIEW?
MR. TRENCH'S ATTEMPTS AT SARCASM ARE TOO FEEBLE TO BE PAINFUL!
I'VE BOOKED ROOMS AT A SKI HOTEL! IT'LL BE QUIET... AN' FAR ENOUGH AWAY FROM THE TOWN, SO CYBER CAN'T GET A LINE ON US!
COMMENDABLE WISDOM, MR. TRENCH!
YEAH...YA DON'T HAVE TO BE OLD, BLIND AN' CHINESE TO BE SMART!
HERE WE ARE, MATES!
HEY, TIM... IT'S POSITIVELY CHARMING!
WE CAN'T DO ANYTHING TONIGHT... EXCEPT POUND A PILLOW! IN THE MORNING, WE CAN HOLD A COUNCIL OF WAR!
I AM TIRED!
REPOSE PROFITS THOSE ENGAGED IN URGENT MATTERS!
DIS VAY, PLEASE! T'REE ROOMS PAST THE DARK AT THE TOP OF THE STAIRS BE YOURS!
SLEEP TIGHT, DI... AN' YOU, TOO, GRAMPS!
BUT DIANA CAN NOT SLEEP ... NOT IMMEDIATELY...
I'M BECOMING FOND OF TIM-- VERY FOND! HE'S CRUSTY... BUT HE'S ALSO STRONG, DECISIVE ... A MAN!
AT TIMES HE MAKES ME FORGET STEVE... ALMOST!
I WONDER IF BEING HUMAN MEANS BEING FICKLE!
17

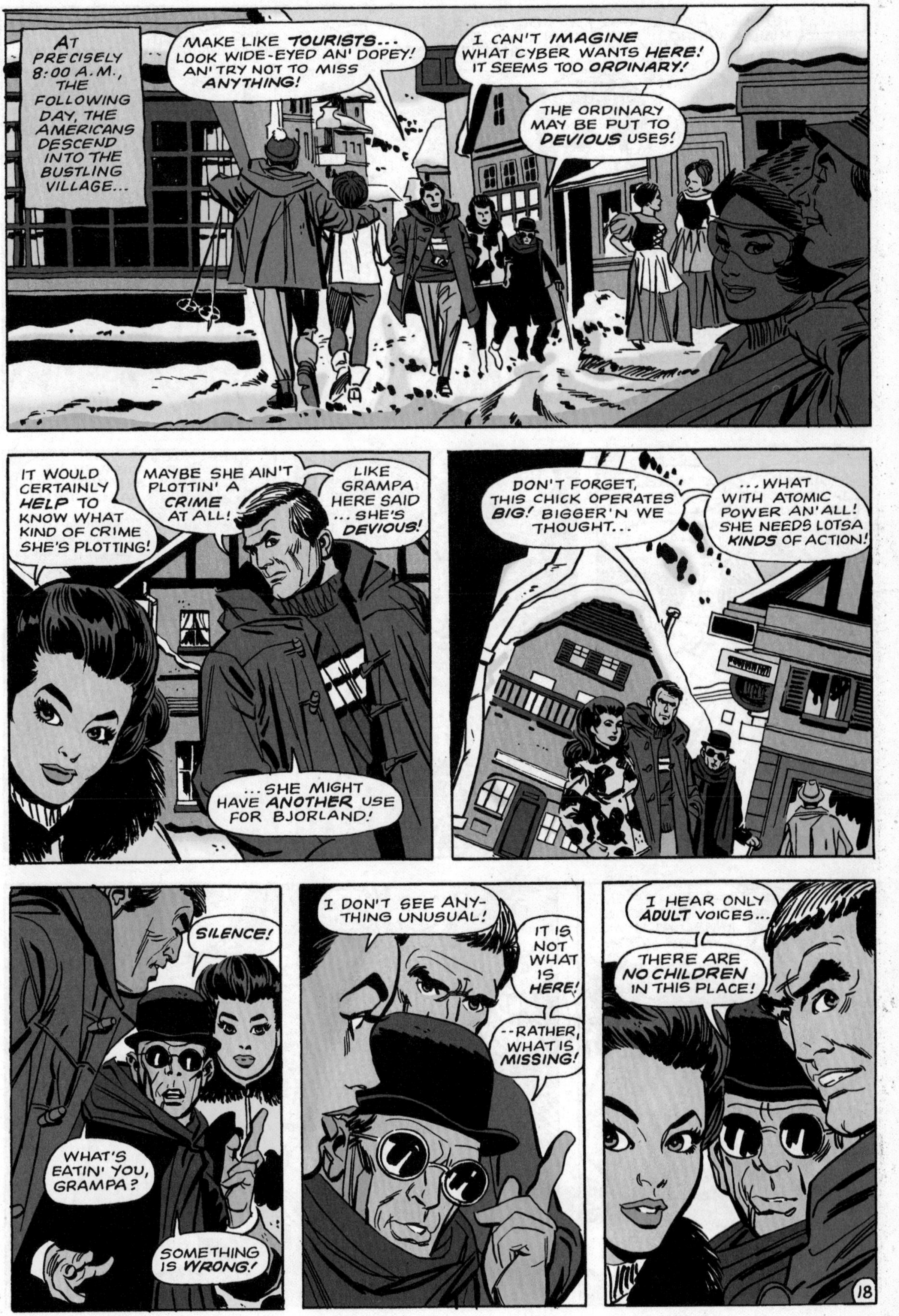
AT PRECISELY 8:00 A.M., THE FOLLOWING DAY, THE AMERICANS DESCEND INTO THE BUSTLING VILLAGE...
MAKE LIKE TOURISTS... LOOK WIDE-EYED AN' DOPEY! AN' TRY NOT TO MISS ANYTHING!
I CAN'T IMAGINE WHAT CYBER WANTS HERE! IT SEEMS TOO ORDINARY!
THE ORDINARY MAY BE PUT TO DEVIOUS USES!
IT WOULD CERTAINLY HELP TO KNOW WHAT KIND OF CRIME SHE'S PLOTTING!
MAYBE SHE AIN'T PLOTTIN' A CRIME AT ALL!
LIKE GRAMPA HERE SAID ... SHE'S DEVIOUS!
...SHE MIGHT HAVE ANOTHER USE FOR BJORLAND!
DON'T FORGET, THIS CHICK OPERATES BIG! BIGGER'N WE THOUGHT...
...WHAT WITH ATOMIC POWER AN' ALL! SHE NEEDS LOTSA KINDS OF ACTION!
SILENCE!
WHAT'S EATIN' YOU, GRAMPA?
SOMETHING IS WRONG!
I DON'T SEE ANYTHING UNUSUAL!
IT IS NOT WHAT IS HERE!
--RATHER, WHAT IS MISSING!
I HEAR ONLY ADULT VOICES...
THERE ARE NO CHILDREN IN THIS PLACE!
18

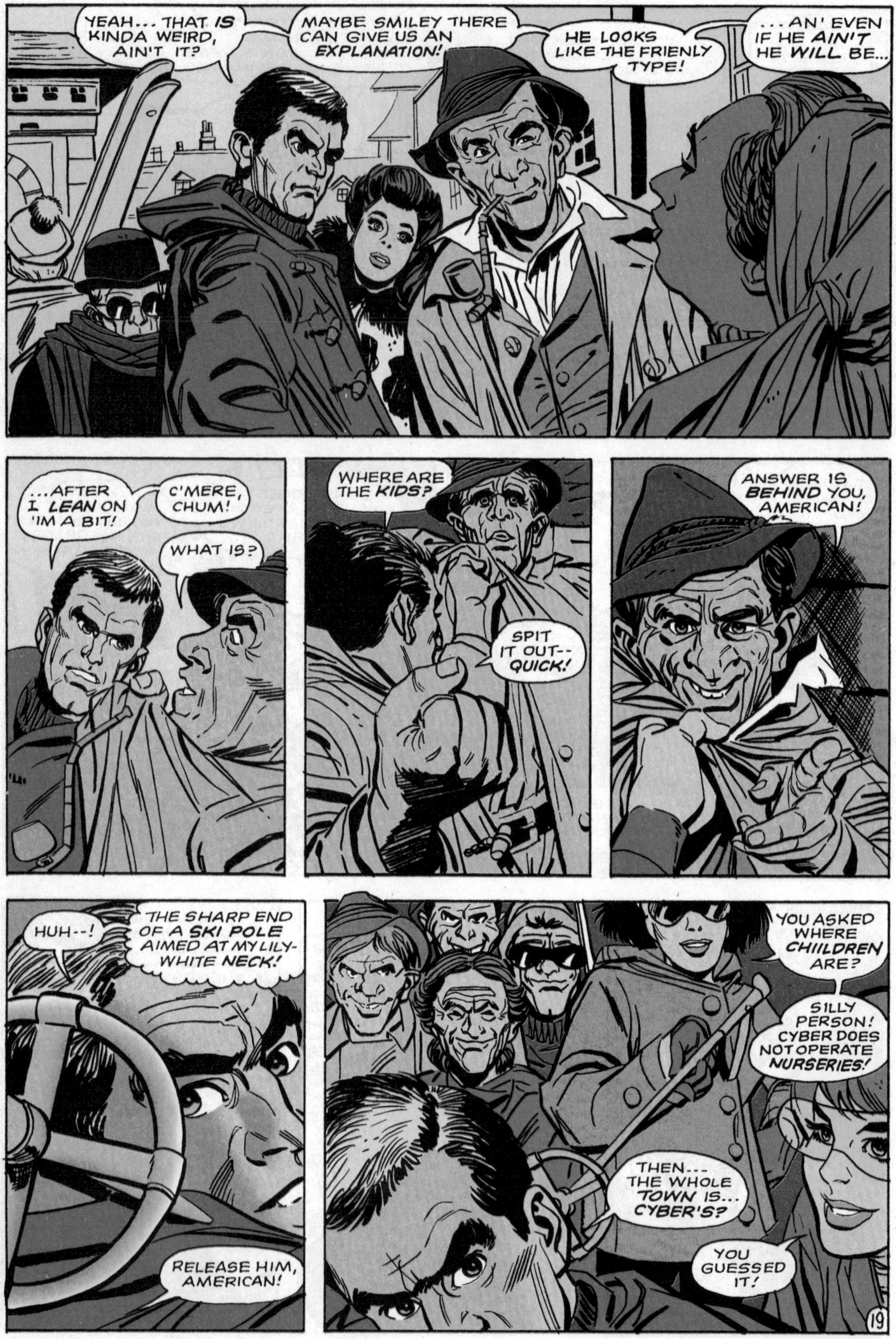
YEAH... THAT IS KINDA WEIRD, AIN'T IT?
MAYBE SMILEY THERE CAN GIVE US AN EXPLANATION!
HE LOOKS LIKE THE FRIENLY TYPE!
...AN' EVEN IF HE AIN'T HE WILL BE...
...AFTER I LEAN ON 'IM A BIT!
C'MERE, CHUM!
WHAT IS?
WHERE ARE THE KIDS?
SPIT IT OUT-- QUICK!
ANSWER IS BEHIND YOU, AMERICAN!
HUH--!
THE SHARP END OF A SKI POLE AIMED AT MY LILY-WHITE NECK!
RELEASE HIM, AMERICAN!
YOU ASKED WHERE CHIILDREN ARE?
SILLY PERSON! CYBER DOES NOT OPERATE NURSERIES!
THEN--- THE WHOLE TOWN IS... CYBER'S?
YOU GUESSED IT!
19

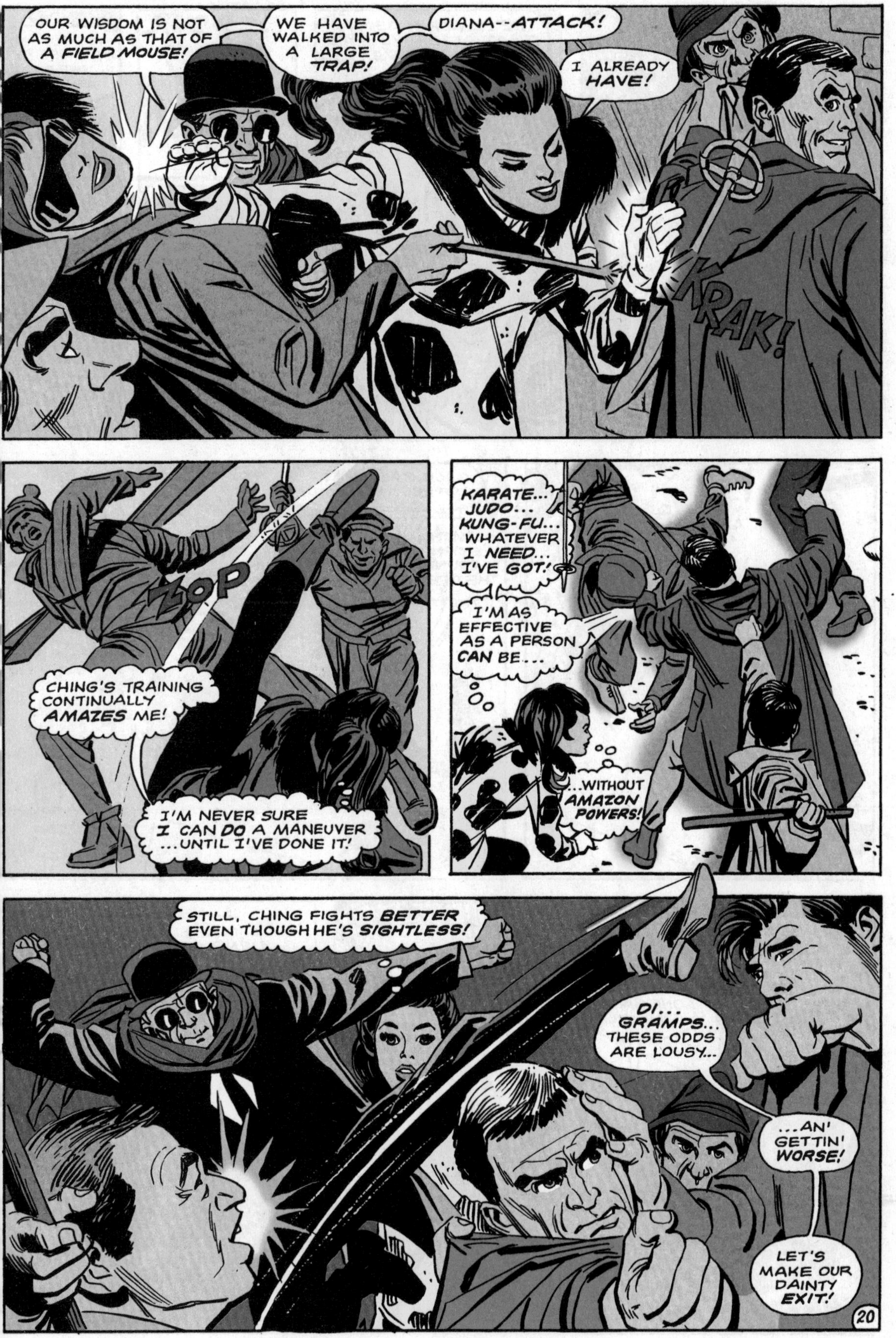
OUR WISDOM IS NOT AS MUCH AS THAT OF A FIELD MOUSE!
WE HAVE WALKED INTO A LARGE TRAP!
DIANA--ATTACK!
I ALREADY HAVE!
KRAK!
ZOP
CHING'S TRAINING CONTINUALLY AMAZES ME!
I'M NEVER SURE I CAN DO A MANEUVER ...UNTIL I'VE DONE IT!
KARATE... JUDO... KUNG-FU... WHATEVER I NEED... I'VE GOT!
I'M AS EFFECTIVE AS A PERSON CAN BE...
...WITHOUT AMAZON POWERS!
STILL, CHING FIGHTS BETTER EVEN THOUGH HE'S SIGHTLESS!
DI... GRAMPS... THESE ODDS ARE LOUSY...
...AN' GETTIN' WORSE!
LET'S MAKE OUR DAINTY EXIT!
20

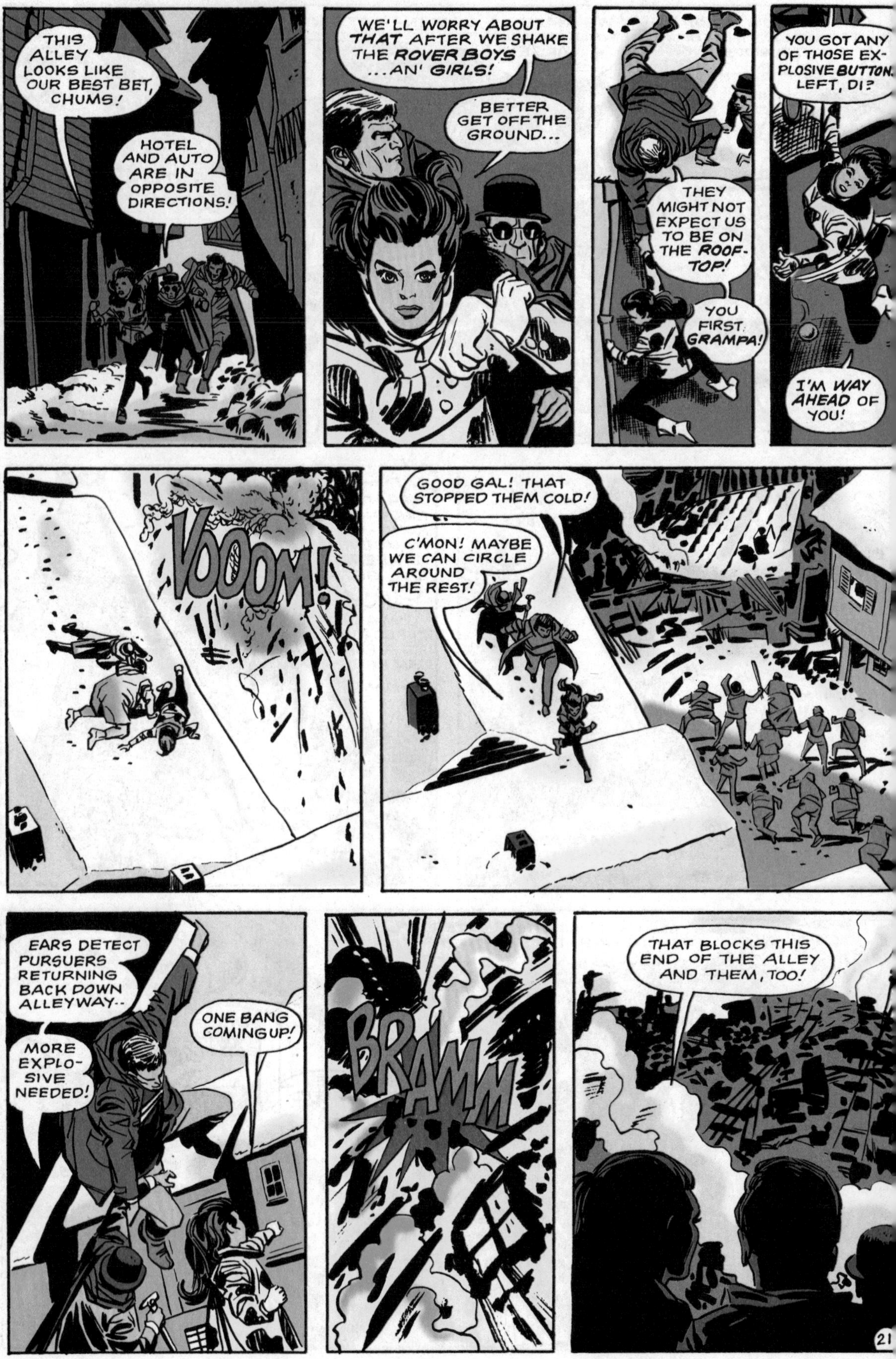
THIS ALLEY LOOKS LIKE OUR BEST BET, CHUMS!
HOTEL AND AUTO ARE IN OPPOSITE DIRECTIONS!
WE'LL WORRY ABOUT THAT AFTER WE SHAKE THE ROVER BOYS ...AN' GIRLS!
BETTER GET OFF THE GROUND...
THEY MIGHT NOT EXPECT US TO BE ON THE ROOF-TOP!
YOU FIRST, GRAMPA!
YOU GOT ANY OF THOSE EX-PLOSIVE BUTTONS LEFT, DI?
I'M WAY AHEAD OF YOU!
VOOOM!
GOOD GAL! THAT STOPPED THEM COLD!
C'MON! MAYBE WE CAN CIRCLE AROUND THE REST!
EARS DETECT PURSUERS RETURNING BACK DOWN ALLEYWAY--
MORE EXPLO-SIVE NEEDED!
ONE BANG COMING UP!
BRAMM
THAT BLOCKS THIS END OF THE ALLEY AND THEM, TOO!
21

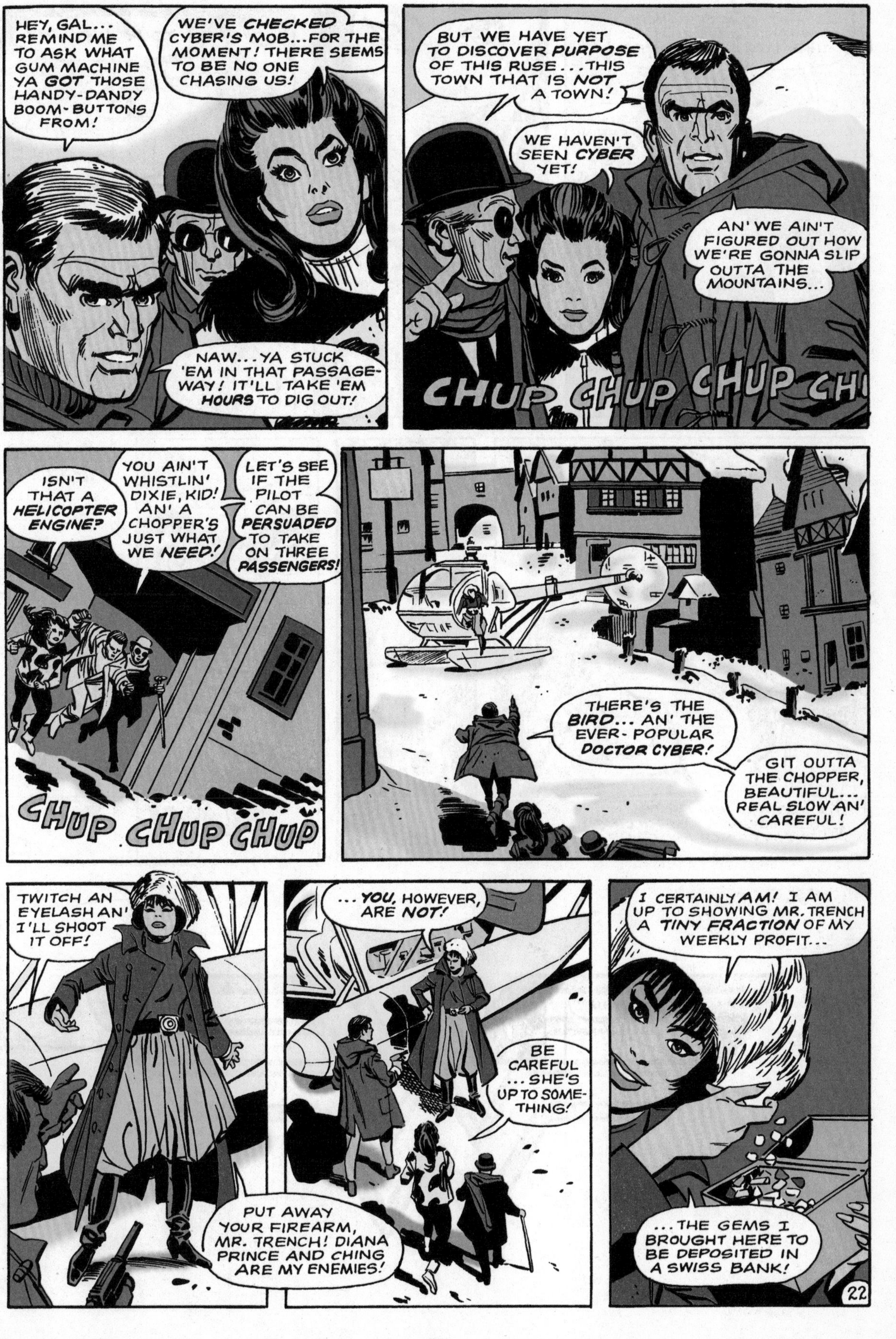
HEY, GAL... REMIND ME TO ASK WHAT GUM MACHINE YA GOT THOSE HANDY-DANDY BOOM-BUTTONS FROM!
WE'VE CHECKED CYBER'S MOB...FOR THE MOMENT! THERE SEEMS TO BE NO ONE CHASING US!
NAW...YA STUCK 'EM IN THAT PASSAGEWAY! IT'LL TAKE 'EM HOURS TO DIG OUT!
BUT WE HAVE YET TO DISCOVER PURPOSE OF THIS RUSE...THIS TOWN THAT IS NOT A TOWN!
WE HAVEN'T SEEN CYBER YET!
AN' WE AIN'T FIGURED OUT HOW WE'RE GONNA SLIP OUTTA THE MOUNTAINS...
CHUP CHUP CHUP CH
ISN'T THAT A HELICOPTER ENGINE?
YOU AIN'T WHISTLIN' DIXIE, KID! AN' A CHOPPER'S JUST WHAT WE NEED!
LET'S SEE IF THE PILOT CAN BE PERSUADED TO TAKE ON THREE PASSENGERS!
CHUP CHUP CHUP
THERE'S THE BIRD... AN' THE EVER-POPULAR DOCTOR CYBER!
GIT OUTTA THE CHOPPER, BEAUTIFUL... REAL SLOW AN' CAREFUL!
TWITCH AN EYELASH AN' I'LL SHOOT IT OFF!
...YOU, HOWEVER, ARE NOT!
BE CAREFUL ...SHE'S UP TO SOMETHING!
PUT AWAY YOUR FIREARM, MR. TRENCH! DIANA PRINCE AND CHING ARE MY ENEMIES!
I CERTAINLY AM! I AM UP TO SHOWING MR. TRENCH A TINY FRACTION OF MY WEEKLY PROFIT...
...THE GEMS I BROUGHT HERE TO BE DEPOSITED IN A SWISS BANK!
22

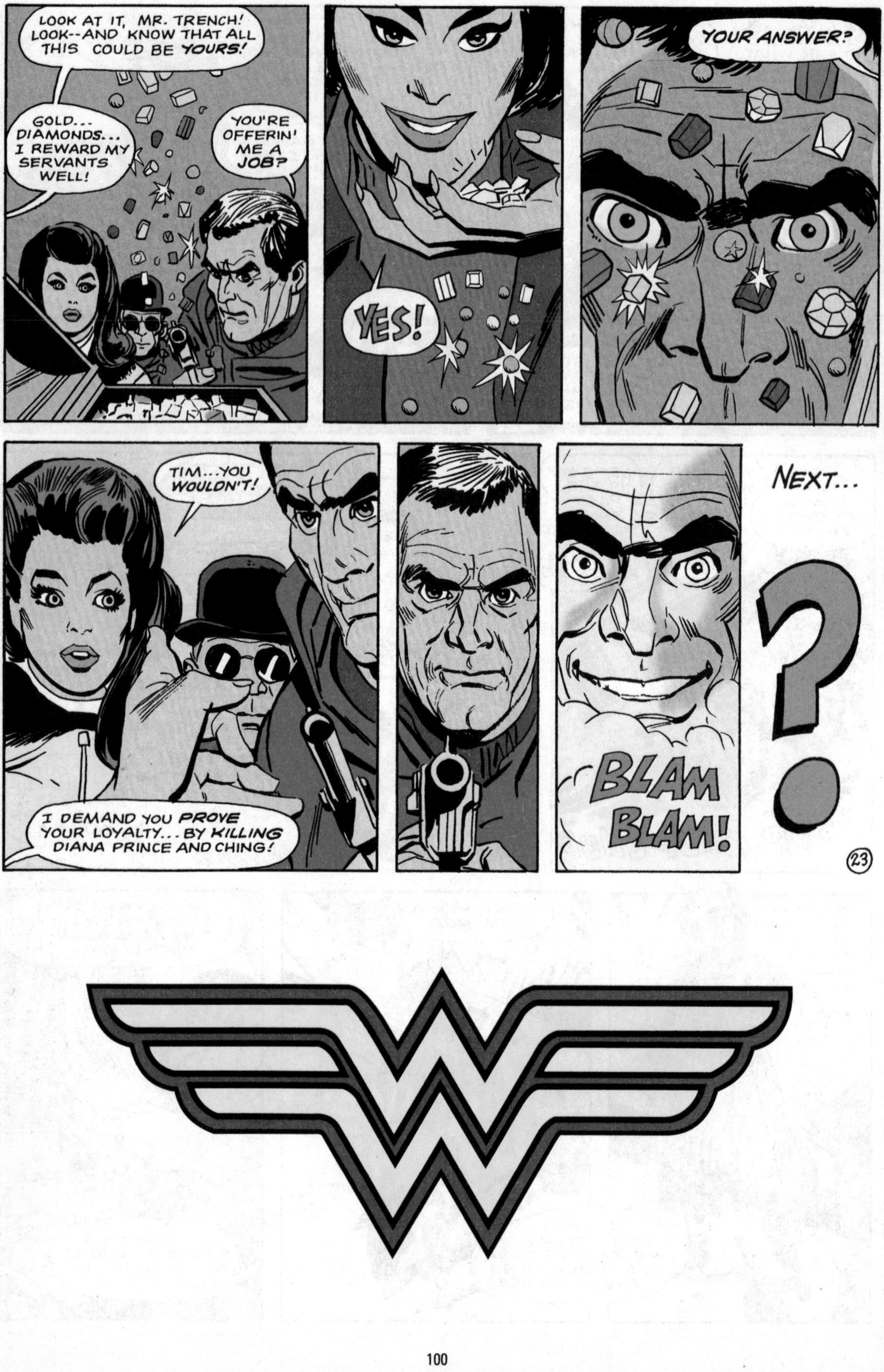
LOOK AT IT, MR. TRENCH! LOOK--AND KNOW THAT ALL THIS COULD BE YOURS!
GOLD... DIAMONDS... I REWARD MY SERVANTS WELL!
YOU'RE OFFERIN' ME A JOB?
YES!
YOUR ANSWER?
TIM...YOU WOULDN'T!
I DEMAND YOU PROVE YOUR LOYALTY... BY KILLING DIANA PRINCE AND CHING!
BLAM BLAM!
NEXT...
?
23

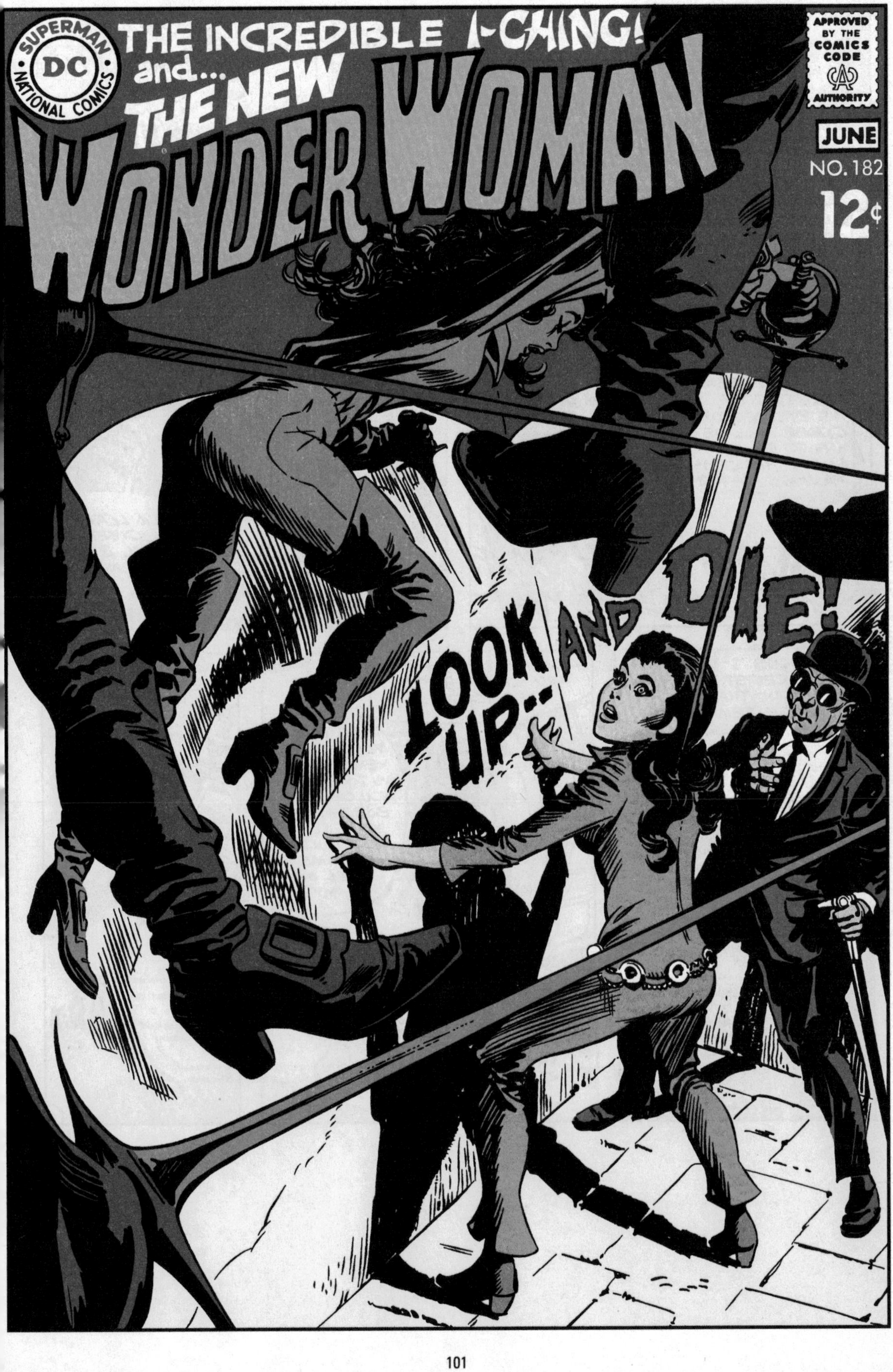
SUPERMAN
DC
NATIONAL COMICS
THE INCREDIBLE I-CHING!
and... THE NEW
WONDER WOMAN
APPROVED BY THE COMICS CODE AUTHORITY
JUNE
NO. 182
12¢
LOOK UP-- AND DIE!

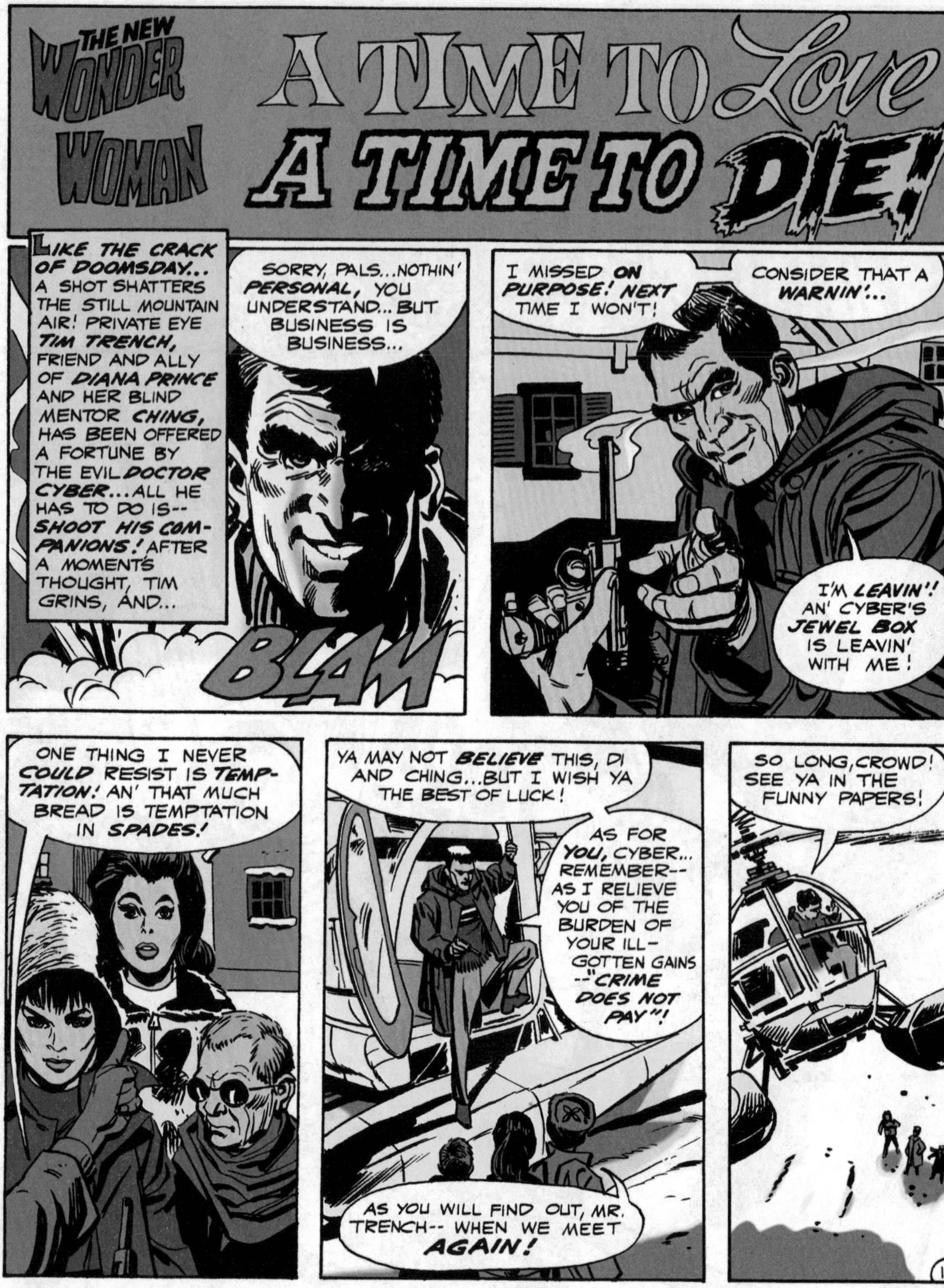
THE NEW WONDER WOMAN
A TIME TO Love A TIME TO DIE!
LIKE THE CRACK OF DOOMSDAY... A SHOT SHATTERS THE STILL MOUNTAIN AIR! PRIVATE EYE TIM TRENCH, FRIEND AND ALLY OF DIANA PRINCE AND HER BLIND MENTOR CHING, HAS BEEN OFFERED A FORTUNE BY THE EVIL DOCTOR CYBER... ALL HE HAS TO DO IS-- SHOOT HIS COMPANIONS! AFTER A MOMENT'S THOUGHT, TIM GRINS, AND...
SORRY, PALS... NOTHIN' PERSONAL, YOU UNDERSTAND... BUT BUSINESS IS BUSINESS...
BLAM
I MISSED ON PURPOSE! NEXT TIME I WON'T!
CONSIDER THAT A WARNIN'...
I'M LEAVIN'! AN' CYBER'S JEWEL BOX IS LEAVIN' WITH ME!
ONE THING I NEVER COULD RESIST IS TEMPTATION! AN' THAT MUCH BREAD IS TEMPTATION IN SPADES!
YA MAY NOT BELIEVE THIS, DI AND CHING... BUT I WISH YA THE BEST OF LUCK!
AS FOR YOU, CYBER... REMEMBER-- AS I RELIEVE YOU OF THE BURDEN OF YOUR ILL-GOTTEN GAINS --"CRIME DOES NOT PAY"!
AS YOU WILL FIND OUT, MR. TRENCH-- WHEN WE MEET AGAIN!
SO LONG, CROWD! SEE YA IN THE FUNNY PAPERS!
1

NO! I CAN'T *BELIEVE* TIM HAS REALLY...*BETRAYED* US! HE *CAN'T* BE BAD!

THE SIGHT OF GOLD MUTES THE VOICE OF MANY A CONSCIENCE TO A WHISPER!

IT'S *YOU,* CYBER! YOUR *EVIL* CORRUPTS EVERYTHING!

HOW *DARE* YOU TOUCH ME!

DIANA! I DETECT THE SOUND OF ENGINES! SOMEONE COMES!

SUDDENLY, FROM ALL SIDES, CYBER'S GIRLS CONVERGE, MOUNTED ON PROPELLER-DRIVEN SNOWMOBILES, AND CARRYING SINISTER, HOODED BIRDS...

VVROOOMM

RELEASE ME, DIANA PRINCE! YOU ARE *SURROUNDED--HELPLESS!*

I SUPPOSE I HAVE--NO CHOICE!

INDEED YOU *DON'T*--NOT IF YOU WISH TO REMAIN AMONG THE *LIVING* A FEW MINUTES MORE!

GIVE ME MY PET!

DO YOU RECOGNIZE MY FEATHERED SERVANTS, DIANA? THEY ARE *HUNTER-FALCONS!*

2

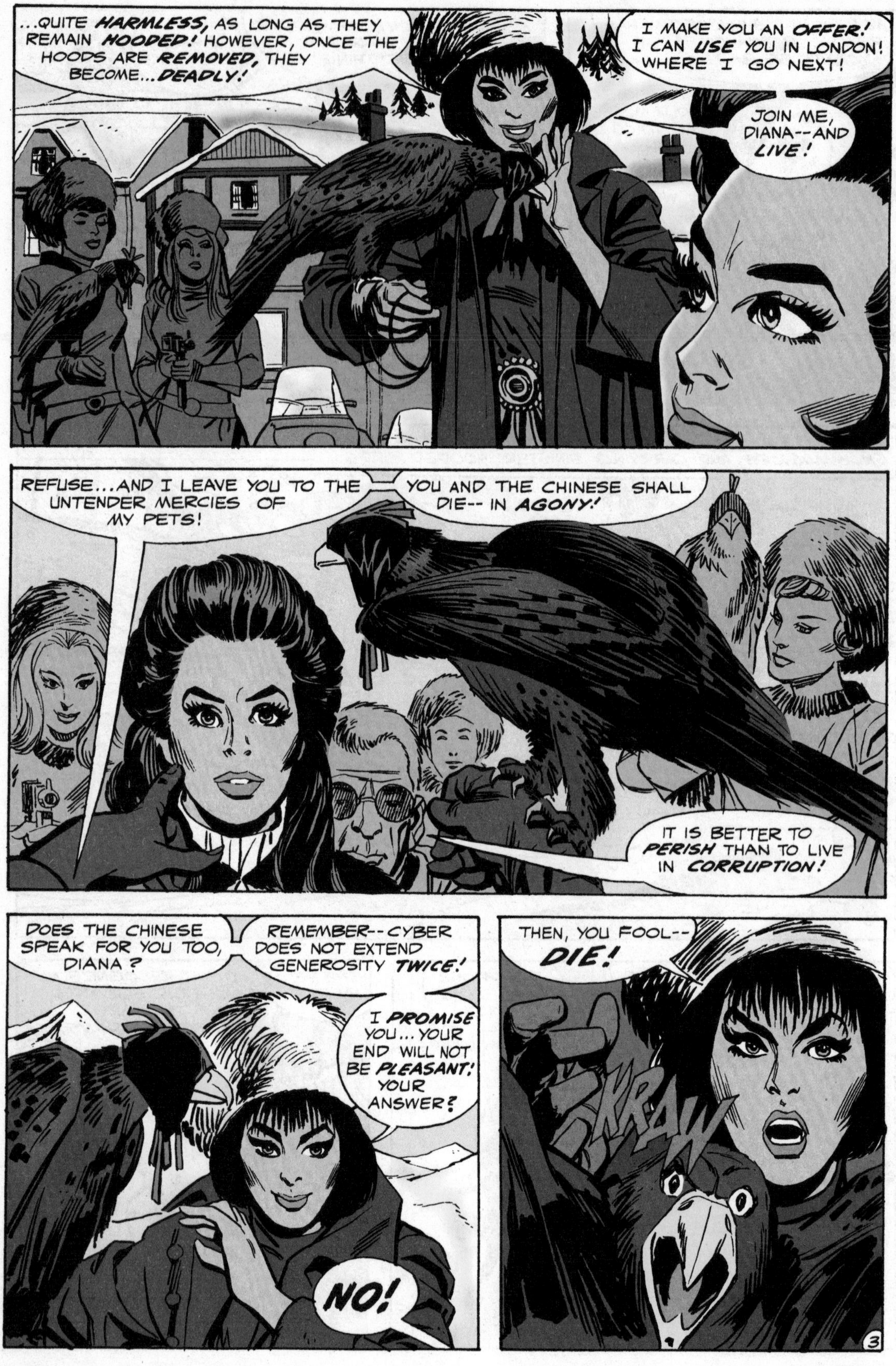
...QUITE HARMLESS, AS LONG AS THEY REMAIN HOODED! HOWEVER, ONCE THE HOODS ARE REMOVED, THEY BECOME...DEADLY!
I MAKE YOU AN OFFER! I CAN USE YOU IN LONDON! WHERE I GO NEXT!
JOIN ME, DIANA--AND LIVE!
REFUSE...AND I LEAVE YOU TO THE UNTENDER MERCIES OF MY PETS!
YOU AND THE CHINESE SHALL DIE-- IN AGONY!
IT IS BETTER TO PERISH THAN TO LIVE IN CORRUPTION!
DOES THE CHINESE SPEAK FOR YOU TOO, DIANA?
REMEMBER--CYBER DOES NOT EXTEND GENEROSITY TWICE!
I PROMISE YOU... YOUR END WILL NOT BE PLEASANT! YOUR ANSWER?
NO!
THEN, YOU FOOL-- DIE!
KRAW
3

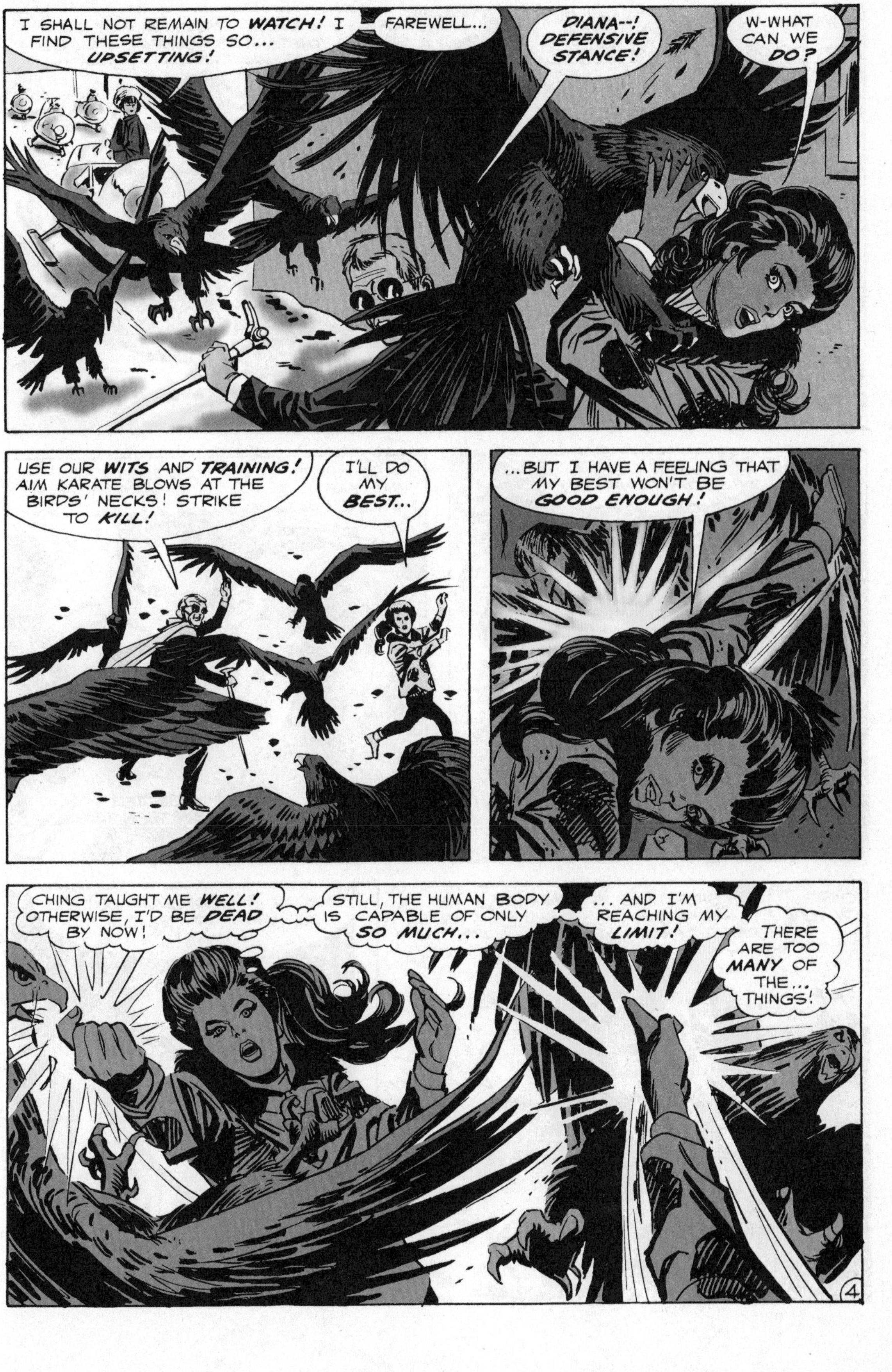

I SHALL NOT REMAIN TO WATCH! I FIND THESE THINGS SO... UPSETTING!
FAREWELL...
DIANA--! DEFENSIVE STANCE!
W-WHAT CAN WE DO?
USE OUR WITS AND TRAINING! AIM KARATE BLOWS AT THE BIRDS' NECKS! STRIKE TO KILL!
I'LL DO MY BEST...
...BUT I HAVE A FEELING THAT MY BEST WON'T BE GOOD ENOUGH!
CHING TAUGHT ME WELL! OTHERWISE, I'D BE DEAD BY NOW!
STILL, THE HUMAN BODY IS CAPABLE OF ONLY SO MUCH...
... AND I'M REACHING MY LIMIT!
THERE ARE TOO MANY OF THE... THINGS!
4

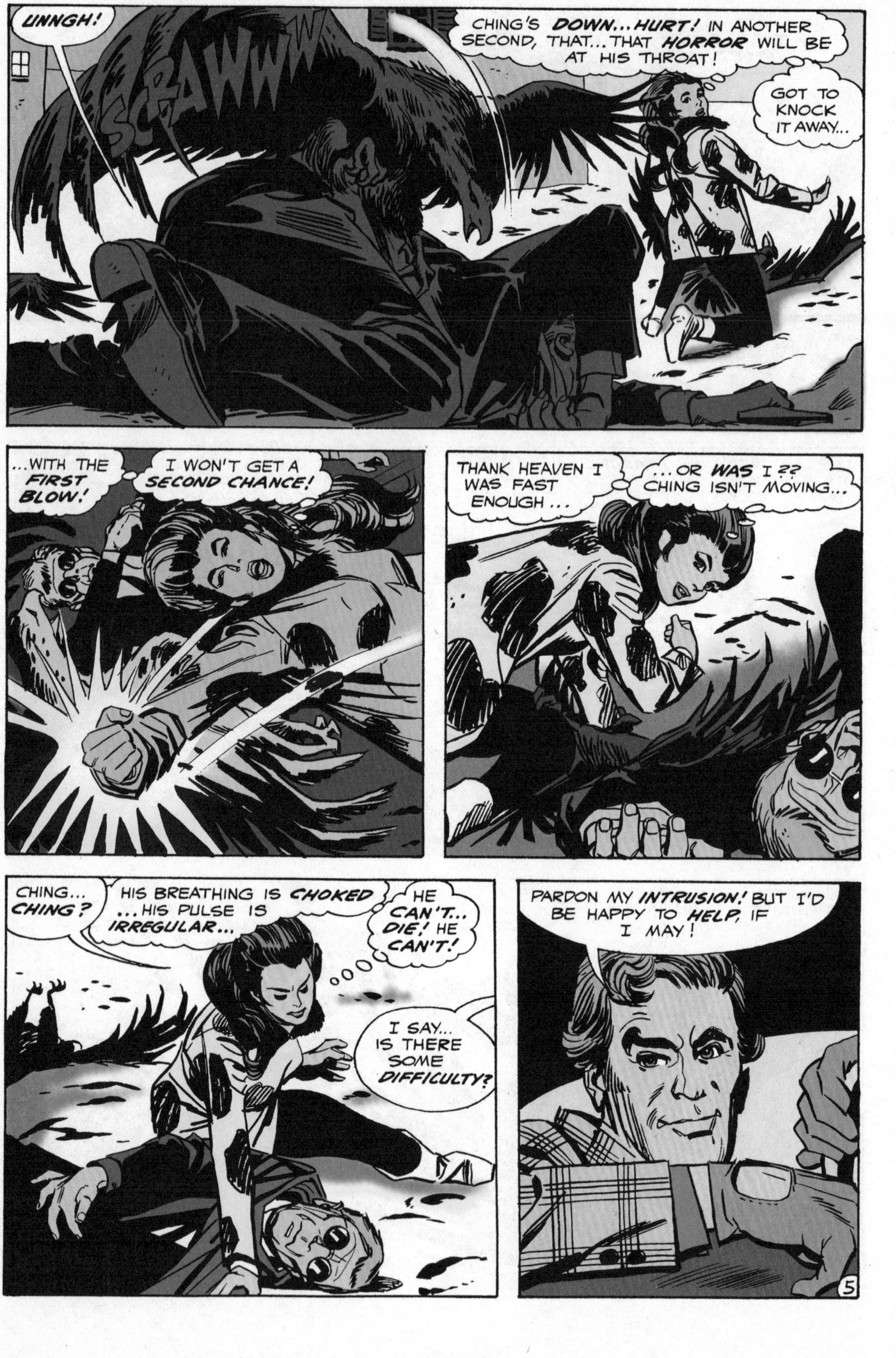
UNNGH!
SCRAWWW
CHING'S DOWN...HURT! IN ANOTHER SECOND, THAT...THAT HORROR WILL BE AT HIS THROAT!
GOT TO KNOCK IT AWAY...
...WITH THE FIRST BLOW!
I WON'T GET A SECOND CHANCE!
THANK HEAVEN I WAS FAST ENOUGH ...
...OR WAS I ??
CHING ISN'T MOVING...
CHING... CHING?
HIS BREATHING IS CHOKED ...HIS PULSE IS IRREGULAR...
HE CAN'T... DIE! HE CAN'T!
I SAY... IS THERE SOME DIFFICULTY?
PARDON MY INTRUSION! BUT I'D BE HAPPY TO HELP, IF I MAY!
5

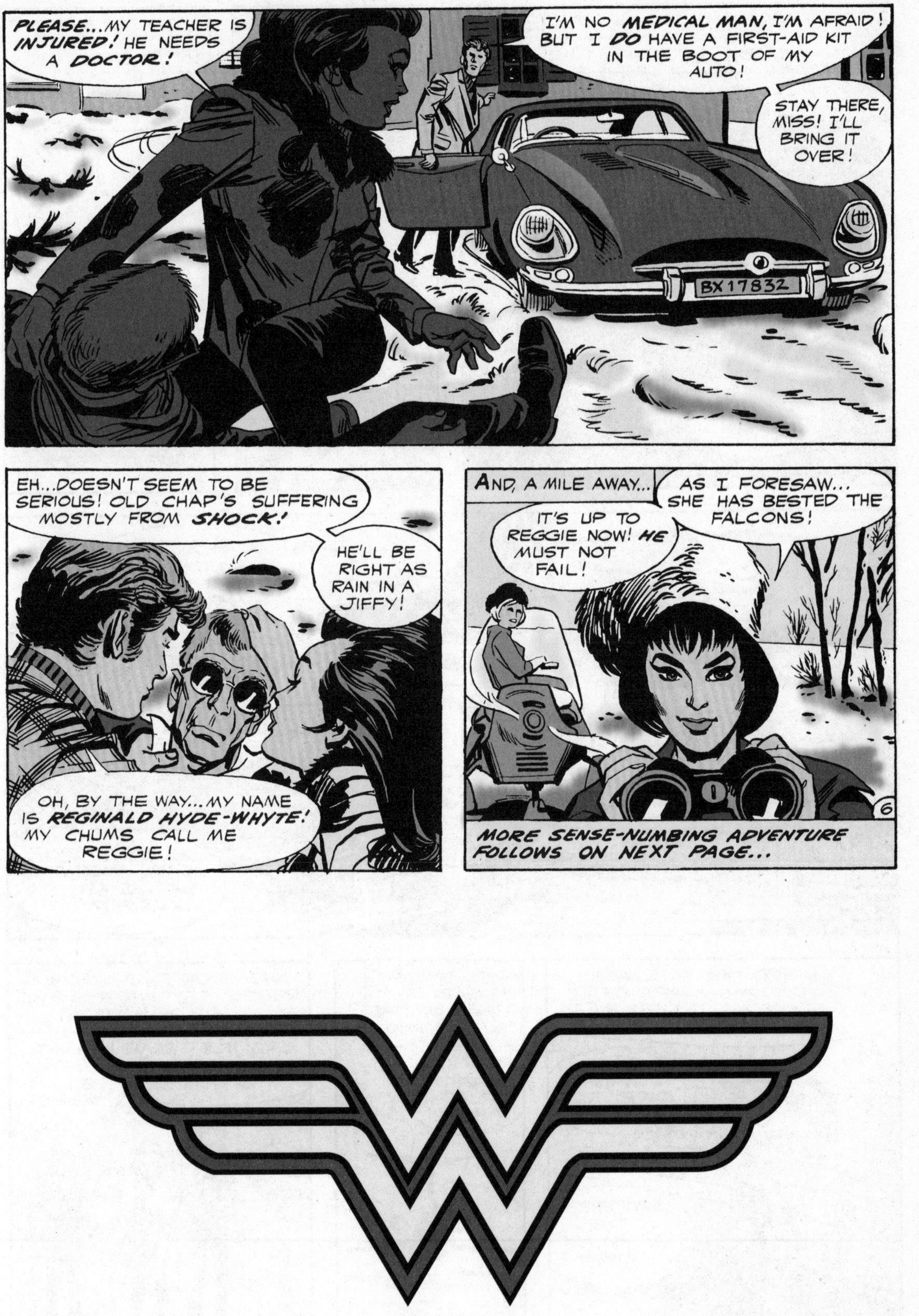
PLEASE...MY TEACHER IS INJURED! HE NEEDS A DOCTOR!
I'M NO MEDICAL MAN, I'M AFRAID! BUT I DO HAVE A FIRST-AID KIT IN THE BOOT OF MY AUTO!
STAY THERE, MISS! I'LL BRING IT OVER!
BX 17832
EH...DOESN'T SEEM TO BE SERIOUS! OLD CHAP'S SUFFERING MOSTLY FROM SHOCK!
HE'LL BE RIGHT AS RAIN IN A JIFFY!
OH, BY THE WAY...MY NAME IS REGINALD HYDE-WHYTE! MY CHUMS CALL ME REGGIE!
AND, A MILE AWAY...
AS I FORESAW... SHE HAS BESTED THE FALCONS!
IT'S UP TO REGGIE NOW! HE MUST NOT FAIL!
6
MORE SENSE-NUMBING ADVENTURE FOLLOWS ON NEXT PAGE...

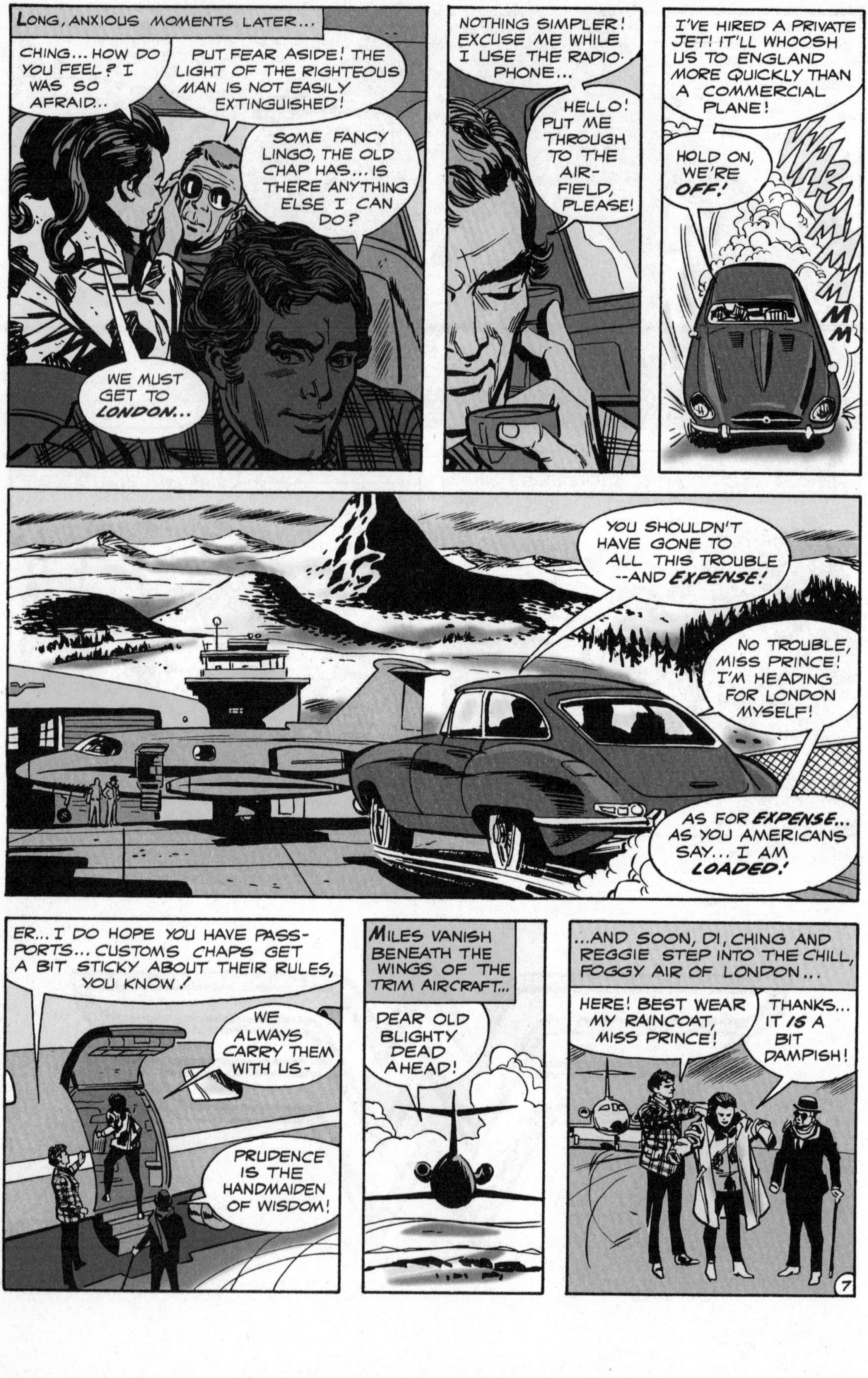
LONG, ANXIOUS MOMENTS LATER...
CHING... HOW DO YOU FEEL? I WAS SO AFRAID...
PUT FEAR ASIDE! THE LIGHT OF THE RIGHTEOUS MAN IS NOT EASILY EXTINGUISHED!
SOME FANCY LINGO, THE OLD CHAP HAS... IS THERE ANYTHING ELSE I CAN DO?
WE MUST GET TO LONDON...
NOTHING SIMPLER! EXCUSE ME WHILE I USE THE RADIO-PHONE...
HELLO! PUT ME THROUGH TO THE AIR-FIELD, PLEASE!
I'VE HIRED A PRIVATE JET! IT'LL WHOOSH US TO ENGLAND MORE QUICKLY THAN A COMMERCIAL PLANE!
HOLD ON, WE'RE OFF!
WHRUMMMMMMM
YOU SHOULDN'T HAVE GONE TO ALL THIS TROUBLE --AND EXPENSE!
NO TROUBLE, MISS PRINCE! I'M HEADING FOR LONDON MYSELF!
AS FOR EXPENSE... AS YOU AMERICANS SAY... I AM LOADED!
ER... I DO HOPE YOU HAVE PASS-PORTS... CUSTOMS CHAPS GET A BIT STICKY ABOUT THEIR RULES, YOU KNOW!
WE ALWAYS CARRY THEM WITH US-
PRUDENCE IS THE HANDMAIDEN OF WISDOM!
MILES VANISH BENEATH THE WINGS OF THE TRIM AIRCRAFT...
DEAR OLD BLIGHTY DEAD AHEAD!
...AND SOON, DI, CHING AND REGGIE STEP INTO THE CHILL, FOGGY AIR OF LONDON...
HERE! BEST WEAR MY RAINCOAT, MISS PRINCE!
THANKS... IT IS A BIT DAMPISH!
7

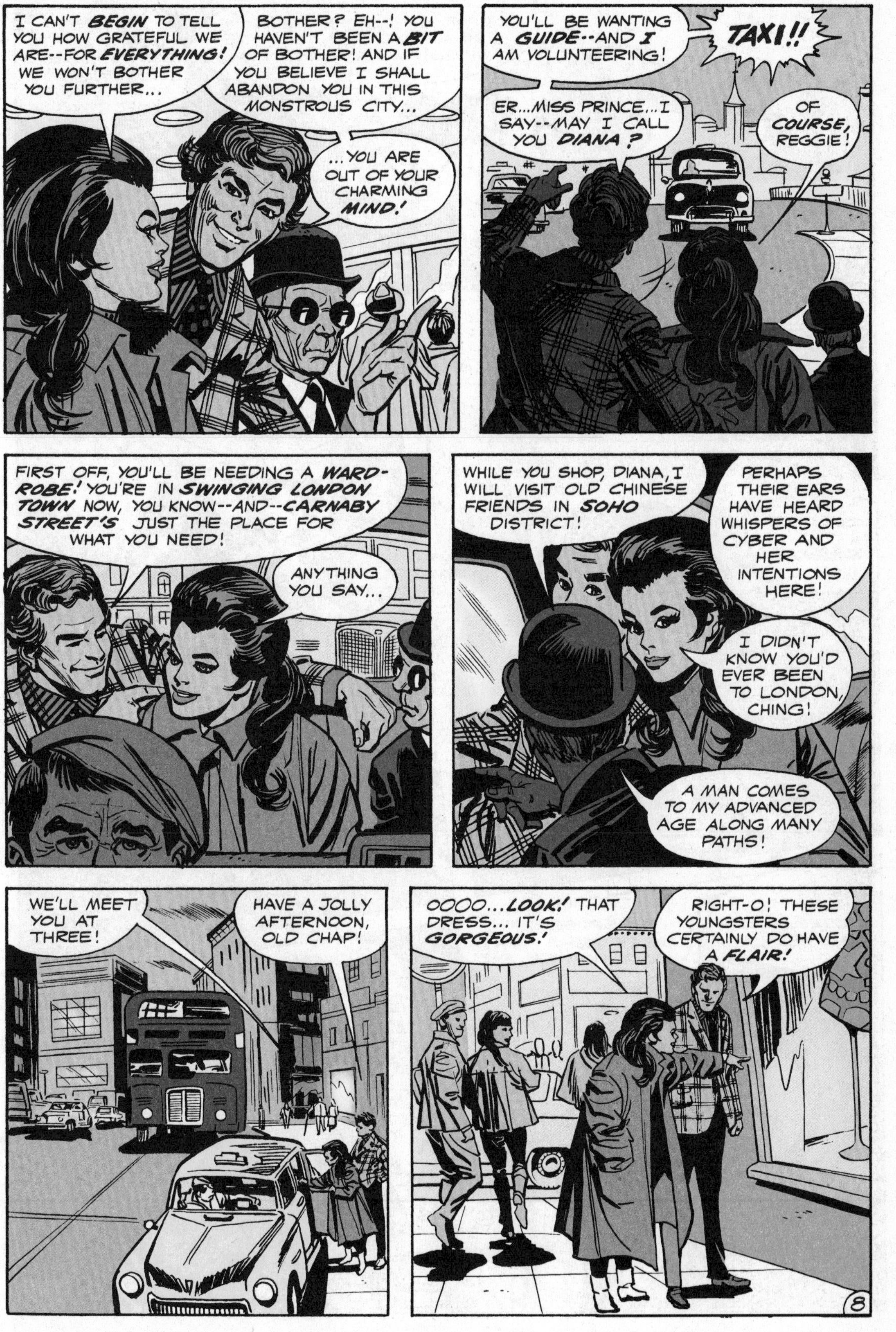
I CAN'T BEGIN TO TELL YOU HOW GRATEFUL WE ARE--FOR EVERYTHING! WE WON'T BOTHER YOU FURTHER...
BOTHER? EH--! YOU HAVEN'T BEEN A BIT OF BOTHER! AND IF YOU BELIEVE I SHALL ABANDON YOU IN THIS MONSTROUS CITY...
...YOU ARE OUT OF YOUR CHARMING MIND!
YOU'LL BE WANTING A GUIDE--AND I AM VOLUNTEERING!
TAXI!!
ER...MISS PRINCE...I SAY--MAY I CALL YOU DIANA?
OF COURSE, REGGIE!
FIRST OFF, YOU'LL BE NEEDING A WARD-ROBE! YOU'RE IN SWINGING LONDON TOWN NOW, YOU KNOW--AND--CARNABY STREET'S JUST THE PLACE FOR WHAT YOU NEED!
ANYTHING YOU SAY...
WHILE YOU SHOP, DIANA, I WILL VISIT OLD CHINESE FRIENDS IN SOHO DISTRICT!
PERHAPS THEIR EARS HAVE HEARD WHISPERS OF CYBER AND HER INTENTIONS HERE!
I DIDN'T KNOW YOU'D EVER BEEN TO LONDON, CHING!
A MAN COMES TO MY ADVANCED AGE ALONG MANY PATHS!
WE'LL MEET YOU AT THREE!
HAVE A JOLLY AFTERNOON, OLD CHAP!
OOOO...LOOK! THAT DRESS... IT'S GORGEOUS!
RIGHT-O! THESE YOUNGSTERS CERTAINLY DO HAVE A FLAIR!
8

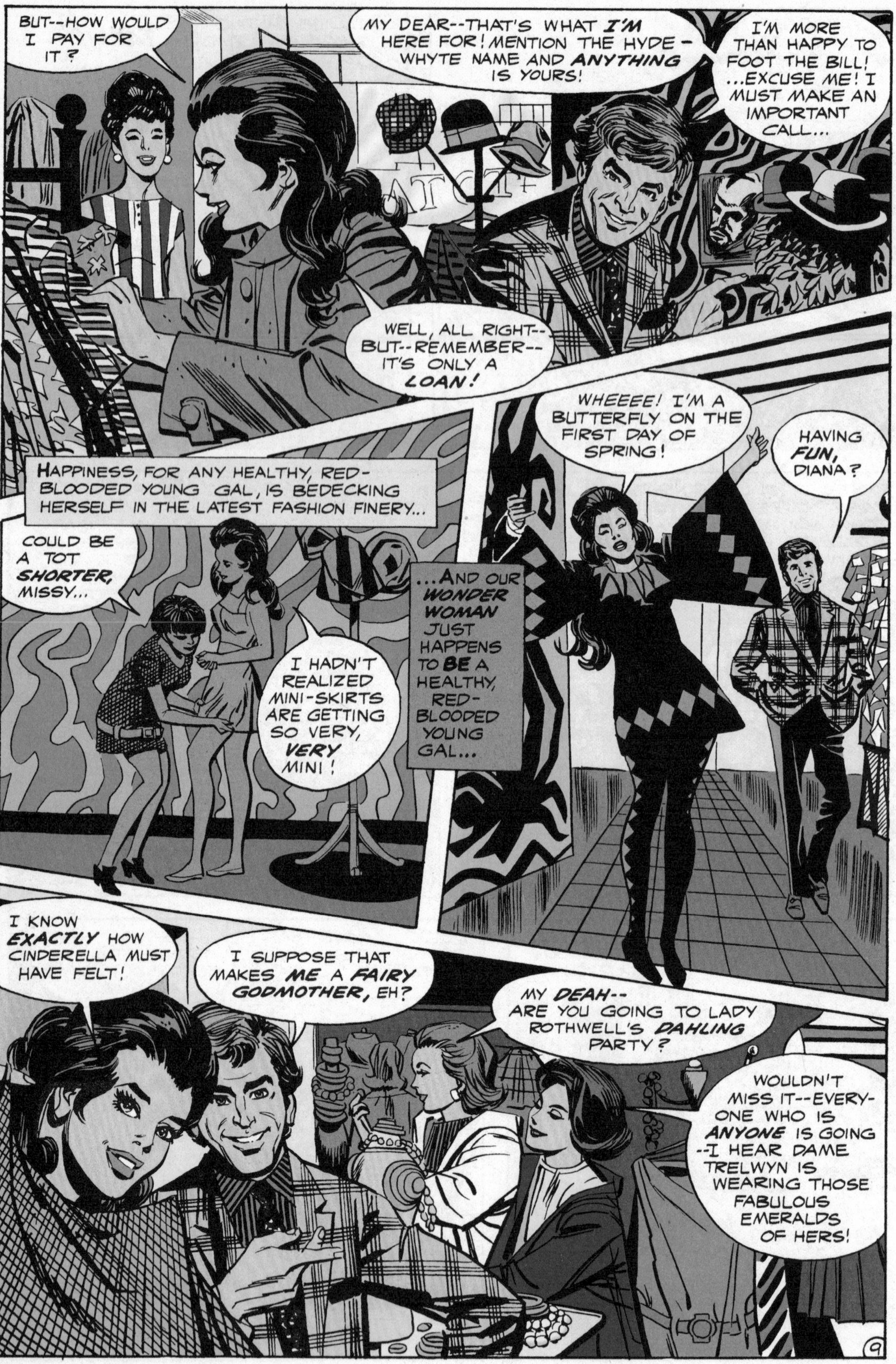
BUT--HOW WOULD I PAY FOR IT?
MY DEAR--THAT'S WHAT I'M HERE FOR! MENTION THE HYDE-WHYTE NAME AND ANYTHING IS YOURS!
I'M MORE THAN HAPPY TO FOOT THE BILL! ...EXCUSE ME! I MUST MAKE AN IMPORTANT CALL...
WELL, ALL RIGHT--BUT--REMEMBER--IT'S ONLY A LOAN!
HAPPINESS, FOR ANY HEALTHY, RED-BLOODED YOUNG GAL, IS BEDECKING HERSELF IN THE LATEST FASHION FINERY...
COULD BE A TOT SHORTER, MISSY...
I HADN'T REALIZED MINI-SKIRTS ARE GETTING SO VERY, VERY MINI!
...AND OUR WONDER WOMAN JUST HAPPENS TO BE A HEALTHY, RED-BLOODED YOUNG GAL...
WHEEEE! I'M A BUTTERFLY ON THE FIRST DAY OF SPRING!
HAVING FUN, DIANA?
I KNOW EXACTLY HOW CINDERELLA MUST HAVE FELT!
I SUPPOSE THAT MAKES ME A FAIRY GODMOTHER, EH?
MY DEAH--ARE YOU GOING TO LADY ROTHWELL'S DAHLING PARTY?
WOULDN'T MISS IT--EVERYONE WHO IS ANYONE IS GOING--I HEAR DAME TRELWYN IS WEARING THOSE FABULOUS EMERALDS OF HERS!
9

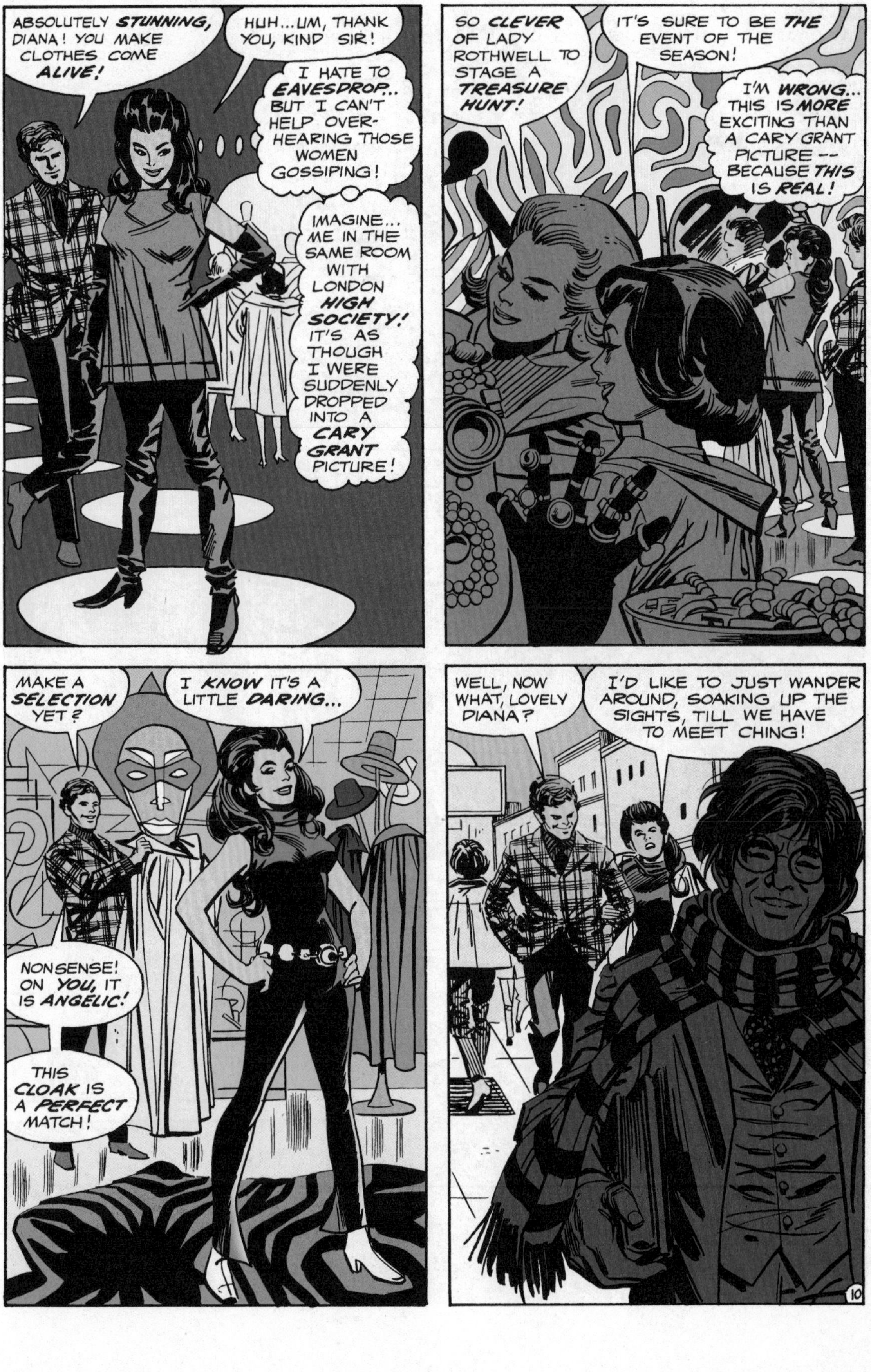
ABSOLUTELY STUNNING, DIANA! YOU MAKE CLOTHES COME ALIVE!
HUH...UM, THANK YOU, KIND SIR!
I HATE TO EAVESDROP... BUT I CAN'T HELP OVER-HEARING THOSE WOMEN GOSSIPING!
IMAGINE... ME IN THE SAME ROOM WITH LONDON HIGH SOCIETY! IT'S AS THOUGH I WERE SUDDENLY DROPPED INTO A CARY GRANT PICTURE!
SO CLEVER OF LADY ROTHWELL TO STAGE A TREASURE HUNT!
IT'S SURE TO BE THE EVENT OF THE SEASON!
I'M WRONG... THIS IS MORE EXCITING THAN A CARY GRANT PICTURE -- BECAUSE THIS IS REAL!
MAKE A SELECTION YET?
I KNOW IT'S A LITTLE DARING...
NONSENSE! ON YOU, IT IS ANGELIC!
THIS CLOAK IS A PERFECT MATCH!
WELL, NOW WHAT, LOVELY DIANA?
I'D LIKE TO JUST WANDER AROUND, SOAKING UP THE SIGHTS, TILL WE HAVE TO MEET CHING!
10

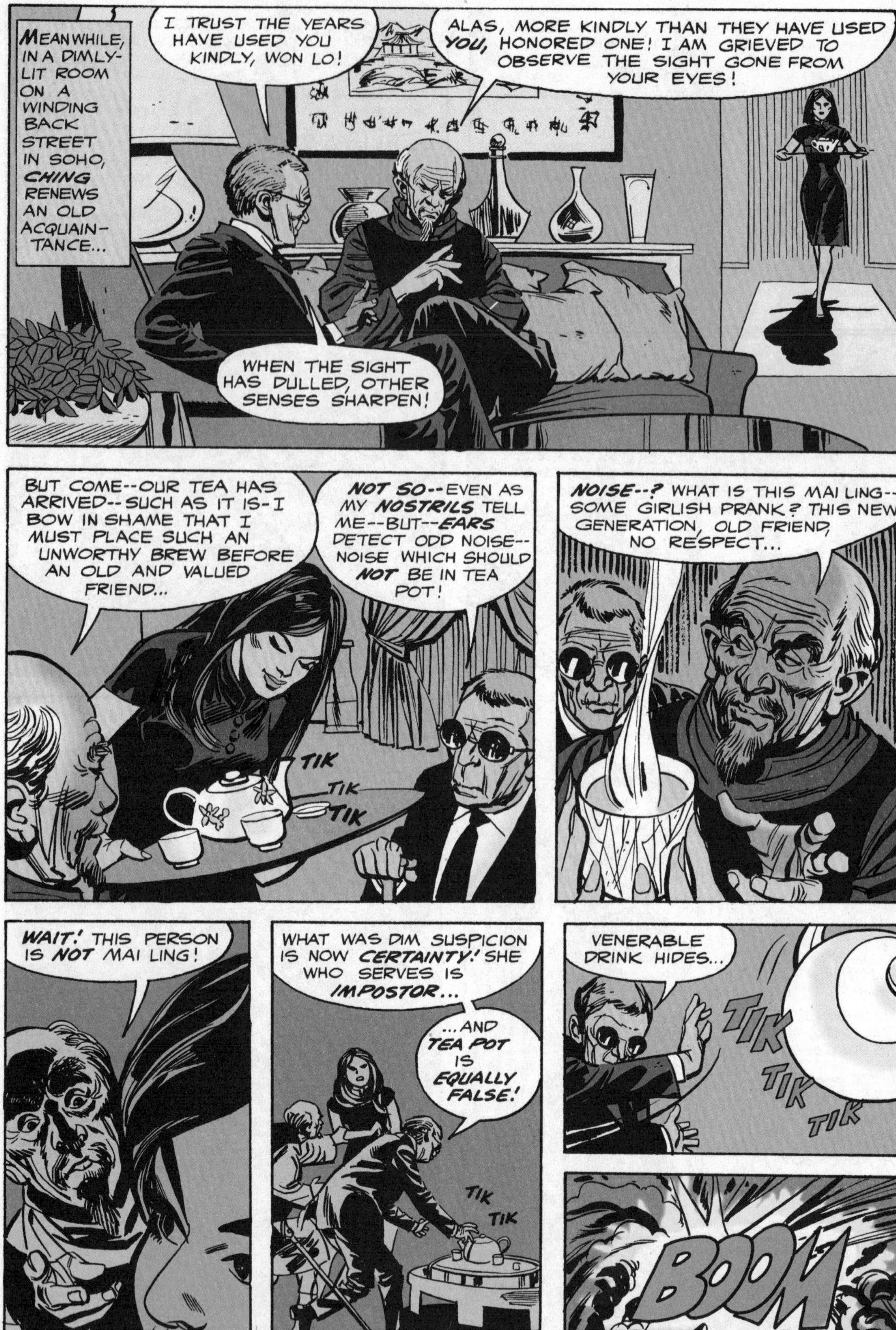
MEANWHILE, IN A DIMLY-LIT ROOM ON A WINDING BACK STREET IN SOHO, CHING RENEWS AN OLD ACQUAINTANCE...
I TRUST THE YEARS HAVE USED YOU KINDLY, WON LO!
ALAS, MORE KINDLY THAN THEY HAVE USED YOU, HONORED ONE! I AM GRIEVED TO OBSERVE THE SIGHT GONE FROM YOUR EYES!
WHEN THE SIGHT HAS DULLED, OTHER SENSES SHARPEN!
BUT COME--OUR TEA HAS ARRIVED--SUCH AS IT IS--I BOW IN SHAME THAT I MUST PLACE SUCH AN UNWORTHY BREW BEFORE AN OLD AND VALUED FRIEND...
NOT SO--EVEN AS MY NOSTRILS TELL ME--BUT--EARS DETECT ODD NOISE--NOISE WHICH SHOULD NOT BE IN TEA POT!
TIK
TIK
TIK
NOISE--? WHAT IS THIS MAI LING--SOME GIRLISH PRANK? THIS NEW GENERATION, OLD FRIEND, NO RESPECT...
WAIT! THIS PERSON IS NOT MAI LING!
WHAT WAS DIM SUSPICION IS NOW CERTAINTY! SHE WHO SERVES IS IMPOSTOR...
...AND TEA POT IS EQUALLY FALSE!
TIK
TIK
VENERABLE DRINK HIDES...
TIK
TIK
TIK
BOOM
11

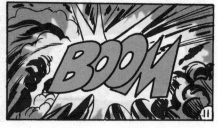

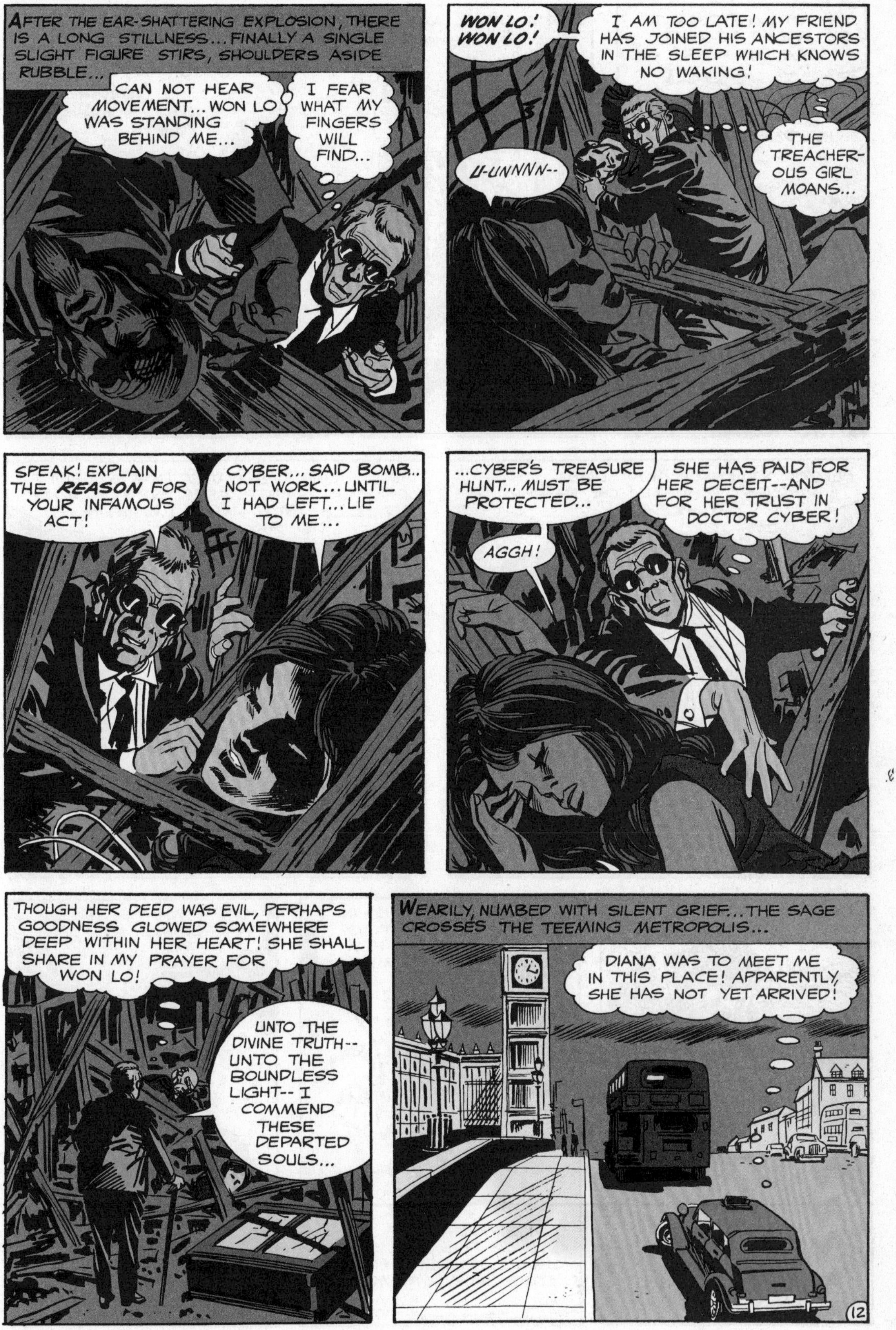
AFTER THE EAR-SHATTERING EXPLOSION, THERE IS A LONG STILLNESS... FINALLY A SINGLE SLIGHT FIGURE STIRS, SHOULDERS ASIDE RUBBLE...
CAN NOT HEAR MOVEMENT... WON LO WAS STANDING BEHIND ME...
I FEAR WHAT MY FINGERS WILL FIND...
WON LO! WON LO!
I AM TOO LATE! MY FRIEND HAS JOINED HIS ANCESTORS IN THE SLEEP WHICH KNOWS NO WAKING!
U-UNNNN--
THE TREACHEROUS GIRL MOANS...
SPEAK! EXPLAIN THE REASON FOR YOUR INFAMOUS ACT!
CYBER... SAID BOMB... NOT WORK... UNTIL I HAD LEFT... LIE TO ME...
...CYBER'S TREASURE HUNT... MUST BE PROTECTED...
AGGH!
SHE HAS PAID FOR HER DECEIT--AND FOR HER TRUST IN DOCTOR CYBER!
THOUGH HER DEED WAS EVIL, PERHAPS GOODNESS GLOWED SOMEWHERE DEEP WITHIN HER HEART! SHE SHALL SHARE IN MY PRAYER FOR WON LO!
UNTO THE DIVINE TRUTH-- UNTO THE BOUNDLESS LIGHT-- I COMMEND THESE DEPARTED SOULS...
WEARILY, NUMBED WITH SILENT GRIEF... THE SAGE CROSSES THE TEEMING METROPOLIS...
DIANA WAS TO MEET ME IN THIS PLACE! APPARENTLY, SHE HAS NOT YET ARRIVED!
12

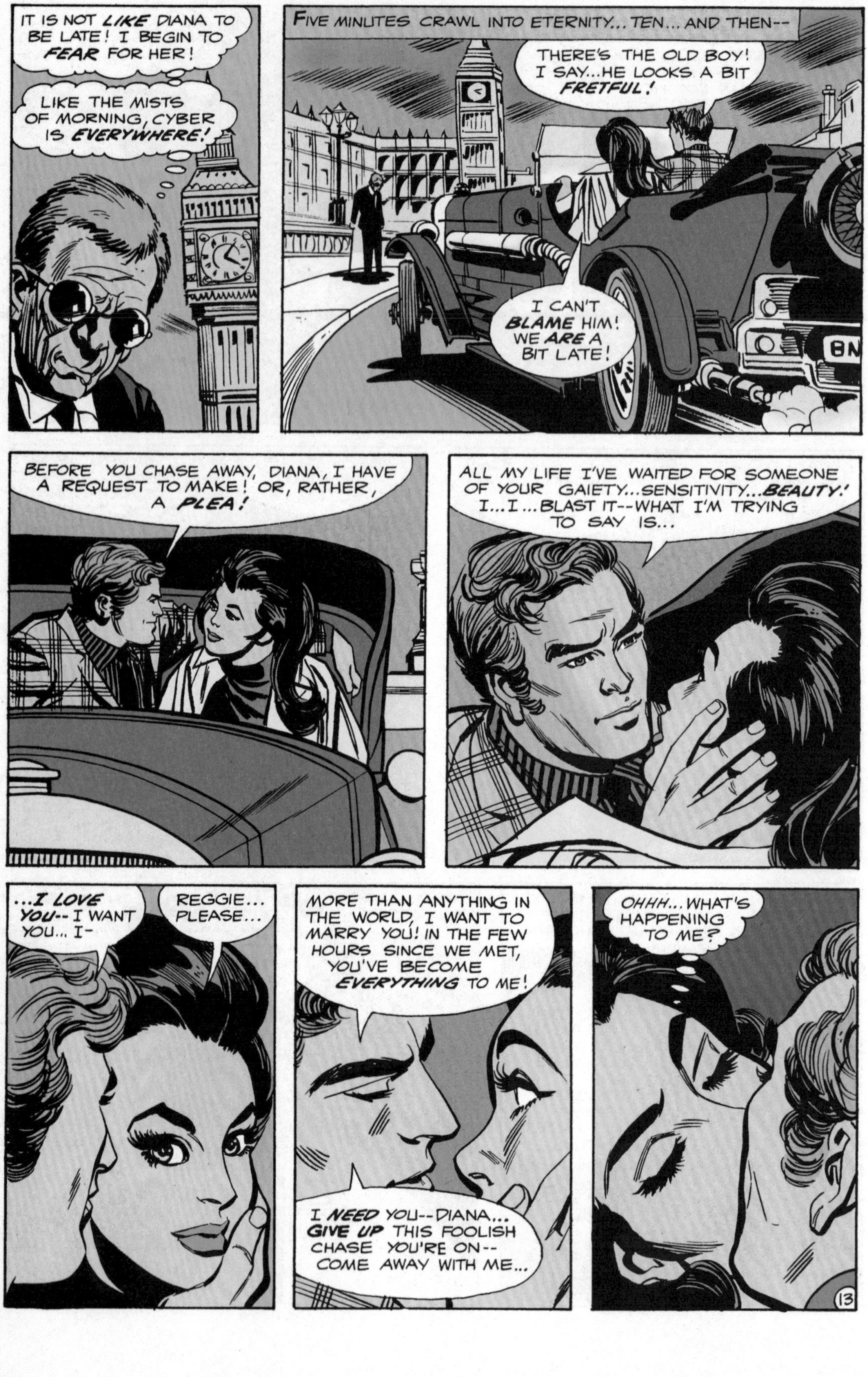
IT IS NOT LIKE DIANA TO BE LATE! I BEGIN TO FEAR FOR HER!
LIKE THE MISTS OF MORNING, CYBER IS EVERYWHERE!
FIVE MINUTES CRAWL INTO ETERNITY... TEN... AND THEN--
THERE'S THE OLD BOY! I SAY...HE LOOKS A BIT FRETFUL!
I CAN'T BLAME HIM! WE ARE A BIT LATE!
BEFORE YOU CHASE AWAY, DIANA, I HAVE A REQUEST TO MAKE! OR, RATHER, A PLEA!
ALL MY LIFE I'VE WAITED FOR SOMEONE OF YOUR GAIETY...SENSITIVITY...BEAUTY! I...I...BLAST IT--WHAT I'M TRYING TO SAY IS...
...I LOVE YOU-- I WANT YOU... I-
REGGIE... PLEASE...
MORE THAN ANYTHING IN THE WORLD, I WANT TO MARRY YOU! IN THE FEW HOURS SINCE WE MET, YOU'VE BECOME EVERYTHING TO ME!
I NEED YOU--DIANA... GIVE UP THIS FOOLISH CHASE YOU'RE ON-- COME AWAY WITH ME...
OHHH... WHAT'S HAPPENING TO ME?
13

I'VE NEVER FELT THIS WAY BEFORE-- BUT... I HARDLY KNOW HIM...I...I...
AHEM!
CHING...I...I FORGOT CHING!
I APOLOGIZE TO YOU BOTH! REGGIE...CHING-- YOU MUST THINK I'M--I'M--
I COULD NEVER THINK ILL OF YOU, DIANA...
THE HEART-- TOO OFTEN-- RULES THE MIND...
AS AN AMAZON PRINCESS-- AS WONDER WOMAN-- I HAD PERFECT CONTROL OF MY EMOTIONS! AS PLAIN DIANA PRINCE, I'M HUMAN --TOO DARN HUMAN!
LEST THIS TIME FOR LOVE CHANGES TO A TIME TO DIE, WE MUST PERFORM A TASK...
A TASK THAT BEGINS AT A TREASURE HUNT!
14
THE HUNT STARTS ON THE PAGE FOLLOWING!

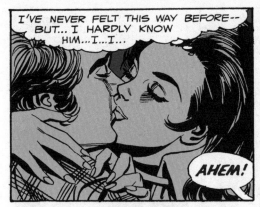

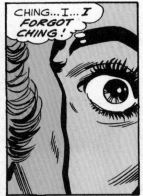

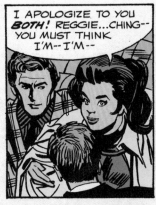

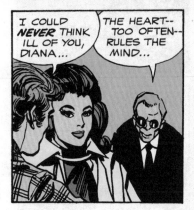

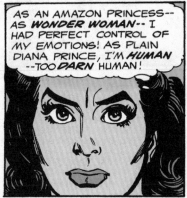

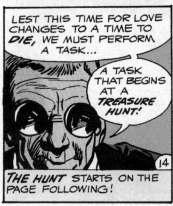

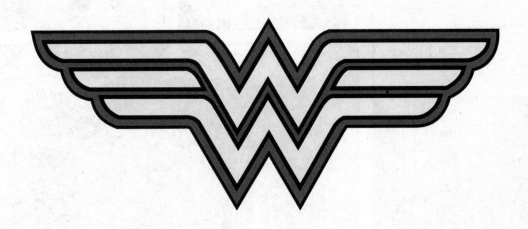

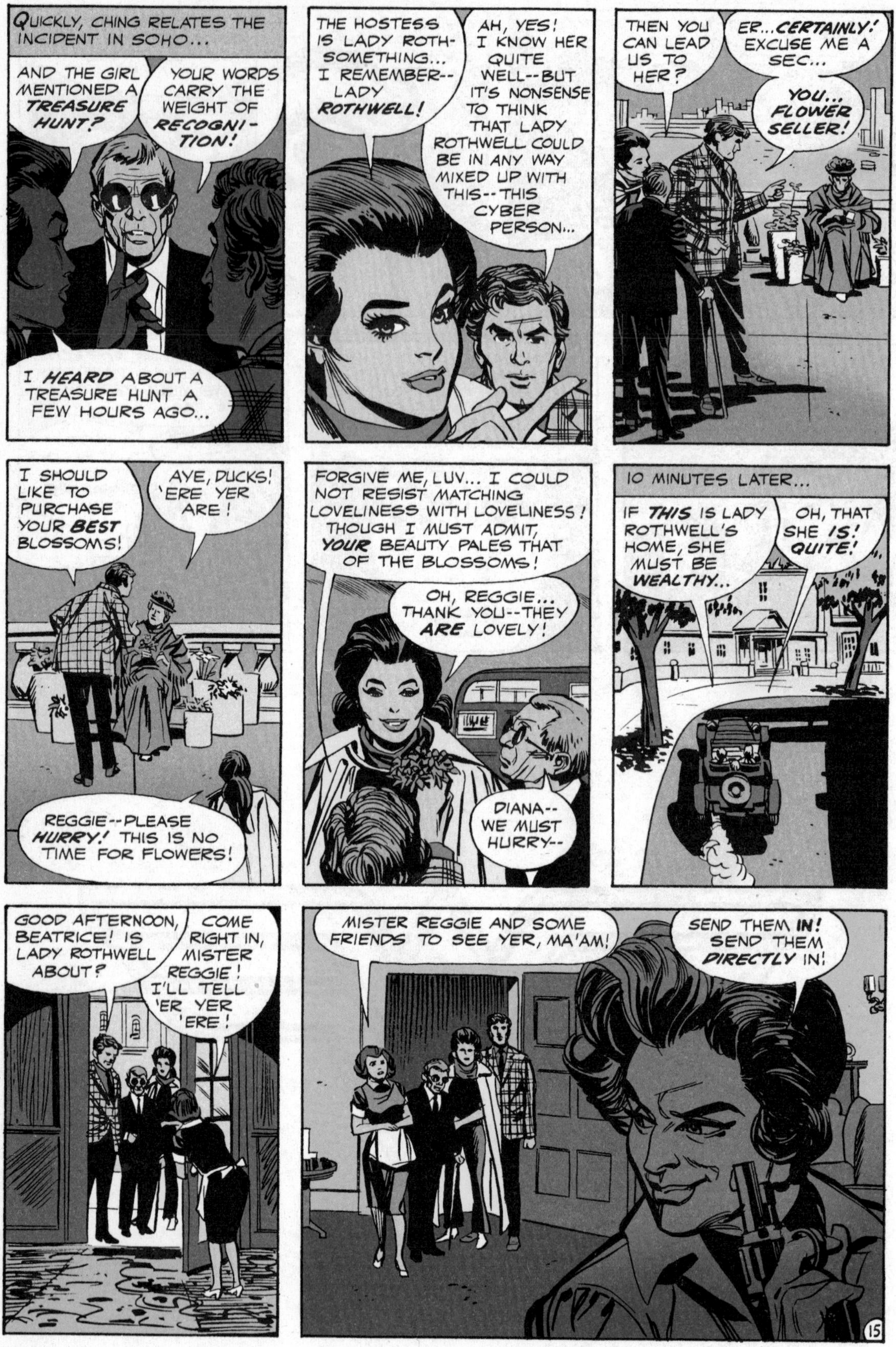
QUICKLY, CHING RELATES THE INCIDENT IN SOHO...
AND THE GIRL MENTIONED A TREASURE HUNT?
YOUR WORDS CARRY THE WEIGHT OF RECOGNITION!
I HEARD ABOUT A TREASURE HUNT A FEW HOURS AGO...
THE HOSTESS IS LADY ROTH-SOMETHING... I REMEMBER-- LADY ROTHWELL!
AH, YES! I KNOW HER QUITE WELL--BUT IT'S NONSENSE TO THINK THAT LADY ROTHWELL COULD BE IN ANY WAY MIXED UP WITH THIS--THIS CYBER PERSON...
THEN YOU CAN LEAD US TO HER?
ER...CERTAINLY! EXCUSE ME A SEC...
YOU... FLOWER SELLER!
I SHOULD LIKE TO PURCHASE YOUR BEST BLOSSOMS!
AYE, DUCKS! 'ERE YER ARE!
REGGIE--PLEASE HURRY! THIS IS NO TIME FOR FLOWERS!
FORGIVE ME, LUV... I COULD NOT RESIST MATCHING LOVELINESS WITH LOVELINESS! THOUGH I MUST ADMIT, YOUR BEAUTY PALES THAT OF THE BLOSSOMS!
OH, REGGIE... THANK YOU--THEY ARE LOVELY!
DIANA-- WE MUST HURRY--
10 MINUTES LATER...
IF THIS IS LADY ROTHWELL'S HOME, SHE MUST BE WEALTHY...
OH, THAT SHE IS! QUITE!
GOOD AFTERNOON, BEATRICE! IS LADY ROTHWELL ABOUT?
COME RIGHT IN, MISTER REGGIE! I'LL TELL 'ER YER 'ERE!
MISTER REGGIE AND SOME FRIENDS TO SEE YER, MA'AM!
SEND THEM IN! SEND THEM DIRECTLY IN!
15

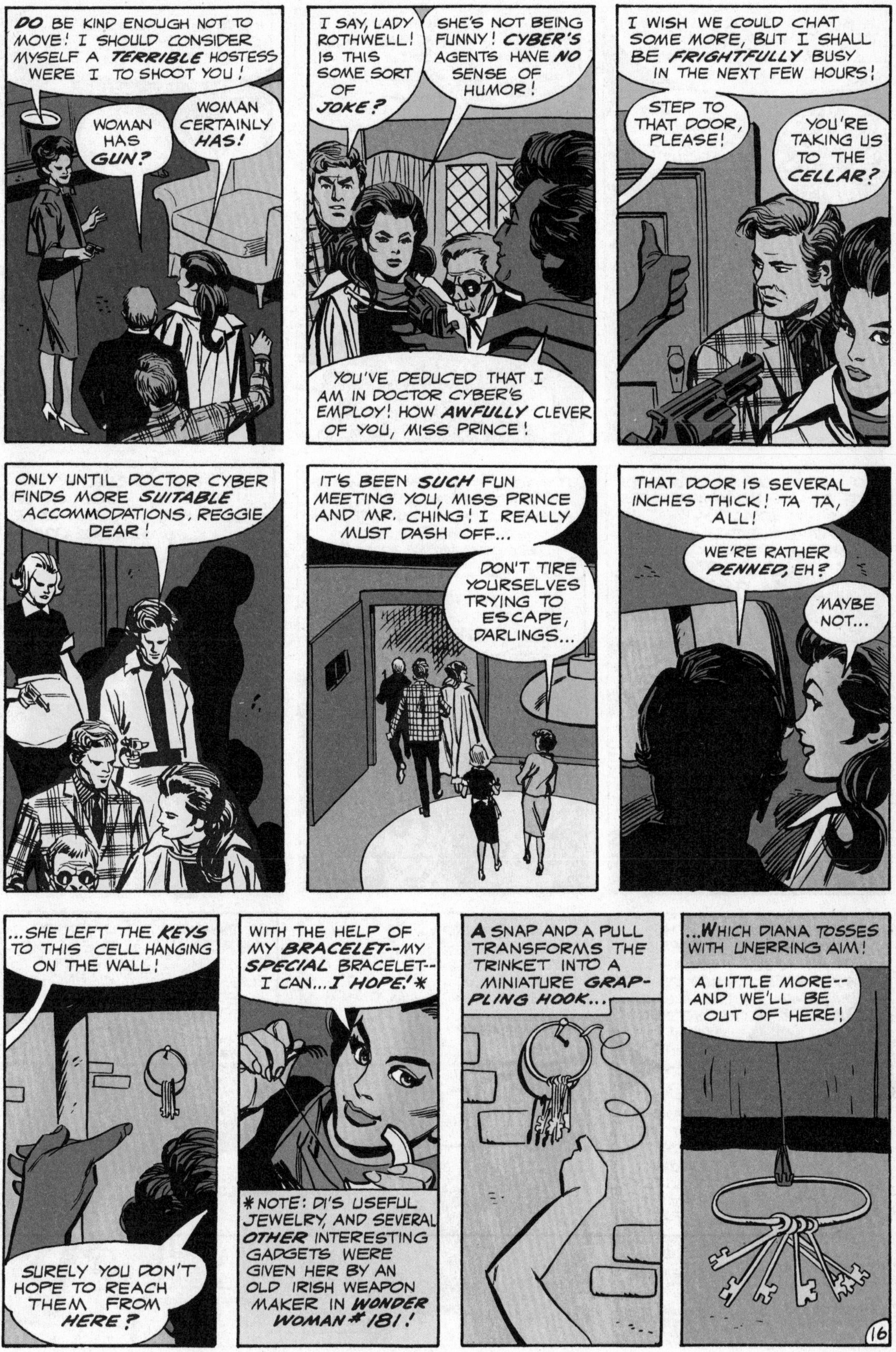
DO BE KIND ENOUGH NOT TO MOVE! I SHOULD CONSIDER MYSELF A TERRIBLE HOSTESS WERE I TO SHOOT YOU!
WOMAN HAS GUN?
WOMAN CERTAINLY HAS!
I SAY, LADY ROTHWELL! IS THIS SOME SORT OF JOKE?
SHE'S NOT BEING FUNNY! CYBER'S AGENTS HAVE NO SENSE OF HUMOR!
YOU'VE DEDUCED THAT I AM IN DOCTOR CYBER'S EMPLOY! HOW AWFULLY CLEVER OF YOU, MISS PRINCE!
I WISH WE COULD CHAT SOME MORE, BUT I SHALL BE FRIGHTFULLY BUSY IN THE NEXT FEW HOURS!
STEP TO THAT DOOR, PLEASE!
YOU'RE TAKING US TO THE CELLAR?
ONLY UNTIL DOCTOR CYBER FINDS MORE SUITABLE ACCOMMODATIONS, REGGIE DEAR!
IT'S BEEN SUCH FUN MEETING YOU, MISS PRINCE AND MR. CHING! I REALLY MUST DASH OFF...
DON'T TIRE YOURSELVES TRYING TO ESCAPE, DARLINGS...
THAT DOOR IS SEVERAL INCHES THICK! TA TA, ALL!
WE'RE RATHER PENNED, EH?
MAYBE NOT...
...SHE LEFT THE KEYS TO THIS CELL HANGING ON THE WALL!
SURELY YOU DON'T HOPE TO REACH THEM FROM HERE?
WITH THE HELP OF MY BRACELET--MY SPECIAL BRACELET--I CAN... I HOPE! *
* NOTE: DI'S USEFUL JEWELRY, AND SEVERAL OTHER INTERESTING GADGETS WERE GIVEN HER BY AN OLD IRISH WEAPON MAKER IN WONDER WOMAN #181!
A SNAP AND A PULL TRANSFORMS THE TRINKET INTO A MINIATURE GRAPPLING HOOK...
...WHICH DIANA TOSSES WITH UNERRING AIM!
A LITTLE MORE--AND WE'LL BE OUT OF HERE!
16

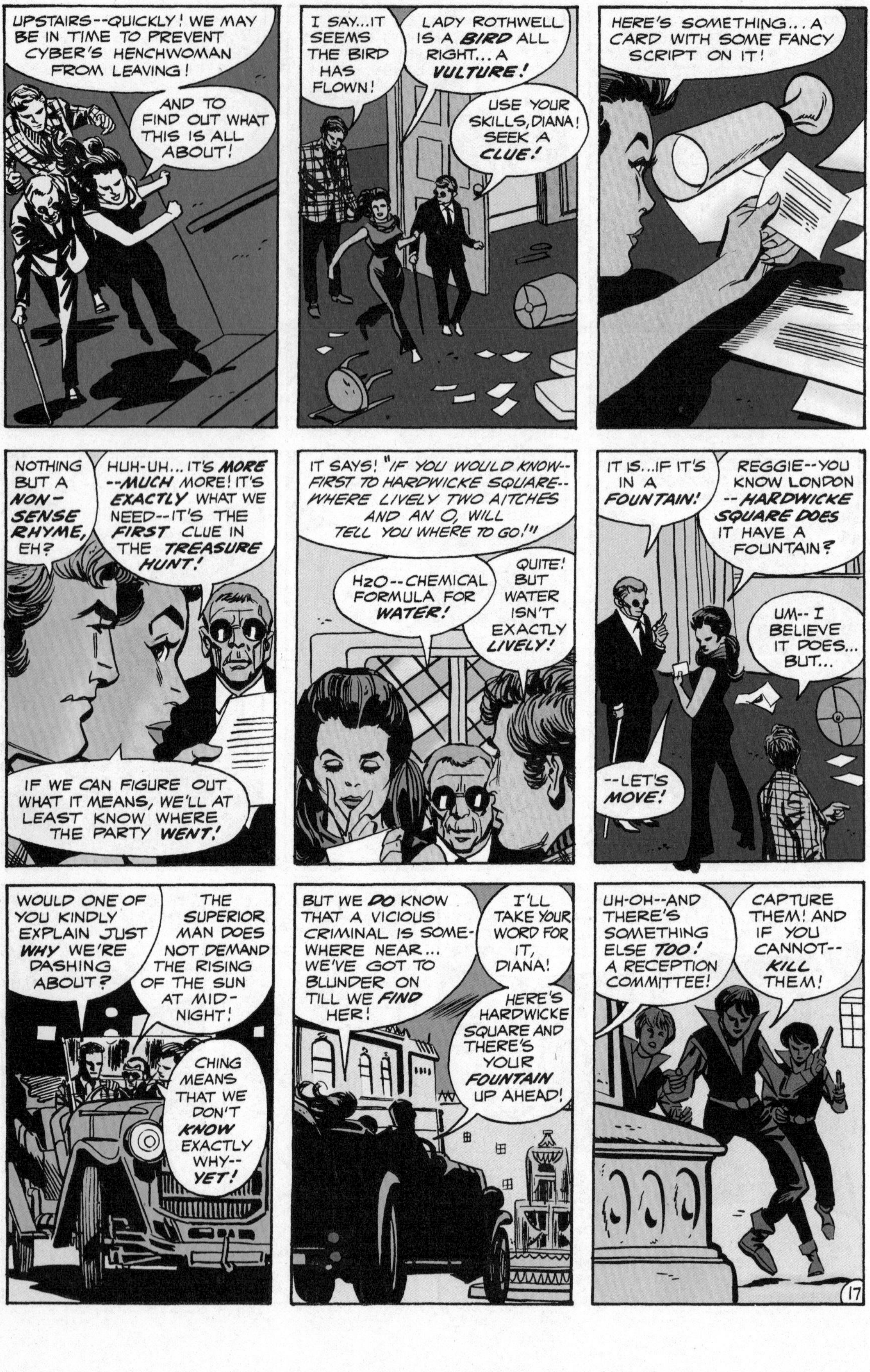
UPSTAIRS--QUICKLY! WE MAY BE IN TIME TO PREVENT CYBER'S HENCHWOMAN FROM LEAVING!
AND TO FIND OUT WHAT THIS IS ALL ABOUT!
I SAY...IT SEEMS THE BIRD HAS FLOWN!
LADY ROTHWELL IS A BIRD ALL RIGHT... A VULTURE!
USE YOUR SKILLS, DIANA! SEEK A CLUE!
HERE'S SOMETHING... A CARD WITH SOME FANCY SCRIPT ON IT!
NOTHING BUT A NON-SENSE RHYME, EH?
HUH-UH... IT'S MORE --MUCH MORE! IT'S EXACTLY WHAT WE NEED--IT'S THE FIRST CLUE IN THE TREASURE HUNT!
IF WE CAN FIGURE OUT WHAT IT MEANS, WE'LL AT LEAST KNOW WHERE THE PARTY WENT!
IT SAYS! "IF YOU WOULD KNOW--FIRST TO HARDWICKE SQUARE--WHERE LIVELY TWO AITCHES AND AN O, WILL TELL YOU WHERE TO GO!"
H2O--CHEMICAL FORMULA FOR WATER!
QUITE! BUT WATER ISN'T EXACTLY LIVELY!
IT IS...IF IT'S IN A FOUNTAIN!
REGGIE--YOU KNOW LONDON --HARDWICKE SQUARE DOES IT HAVE A FOUNTAIN?
UM-- I BELIEVE IT DOES... BUT...
--LET'S MOVE!
WOULD ONE OF YOU KINDLY EXPLAIN JUST WHY WE'RE DASHING ABOUT?
THE SUPERIOR MAN DOES NOT DEMAND THE RISING OF THE SUN AT MID-NIGHT!
CHING MEANS THAT WE DON'T KNOW EXACTLY WHY--YET!
BUT WE DO KNOW THAT A VICIOUS CRIMINAL IS SOME-WHERE NEAR... WE'VE GOT TO BLUNDER ON TILL WE FIND HER!
I'LL TAKE YOUR WORD FOR IT, DIANA!
HERE'S HARDWICKE SQUARE AND THERE'S YOUR FOUNTAIN UP AHEAD!
UH-OH--AND THERE'S SOMETHING ELSE TOO! A RECEPTION COMMITTEE!
CAPTURE THEM! AND IF YOU CANNOT-- KILL THEM!
17

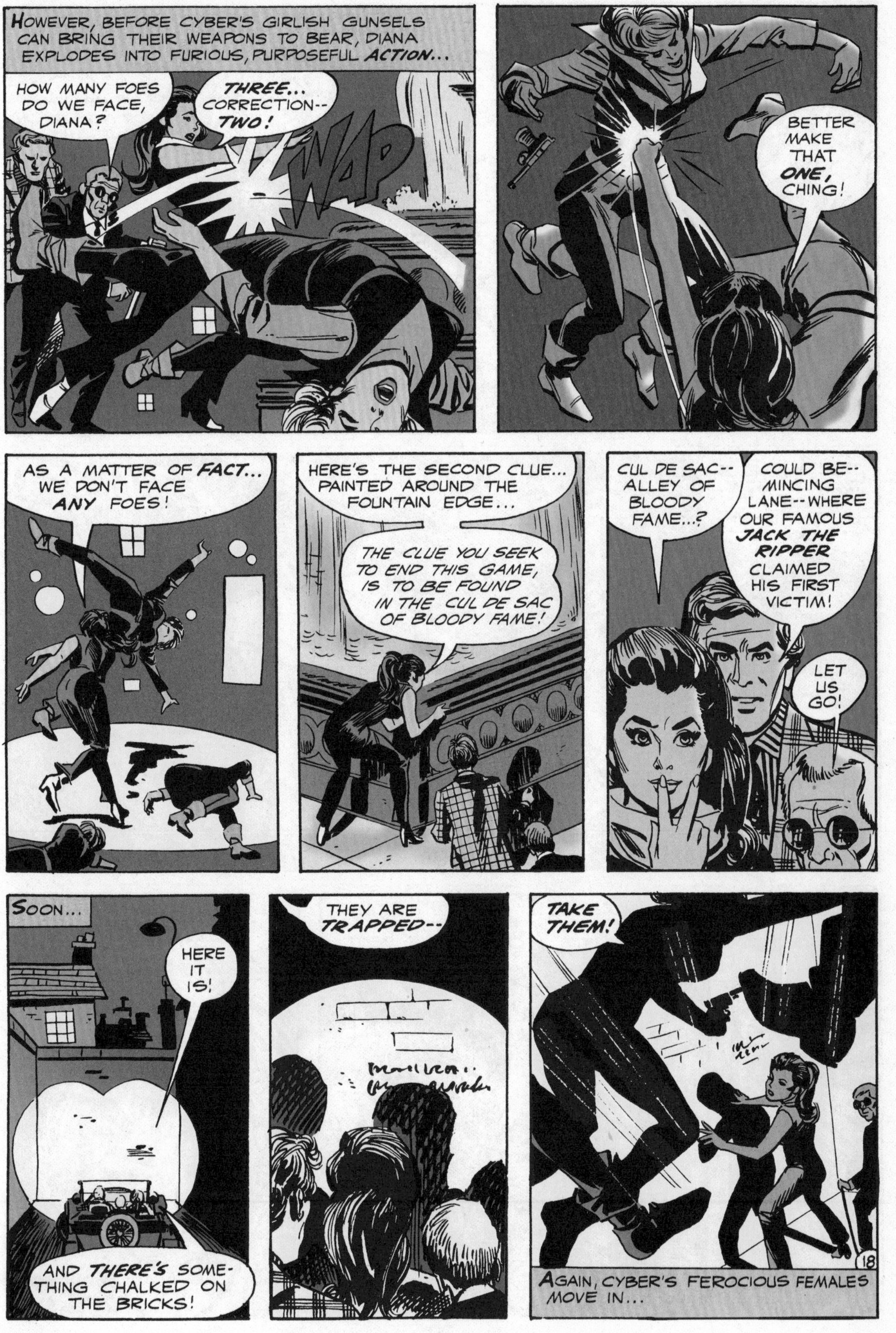
HOWEVER, BEFORE CYBER'S GIRLISH GUNSELS CAN BRING THEIR WEAPONS TO BEAR, DIANA EXPLODES INTO FURIOUS, PURPOSEFUL ACTION...
HOW MANY FOES DO WE FACE, DIANA?
THREE... CORRECTION-- TWO!
WAP
BETTER MAKE THAT ONE, CHING!
AS A MATTER OF FACT... WE DON'T FACE ANY FOES!
HERE'S THE SECOND CLUE... PAINTED AROUND THE FOUNTAIN EDGE...
THE CLUE YOU SEEK TO END THIS GAME, IS TO BE FOUND IN THE CUL DE SAC OF BLOODY FAME!
CUL DE SAC-- ALLEY OF BLOODY FAME...?
COULD BE-- MINCING LANE--WHERE OUR FAMOUS JACK THE RIPPER CLAIMED HIS FIRST VICTIM!
LET US GO!
SOON...
HERE IT IS!
AND THERE'S SOME-THING CHALKED ON THE BRICKS!
THEY ARE TRAPPED--
TAKE THEM!
18
AGAIN, CYBER'S FEROCIOUS FEMALES MOVE IN...

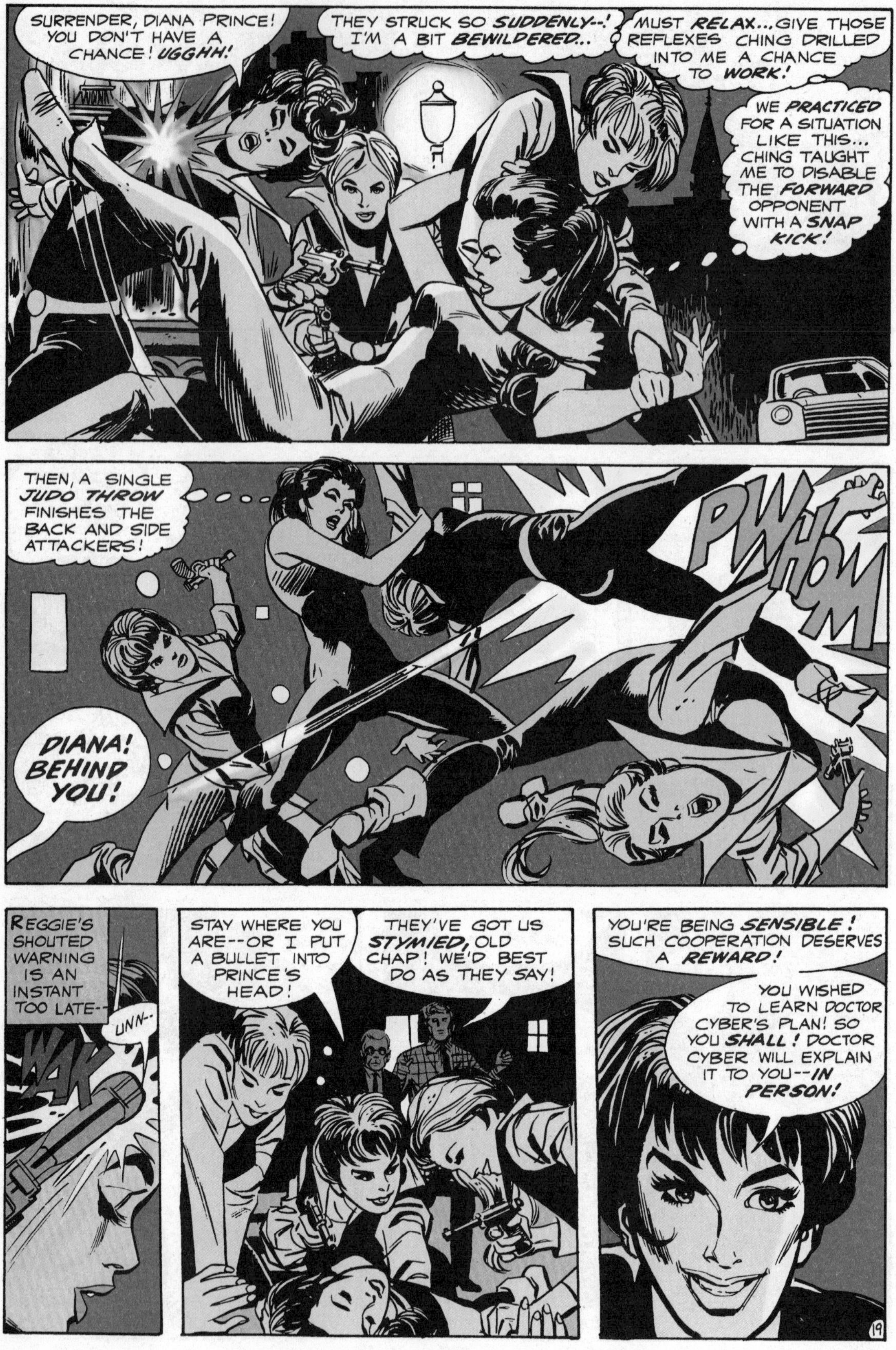

SURRENDER, DIANA PRINCE! YOU DON'T HAVE A CHANCE! UGGHH!
THEY STRUCK SO SUDDENLY--! I'M A BIT BEWILDERED..
MUST RELAX...GIVE THOSE REFLEXES CHING DRILLED INTO ME A CHANCE TO WORK!
WE PRACTICED FOR A SITUATION LIKE THIS... CHING TAUGHT ME TO DISABLE THE FORWARD OPPONENT WITH A SNAP KICK!
THEN, A SINGLE JUDO THROW FINISHES THE BACK AND SIDE ATTACKERS!
PWHOM
DIANA! BEHIND YOU!
REGGIE'S SHOUTED WARNING IS AN INSTANT TOO LATE--
UNN--
WAK
STAY WHERE YOU ARE--OR I PUT A BULLET INTO PRINCE'S HEAD!
THEY'VE GOT US STYMIED, OLD CHAP! WE'D BEST DO AS THEY SAY!
YOU'RE BEING SENSIBLE! SUCH COOPERATION DESERVES A REWARD!
YOU WISHED TO LEARN DOCTOR CYBER'S PLAN! SO YOU SHALL! DOCTOR CYBER WILL EXPLAIN IT TO YOU--IN PERSON!
19

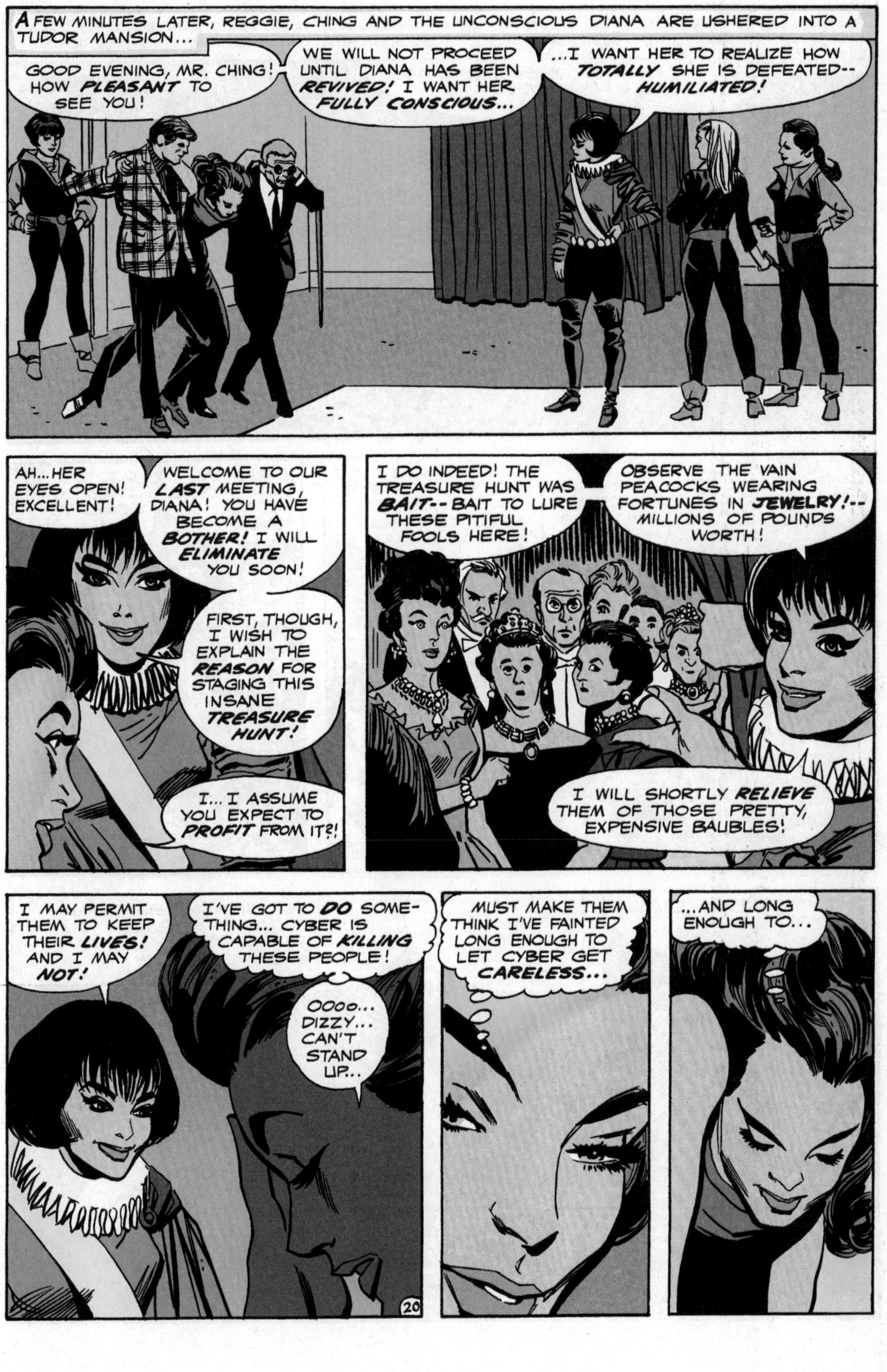
A FEW MINUTES LATER, REGGIE, CHING AND THE UNCONSCIOUS DIANA ARE USHERED INTO A TUDOR MANSION...
GOOD EVENING, MR. CHING! HOW PLEASANT TO SEE YOU!
WE WILL NOT PROCEED UNTIL DIANA HAS BEEN REVIVED! I WANT HER FULLY CONSCIOUS...
...I WANT HER TO REALIZE HOW TOTALLY SHE IS DEFEATED-- HUMILIATED!
AH... HER EYES OPEN! EXCELLENT!
WELCOME TO OUR LAST MEETING, DIANA! YOU HAVE BECOME A BOTHER! I WILL ELIMINATE YOU SOON!
FIRST, THOUGH, I WISH TO EXPLAIN THE REASON FOR STAGING THIS INSANE TREASURE HUNT!
I... I ASSUME YOU EXPECT TO PROFIT FROM IT?!
I DO INDEED! THE TREASURE HUNT WAS BAIT-- BAIT TO LURE THESE PITIFUL FOOLS HERE!
OBSERVE THE VAIN PEACOCKS WEARING FORTUNES IN JEWELRY!-- MILLIONS OF POUNDS WORTH!
I WILL SHORTLY RELIEVE THEM OF THOSE PRETTY, EXPENSIVE BAUBLES!
I MAY PERMIT THEM TO KEEP THEIR LIVES! AND I MAY NOT!
I'VE GOT TO DO SOMETHING... CYBER IS CAPABLE OF KILLING THESE PEOPLE!
OOOO... DIZZY... CAN'T STAND UP...
20
MUST MAKE THEM THINK I'VE FAINTED LONG ENOUGH TO LET CYBER GET CARELESS...
...AND LONG ENOUGH TO...

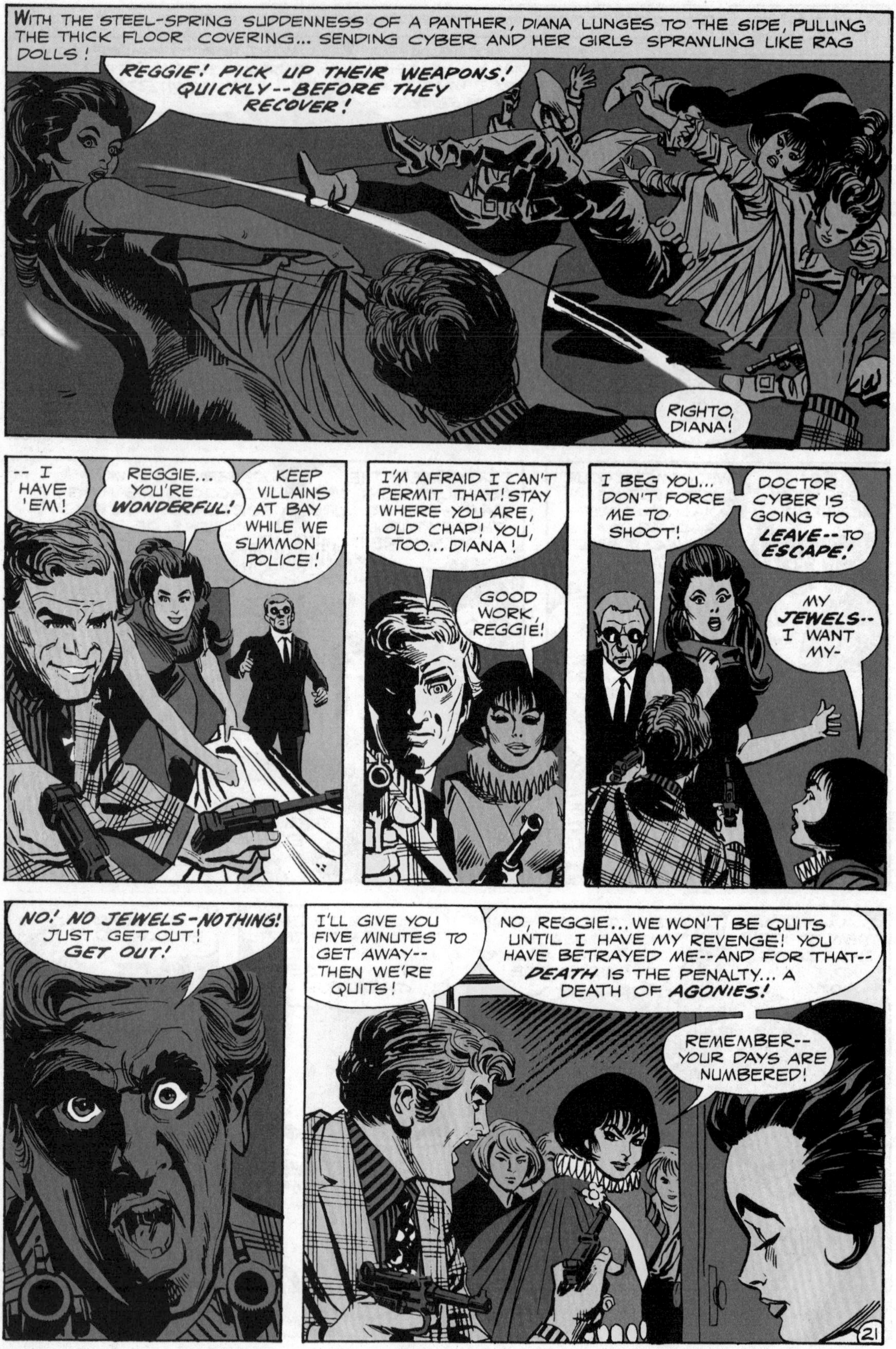

WITH THE STEEL-SPRING SUDDENNESS OF A PANTHER, DIANA LUNGES TO THE SIDE, PULLING THE THICK FLOOR COVERING... SENDING CYBER AND HER GIRLS SPRAWLING LIKE RAG DOLLS!
REGGIE! PICK UP THEIR WEAPONS! QUICKLY--BEFORE THEY RECOVER!
RIGHTO, DIANA!
-- I HAVE 'EM!
REGGIE... YOU'RE WONDERFUL!
KEEP VILLAINS AT BAY WHILE WE SUMMON POLICE!
I'M AFRAID I CAN'T PERMIT THAT! STAY WHERE YOU ARE, OLD CHAP! YOU, TOO... DIANA!
GOOD WORK, REGGIE!
I BEG YOU... DON'T FORCE ME TO SHOOT!
DOCTOR CYBER IS GOING TO LEAVE--TO ESCAPE!
MY JEWELS-- I WANT MY-
NO! NO JEWELS-NOTHING! JUST GET OUT! GET OUT!
I'LL GIVE YOU FIVE MINUTES TO GET AWAY-- THEN WE'RE QUITS!
NO, REGGIE... WE WON'T BE QUITS UNTIL I HAVE MY REVENGE! YOU HAVE BETRAYED ME--AND FOR THAT-- DEATH IS THE PENALTY... A DEATH OF AGONIES!
REMEMBER-- YOUR DAYS ARE NUMBERED!
21

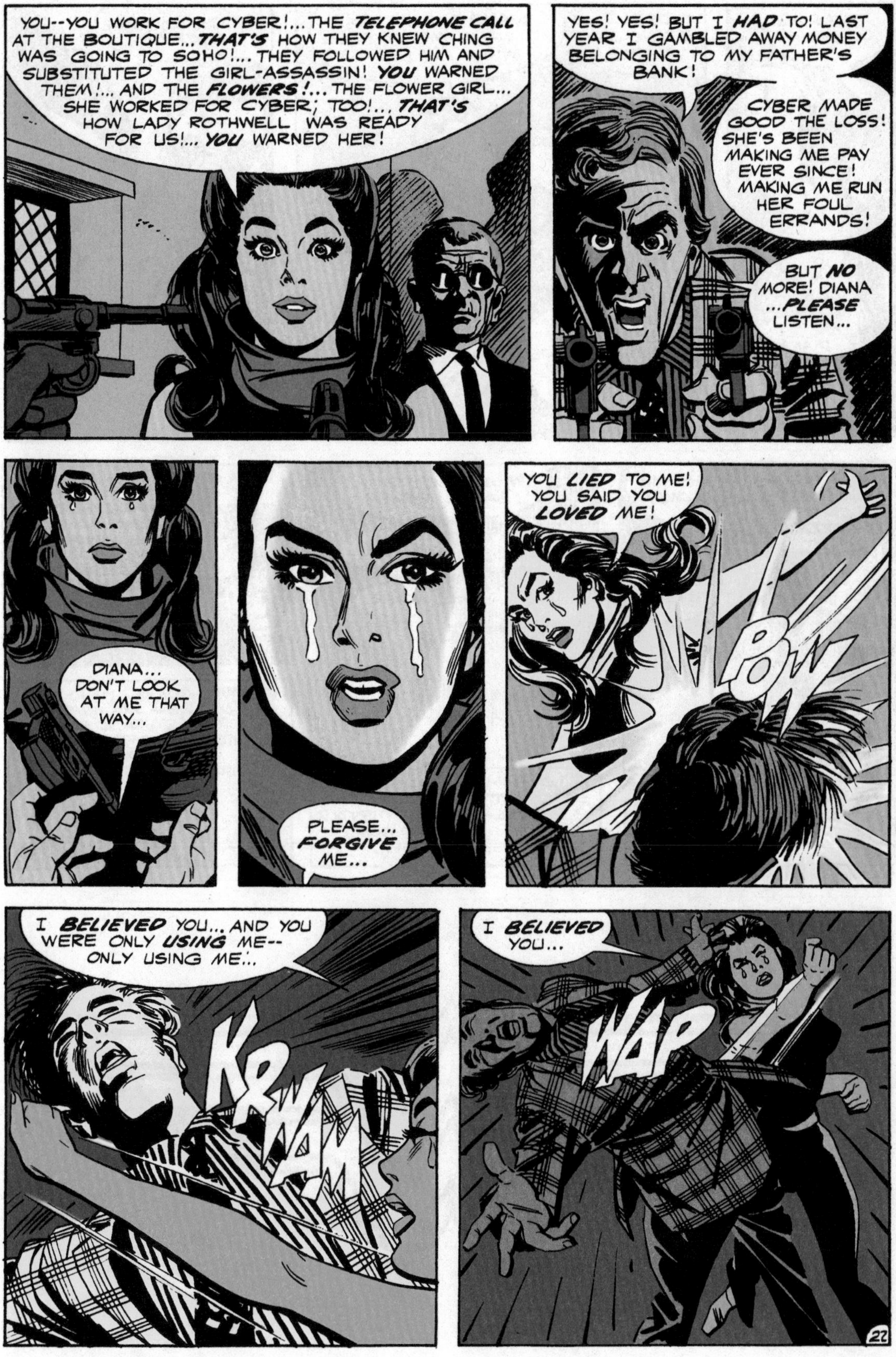
YOU--YOU WORK FOR CYBER!... THE TELEPHONE CALL AT THE BOUTIQUE... THAT'S HOW THEY KNEW CHING WAS GOING TO SOHO!... THEY FOLLOWED HIM AND SUBSTITUTED THE GIRL-ASSASSIN! YOU WARNED THEM!... AND THE FLOWERS!... THE FLOWER GIRL... SHE WORKED FOR CYBER, TOO!... THAT'S HOW LADY ROTHWELL WAS READY FOR US!... YOU WARNED HER!
YES! YES! BUT I HAD TO! LAST YEAR I GAMBLED AWAY MONEY BELONGING TO MY FATHER'S BANK!
CYBER MADE GOOD THE LOSS! SHE'S BEEN MAKING ME PAY EVER SINCE! MAKING ME RUN HER FOUL ERRANDS!
BUT NO MORE! DIANA ...PLEASE LISTEN...
DIANA... DON'T LOOK AT ME THAT WAY...
PLEASE... FORGIVE ME...
YOU LIED TO ME! YOU SAID YOU LOVED ME!
POW
I BELIEVED YOU... AND YOU WERE ONLY USING ME-- ONLY USING ME!...
KRWAM
I BELIEVED YOU...
WAP
22

IT WAS ALL A *LIE*--!

DIANA... *STOP!*

THOSE BLOWS CAN *CRIPPLE!*

I *WANT* TO HURT HIM... I WANT *HIM* TO FEEL WHAT *I'M* FEELING!

STOP! THE SUPERIOR PERSON HOLDS EMOTIONS IN CHECK!

OH, CHING... *SHUT UP!*

I'M *SICK* OF YOUR WISDOM... SICK OF *EVERYTHING!*

LET ME *ALONE!*

DIANA... *COME BACK!*

23

I'M *NEVER* COMING BACK...*NEVER!*

NEVER...

NEVER...

A LOVELY GIRL WHOSE VERY SOUL WRITHES IN TORMENT RUNS WEEPING INTO THE COLD, GREY FOG, TOWARD SOME NAMELESS DESTINY...

...AND A GRIM-FACED FIGURE MAKES A SILENT VOW...

DR. CYBER, TOO *LONG* HAVE YOU GONE *UNPUNISHED*-- I VOW-- BY MY ANCESTORS--THAT SOON, YOU WILL PAY FOR YOUR CRIMES, *IN FULL!*

And FAR AWAY... ANOTHER TORMENTED SOUL CRIES OUT... IN HER AGONY...

GO! AND HURRY! TELL DIANA SHE *MUST* RETURN TO *PARADISE ISLAND!* TELL HER-- HER *MOTHER* NEEDS HER!

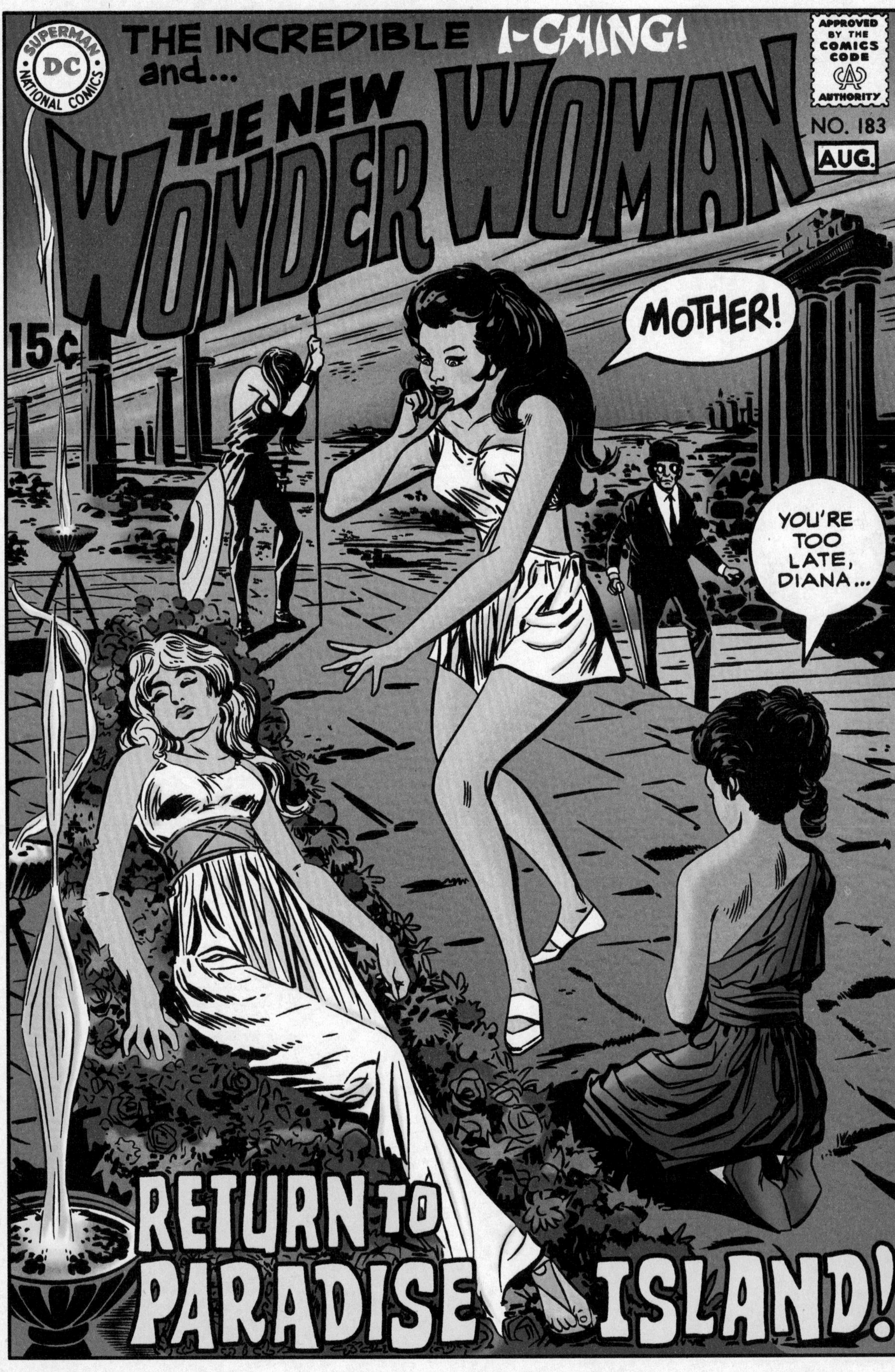

SUPERMAN
DC
NATIONAL COMICS
THE INCREDIBLE I-CHING!
and...
THE NEW WONDER WOMAN
APPROVED BY THE COMICS CODE AUTHORITY
NO. 183
AUG.
15¢
MOTHER!
YOU'RE TOO LATE, DIANA...
RETURN TO PARADISE ISLAND!

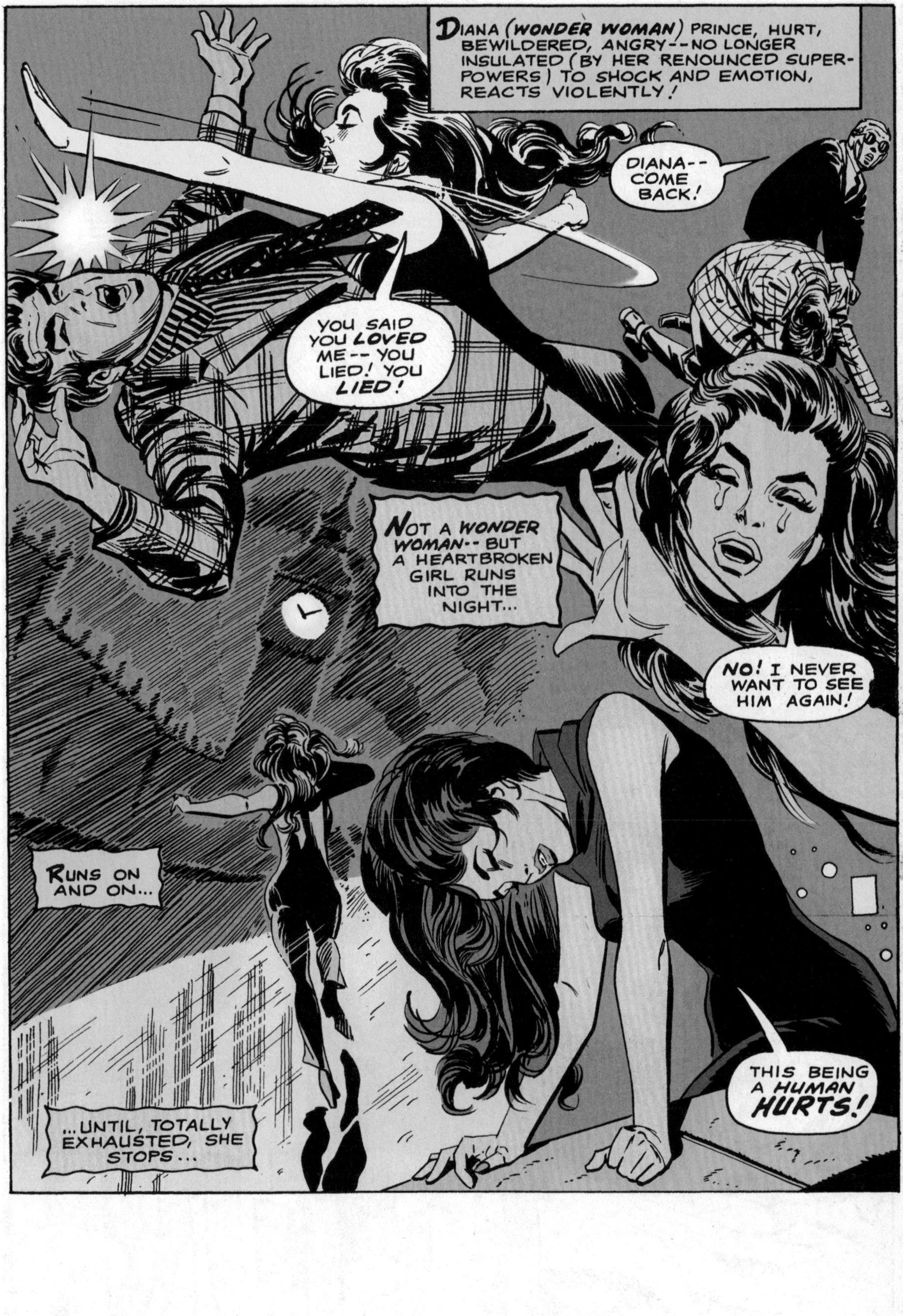
DIANA (WONDER WOMAN) PRINCE, HURT, BEWILDERED, ANGRY--NO LONGER INSULATED (BY HER RENOUNCED SUPER-POWERS) TO SHOCK AND EMOTION, REACTS VIOLENTLY!
DIANA--COME BACK!
YOU SAID YOU LOVED ME--YOU LIED! YOU LIED!
NOT A WONDER WOMAN--BUT A HEARTBROKEN GIRL RUNS INTO THE NIGHT...
NO! I NEVER WANT TO SEE HIM AGAIN!
RUNS ON AND ON...
THIS BEING A HUMAN HURTS!
...UNTIL, TOTALLY EXHAUSTED, SHE STOPS...

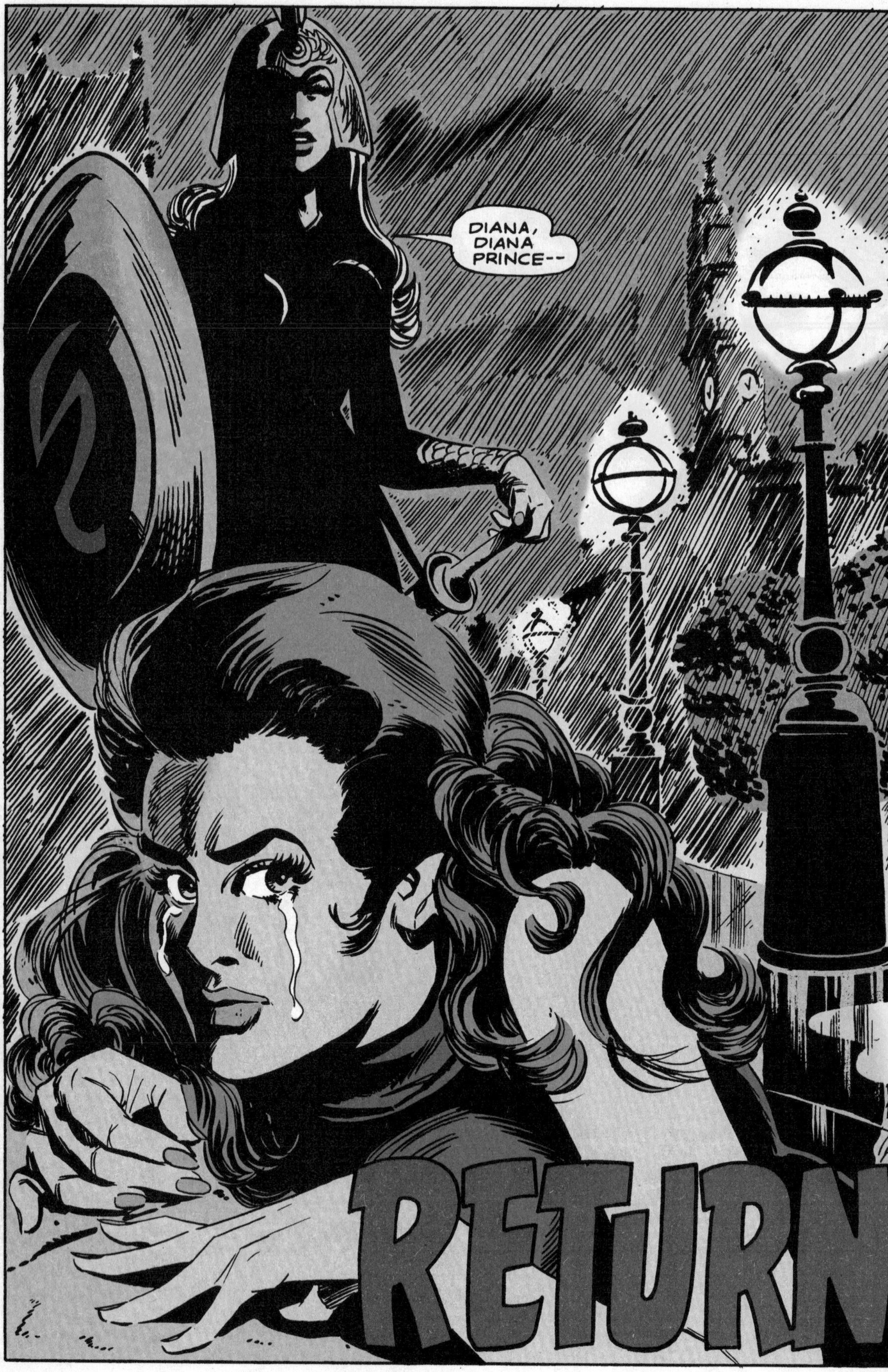
DIANA, DIANA PRINCE--
RETURN

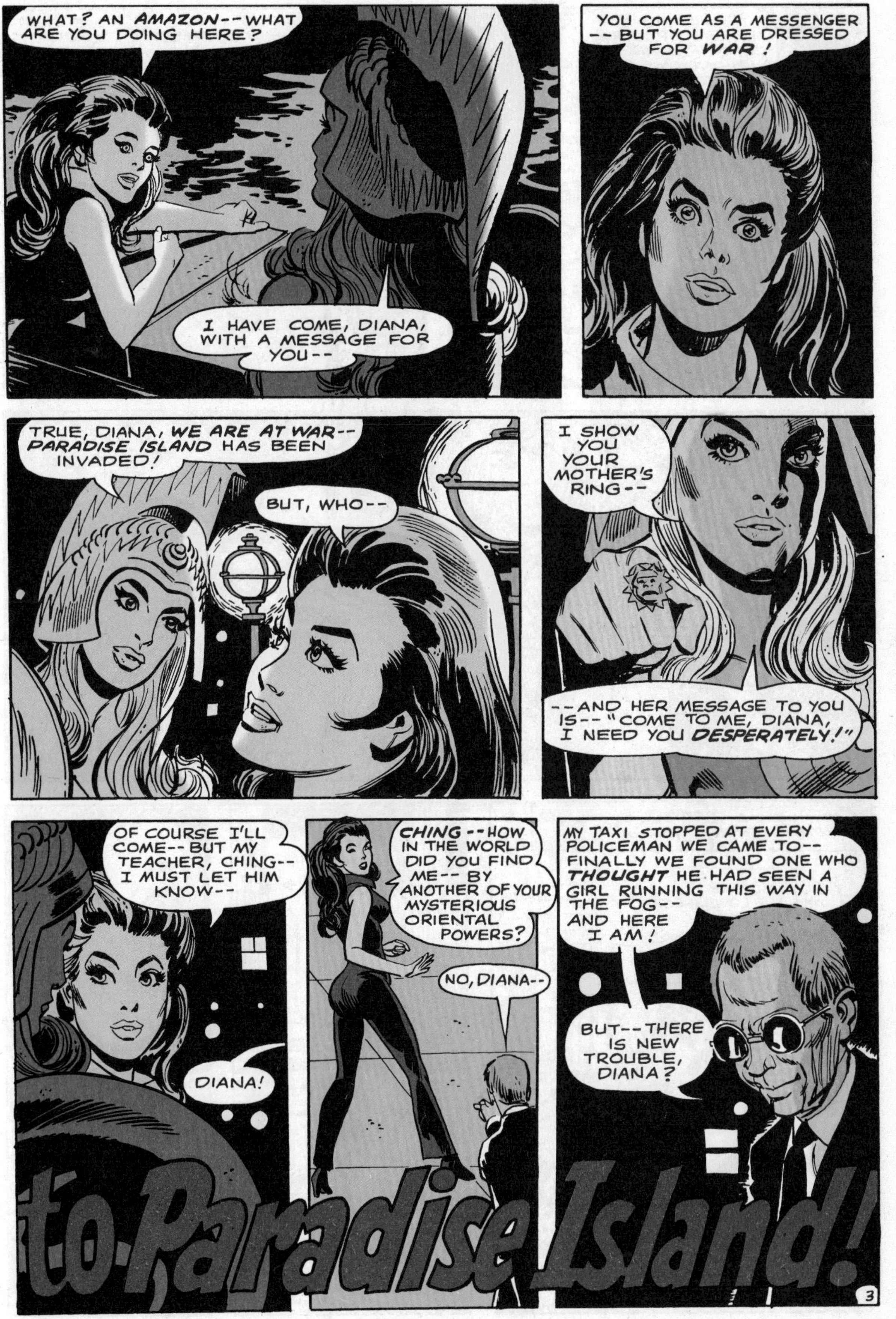

WHAT? AN AMAZON--WHAT ARE YOU DOING HERE?
I HAVE COME, DIANA, WITH A MESSAGE FOR YOU--
YOU COME AS A MESSENGER -- BUT YOU ARE DRESSED FOR WAR!
TRUE, DIANA, WE ARE AT WAR-- PARADISE ISLAND HAS BEEN INVADED!
BUT, WHO--
I SHOW YOU YOUR MOTHER'S RING--
--AND HER MESSAGE TO YOU IS-- "COME TO ME, DIANA, I NEED YOU DESPERATELY!"
OF COURSE I'LL COME-- BUT MY TEACHER, CHING-- I MUST LET HIM KNOW--
DIANA!
CHING--HOW IN THE WORLD DID YOU FIND ME-- BY ANOTHER OF YOUR MYSTERIOUS ORIENTAL POWERS?
NO, DIANA--
MY TAXI STOPPED AT EVERY POLICEMAN WE CAME TO-- FINALLY WE FOUND ONE WHO THOUGHT HE HAD SEEN A GIRL RUNNING THIS WAY IN THE FOG-- AND HERE I AM!
BUT--THERE IS NEW TROUBLE, DIANA?
to Paradise Island!
3

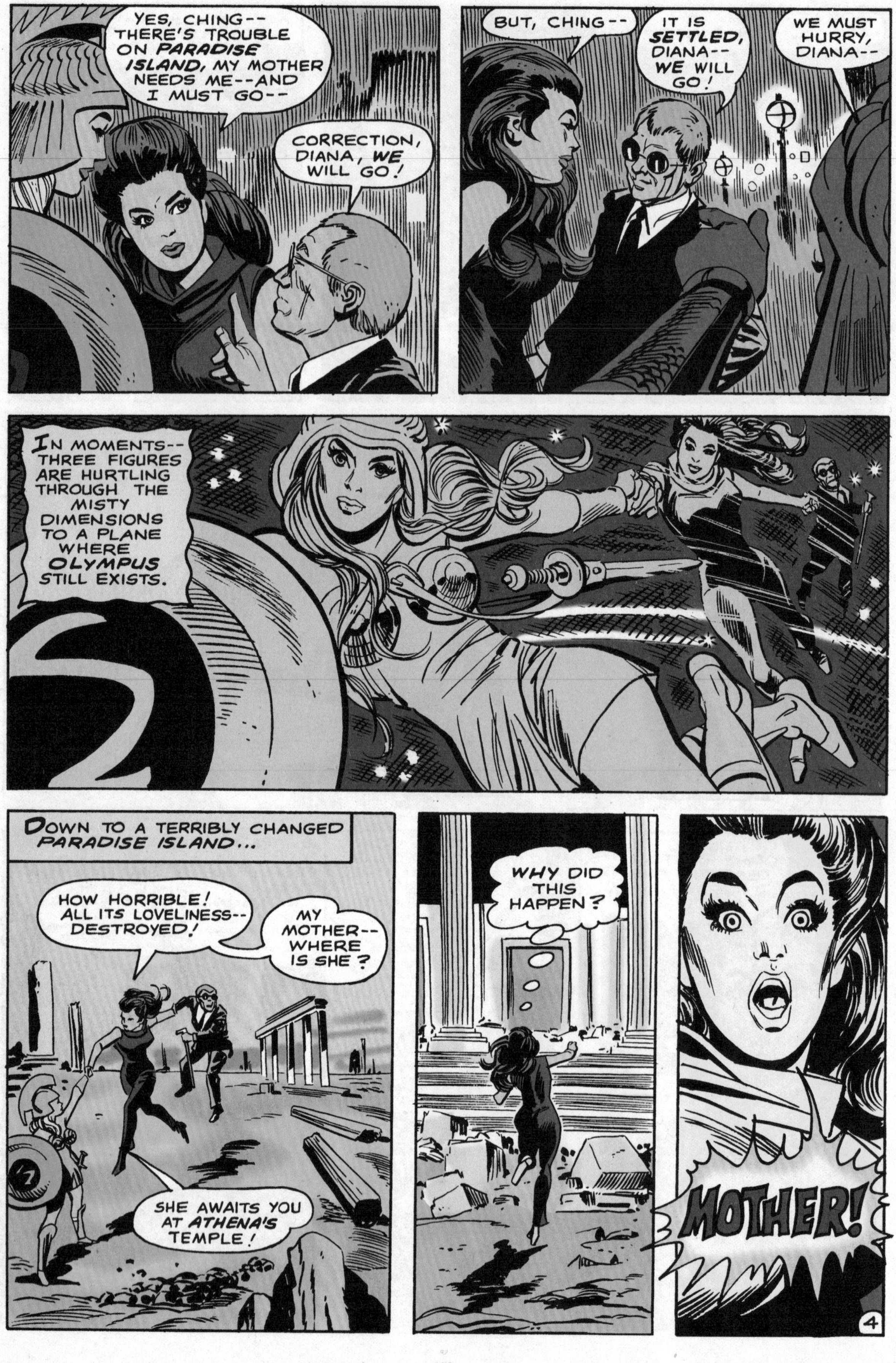
YES, CHING-- THERE'S TROUBLE ON PARADISE ISLAND, MY MOTHER NEEDS ME--AND I MUST GO--
CORRECTION, DIANA, WE WILL GO!
BUT, CHING--
IT IS SETTLED, DIANA-- WE WILL GO!
WE MUST HURRY, DIANA--
IN MOMENTS-- THREE FIGURES ARE HURTLING THROUGH THE MISTY DIMENSIONS TO A PLANE WHERE OLYMPUS STILL EXISTS.
DOWN TO A TERRIBLY CHANGED PARADISE ISLAND...
HOW HORRIBLE! ALL ITS LOVELINESS-- DESTROYED!
MY MOTHER-- WHERE IS SHE?
SHE AWAITS YOU AT ATHENA'S TEMPLE!
WHY DID THIS HAPPEN?
MOTHER!
4

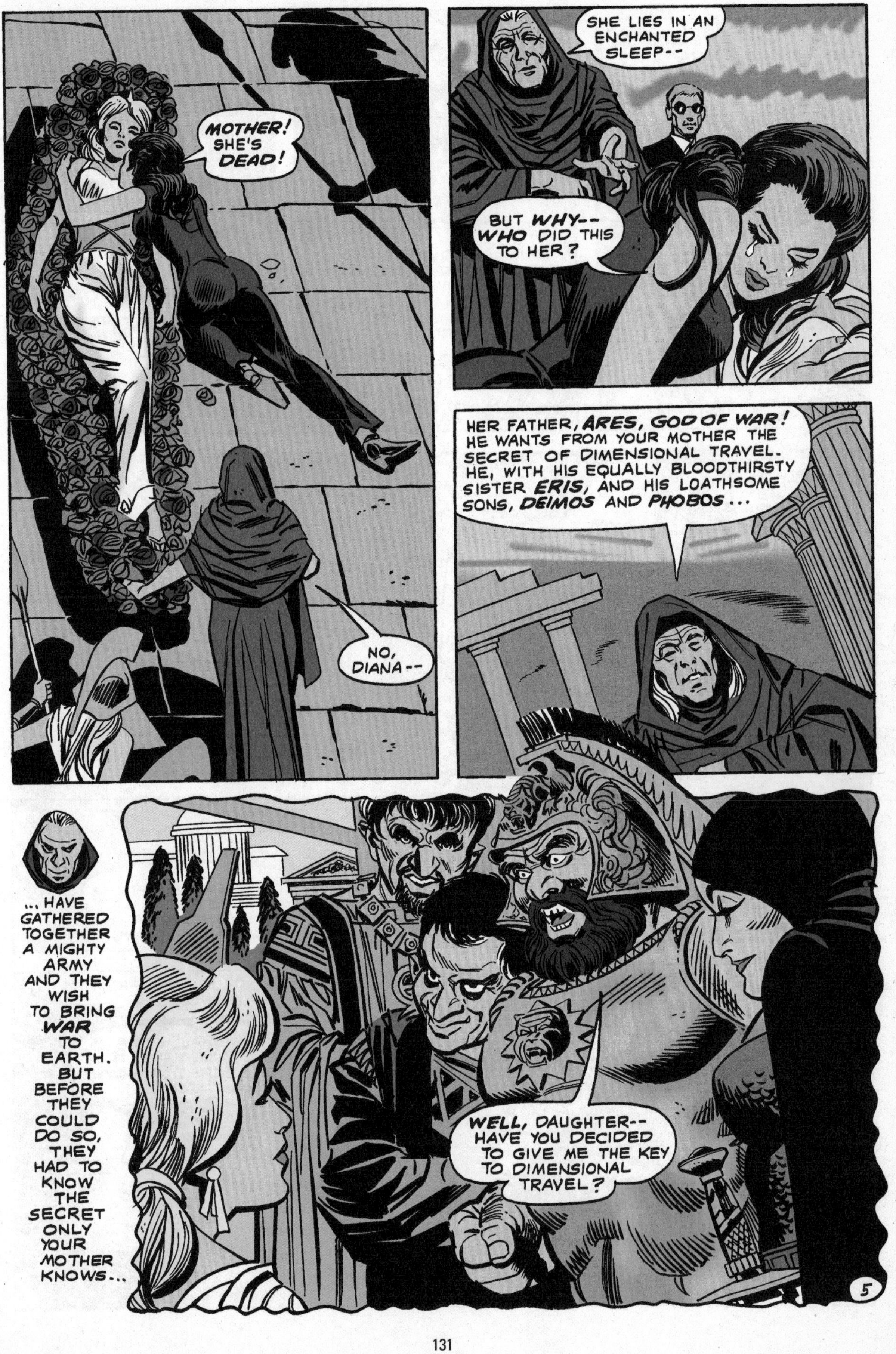
MOTHER! SHE'S DEAD!
NO, DIANA--
SHE LIES IN AN ENCHANTED SLEEP--
BUT WHY-- WHO DID THIS TO HER?
HER FATHER, ARES, GOD OF WAR! HE WANTS FROM YOUR MOTHER THE SECRET OF DIMENSIONAL TRAVEL. HE, WITH HIS EQUALLY BLOODTHIRSTY SISTER ERIS, AND HIS LOATHSOME SONS, DEIMOS AND PHOBOS ...
... HAVE GATHERED TOGETHER A MIGHTY ARMY AND THEY WISH TO BRING WAR TO EARTH. BUT BEFORE THEY COULD DO SO, THEY HAD TO KNOW THE SECRET ONLY YOUR MOTHER KNOWS ...
WELL, DAUGHTER-- HAVE YOU DECIDED TO GIVE ME THE KEY TO DIMENSIONAL TRAVEL?
5

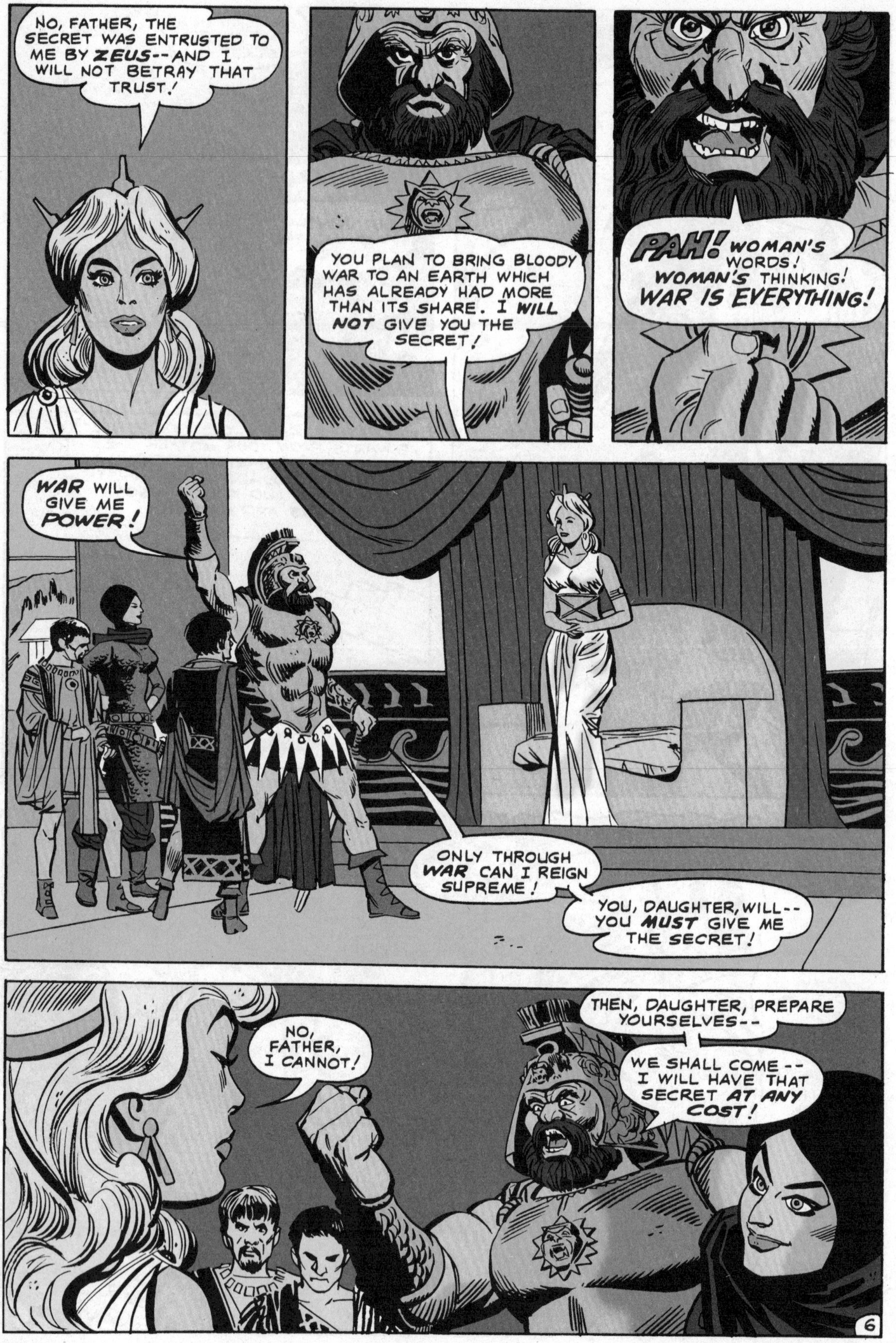

NO, FATHER, THE SECRET WAS ENTRUSTED TO ME BY ZEUS--AND I WILL NOT BETRAY THAT TRUST!
YOU PLAN TO BRING BLOODY WAR TO AN EARTH WHICH HAS ALREADY HAD MORE THAN ITS SHARE. I WILL NOT GIVE YOU THE SECRET!
PAH! WOMAN'S WORDS! WOMAN'S THINKING! WAR IS EVERYTHING!
WAR WILL GIVE ME POWER!
ONLY THROUGH WAR CAN I REIGN SUPREME!
YOU, DAUGHTER, WILL-- YOU MUST GIVE ME THE SECRET!
NO, FATHER, I CANNOT!
THEN, DAUGHTER, PREPARE YOURSELVES--
WE SHALL COME-- I WILL HAVE THAT SECRET AT ANY COST!
6

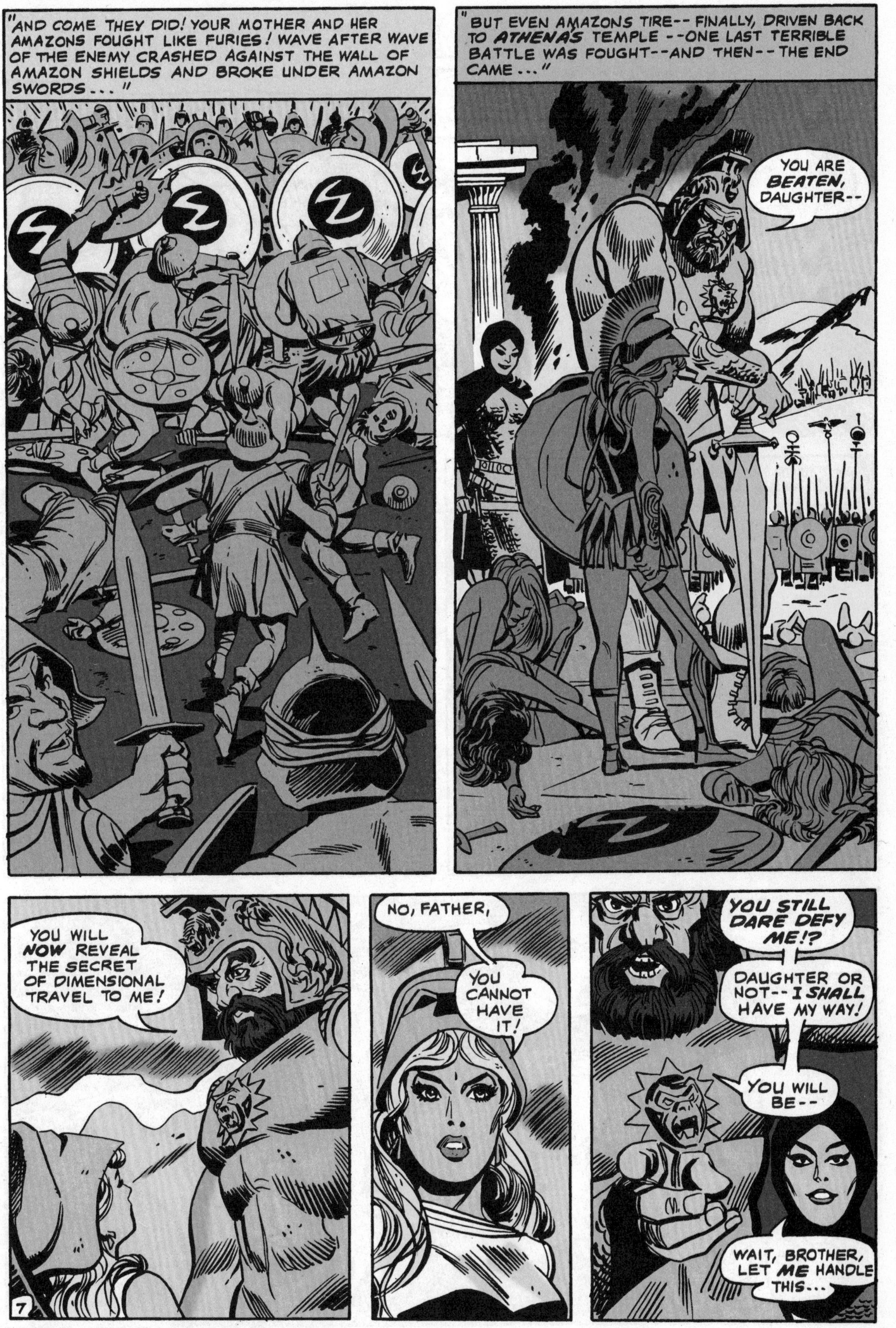

"AND COME THEY DID! YOUR MOTHER AND HER AMAZONS FOUGHT LIKE FURIES! WAVE AFTER WAVE OF THE ENEMY CRASHED AGAINST THE WALL OF AMAZON SHIELDS AND BROKE UNDER AMAZON SWORDS..."
"BUT EVEN AMAZONS TIRE-- FINALLY, DRIVEN BACK TO ATHENA'S TEMPLE --ONE LAST TERRIBLE BATTLE WAS FOUGHT--AND THEN--THE END CAME..."
YOU ARE BEATEN, DAUGHTER--
YOU WILL NOW REVEAL THE SECRET OF DIMENSIONAL TRAVEL TO ME!
7
NO, FATHER,
YOU CANNOT HAVE IT!
YOU STILL DARE DEFY ME!?
DAUGHTER OR NOT-- I SHALL HAVE MY WAY!
YOU WILL BE--
WAIT, BROTHER, LET ME HANDLE THIS...

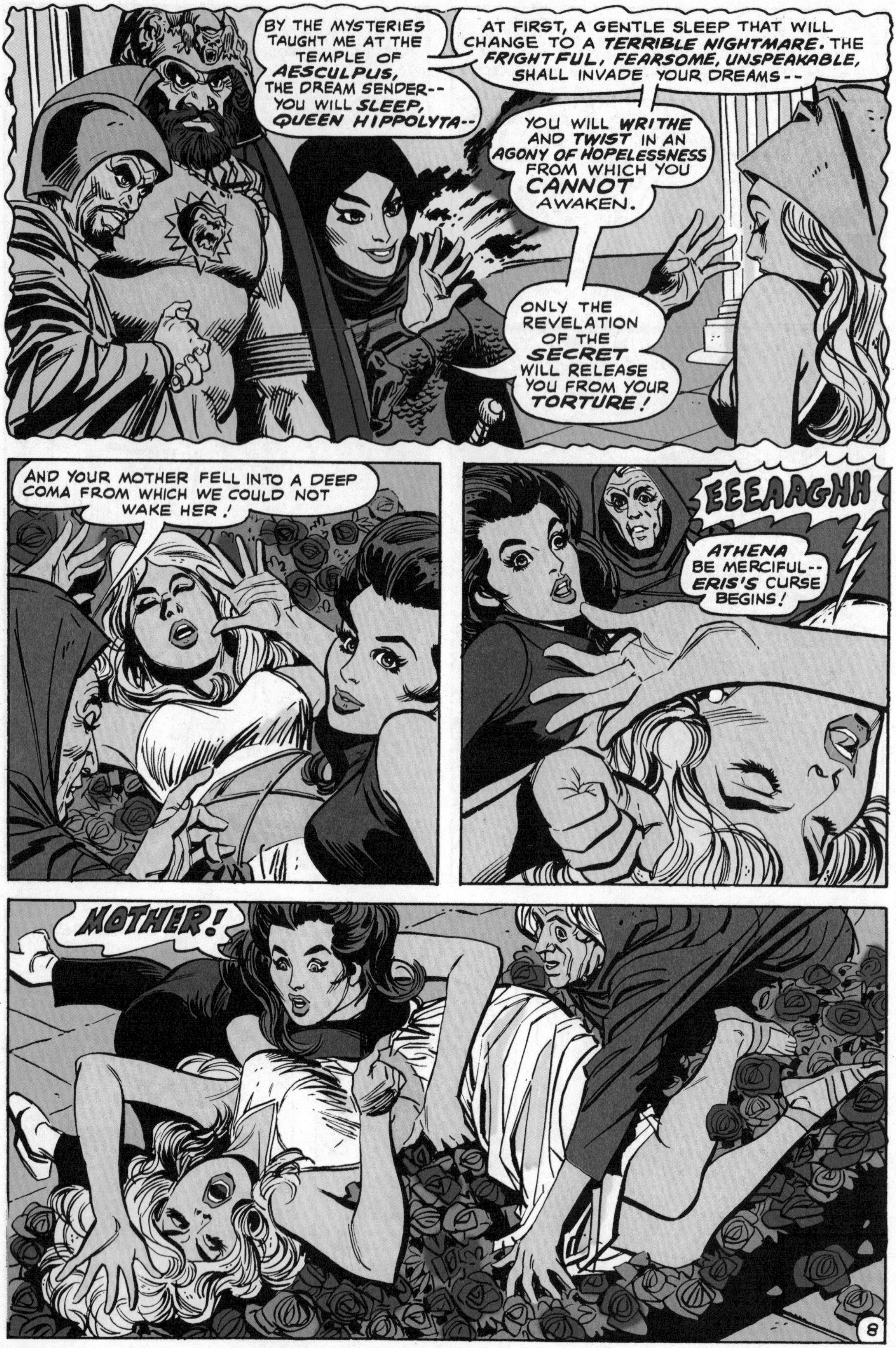
BY THE MYSTERIES TAUGHT ME AT THE TEMPLE OF AESCULPUS, THE DREAM SENDER-- YOU WILL SLEEP, QUEEN HIPPOLYTA--
AT FIRST, A GENTLE SLEEP THAT WILL CHANGE TO A TERRIBLE NIGHTMARE. THE FRIGHTFUL, FEARSOME, UNSPEAKABLE, SHALL INVADE YOUR DREAMS--
YOU WILL WRITHE AND TWIST IN AN AGONY OF HOPELESSNESS FROM WHICH YOU CANNOT AWAKEN.
ONLY THE REVELATION OF THE SECRET WILL RELEASE YOU FROM YOUR TORTURE!
AND YOUR MOTHER FELL INTO A DEEP COMA FROM WHICH WE COULD NOT WAKE HER!
EEEAAAGHH
ATHENA BE MERCIFUL-- ERIS'S CURSE BEGINS!
MOTHER!
8

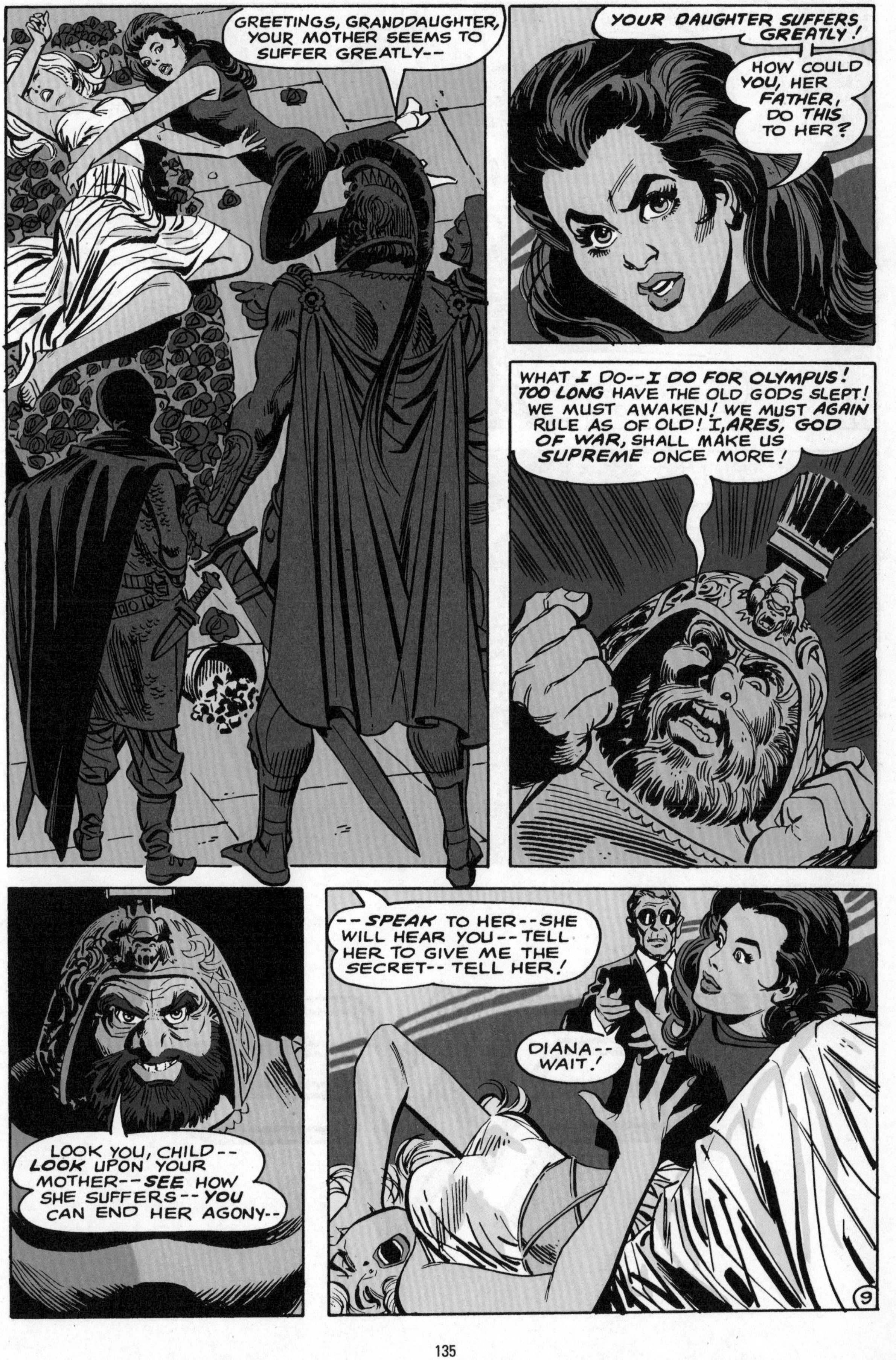
GREETINGS, GRANDDAUGHTER, YOUR MOTHER SEEMS TO SUFFER GREATLY--
YOUR DAUGHTER SUFFERS GREATLY!
HOW COULD YOU, HER FATHER, DO THIS TO HER?
WHAT I DO--I DO FOR OLYMPUS! TOO LONG HAVE THE OLD GODS SLEPT! WE MUST AWAKEN! WE MUST AGAIN RULE AS OF OLD! I, ARES, GOD OF WAR, SHALL MAKE US SUPREME ONCE MORE!
LOOK YOU, CHILD-- LOOK UPON YOUR MOTHER--SEE HOW SHE SUFFERS--YOU CAN END HER AGONY--
--SPEAK TO HER--SHE WILL HEAR YOU--TELL HER TO GIVE ME THE SECRET-- TELL HER!
DIANA-- WAIT!
9

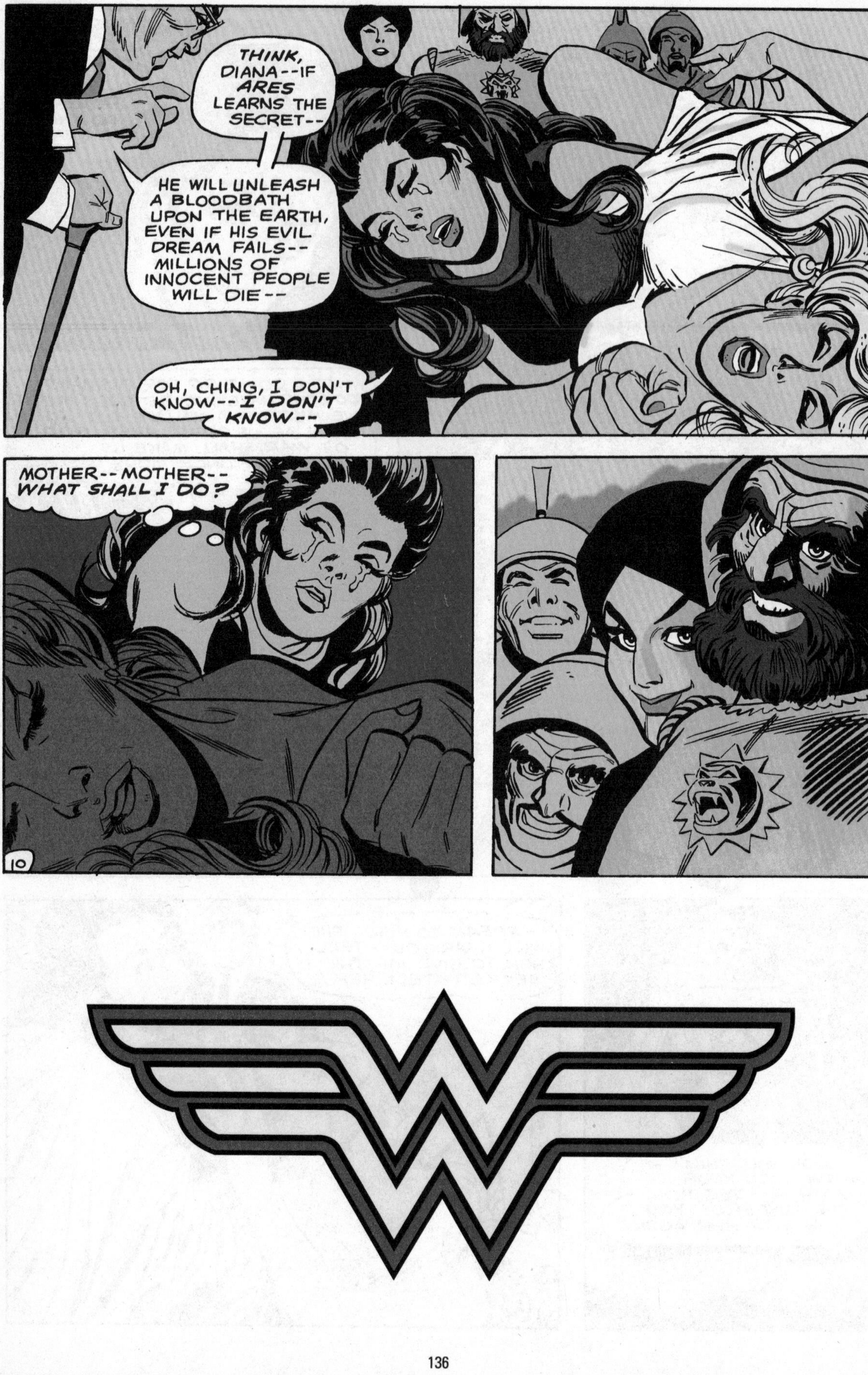
THINK, DIANA--IF ARES LEARNS THE SECRET--
HE WILL UNLEASH A BLOODBATH UPON THE EARTH, EVEN IF HIS EVIL DREAM FAILS-- MILLIONS OF INNOCENT PEOPLE WILL DIE--
OH, CHING, I DON'T KNOW--I DON'T KNOW--
MOTHER--MOTHER-- WHAT SHALL I DO?
10

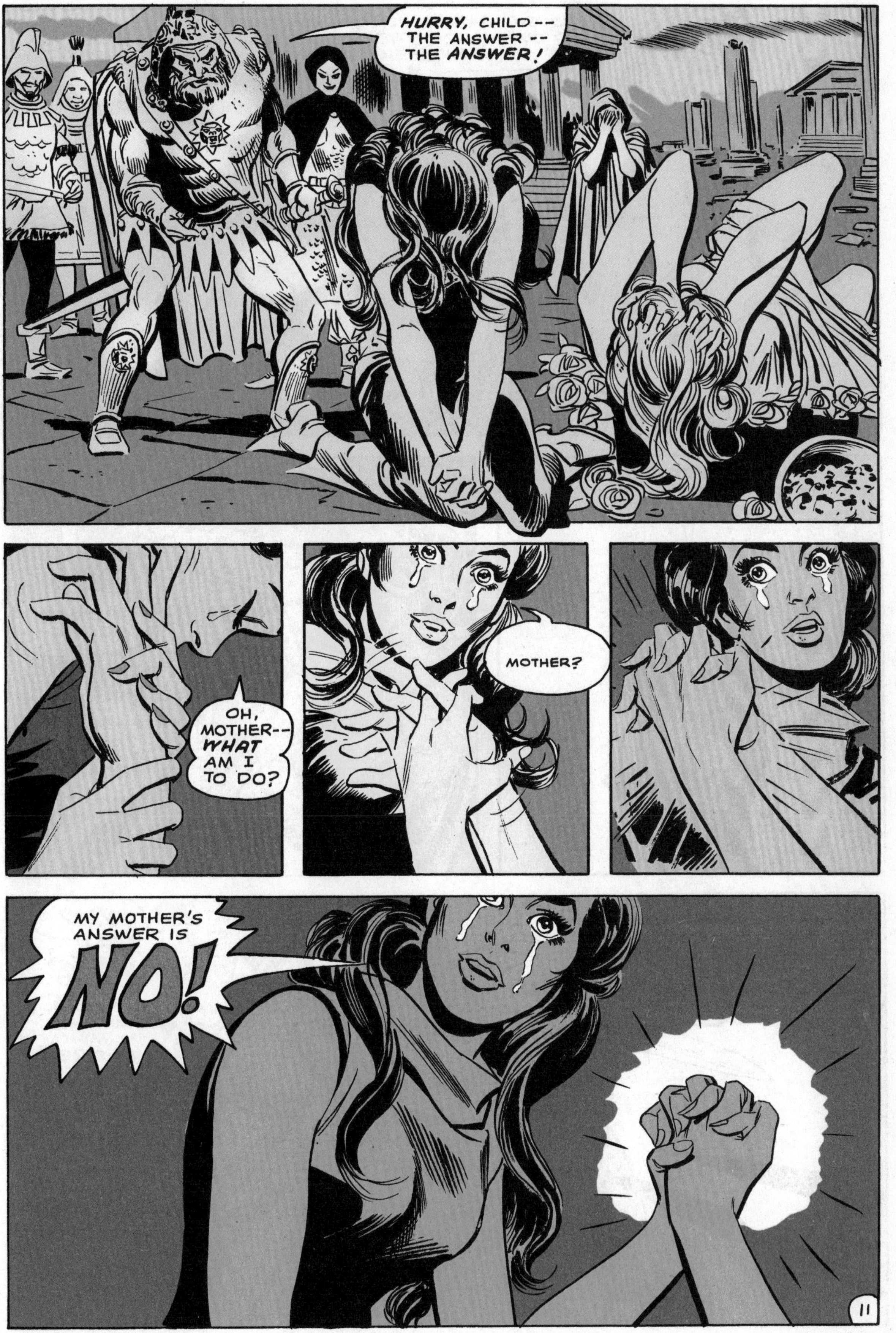
HURRY, CHILD-- THE ANSWER -- THE ANSWER!
OH, MOTHER-- WHAT AM I TO DO?
MOTHER?
MY MOTHER'S ANSWER IS NO!
11

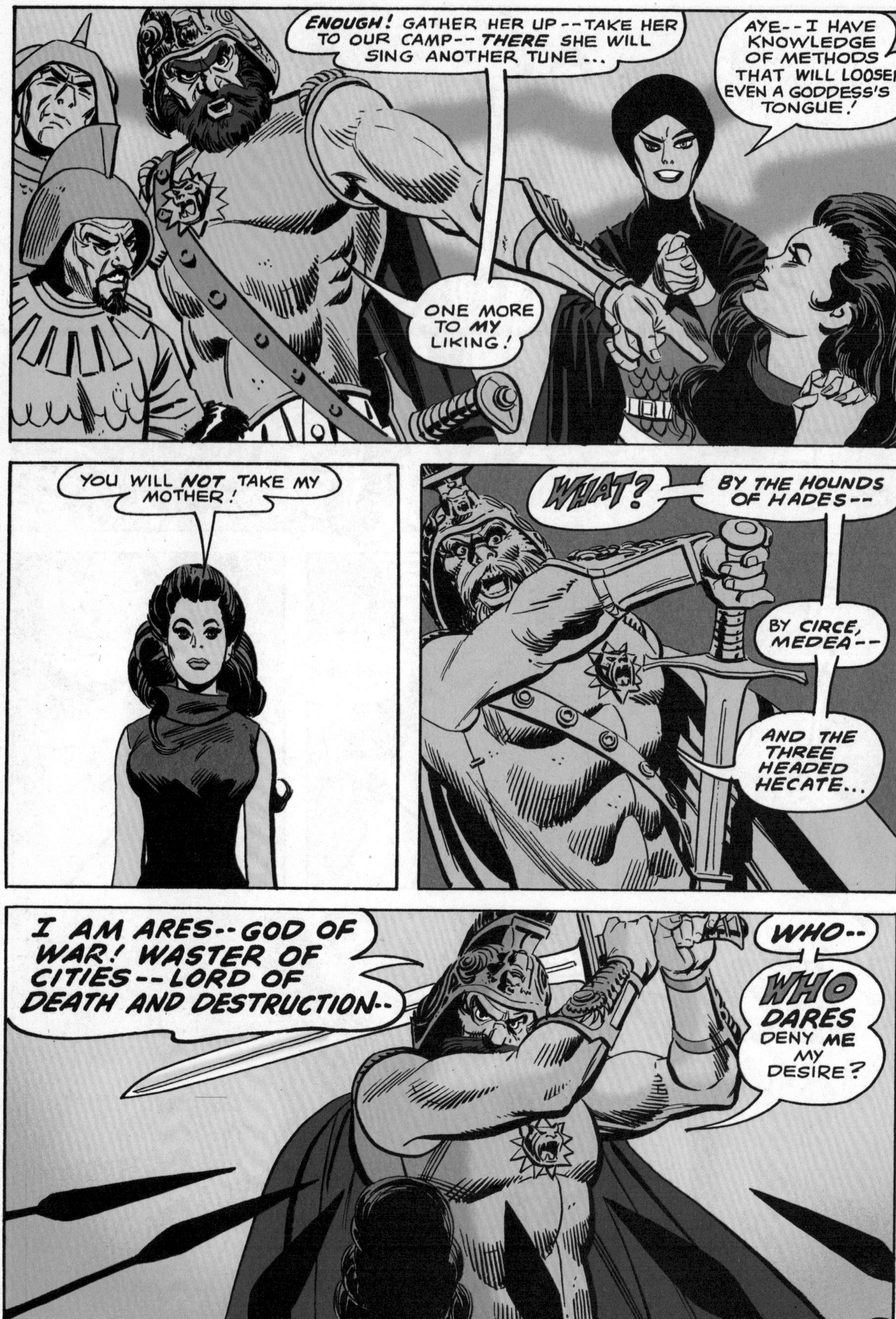
ENOUGH! GATHER HER UP--TAKE HER TO OUR CAMP--THERE SHE WILL SING ANOTHER TUNE...
ONE MORE TO MY LIKING!
AYE--I HAVE KNOWLEDGE OF METHODS THAT WILL LOOSEN EVEN A GODDESS'S TONGUE!
YOU WILL NOT TAKE MY MOTHER!
WHAT?
BY THE HOUNDS OF HADES--
BY CIRCE, MEDEA--
AND THE THREE HEADED HECATE...
I AM ARES--GOD OF WAR! WASTER OF CITIES--LORD OF DEATH AND DESTRUCTION--
WHO--
WHO DARES DENY ME MY DESIRE?
12

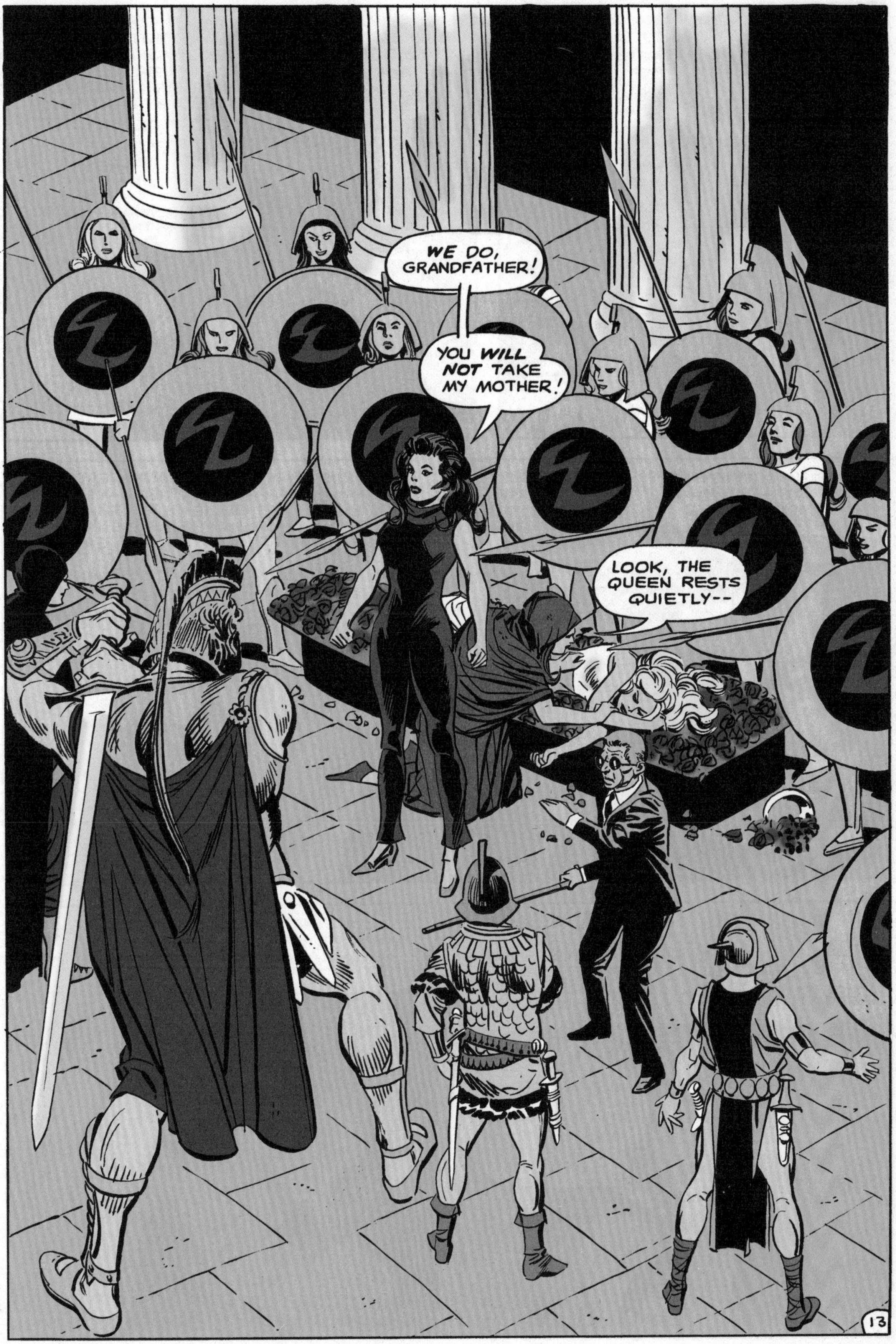
WE DO, GRANDFATHER!
YOU WILL NOT TAKE MY MOTHER!
LOOK, THE QUEEN RESTS QUIETLY--
13

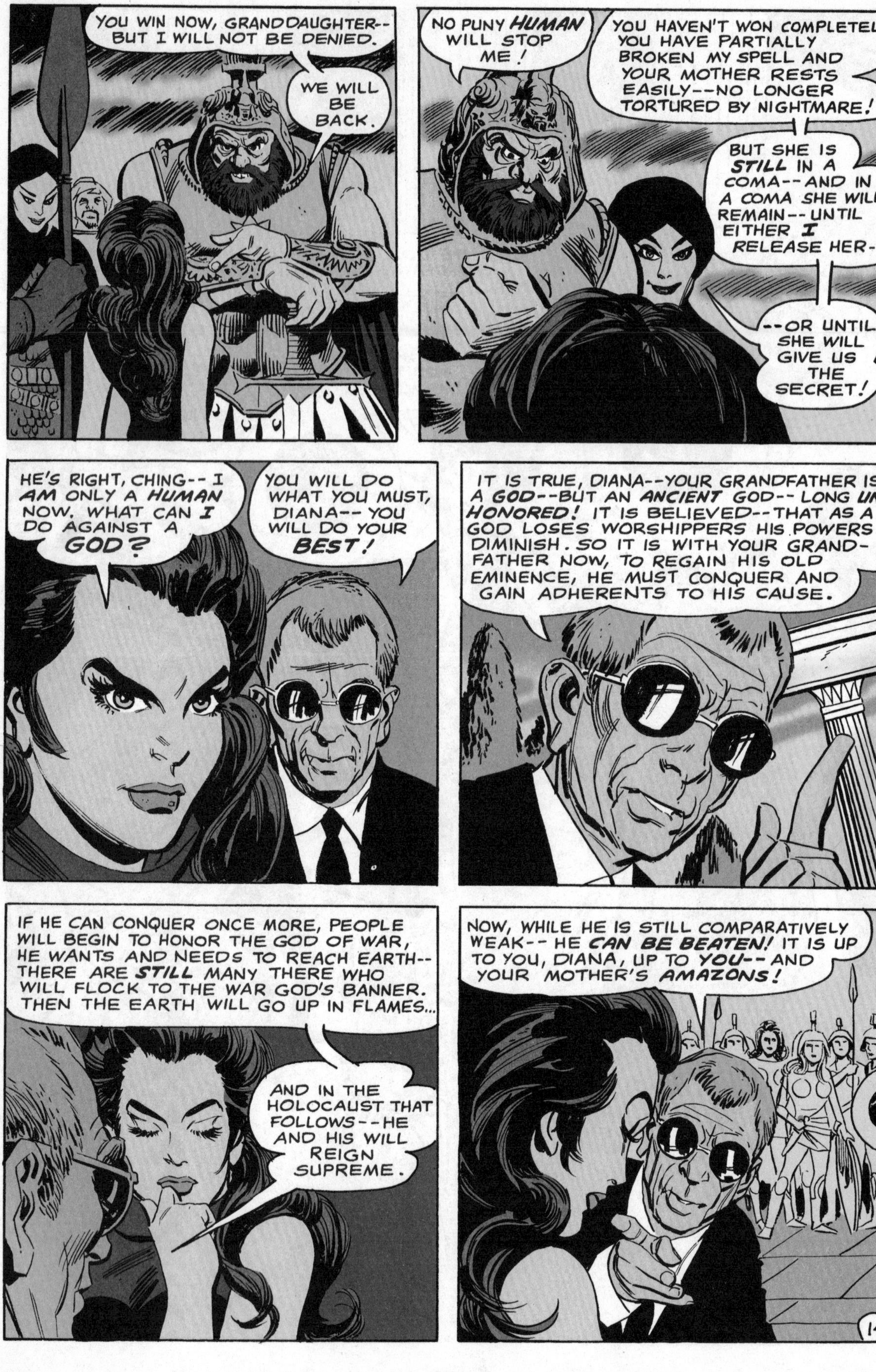
YOU WIN NOW, GRANDDAUGHTER-- BUT I WILL NOT BE DENIED.
WE WILL BE BACK.
NO PUNY HUMAN WILL STOP ME!
YOU HAVEN'T WON COMPLETELY, YOU HAVE PARTIALLY BROKEN MY SPELL AND YOUR MOTHER RESTS EASILY--NO LONGER TORTURED BY NIGHTMARE!
BUT SHE IS STILL IN A COMA--AND IN A COMA SHE WILL REMAIN--UNTIL EITHER I RELEASE HER--
--OR UNTIL SHE WILL GIVE US THE SECRET!
HE'S RIGHT, CHING-- I AM ONLY A HUMAN NOW. WHAT CAN I DO AGAINST A GOD?
YOU WILL DO WHAT YOU MUST, DIANA-- YOU WILL DO YOUR BEST!
IT IS TRUE, DIANA--YOUR GRANDFATHER IS A GOD--BUT AN ANCIENT GOD-- LONG UN-HONORED! IT IS BELIEVED--THAT AS A GOD LOSES WORSHIPPERS HIS POWERS DIMINISH. SO IT IS WITH YOUR GRAND-FATHER NOW, TO REGAIN HIS OLD EMINENCE, HE MUST CONQUER AND GAIN ADHERENTS TO HIS CAUSE.
IF HE CAN CONQUER ONCE MORE, PEOPLE WILL BEGIN TO HONOR THE GOD OF WAR, HE WANTS AND NEEDS TO REACH EARTH-- THERE ARE STILL MANY THERE WHO WILL FLOCK TO THE WAR GOD'S BANNER. THEN THE EARTH WILL GO UP IN FLAMES...
AND IN THE HOLOCAUST THAT FOLLOWS--HE AND HIS WILL REIGN SUPREME.
NOW, WHILE HE IS STILL COMPARATIVELY WEAK-- HE CAN BE BEATEN! IT IS UP TO YOU, DIANA, UP TO YOU--AND YOUR MOTHER'S AMAZONS!
14

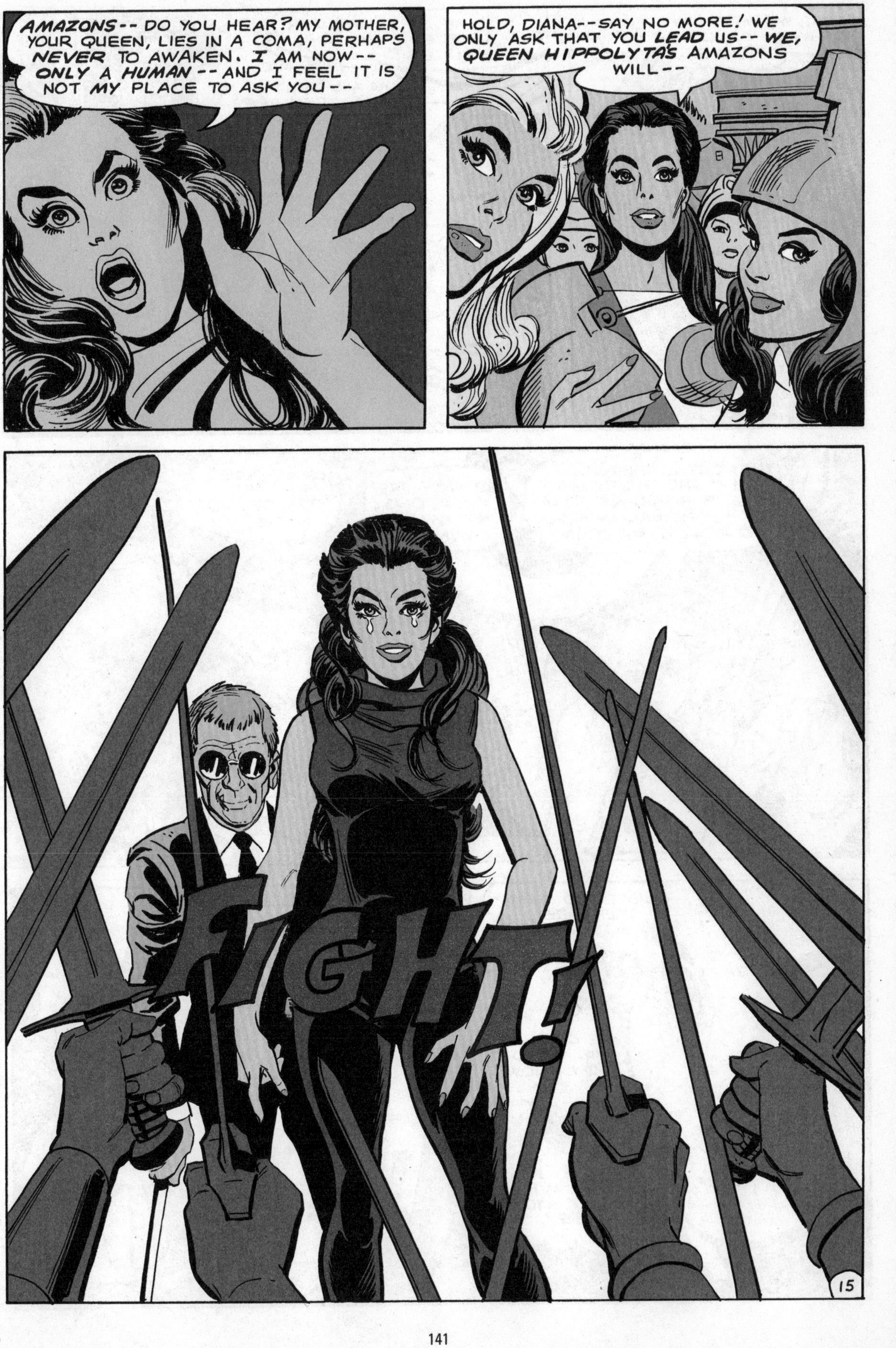
AMAZONS-- DO YOU HEAR? MY MOTHER, YOUR QUEEN, LIES IN A COMA, PERHAPS NEVER TO AWAKEN. I AM NOW-- ONLY A HUMAN--AND I FEEL IT IS NOT MY PLACE TO ASK YOU--
HOLD, DIANA--SAY NO MORE! WE ONLY ASK THAT YOU LEAD US--WE, QUEEN HIPPOLYTA'S AMAZONS WILL--
FIGHT!
15

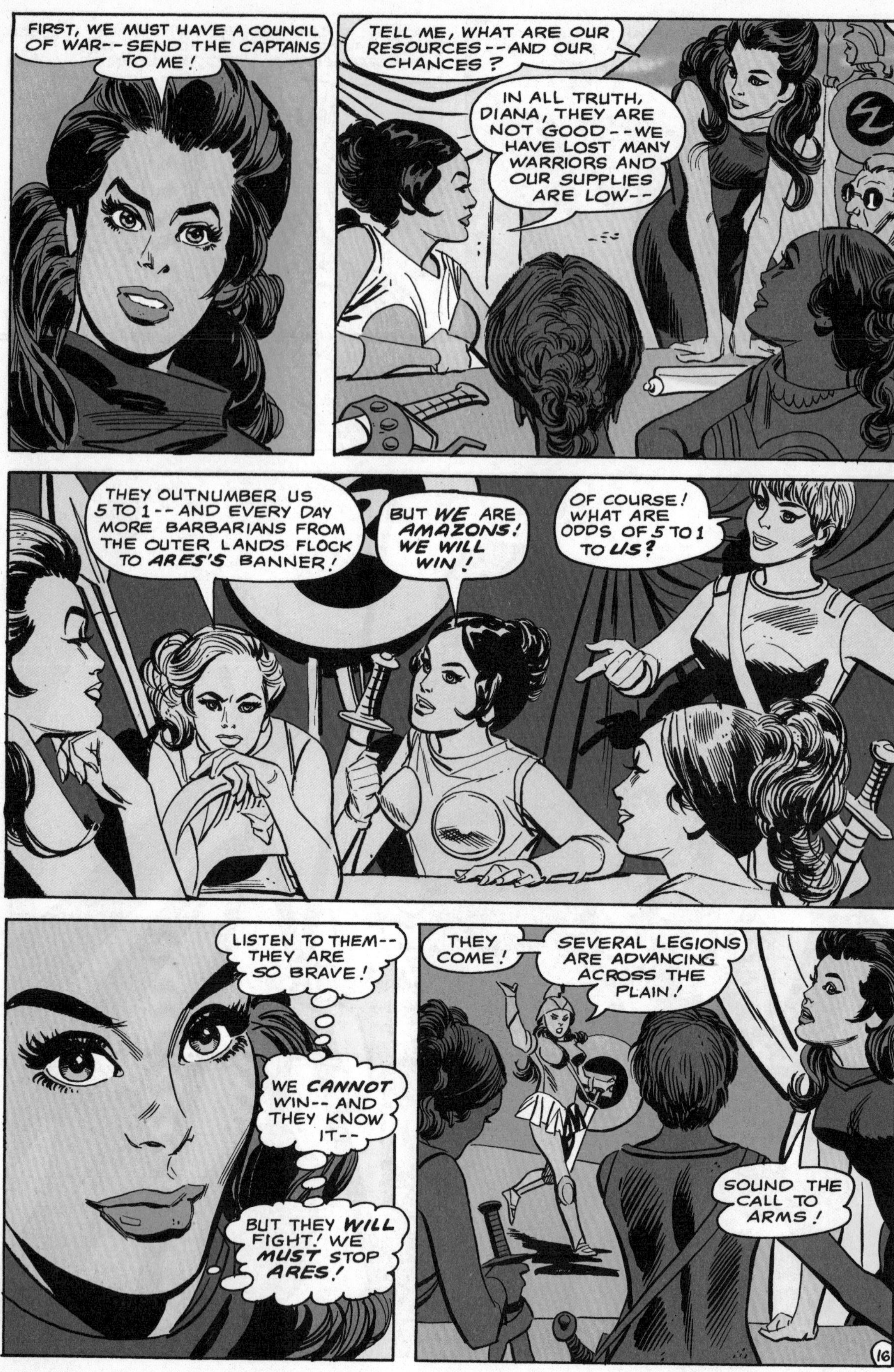
FIRST, WE MUST HAVE A COUNCIL OF WAR--SEND THE CAPTAINS TO ME!
TELL ME, WHAT ARE OUR RESOURCES--AND OUR CHANCES?
IN ALL TRUTH, DIANA, THEY ARE NOT GOOD--WE HAVE LOST MANY WARRIORS AND OUR SUPPLIES ARE LOW--
THEY OUTNUMBER US 5 TO 1--AND EVERY DAY MORE BARBARIANS FROM THE OUTER LANDS FLOCK TO ARES'S BANNER!
BUT WE ARE AMAZONS! WE WILL WIN!
OF COURSE! WHAT ARE ODDS OF 5 TO 1 TO US?
LISTEN TO THEM--THEY ARE SO BRAVE!
WE CANNOT WIN--AND THEY KNOW IT--
BUT THEY WILL FIGHT! WE MUST STOP ARES!
THEY COME!
SEVERAL LEGIONS ARE ADVANCING ACROSS THE PLAIN!
SOUND THE CALL TO ARMS!
16

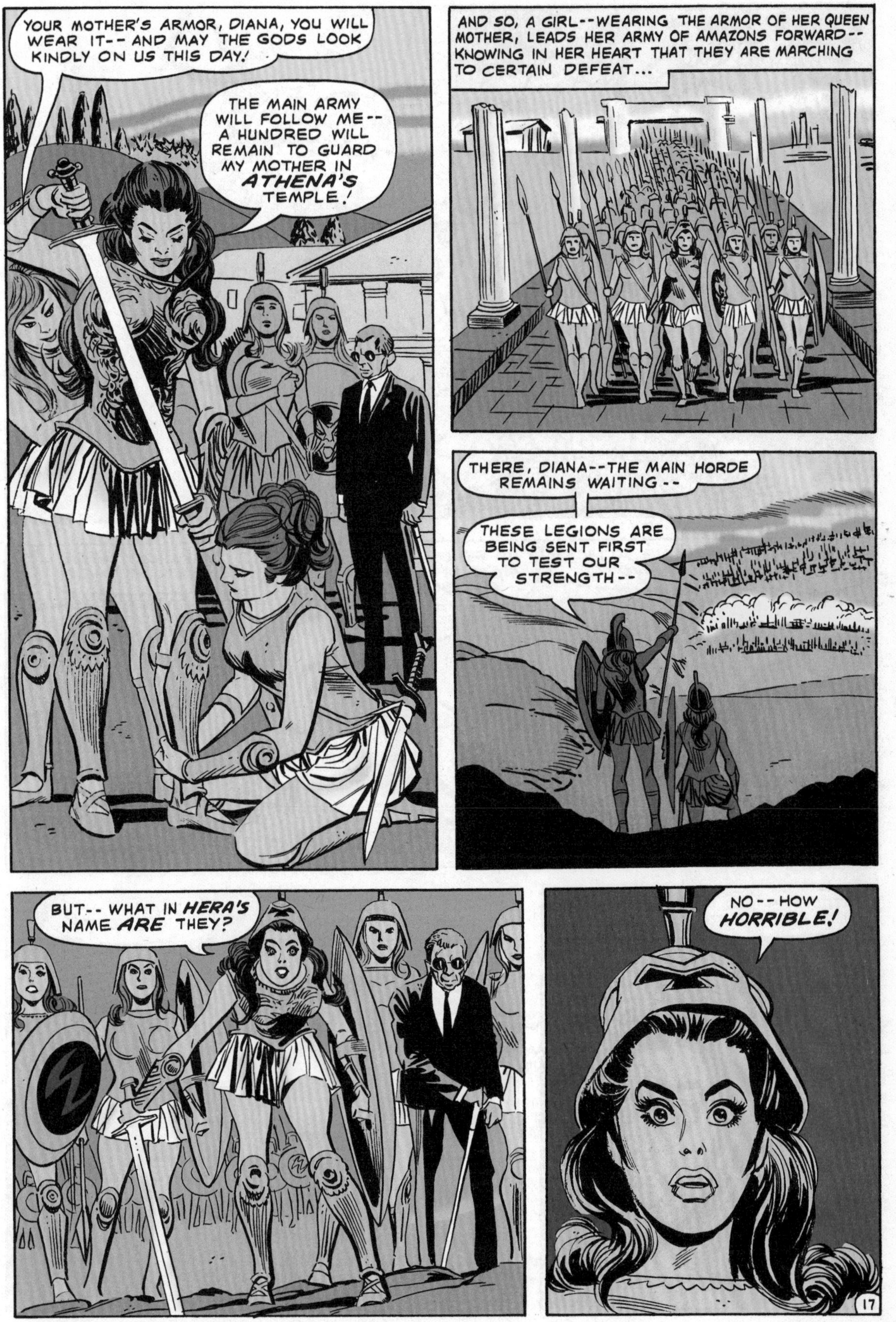
YOUR MOTHER'S ARMOR, DIANA, YOU WILL WEAR IT-- AND MAY THE GODS LOOK KINDLY ON US THIS DAY!
THE MAIN ARMY WILL FOLLOW ME-- A HUNDRED WILL REMAIN TO GUARD MY MOTHER IN ATHENA'S TEMPLE!
AND SO, A GIRL--WEARING THE ARMOR OF HER QUEEN MOTHER, LEADS HER ARMY OF AMAZONS FORWARD-- KNOWING IN HER HEART THAT THEY ARE MARCHING TO CERTAIN DEFEAT...
THERE, DIANA--THE MAIN HORDE REMAINS WAITING--
THESE LEGIONS ARE BEING SENT FIRST TO TEST OUR STRENGTH--
BUT-- WHAT IN HERA'S NAME ARE THEY?
NO--HOW HORRIBLE!
17

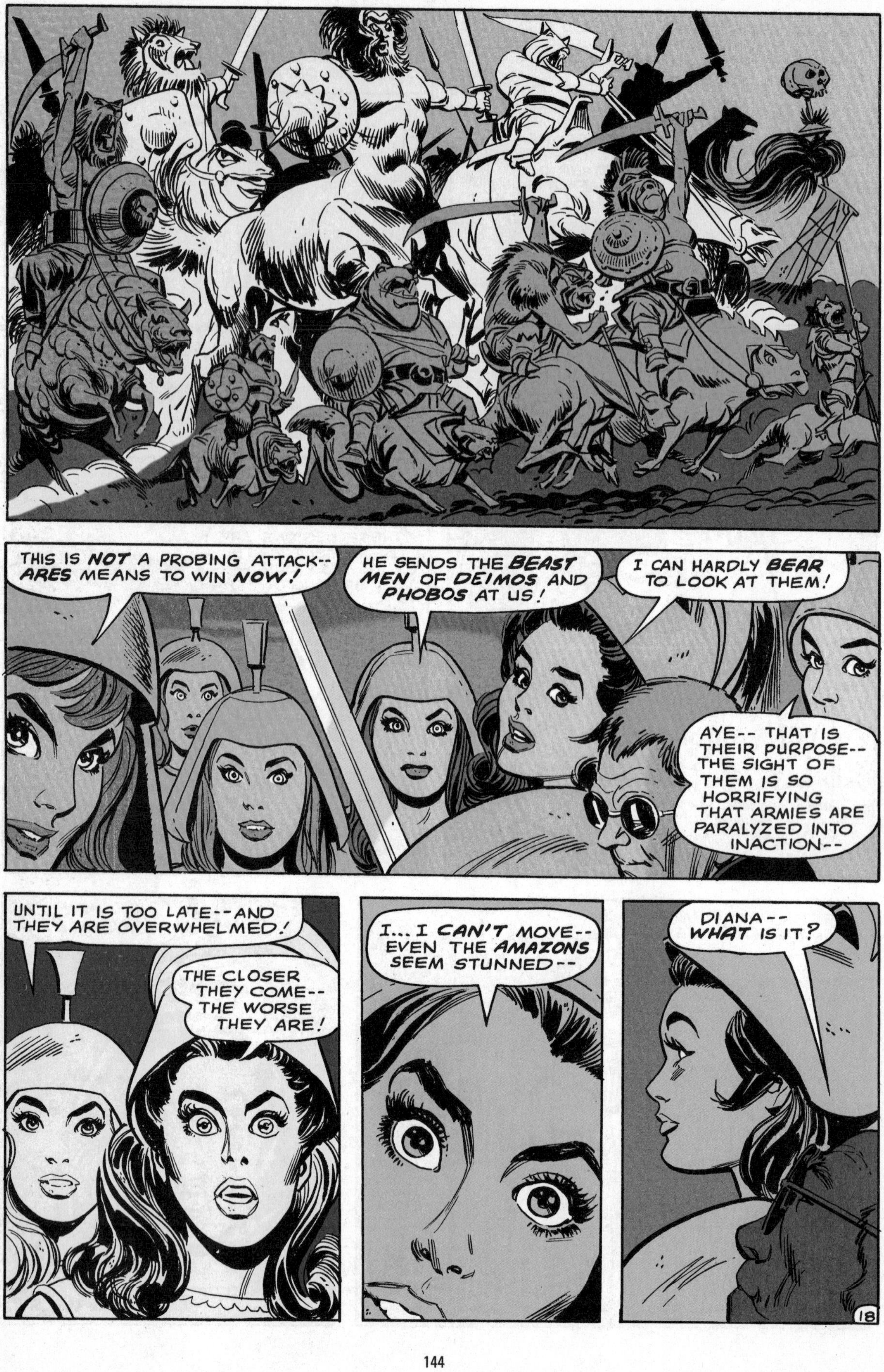
THIS IS NOT A PROBING ATTACK-- ARES MEANS TO WIN NOW!
HE SENDS THE BEAST MEN OF DEIMOS AND PHOBOS AT US!
I CAN HARDLY BEAR TO LOOK AT THEM!
AYE-- THAT IS THEIR PURPOSE-- THE SIGHT OF THEM IS SO HORRIFYING THAT ARMIES ARE PARALYZED INTO INACTION--
UNTIL IT IS TOO LATE--AND THEY ARE OVERWHELMED!
THE CLOSER THEY COME-- THE WORSE THEY ARE!
I... I CAN'T MOVE-- EVEN THE AMAZONS SEEM STUNNED--
DIANA-- WHAT IS IT?
18

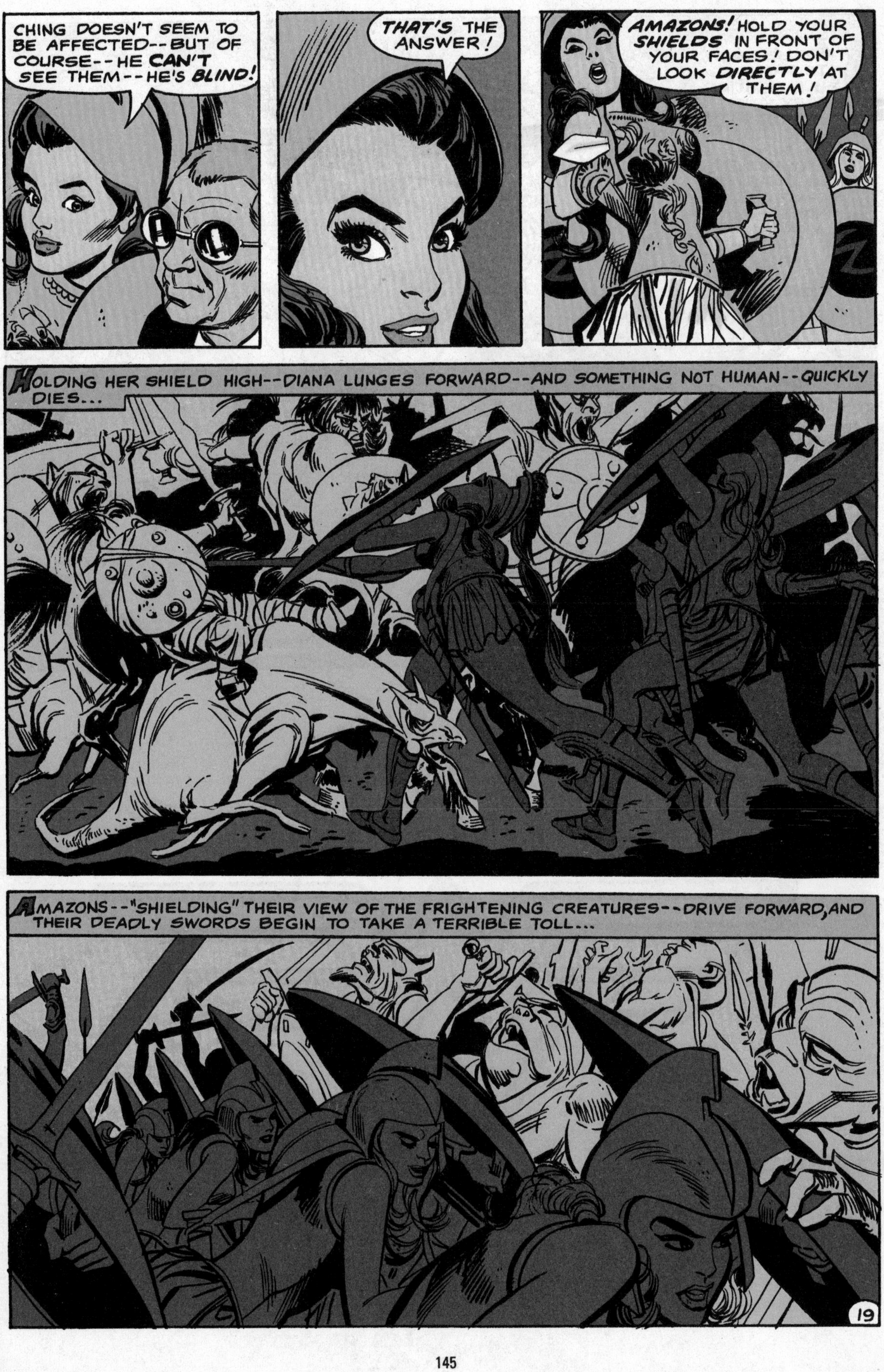
CHING DOESN'T SEEM TO BE AFFECTED--BUT OF COURSE--HE CAN'T SEE THEM--HE'S BLIND!
THAT'S THE ANSWER!
AMAZONS! HOLD YOUR SHIELDS IN FRONT OF YOUR FACES! DON'T LOOK DIRECTLY AT THEM!
HOLDING HER SHIELD HIGH--DIANA LUNGES FORWARD--AND SOMETHING NOT HUMAN--QUICKLY DIES...
AMAZONS--"SHIELDING" THEIR VIEW OF THE FRIGHTENING CREATURES--DRIVE FORWARD, AND THEIR DEADLY SWORDS BEGIN TO TAKE A TERRIBLE TOLL...
19

AROUSED NOW, TO THEIR FULL FIGHTING FURY, THE AMAZONS MERCILESSLY MOVE FORWARD. GIVING NO QUARTER AND ASKING NONE, BEAST-MAN AND AMAZON FALL...
STORY CONTINUES ON THE FOLLOWING PAGE...
20

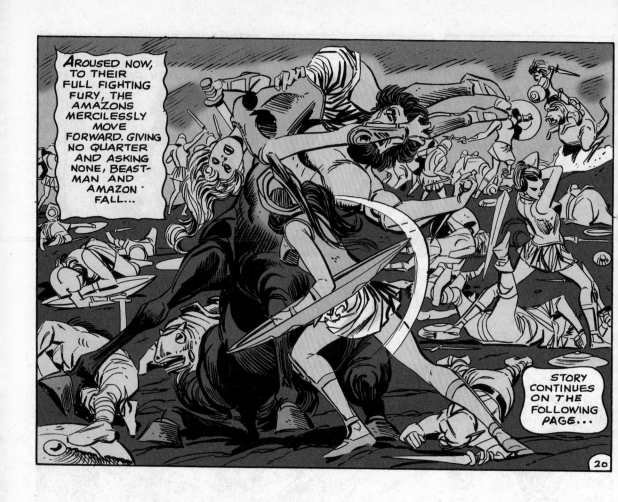

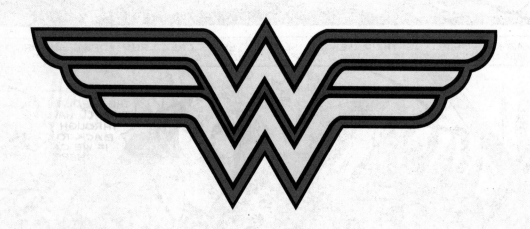

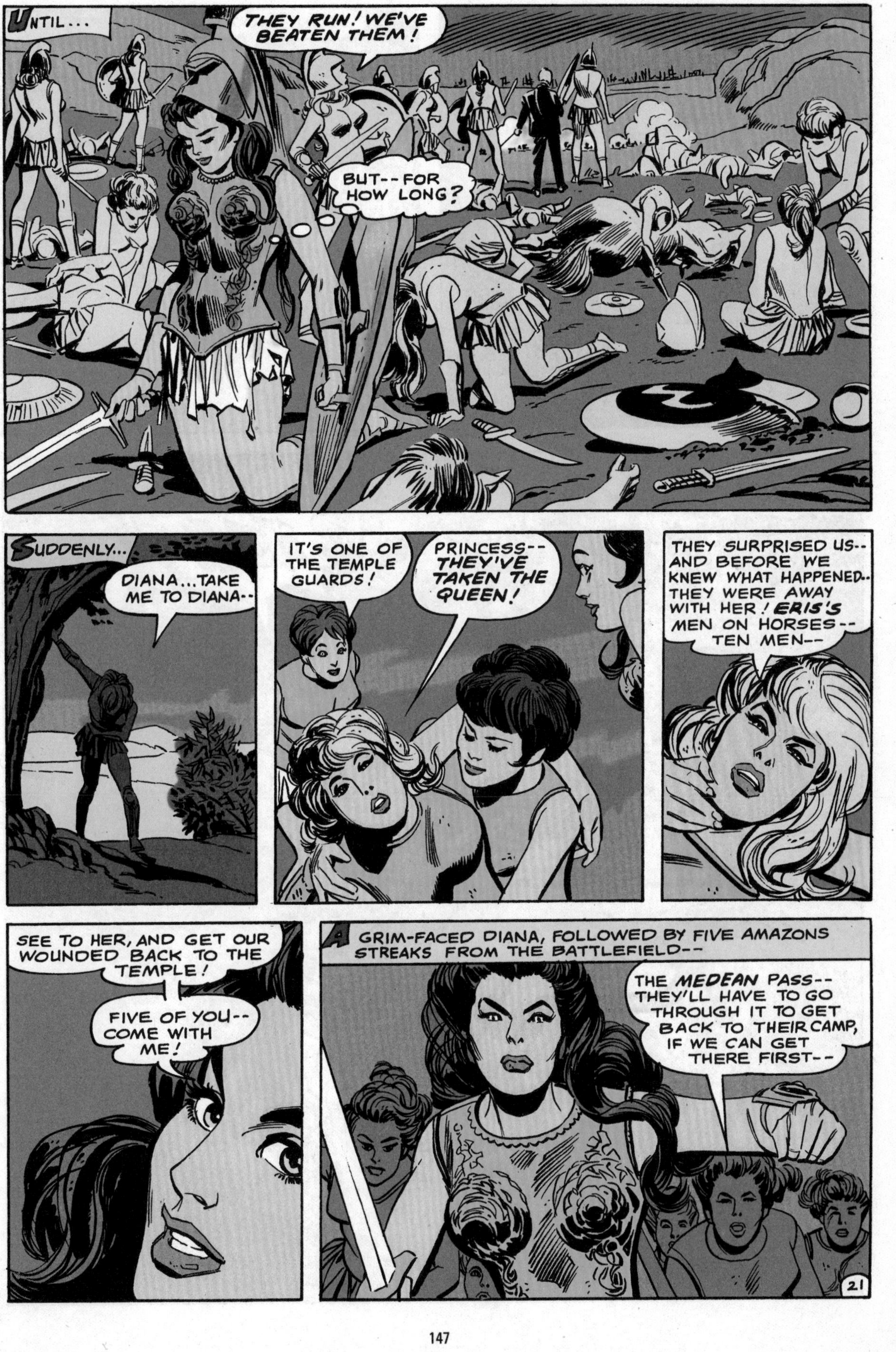
UNTIL...
THEY RUN! WE'VE BEATEN THEM!
BUT--FOR HOW LONG?
SUDDENLY...
DIANA...TAKE ME TO DIANA--
IT'S ONE OF THE TEMPLE GUARDS!
PRINCESS-- THEY'VE TAKEN THE QUEEN!
THEY SURPRISED US-- AND BEFORE WE KNEW WHAT HAPPENED.. THEY WERE AWAY WITH HER! ERIS'S MEN ON HORSES-- TEN MEN--
SEE TO HER, AND GET OUR WOUNDED BACK TO THE TEMPLE!
FIVE OF YOU-- COME WITH ME!
A GRIM-FACED DIANA, FOLLOWED BY FIVE AMAZONS STREAKS FROM THE BATTLEFIELD--
THE MEDEAN PASS-- THEY'LL HAVE TO GO THROUGH IT TO GET BACK TO THEIR CAMP, IF WE CAN GET THERE FIRST--
21

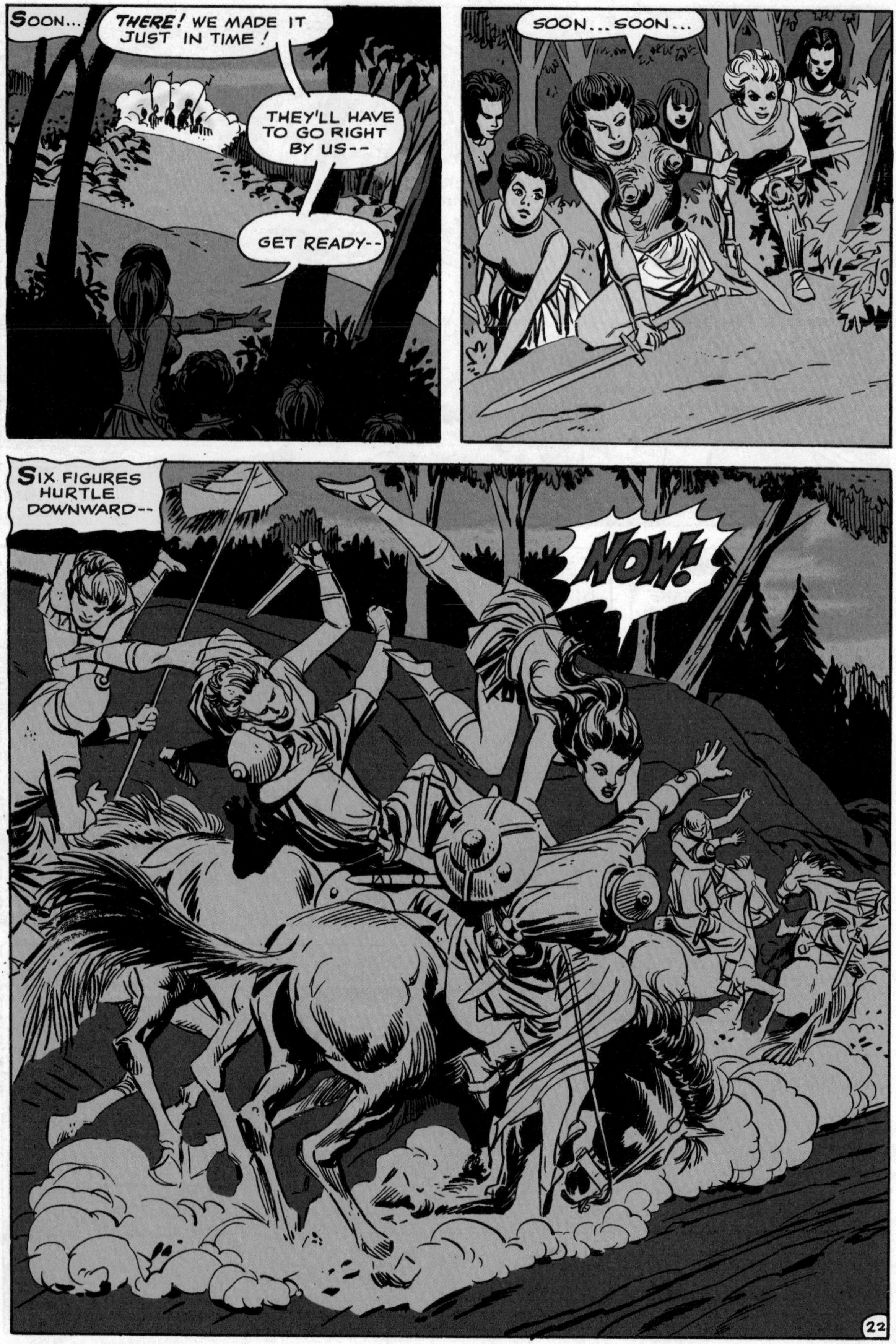
SOON...
THERE! WE MADE IT JUST IN TIME!
THEY'LL HAVE TO GO RIGHT BY US--
GET READY--
SOON... SOON...
SIX FIGURES HURTLE DOWNWARD--
NOW!
22

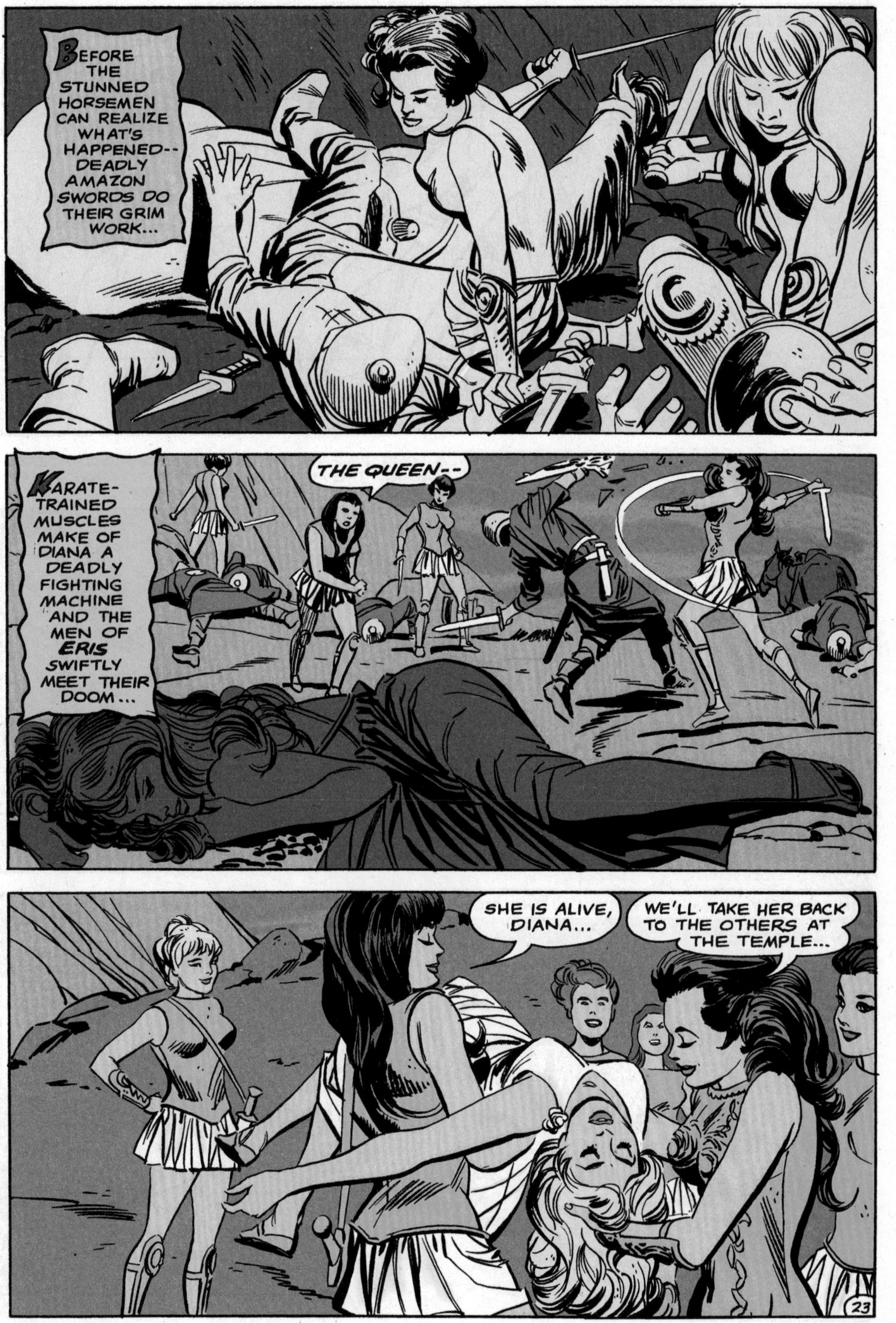
BEFORE THE STUNNED HORSEMEN CAN REALIZE WHAT'S HAPPENED-- DEADLY AMAZON SWORDS DO THEIR GRIM WORK...
KARATE-TRAINED MUSCLES MAKE OF DIANA A DEADLY FIGHTING MACHINE AND THE MEN OF ERIS SWIFTLY MEET THEIR DOOM...
THE QUEEN--
SHE IS ALIVE, DIANA...
WE'LL TAKE HER BACK TO THE OTHERS AT THE TEMPLE...
23

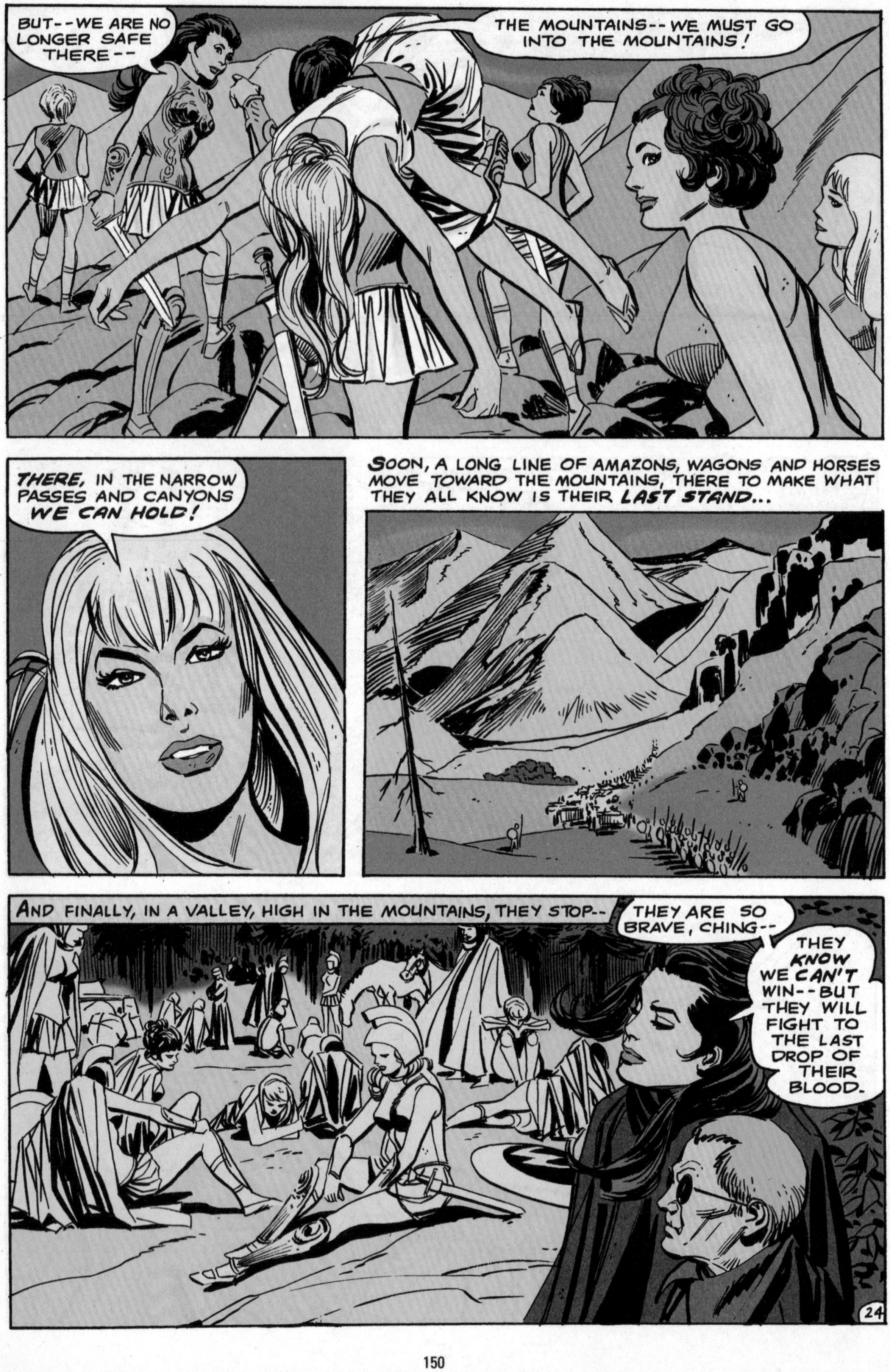
BUT--WE ARE NO LONGER SAFE THERE--
THE MOUNTAINS--WE MUST GO INTO THE MOUNTAINS!
THERE, IN THE NARROW PASSES AND CANYONS WE CAN HOLD!
SOON, A LONG LINE OF AMAZONS, WAGONS AND HORSES MOVE TOWARD THE MOUNTAINS, THERE TO MAKE WHAT THEY ALL KNOW IS THEIR LAST STAND...
AND FINALLY, IN A VALLEY, HIGH IN THE MOUNTAINS, THEY STOP--
THEY ARE SO BRAVE, CHING--
THEY KNOW WE CAN'T WIN--BUT THEY WILL FIGHT TO THE LAST DROP OF THEIR BLOOD.
24

I *MUST* THINK OF A WAY--THERE *MUST* BE A WAY TO *SAVE* THEM AND STOP *ARES*--

YOU ARE TIRED, TOO, DIANA. REST-- AND IN THE MORNING--

NO, CHING--I MUST FIND THE ANSWER NOW--

TONIGHT!

THERE IS SO *LITTLE* TIME LEFT BEFORE *ARES* COMES!

*A*ND SO, DIANA, TIRED AND BATTLE-WEARY, STANDS ALONE--HER HEAD BOWED--AND DESPERATELY WRACKS HER BRAIN FOR A SOLUTION...

END OF PART ONE...

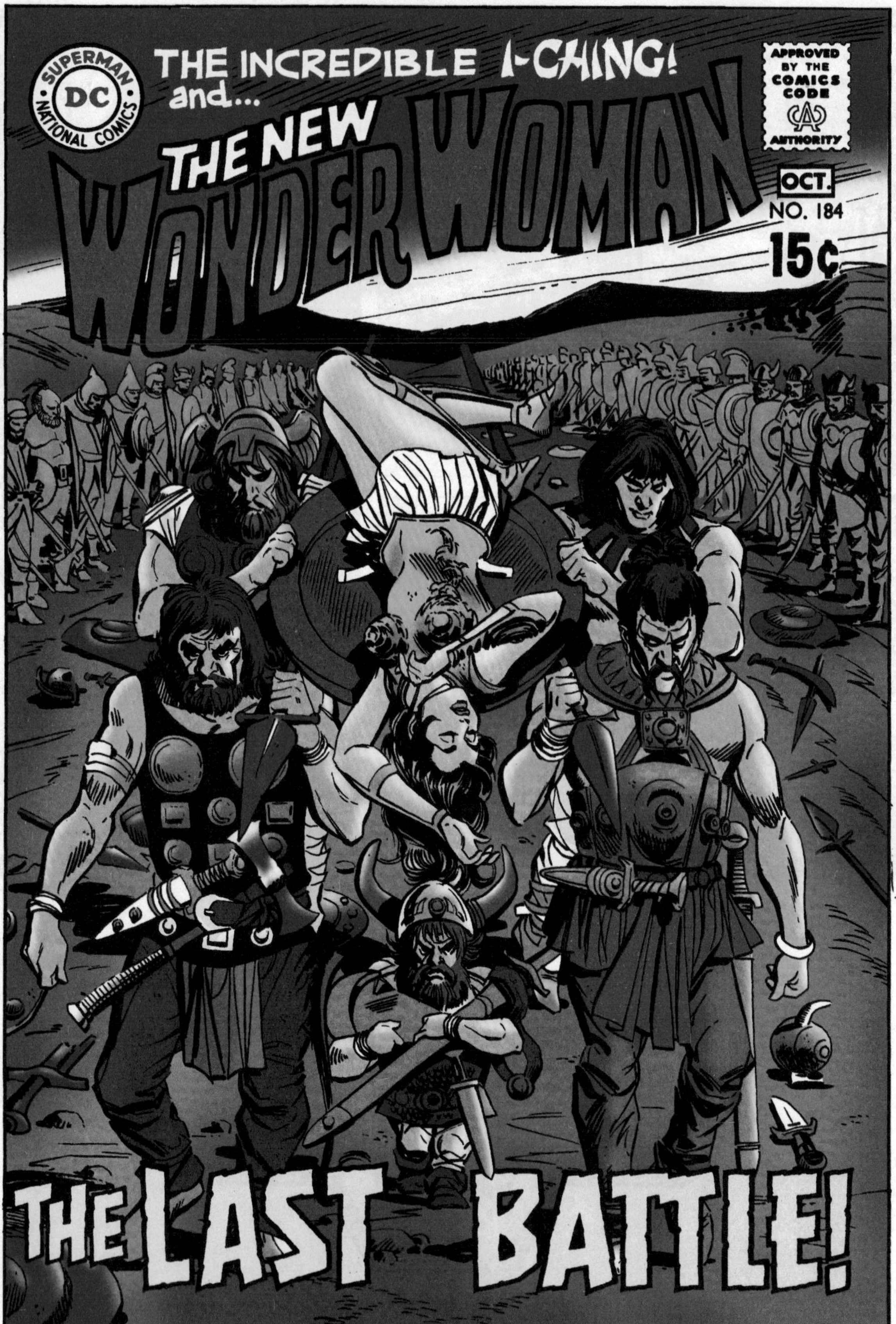
SUPERMAN DC NATIONAL COMICS
THE INCREDIBLE I-CHING!
and...
THE NEW
WONDER WOMAN
APPROVED BY THE COMICS CODE AUTHORITY
OCT.
NO. 184
15¢
THE LAST BATTLE!

THE NEW WONDER WOMAN

Answering her mother's call for help, DIANA (*WONDER WOMAN*) PRINCE AND **I CHING** ARRIVE ON **PARADISE ISLAND**, ONLY TO FIND HER MOTHER LYING IN AN ENCHANTED SLEEP FROM WHICH SHE CANNOT BE AWAKENED! PARADISE ISLAND IS TERRIBLY RAVAGED BY WAR, A WAR BROUGHT ON BY DIANA'S GRANDFATHER, **ARES**, **GOD OF WAR**, WHO IN HIS MAD DESIRE TO WREST FROM HIS DAUGHTER, **HIPPOLYTA**, QUEEN OF THE AMAZONS, THE SECRET OF DIMENSIONAL TRAVEL. A SECRET THAT HE NEEDS AND WANTS SO THAT HE MAY POUR HIS ARMIES ONTO EARTH AND OTHER WORLDS, KNOWING THAT ONLY THROUGH WAR CAN HE AGAIN BE THE POWERFUL GOD HE ONCE WAS. RALLYING HER MOTHER'S AMAZONS TO HER, DIANA LEADS THEM AGAINST **ARES** IN A DESPERATE ATTEMPT TO STOP HIM. BRAVELY THEY FIGHT--BUT AGAINST SUCH OVERWHELMING ODDS AS **ARES** THROWS AT THEM--EVEN AMAZON BRAVERY AND COURAGE CANNOT PREVAIL. NOW, DRIVEN BACK INTO THE MOUNTAINS, DIANA AND HER AMAZONS WAIT-- WAIT FOR THE BATTLE THEY **MUST** FIGHT--AND THE BATTLE THEY **KNOW** THEY **CANNOT** WIN--

THE Last BATTLE!

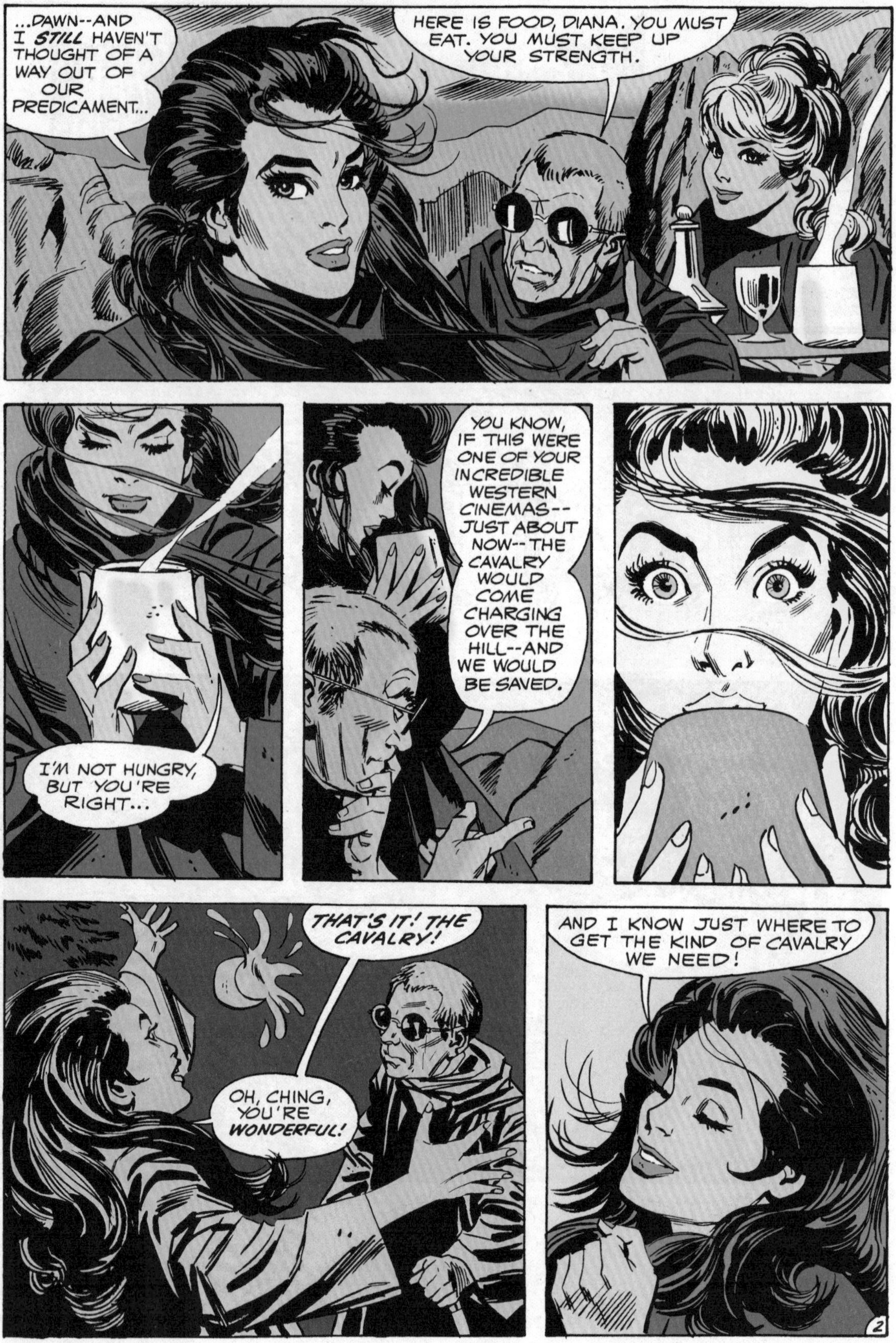
...DAWN--AND I STILL HAVEN'T THOUGHT OF A WAY OUT OF OUR PREDICAMENT...
HERE IS FOOD, DIANA. YOU MUST EAT. YOU MUST KEEP UP YOUR STRENGTH.
I'M NOT HUNGRY, BUT YOU'RE RIGHT...
YOU KNOW, IF THIS WERE ONE OF YOUR INCREDIBLE WESTERN CINEMAS-- JUST ABOUT NOW--THE CAVALRY WOULD COME CHARGING OVER THE HILL--AND WE WOULD BE SAVED.
THAT'S IT! THE CAVALRY!
OH, CHING, YOU'RE WONDERFUL!
AND I KNOW JUST WHERE TO GET THE KIND OF CAVALRY WE NEED!
2

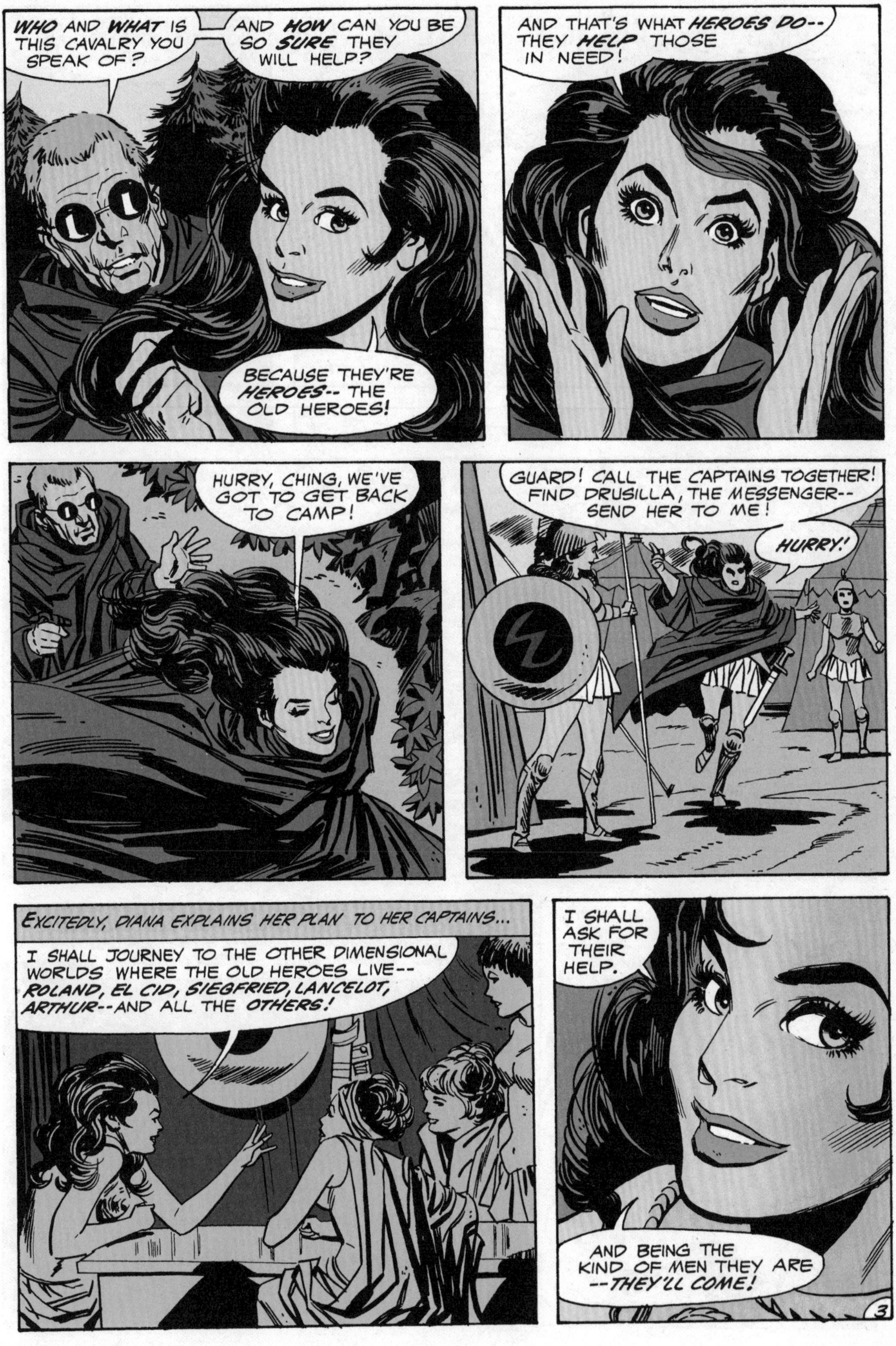
WHO AND WHAT IS THIS CAVALRY YOU SPEAK OF?
AND HOW CAN YOU BE SO SURE THEY WILL HELP?
BECAUSE THEY'RE HEROES-- THE OLD HEROES!
AND THAT'S WHAT HEROES DO-- THEY HELP THOSE IN NEED!
HURRY, CHING, WE'VE GOT TO GET BACK TO CAMP!
GUARD! CALL THE CAPTAINS TOGETHER! FIND DRUSILLA, THE MESSENGER-- SEND HER TO ME!
HURRY!
EXCITEDLY, DIANA EXPLAINS HER PLAN TO HER CAPTAINS...
I SHALL JOURNEY TO THE OTHER DIMENSIONAL WORLDS WHERE THE OLD HEROES LIVE-- ROLAND, EL CID, SIEGFRIED, LANCELOT, ARTHUR--AND ALL THE OTHERS!
I SHALL ASK FOR THEIR HELP.
AND BEING THE KIND OF MEN THEY ARE --THEY'LL COME!
3

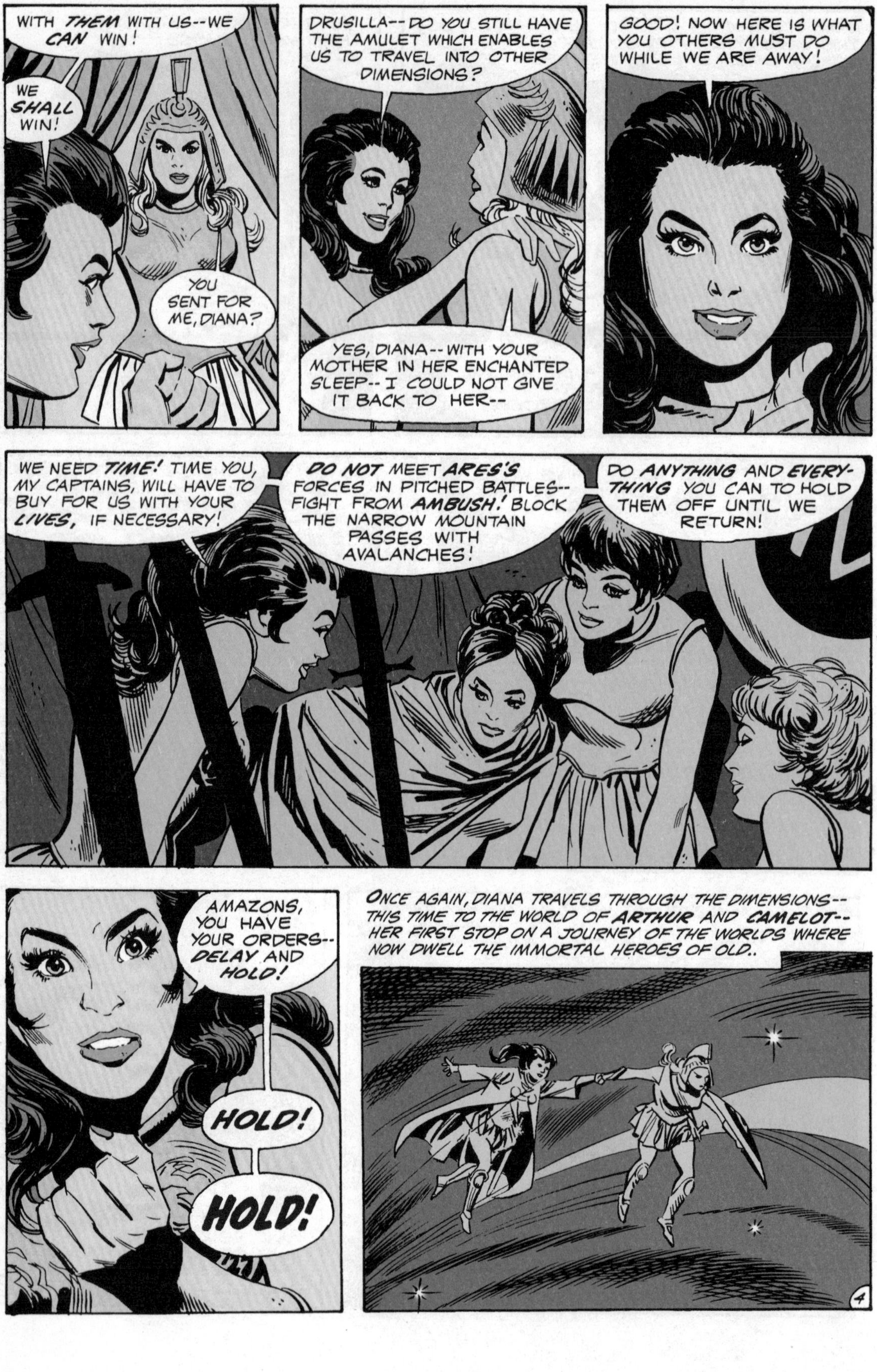

WITH THEM WITH US--WE CAN WIN!
WE SHALL WIN!
YOU SENT FOR ME, DIANA?
DRUSILLA--DO YOU STILL HAVE THE AMULET WHICH ENABLES US TO TRAVEL INTO OTHER DIMENSIONS?
YES, DIANA--WITH YOUR MOTHER IN HER ENCHANTED SLEEP--I COULD NOT GIVE IT BACK TO HER--
GOOD! NOW HERE IS WHAT YOU OTHERS MUST DO WHILE WE ARE AWAY!
WE NEED TIME! TIME YOU, MY CAPTAINS, WILL HAVE TO BUY FOR US WITH YOUR LIVES, IF NECESSARY!
DO NOT MEET ARES'S FORCES IN PITCHED BATTLES--FIGHT FROM AMBUSH! BLOCK THE NARROW MOUNTAIN PASSES WITH AVALANCHES!
DO ANYTHING AND EVERYTHING YOU CAN TO HOLD THEM OFF UNTIL WE RETURN!
AMAZONS, YOU HAVE YOUR ORDERS--DELAY AND HOLD!
HOLD!
HOLD!
ONCE AGAIN, DIANA TRAVELS THROUGH THE DIMENSIONS--THIS TIME TO THE WORLD OF ARTHUR AND CAMELOT--HER FIRST STOP ON A JOURNEY OF THE WORLDS WHERE NOW DWELL THE IMMORTAL HEROES OF OLD..
4

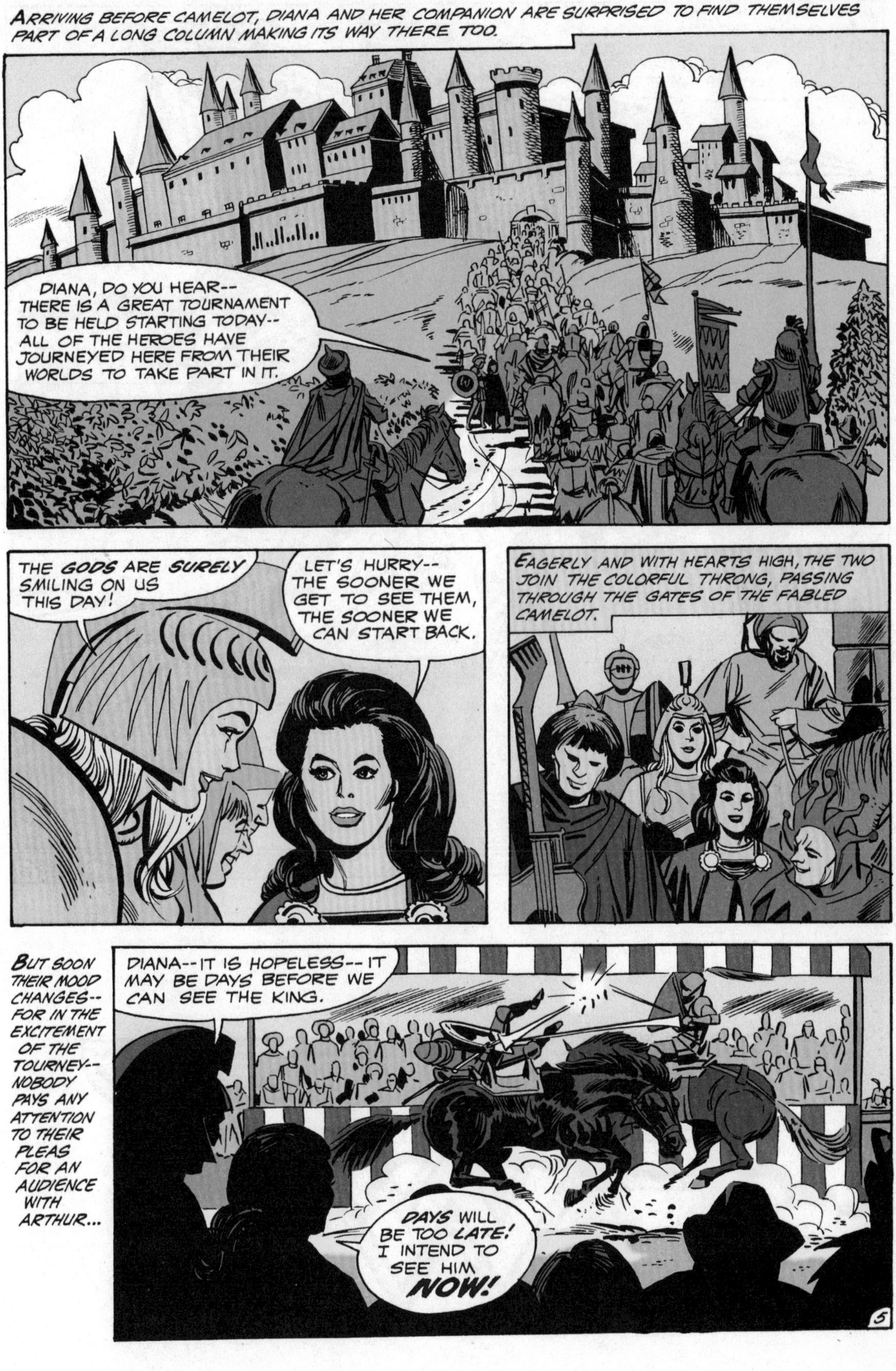
ARRIVING BEFORE CAMELOT, DIANA AND HER COMPANION ARE SURPRISED TO FIND THEMSELVES PART OF A LONG COLUMN MAKING ITS WAY THERE TOO.
DIANA, DO YOU HEAR-- THERE IS A GREAT TOURNAMENT TO BE HELD STARTING TODAY-- ALL OF THE HEROES HAVE JOURNEYED HERE FROM THEIR WORLDS TO TAKE PART IN IT.
THE GODS ARE SURELY SMILING ON US THIS DAY!
LET'S HURRY-- THE SOONER WE GET TO SEE THEM, THE SOONER WE CAN START BACK.
EAGERLY AND WITH HEARTS HIGH, THE TWO JOIN THE COLORFUL THRONG, PASSING THROUGH THE GATES OF THE FABLED CAMELOT.
BUT SOON THEIR MOOD CHANGES-- FOR IN THE EXCITEMENT OF THE TOURNEY-- NOBODY PAYS ANY ATTENTION TO THEIR PLEAS FOR AN AUDIENCE WITH ARTHUR...
DIANA-- IT IS HOPELESS-- IT MAY BE DAYS BEFORE WE CAN SEE THE KING.
DAYS WILL BE TOO LATE! I INTEND TO SEE HIM NOW!
5

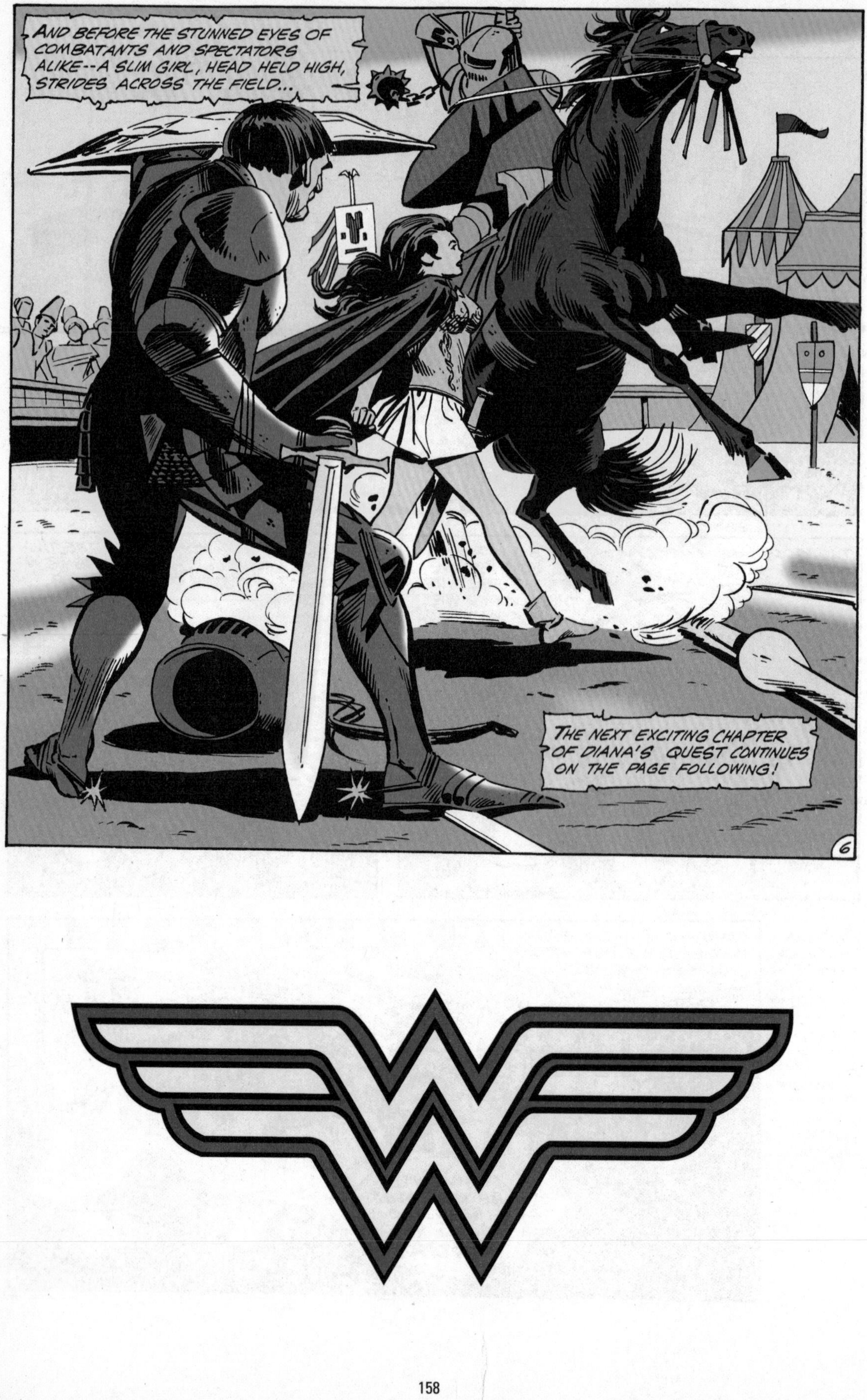
AND BEFORE THE STUNNED EYES OF COMBATANTS AND SPECTATORS ALIKE--A SLIM GIRL, HEAD HELD HIGH, STRIDES ACROSS THE FIELD...
THE NEXT EXCITING CHAPTER OF DIANA'S QUEST CONTINUES ON THE PAGE FOLLOWING!
6

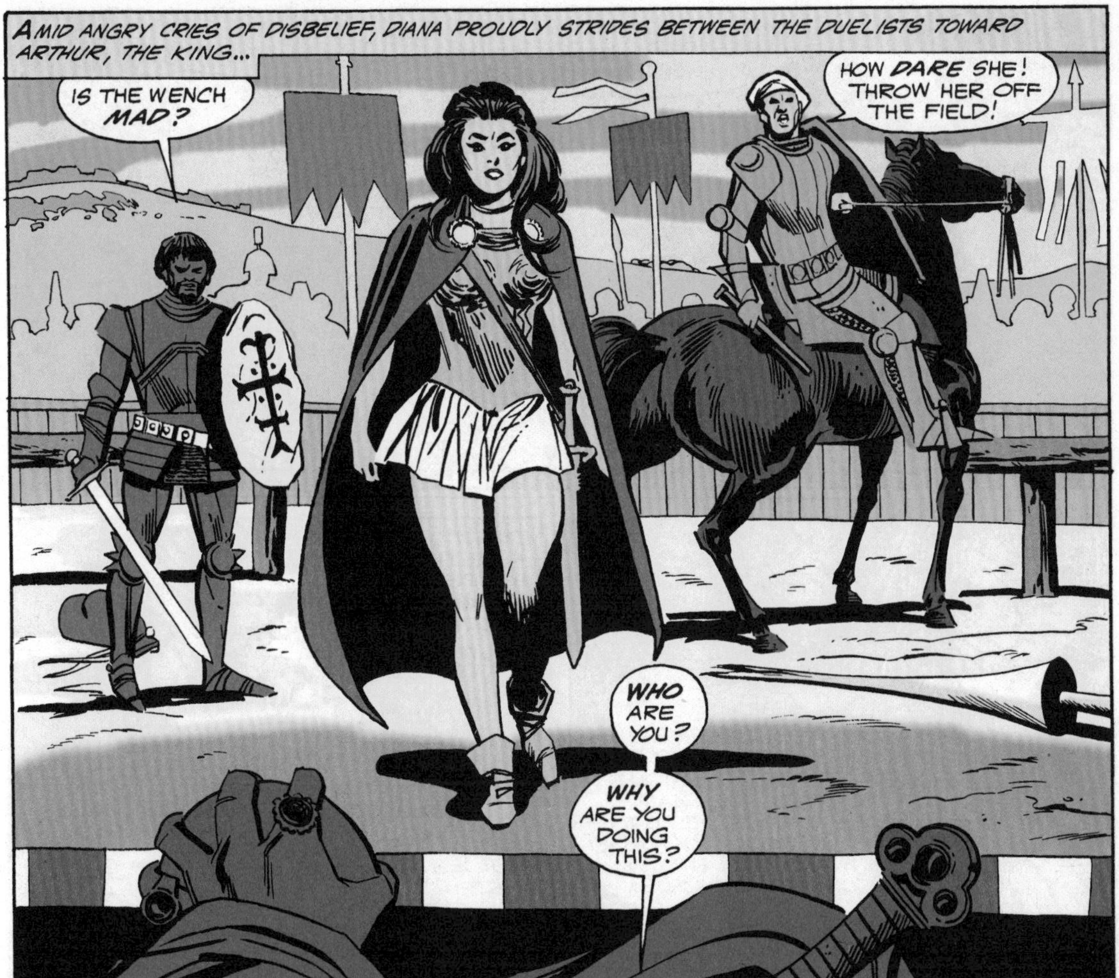
AMID ANGRY CRIES OF DISBELIEF, DIANA PROUDLY STRIDES BETWEEN THE DUELISTS TOWARD ARTHUR, THE KING...
IS THE WENCH MAD?
HOW DARE SHE! THROW HER OFF THE FIELD!
WHO ARE YOU?
WHY ARE YOU DOING THIS?

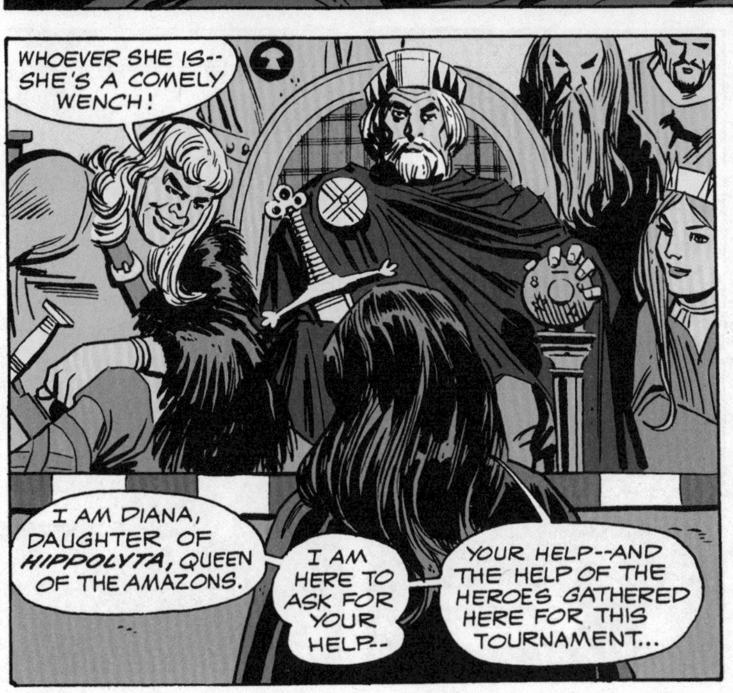
WHOEVER SHE IS--SHE'S A COMELY WENCH!
I AM DIANA, DAUGHTER OF HIPPOLYTA, QUEEN OF THE AMAZONS.
I AM HERE TO ASK FOR YOUR HELP--
YOUR HELP--AND THE HELP OF THE HEROES GATHERED HERE FOR THIS TOURNAMENT...

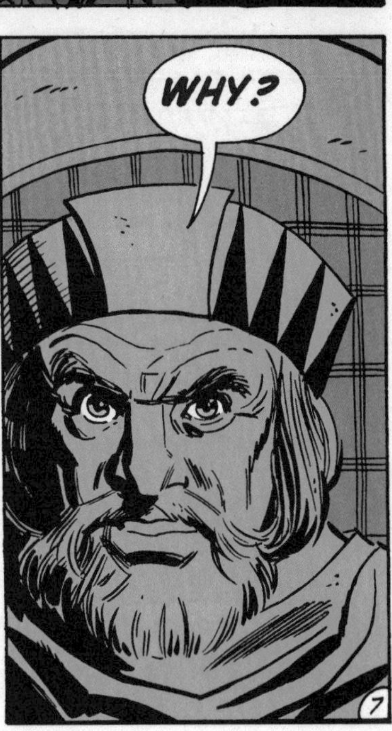
WHY?
7

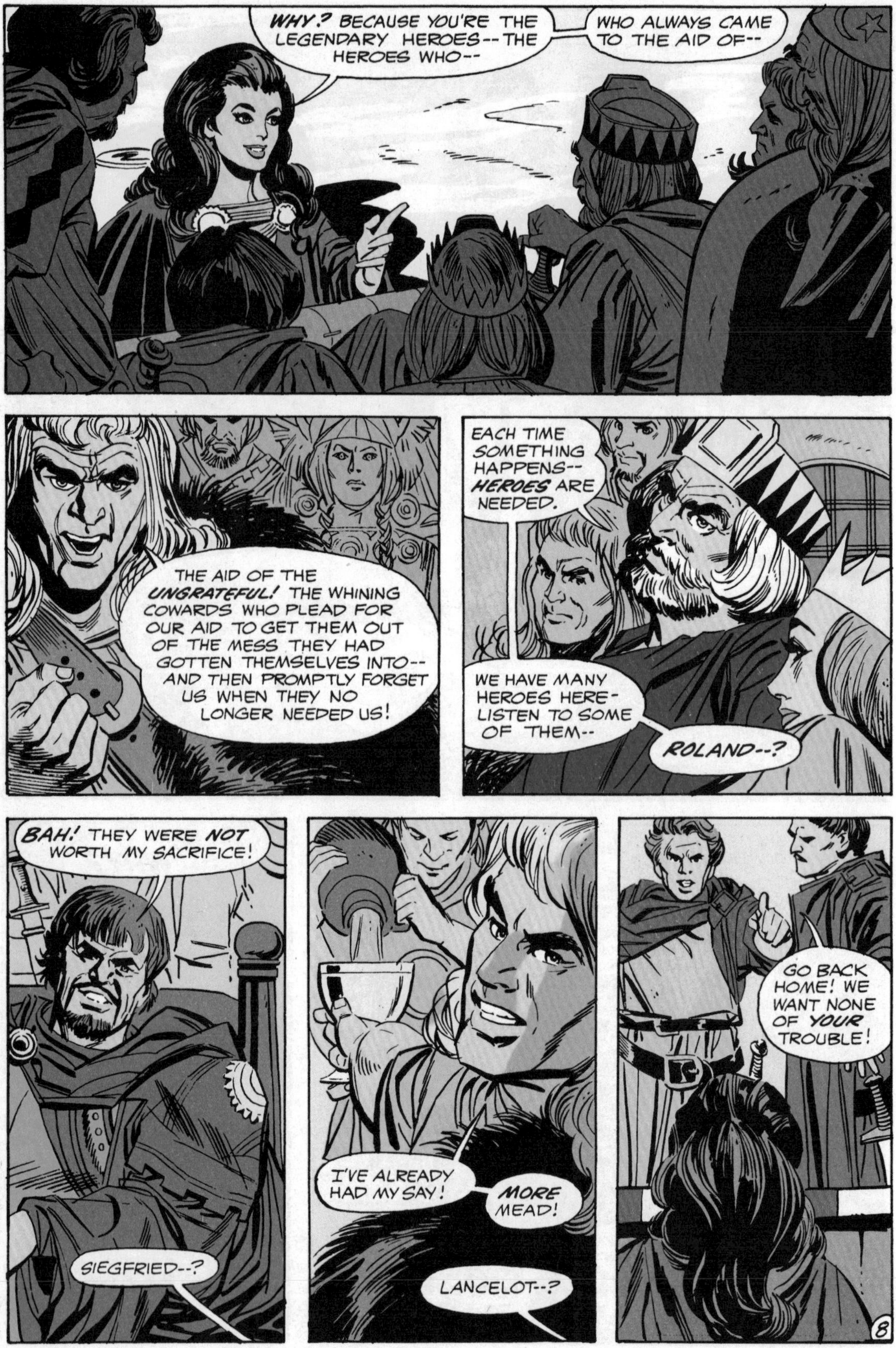
WHY? BECAUSE YOU'RE THE LEGENDARY HEROES--THE HEROES WHO--
WHO ALWAYS CAME TO THE AID OF--
THE AID OF THE UNGRATEFUL! THE WHINING COWARDS WHO PLEAD FOR OUR AID TO GET THEM OUT OF THE MESS THEY HAD GOTTEN THEMSELVES INTO-- --AND THEN PROMPTLY FORGET US WHEN THEY NO LONGER NEEDED US!
EACH TIME SOMETHING HAPPENS-- HEROES ARE NEEDED.
WE HAVE MANY HEROES HERE- LISTEN TO SOME OF THEM--
ROLAND--?
BAH! THEY WERE NOT WORTH MY SACRIFICE!
SIEGFRIED--?
I'VE ALREADY HAD MY SAY!
MORE MEAD!
LANCELOT--?
GO BACK HOME! WE WANT NONE OF YOUR TROUBLE!
8

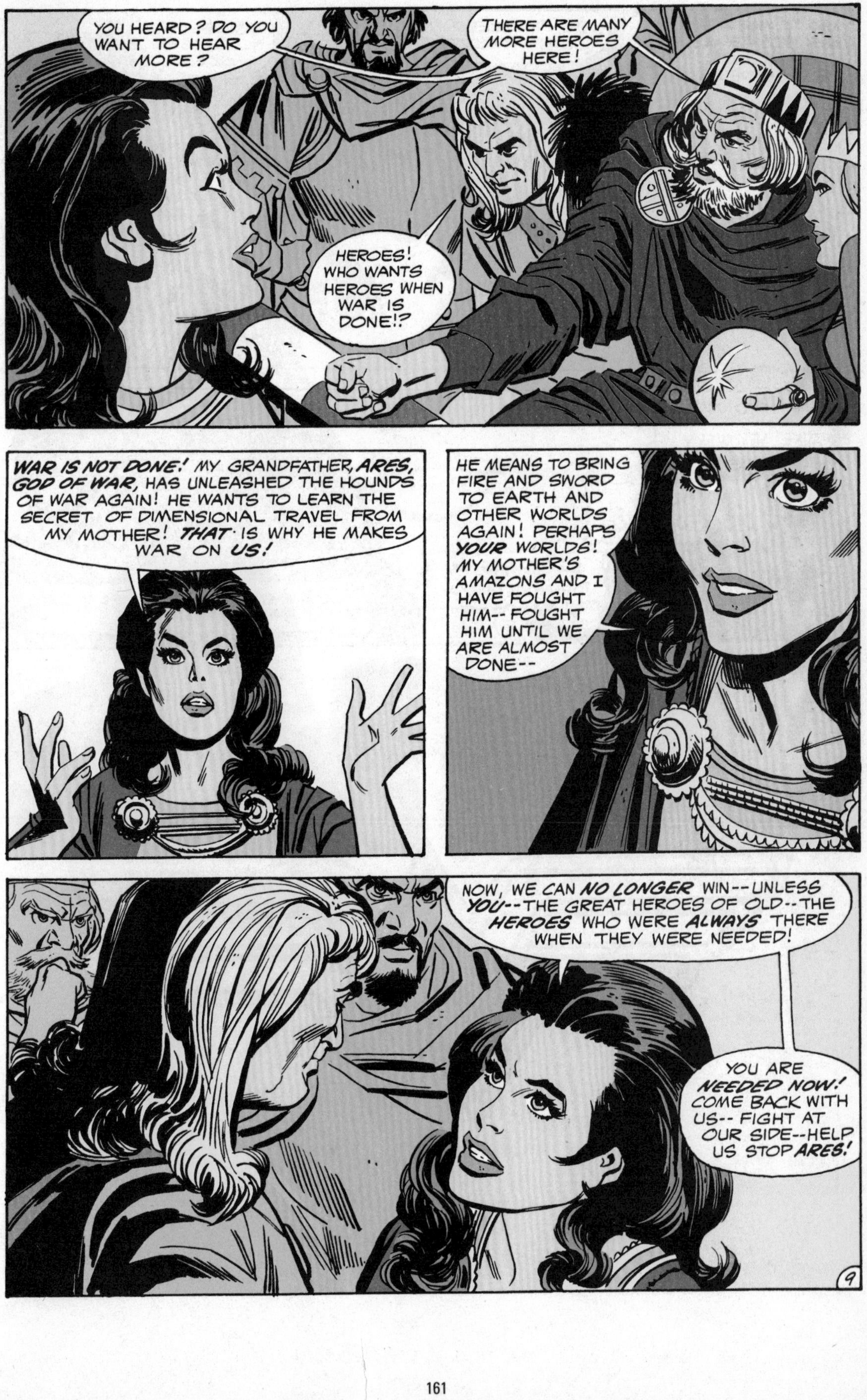
YOU HEARD? DO YOU WANT TO HEAR MORE?
THERE ARE MANY MORE HEROES HERE!
HEROES! WHO WANTS HEROES WHEN WAR IS DONE!?
WAR IS NOT DONE! MY GRANDFATHER, ARES, GOD OF WAR, HAS UNLEASHED THE HOUNDS OF WAR AGAIN! HE WANTS TO LEARN THE SECRET OF DIMENSIONAL TRAVEL FROM MY MOTHER! THAT IS WHY HE MAKES WAR ON US!
HE MEANS TO BRING FIRE AND SWORD TO EARTH AND OTHER WORLDS AGAIN! PERHAPS YOUR WORLDS! MY MOTHER'S AMAZONS AND I HAVE FOUGHT HIM-- FOUGHT HIM UNTIL WE ARE ALMOST DONE--
NOW, WE CAN NO LONGER WIN--UNLESS YOU--THE GREAT HEROES OF OLD--THE HEROES WHO WERE ALWAYS THERE WHEN THEY WERE NEEDED!
YOU ARE NEEDED NOW! COME BACK WITH US-- FIGHT AT OUR SIDE--HELP US STOP ARES!
9

GO TO WAR AGAIN? NEVER! WE ARE DONE WITH SUCH FOOLISHNESS!
AYE--TO BLEED AND DIE--FOR NOTHING!
HEROES--BUT NO LONGER FOOLS!
GO AWAY!
ART AND STORY by MIKE SEKOWSKY
INKING by DICK GIORDANO
LETTERING by JOHN COSTANZA
FOR THE STUNNING CONCLUSION TURN TO THE PAGE FOLLOWING!
10

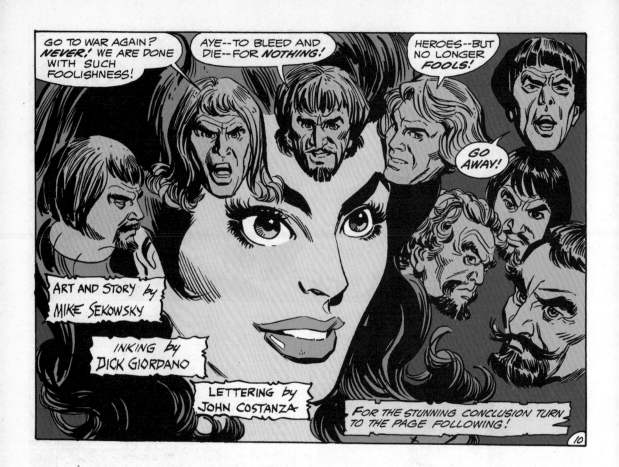

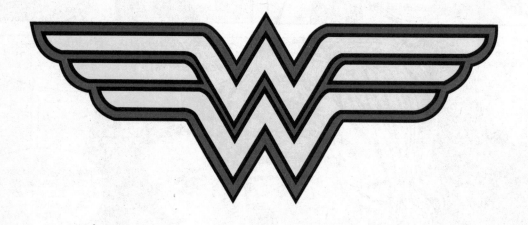

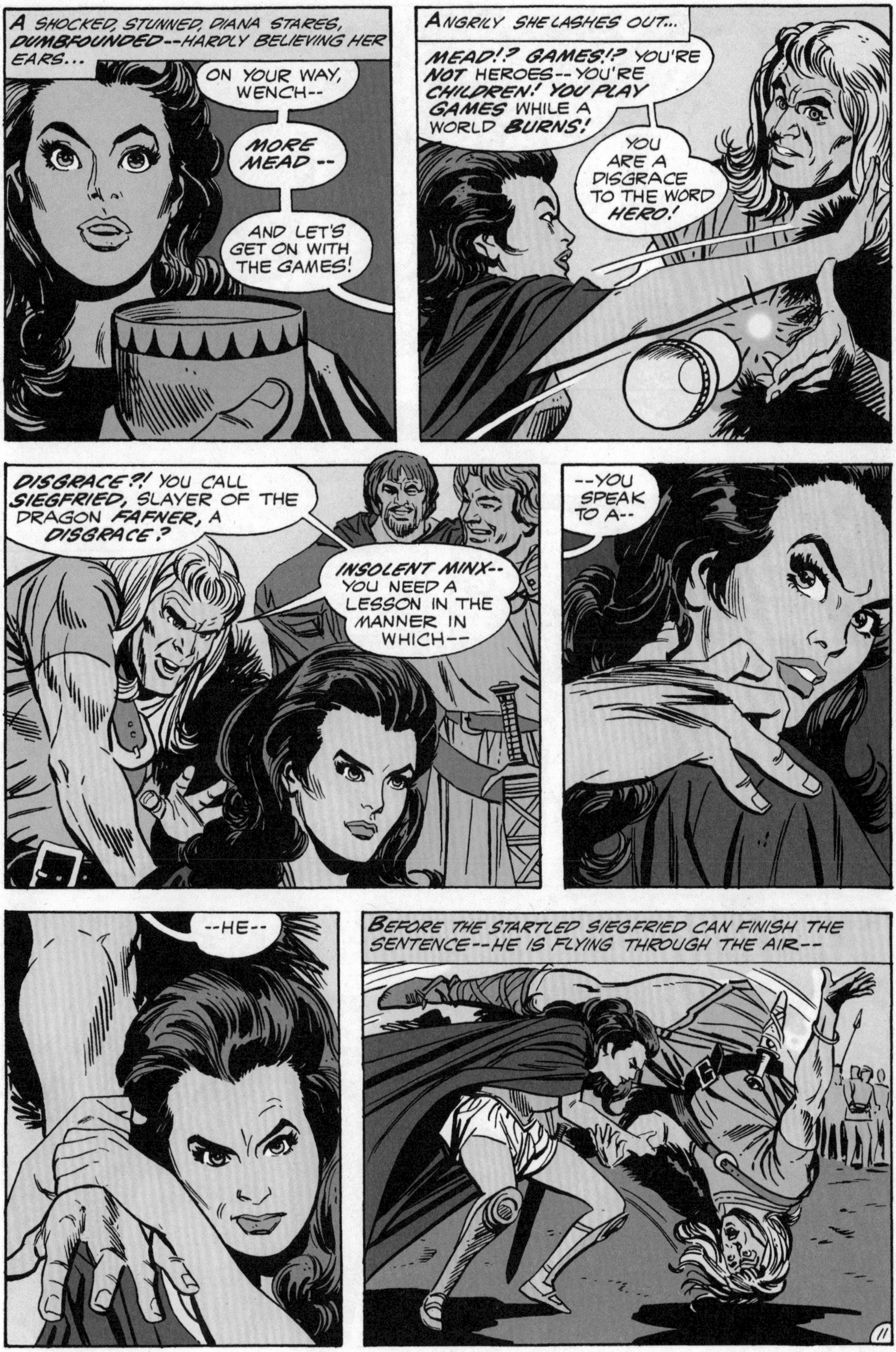
A SHOCKED, STUNNED, DIANA STARES, DUMBFOUNDED--HARDLY BELIEVING HER EARS...
ON YOUR WAY, WENCH--
MORE MEAD--
AND LET'S GET ON WITH THE GAMES!
ANGRILY SHE LASHES OUT...
MEAD!? GAMES!? YOU'RE NOT HEROES--YOU'RE CHILDREN! YOU PLAY GAMES WHILE A WORLD BURNS!
YOU ARE A DISGRACE TO THE WORD HERO!
DISGRACE?! YOU CALL SIEGFRIED, SLAYER OF THE DRAGON FAFNER, A DISGRACE?
INSOLENT MINX--YOU NEED A LESSON IN THE MANNER IN WHICH--
--YOU SPEAK TO A--
--HE--
BEFORE THE STARTLED SIEGFRIED CAN FINISH THE SENTENCE--HE IS FLYING THROUGH THE AIR--
11

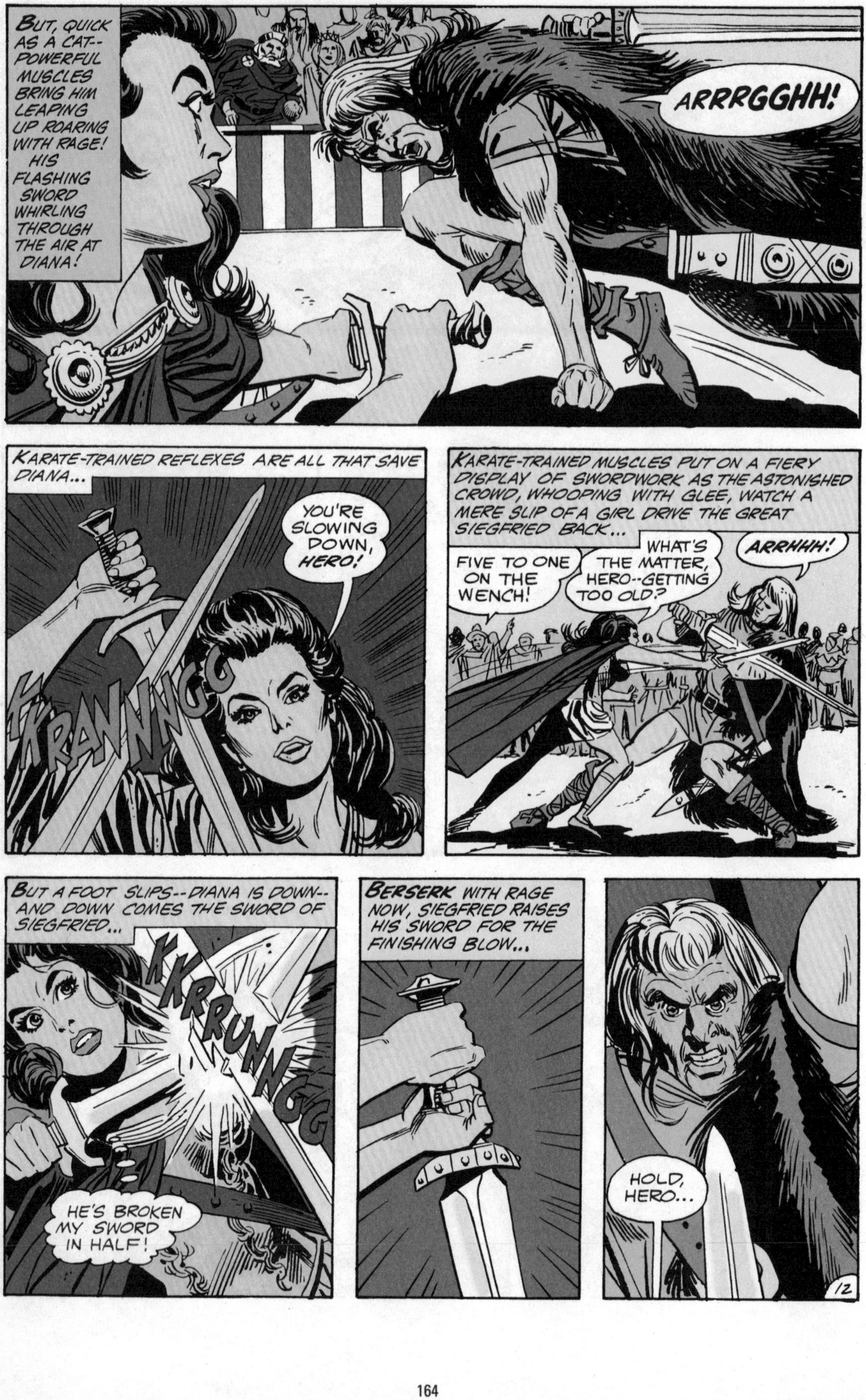
BUT, QUICK AS A CAT-- POWERFUL MUSCLES BRING HIM LEAPING UP ROARING WITH RAGE! HIS FLASHING SWORD WHIRLING THROUGH THE AIR AT DIANA!
ARRRGGHH!
KARATE-TRAINED REFLEXES ARE ALL THAT SAVE DIANA...
YOU'RE SLOWING DOWN, HERO!
KRANNNGG
KARATE-TRAINED MUSCLES PUT ON A FIERY DISPLAY OF SWORDWORK AS THE ASTONISHED CROWD, WHOOPING WITH GLEE, WATCH A MERE SLIP OF A GIRL DRIVE THE GREAT SIEGFRIED BACK...
FIVE TO ONE ON THE WENCH!
WHAT'S THE MATTER, HERO--GETTING TOO OLD?
ARRHHH!
BUT A FOOT SLIPS--DIANA IS DOWN-- AND DOWN COMES THE SWORD OF SIEGFRIED...
KKRRUNNGG
HE'S BROKEN MY SWORD IN HALF!
BERSERK WITH RAGE NOW, SIEGFRIED RAISES HIS SWORD FOR THE FINISHING BLOW...
HOLD, HERO...
12

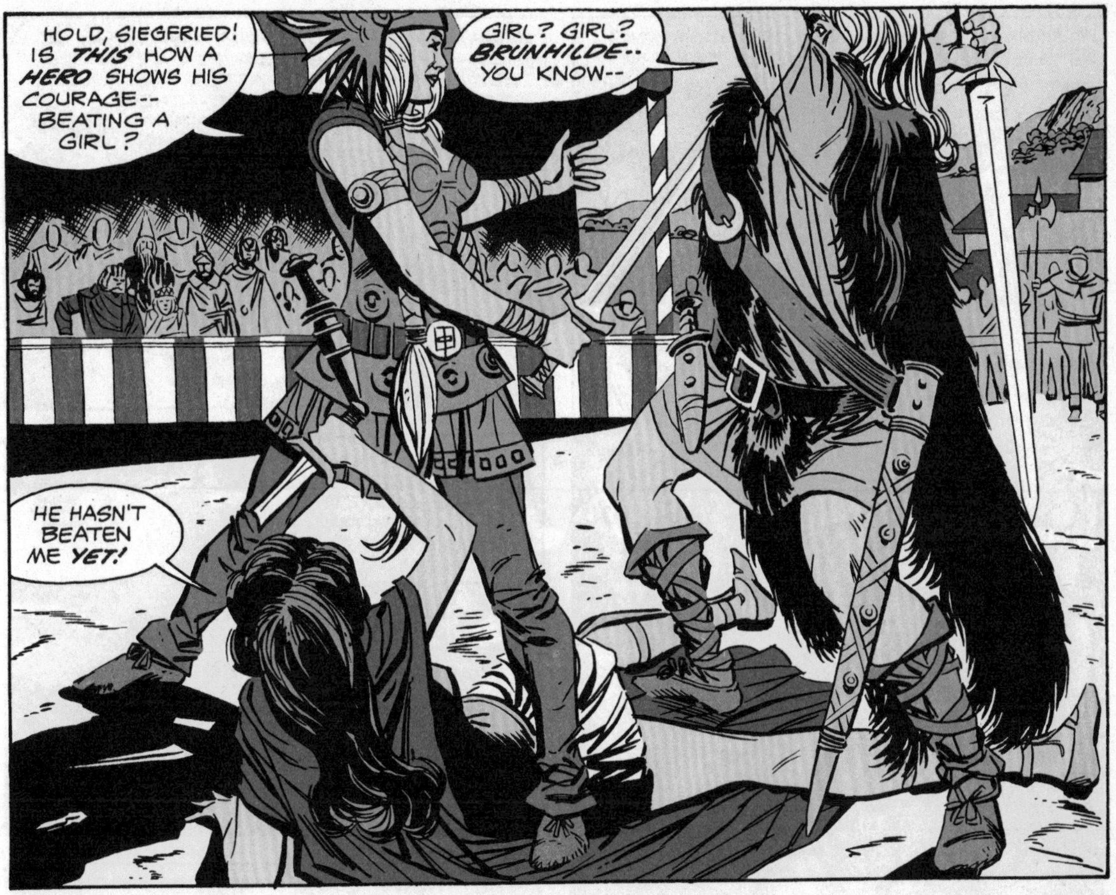
HOLD, SIEGFRIED! IS THIS HOW A HERO SHOWS HIS COURAGE-- BEATING A GIRL?
GIRL? GIRL? BRUNHILDE-- YOU KNOW--
HE HASN'T BEATEN ME YET!

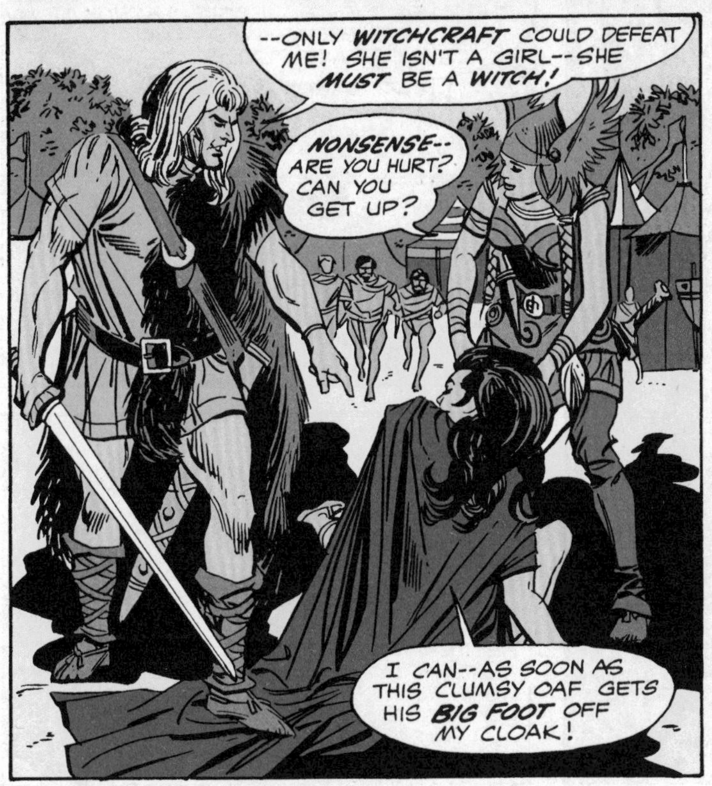
--ONLY WITCHCRAFT COULD DEFEAT ME! SHE ISN'T A GIRL--SHE MUST BE A WITCH!
NONSENSE-- ARE YOU HURT? CAN YOU GET UP?
I CAN--AS SOON AS THIS CLUMSY OAF GETS HIS BIG FOOT OFF MY CLOAK!

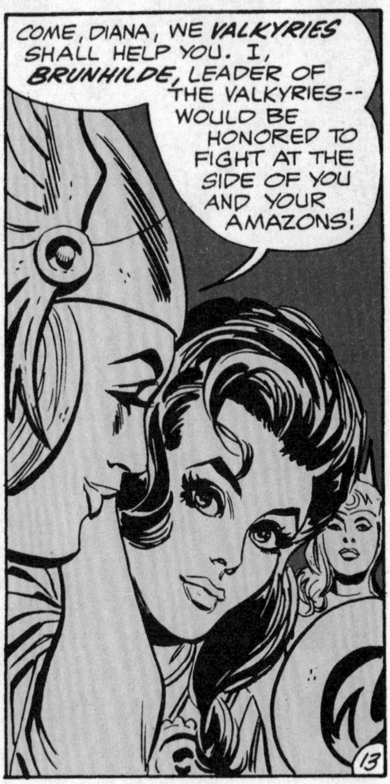
COME, DIANA, WE VALKYRIES SHALL HELP YOU. I, BRUNHILDE, LEADER OF THE VALKYRIES-- WOULD BE HONORED TO FIGHT AT THE SIDE OF YOU AND YOUR AMAZONS!
13

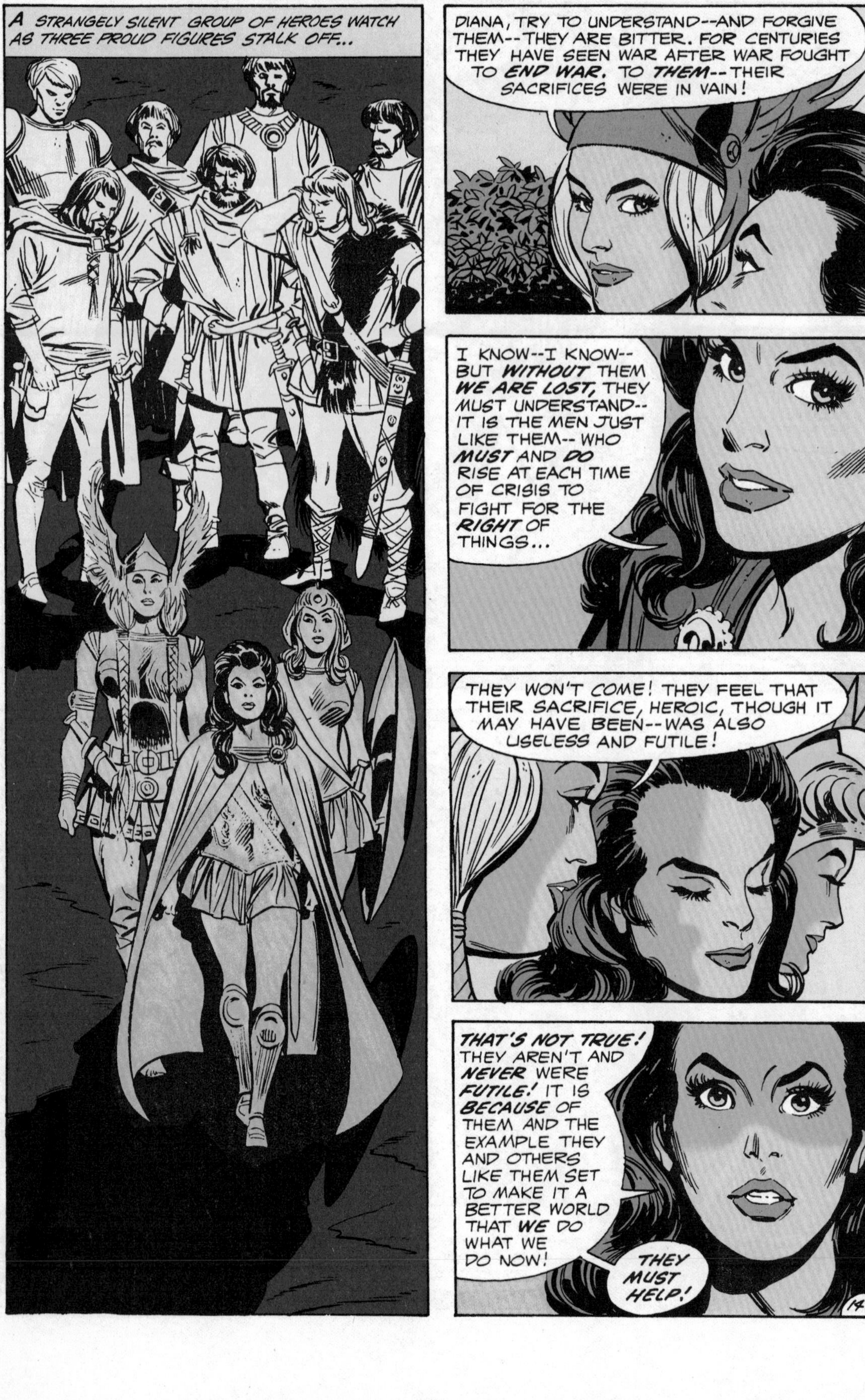
A STRANGELY SILENT GROUP OF HEROES WATCH AS THREE PROUD FIGURES STALK OFF...
DIANA, TRY TO UNDERSTAND--AND FORGIVE THEM--THEY ARE BITTER. FOR CENTURIES THEY HAVE SEEN WAR AFTER WAR FOUGHT TO END WAR. TO THEM--THEIR SACRIFICES WERE IN VAIN!
I KNOW--I KNOW--BUT WITHOUT THEM WE ARE LOST, THEY MUST UNDERSTAND--IT IS THE MEN JUST LIKE THEM--WHO MUST AND DO RISE AT EACH TIME OF CRISIS TO FIGHT FOR THE RIGHT OF THINGS...
THEY WON'T COME! THEY FEEL THAT THEIR SACRIFICE, HEROIC, THOUGH IT MAY HAVE BEEN--WAS ALSO USELESS AND FUTILE!
THAT'S NOT TRUE! THEY AREN'T AND NEVER WERE FUTILE! IT IS BECAUSE OF THEM AND THE EXAMPLE THEY AND OTHERS LIKE THEM SET TO MAKE IT A BETTER WORLD THAT WE DO WHAT WE DO NOW!
THEY MUST HELP!
14

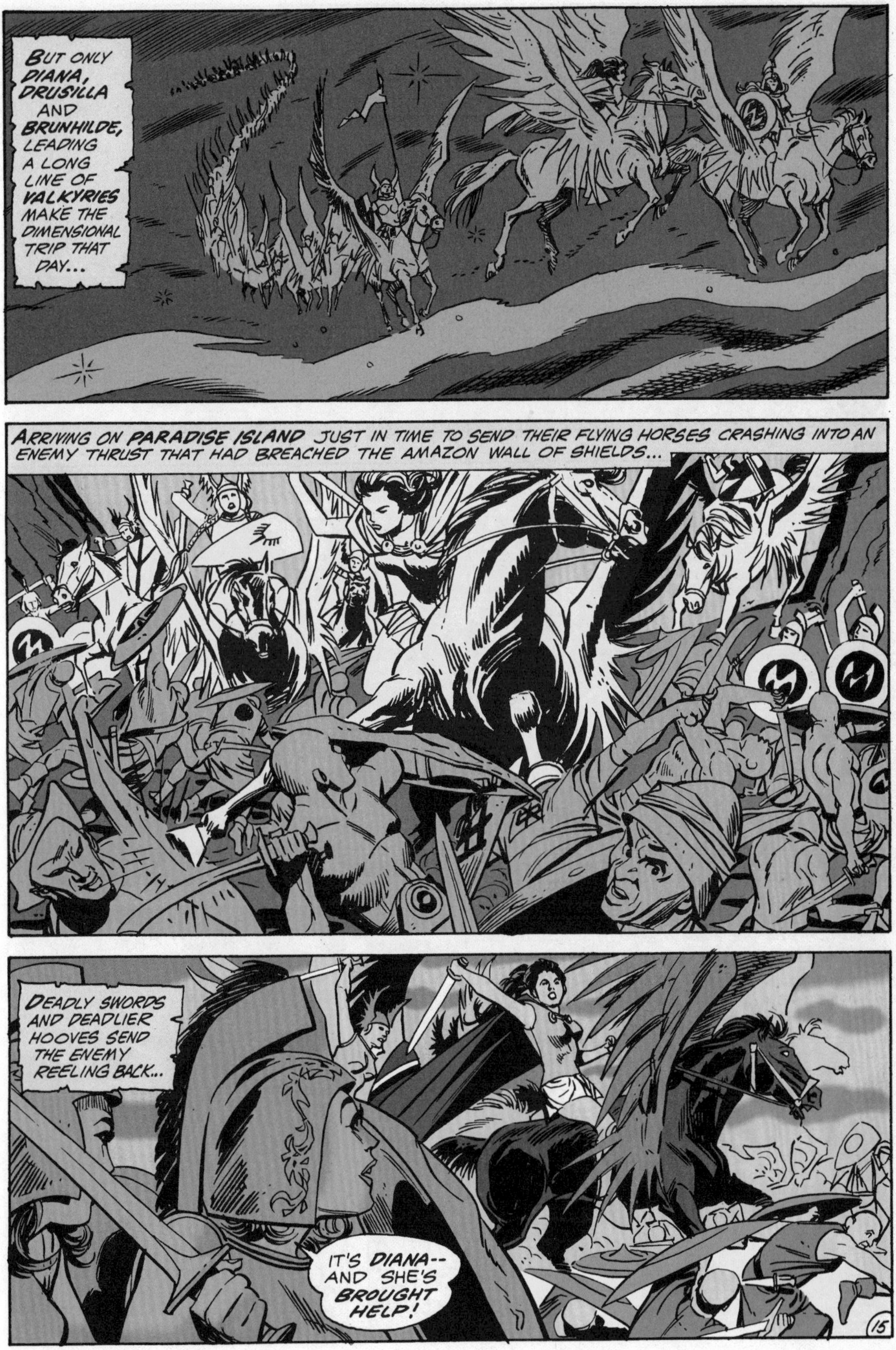

BUT ONLY DIANA, DRUSILLA AND BRUNHILDE, LEADING A LONG LINE OF VALKYRIES MAKE THE DIMENSIONAL TRIP THAT DAY...
ARRIVING ON PARADISE ISLAND JUST IN TIME TO SEND THEIR FLYING HORSES CRASHING INTO AN ENEMY THRUST THAT HAD BREACHED THE AMAZON WALL OF SHIELDS...
DEADLY SWORDS AND DEADLIER HOOVES SEND THE ENEMY REELING BACK...
IT'S DIANA-- AND SHE'S BROUGHT HELP!
15

WHAT SEEMED TO BE CERTAIN DEFEAT BECOMES *VICTORY!* AMAZON AND VALKYRIE DRIVE FORWARD AND THE ENEMY RETREAT BECOMES A RACE FOR LIFE!

HALT! RE-FORM LINES! THEY ARE BEATEN!

FOR TODAY ANYWAY--

LONG INTO THE NIGHT--*DIANA, AMAZON* AND *VALKYRIE* TALK, PLAN--BUT *EACH IN HER OWN HEART* KNOWS THAT TOMORROW WOULD END IN *DEFEAT* AND *DEATH!*

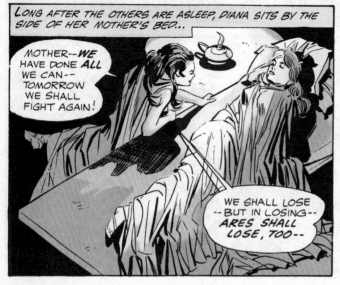

LONG AFTER THE OTHERS ARE ASLEEP, DIANA SITS BY THE SIDE OF HER MOTHER'S BED...

MOTHER--*WE* HAVE DONE *ALL* WE CAN--TOMORROW WE SHALL FIGHT AGAIN!

WE SHALL LOSE --BUT IN LOSING-- *ARES* SHALL LOSE, TOO--

FOR I SWEAR TO YOU, MOTHER --HE *SHALL NOT* GET THE SECRET OF DIMENSIONAL TRAVEL FROM YOU--

I KNOW WHAT I MUST DO-- WHAT *YOU* WOULD *WANT* ME TO DO--

GOODBYE-- FORGIVE ME, MOTHER--

16

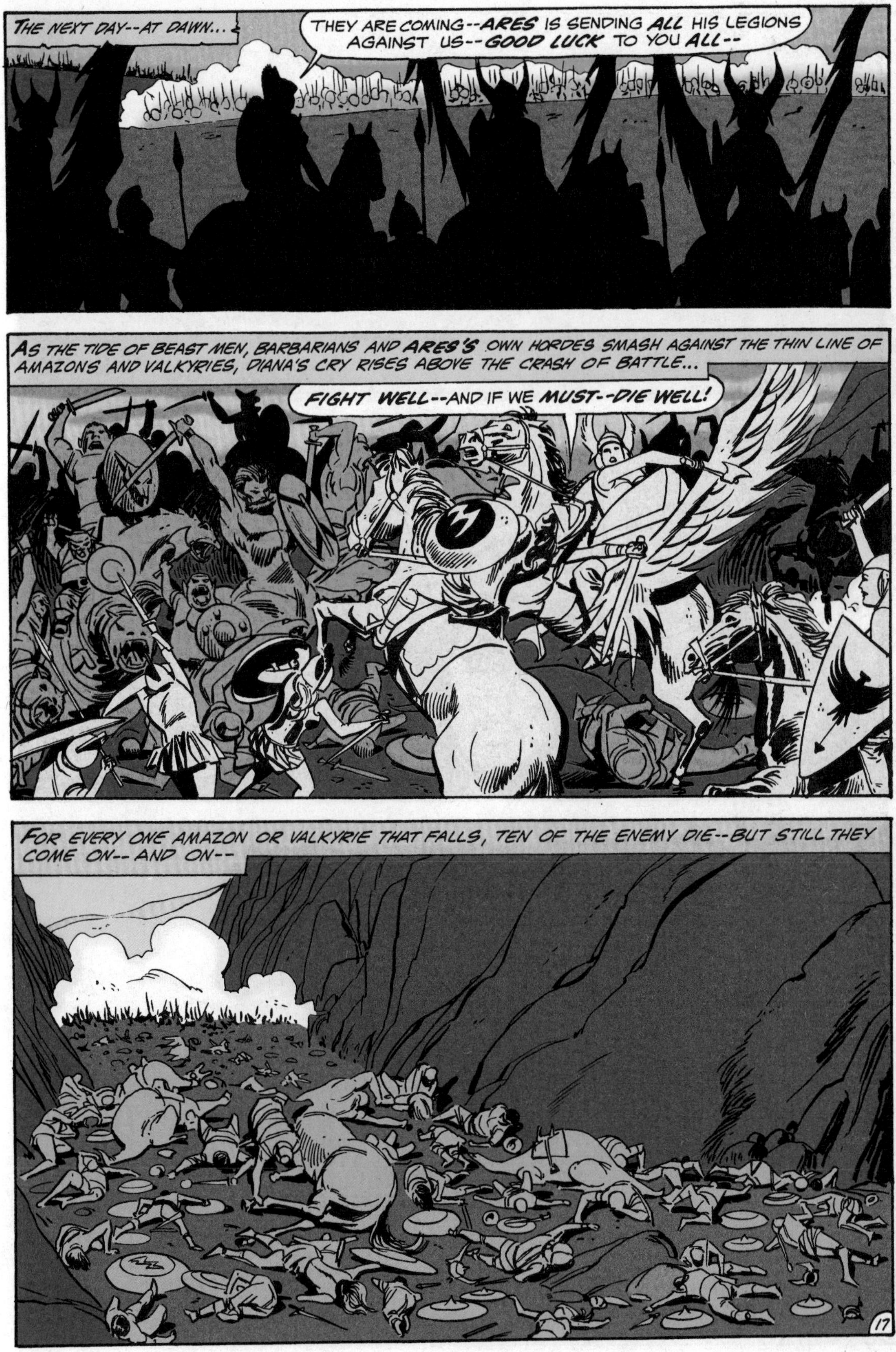
THE NEXT DAY--AT DAWN...
THEY ARE COMING--ARES IS SENDING ALL HIS LEGIONS AGAINST US--GOOD LUCK TO YOU ALL--
AS THE TIDE OF BEAST MEN, BARBARIANS AND ARES'S OWN HORDES SMASH AGAINST THE THIN LINE OF AMAZONS AND VALKYRIES, DIANA'S CRY RISES ABOVE THE CRASH OF BATTLE...
FIGHT WELL--AND IF WE MUST--DIE WELL!
FOR EVERY ONE AMAZON OR VALKYRIE THAT FALLS, TEN OF THE ENEMY DIE--BUT STILL THEY COME ON--AND ON--
17

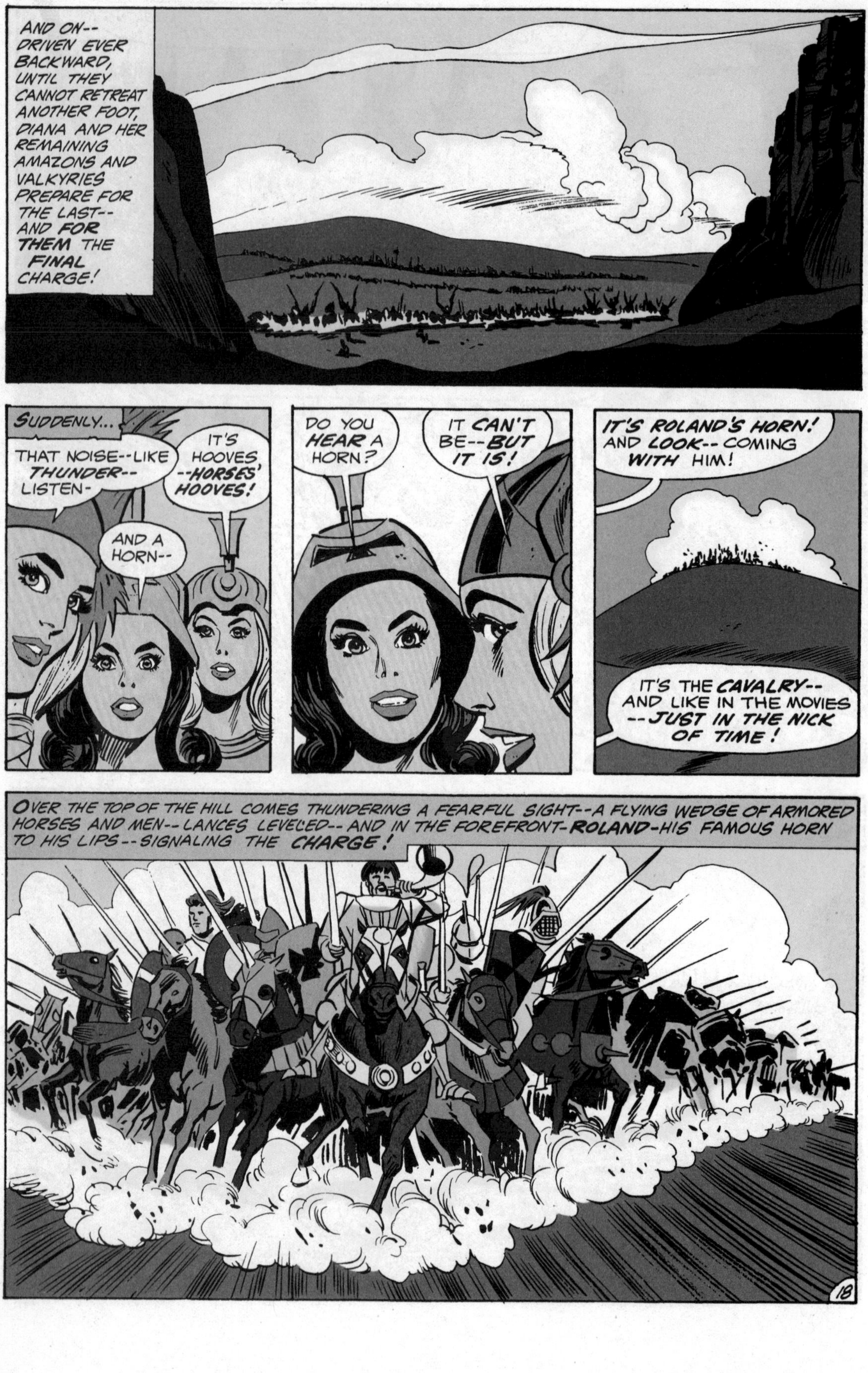
AND ON-- DRIVEN EVER BACKWARD, UNTIL THEY CANNOT RETREAT ANOTHER FOOT, DIANA AND HER REMAINING AMAZONS AND VALKYRIES PREPARE FOR THE LAST-- AND FOR THEM THE FINAL CHARGE!
SUDDENLY...
THAT NOISE--LIKE THUNDER-- LISTEN-
IT'S HOOVES --HORSES' HOOVES!
AND A HORN--
DO YOU HEAR A HORN?
IT CAN'T BE--BUT IT IS!
IT'S ROLAND'S HORN! AND LOOK-- COMING WITH HIM!
IT'S THE CAVALRY-- --AND LIKE IN THE MOVIES --JUST IN THE NICK OF TIME!
OVER THE TOP OF THE HILL COMES THUNDERING A FEARFUL SIGHT--A FLYING WEDGE OF ARMORED HORSES AND MEN--LANCES LEVELED--AND IN THE FOREFRONT-ROLAND-HIS FAMOUS HORN TO HIS LIPS--SIGNALING THE CHARGE!
18

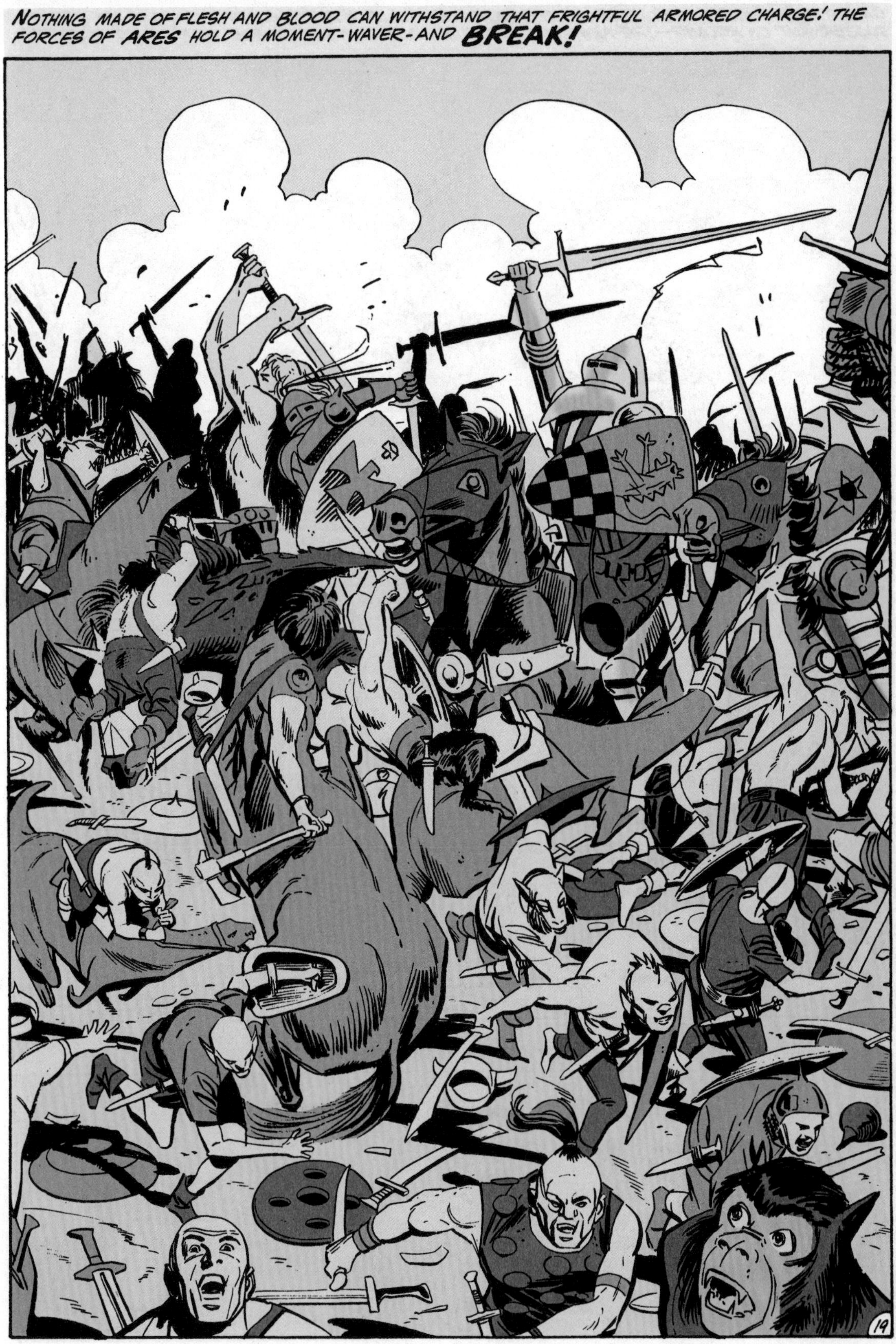
NOTHING MADE OF FLESH AND BLOOD CAN WITHSTAND THAT FRIGHTFUL ARMORED CHARGE! THE FORCES OF ARES HOLD A MOMENT-WAVER-AND BREAK!
19

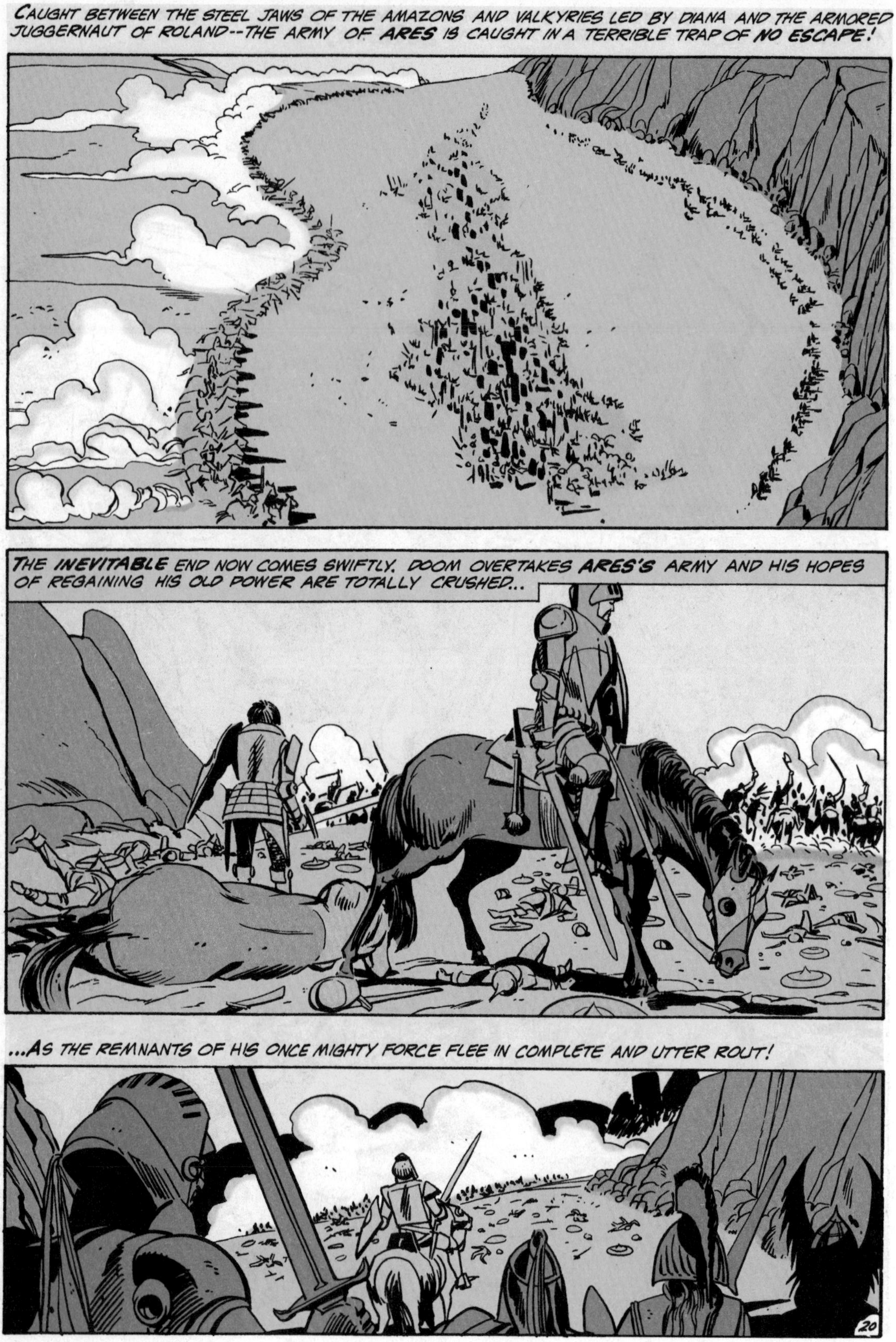
CAUGHT BETWEEN THE STEEL JAWS OF THE AMAZONS AND VALKYRIES LED BY DIANA AND THE ARMORED JUGGERNAUT OF ROLAND--THE ARMY OF ARES IS CAUGHT IN A TERRIBLE TRAP OF NO ESCAPE!
THE INEVITABLE END NOW COMES SWIFTLY. DOOM OVERTAKES ARES'S ARMY AND HIS HOPES OF REGAINING HIS OLD POWER ARE TOTALLY CRUSHED...
...AS THE REMNANTS OF HIS ONCE MIGHTY FORCE FLEE IN COMPLETE AND UTTER ROUT!
20

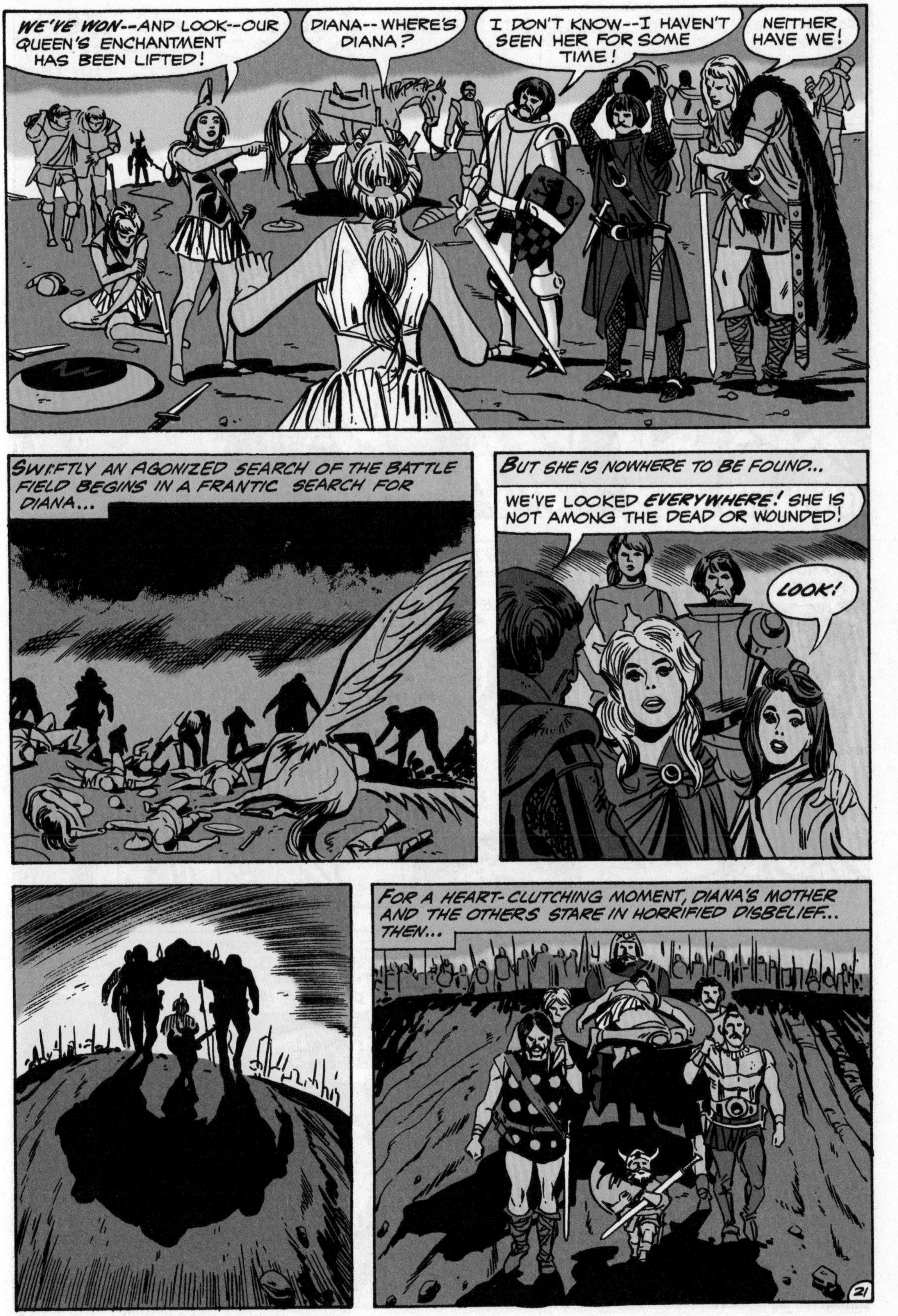
WE'VE WON--AND LOOK--OUR QUEEN'S ENCHANTMENT HAS BEEN LIFTED!
DIANA-- WHERE'S DIANA?
I DON'T KNOW--I HAVEN'T SEEN HER FOR SOME TIME!
NEITHER HAVE WE!
SWIFTLY AN AGONIZED SEARCH OF THE BATTLE FIELD BEGINS IN A FRANTIC SEARCH FOR DIANA...
BUT SHE IS NOWHERE TO BE FOUND...
WE'VE LOOKED EVERYWHERE! SHE IS NOT AMONG THE DEAD OR WOUNDED!
LOOK!
FOR A HEART-CLUTCHING MOMENT, DIANA'S MOTHER AND THE OTHERS STARE IN HORRIFIED DISBELIEF... THEN...
21

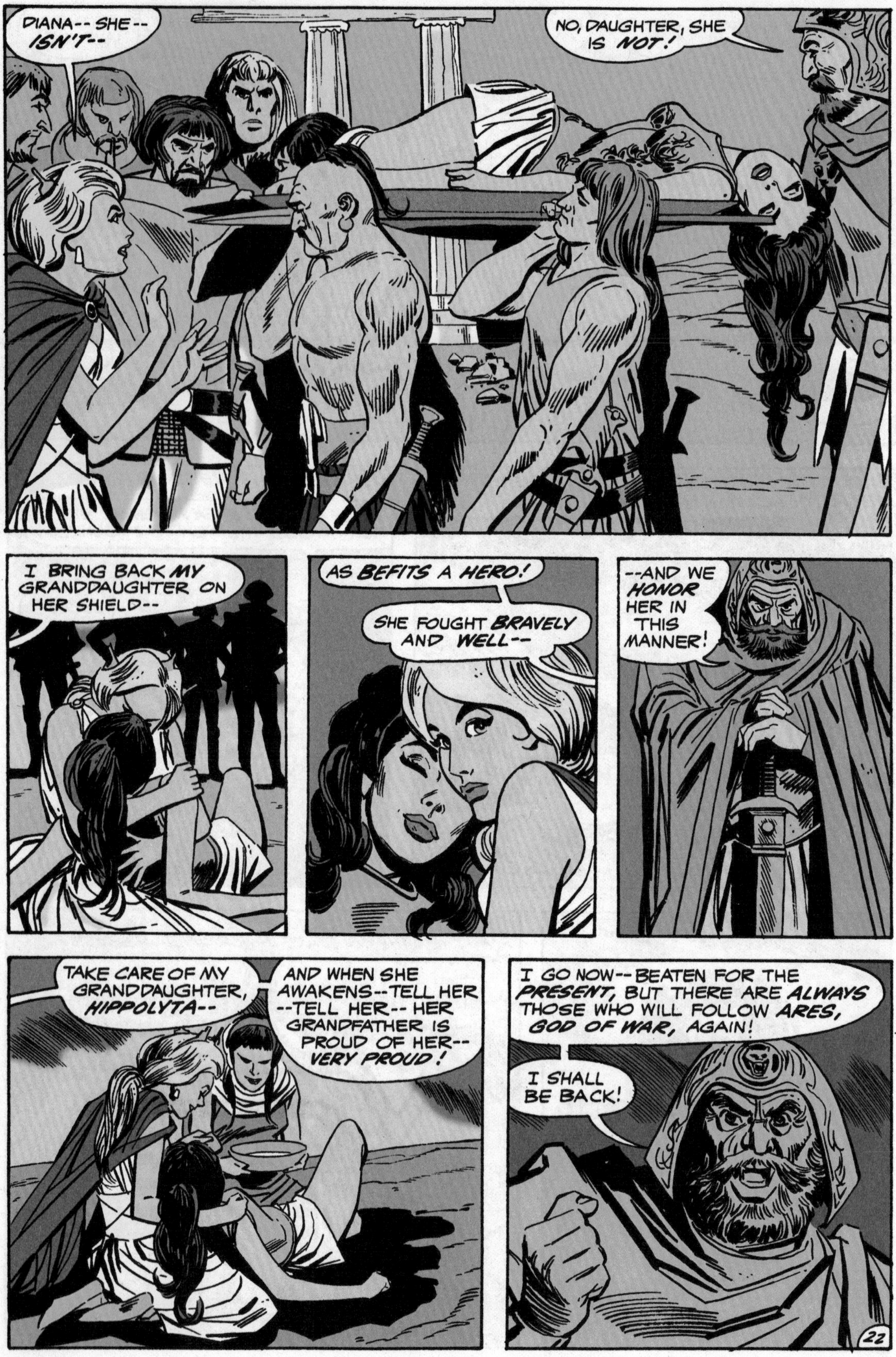
DIANA-- SHE-- ISN'T--
NO, DAUGHTER, SHE IS NOT!
I BRING BACK MY GRANDDAUGHTER ON HER SHIELD--
AS BEFITS A HERO!
SHE FOUGHT BRAVELY AND WELL--
--AND WE HONOR HER IN THIS MANNER!
TAKE CARE OF MY GRANDDAUGHTER, HIPPOLYTA--
AND WHEN SHE AWAKENS--TELL HER --TELL HER-- HER GRANDFATHER IS PROUD OF HER-- VERY PROUD!
I GO NOW-- BEATEN FOR THE PRESENT, BUT THERE ARE ALWAYS THOSE WHO WILL FOLLOW ARES, GOD OF WAR, AGAIN!
I SHALL BE BACK!
22

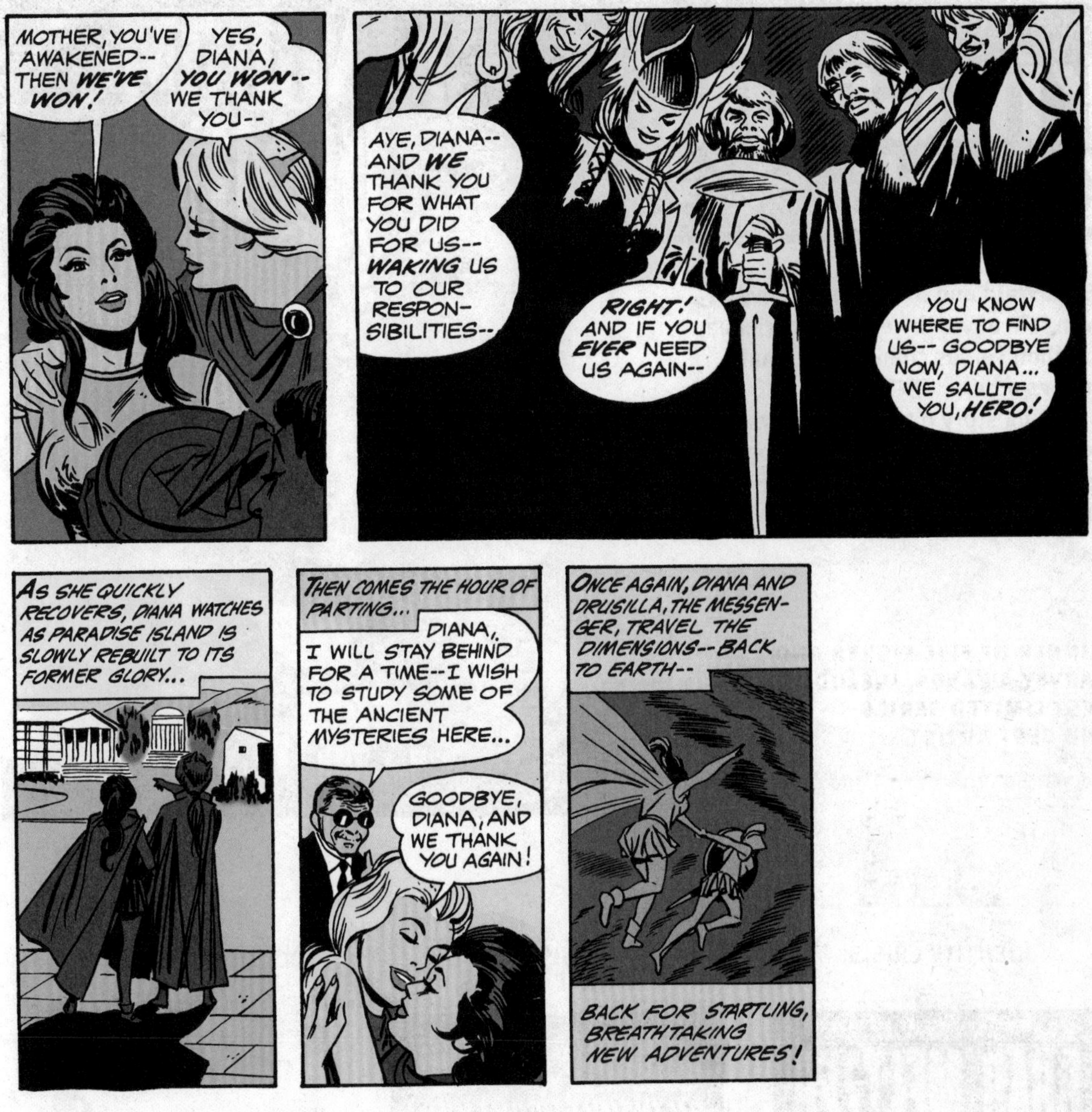
MOTHER, YOU'VE AWAKENED-- THEN WE'VE WON!
YES, DIANA, YOU WON-- WE THANK YOU--
AYE, DIANA-- AND WE THANK YOU FOR WHAT YOU DID FOR US-- WAKING US TO OUR RESPON-SIBILITIES--
RIGHT! AND IF YOU EVER NEED US AGAIN--
YOU KNOW WHERE TO FIND US-- GOODBYE NOW, DIANA... WE SALUTE YOU, HERO!
AS SHE QUICKLY RECOVERS, DIANA WATCHES AS PARADISE ISLAND IS SLOWLY REBUILT TO ITS FORMER GLORY...
THEN COMES THE HOUR OF PARTING...
DIANA, I WILL STAY BEHIND FOR A TIME--I WISH TO STUDY SOME OF THE ANCIENT MYSTERIES HERE...
GOODBYE, DIANA, AND WE THANK YOU AGAIN!
ONCE AGAIN, DIANA AND DRUSILLA, THE MESSEN-GER, TRAVEL THE DIMENSIONS--BACK TO EARTH--
BACK FOR STARTLING, BREATHTAKING NEW ADVENTURES!

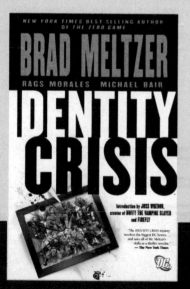